THE COMPLETE BRITISH ISLES COLLECTION

THE COMPLETE BRITISH ISLES COLLECTION

FREE BONUS FROM HBA: EBOOK BUNDLE

Greetings!

First of all, thank you for reading our books. As fellow passionate readers of History and Mythology, we aim to create the very best books for our readers.

Now, we invite you to join our VIP list. As a welcome gift, we offer the History & Mythology Ebook Bundle below for free. Plus, you can be the first to receive new books and exclusives! Remember it's 100% free to join.

Simply scan the QR code down below to join.

https://www.subscribepage.com/hba

Keep up to date with us on:

YouTube: History Brought Alive

Facebook: History Brought Alive

WWW.HISTORYBROUGHTALIVE.COM

CONTENTS

THE HISTORY OF ENGLAND

IRISH HISTORY & MYHTOLOGY

CONCLUSION 265

SCOTLAND

WALES HISTORY

THE HISTORY OF ENGLAND

INTRODUCTION

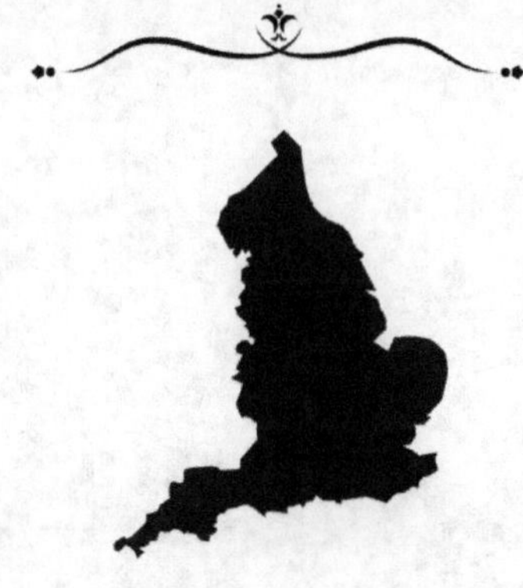

The history of any country is complex. However, that of England is perhaps one of the most complex and varied histories of any country. This is not to say that England's history is especially more misunderstood, misrepresented, or intricate. Nor is it to imply that the history of other countries, Western or otherwise, is of inferior interest or development when compared to England's. But when a country has a history with such substantial longevity as England's, it is bound to be intimidating to those hoping for a succinct summary.

Many historians, educators, and general authors alike have attempted to tackle England's history. There have been countless textbooks, guidebooks, and tomes that attempt to give a clear and concise image of England's chronology. Many of them follow the same chronological structure that will be adhered to in this book, but the difference among many of those books is the pacing, tone, and energy. To put it bluntly, it is easy to write a dense book on England's history. If they do not follow a clear chronological timeline, then they can be difficult to follow. The sheer amount of events, characters, and settings within England's history makes it nearly impossible to structure a book in any other way than according to time. To create themes or sections devoted to any other categorization is to confuse the reader, giving a false understanding of the series of events and the cultural and social factors that contributed to the development of England's history as a whole. But books following the chronological structure are not exempt from fault either. Some adhere to a strong academic and/or scholarly tone. They expect readers to be experts in the field they are entering, omitting opportunities to give a clear background on events and changes throughout history. This is understandable, considering that to give a comprehensive history of England is to demand a substantial effort from the reader. Unfortunately, many historians and scholars see this as a challenge worth facing, writing books that only fellow scholars can understand. This makes it difficult for the common person to approach the topic of England's history outside of an Advanced Placement history class.

In an effort to even dip one's toe into the history of England, the amateur scholar is thrown back, ostracized by the overcomplicated and dull quality of rigorous history books. To be clear, there is a time and a place for these books. Scholars and historians, and students of these areas, are likely to gravitate toward specialized books. They are the demographic that these books are geared toward and written for. But, for the common person, who Shakespeare can attest is arguably the most important member of the population, this level of complexity is unnecessary. You do not begin to study history as an expert.

The book you hold in your hands attempts to combat this. The History of England is neither comprehensive nor of the same caliber as high-brow academic or rigorous scholarly texts. It does not attempt to be either of these, though, as you will discover throughout the narrative. Its goal is, instead, to show the reader a different side of the study of history. History, as a general area of interest, does not need to be dull or heavy material. In fact, it should be as fascinating and thrilling as history itself. We do not read stories to prove to others our literary endurance nor to flex our vocabulary. We read stories to be entertained, to discover ourselves within them. We read about the past to better understand our own present.

In The History of England, the reader will encounter poignant and verifiably factual information. It will cover a broad overview of England's most pertinent historical events and figures. It will detail key cultural, social, and economic changes. Compared to other history books addressing England's history, it is a refreshing read that is both easily comprehensible and factually correct. The book will give a more concise history, told in chronological order and supplemented with an additional list of the English monarchy and heads of Parliament in order to help guide further research.

History Brought Alive is made up of a team of experts in history and mythology. Their writers have established credibility in their fields and aim to create a pleasant, genuine, and educational reading experience for anyone interested in broadening their historical studies. History Brought Alive's writers take pride in their work and strive to make academic and scholarly material accessible to anyone. They have a wide variety of writers, each with expertise in different geographical histories, spanning from Norse mythology to Roman history to Hoodoo, the history of ancient spiritual connections. Their books are well-referenced and accurate, supporting the History Brought Alive name and creating a foundation of meaningful historical texts.

The writers at History Brought Alive understand the importance of creating a beneficial historical text. As a result, The History of England presents highlights of the key events in England's history. It aims not to confuse or intimidate but to entice and engage, creating a satisfying read of a true account. It gives readers a taste of the country's rich history in a variety of different areas.

The History of England is a masterful book for anyone wanting to learn more about English history and culture. It  takes the reader through a panorama of historical events, giving the reader an emotional and human experience. It doesn't drown the reader in statistics but appeals, instead, to the origin of storytelling. It is a narrative, first and foremost, to be enjoyed and to elicit passion from the reader. For anyone, whether you are a scholar, a student, a casual reader, or someone who simply hopes to have an intelligent conversational topic for next year's Thanksgiving dinner, this is a must-have for your library.

Reading other books on England's history, especially as an introduction to the topic, is time-consuming and could result in the reader simply disliking a topic out of misunderstanding. In order to best understand the true, fascinating nature of England's history, The History of England is the text at the top of your list. History is not meant to be sitting on a dusty shelf or at the bottom of your reading pile. It is not meant to remain inside the classroom. It is not a subject for the elite, for a specialized few who choose to remain within the confines of the university system. History is for everyone. History is intended to be brought alive and to live alongside us.

CHAPTER 1
STORIES ABOUT ENGLAND

England is already a land of stories, as long as we are only willing to recognize which ones are truthful and which ones are simply reflections of our own contemporary beliefs about the country. Considering how long England has been around and how much of an impact it has had on the world, it comes as no surprise that stories about the country are infinite and span from incredible cultural and social commentary that has left a meaningful stamp on the nation, to incorrect stereotypes. It has been the center of folklore, television shows, myths, and movies. Both the stories that have originated in England and those that seek to portray it from an outsider's perspective have had lasting impacts on our impressions of the English people as well as English history and culture.

In this section, you will be given a brief overview of how both scholars and common people consider modern England today. Like any other nation, England has been affected (both internally and externally) by the stories told about it and the stories that have been told within its borders. A story makes a story, in truth, and England's history and present time would not be the same without the stories that came out of its nation. Some of the most influential myths and legends of England's history have shaped the moral conduct and beliefs of its people. Similarly, the media concerning England today still impacts how the British people think of themselves and how others think of them. While the history of a place must be understood to see the place for what it is now, it is equally important to first assess where you, as the reader, stand now: Evaluate the language you use and the knowledge that you currently have. It is important to begin with what you know and to ask yourself how you know it. A beginning is always the start before one dive into the past.

Myths and Legends

The myths and legends that have perpetuated English history and culture are similar to other countries' myths and legends in that they act as mirrors for what their people value as well as reinforce the forward progression of the country's future. One of England's most popular and enduring myths is that of Robin Hood. Though some may only recognize him as Kevin Costner and others might identify with the Disney production featuring foxes, a lion king who sucks his thumb, and a bear with a rather striking resemblance to Baloo from a sister Disney film, the true legend appears in history around the 12th century, during King John of England's reign. While the man himself is still unidentified, there are several theories as to who such a humanitarian and vigilante might have been. The time and origin of the myth suggest, though, that the factuality of such a myth is irrelevant when it comes to the importance that it bore on popular culture and English culture.

If you're unfamiliar with the myth of Robin Hood, it goes

as follows: A young man during the 12th century robs from the rich to feed the poor, gaining help from his band of Merry Men and his faithful friend Little John. Now, given the time period in which this myth arises, it is no surprise that such a legend became necessary. The origin of any myth or legend is in necessity, a desperation of the people to believe in something. This can be seen in contemporary myths as well. Superheroes are created for the same purpose: They provide beacons of hope for both the young and old in times that challenge the hearts and souls of the common people. During King John of England's reign, the people of England were indeed heavily taxed; this much is true from the original Robin Hood myth. King John's reign ended with the signing of the Magna Carta, a momentous event that will be detailed later in Chapter Three, and the subsequent cessation of the feudal system in England. Citizens of the country were growing tired of a system that relied on their hard work and left them with nothing to their name, all for the greater good of the monarchy overseeing their homelands. A vigilante romanticized or not, who restored some of the power to the common people was necessitated at the time and, therefore, became incredibly popular. It would prove to have lasting effects on the people and the modern impression of England.

One theory of the true Robin Hood is that it was really a man named Robert Godberd, who did in fact travel around Nottinghamshire to rob the rich. However, his "robbing the rich to feed the poor" narrative has been gentrified to meet a modern audience. His true actions, according to historians, would have more likely been murder, arson, burgling, and harassment of travelers and clergy. Where the contemporary myth draws more inspiration from true history is in King John's passing of the Forest Law, which gave private access to forested hunting grounds to the monarchy as well as the feudal lords. Unsurprisingly, it was unpopular among the public, and Godberd's actions against the clergy and feudal lords seemed heroic at the time, as he and his band of "merry men" fought back against the iron grip of their government.

The debates among historians regarding the myth of King Arthur are similar to that of Robin Hood. The chances that such a legend existed are probable, considering the circumstances of the time in which King Arthur was supposed to have lived, though historians have yet to confirm whether this is true. With a history as long as England's, it is difficult to differentiate the truth from a perpetuated myth that has become so ingrained in the culture that it seems plausible.

The myth of King Arthur first appears in Welsh poetry around the 10th century, claiming that King Arthur won 12 battles against too many different enemies to make such a story possible. Furthermore, the stories detailed in the poems document that the battles took place in disparate locations, making it impossible for a single  person to have been at all 12. That being said, the myth of a King Arthur stuck and continued to spread throughout English history. King Arthur earns his first full life story in the 12th-century book The History of the Kings of Britain, in which Lancelot, Guinevere, and Excalibur make their first appearances. The story was a perfect combination of myth and truth, pulled from other stories of real kings and heroes of the time, creating an invaluable narrative for English culture.

The power of the King Arthur myth was lasting in English culture, in that as it developed, it evolved from a single tale of a powerful king to a tale of a young stable hand rising to power. In essence, it is one of the oldest rags-to-riches stories to have entered the modern canon. Its mythic power grew extensively as time went on, becoming a common tale for everyone to point to for inspiration and heroism. Kings and queens, as well as artists, poets, and the common citizens of England, would herald the myth of King Arthur as truth for centuries to come.

Though the story of Jack and the Beanstalk might not carry as much weight as the former English stories, its importance in English culture cannot be understated. The story was documented in its first written form in 1734 under the name "The Story of Jack Spriggins and the Enchanted Bean." Prior to this, though, it is perhaps one of the oldest oral stories of English culture. Some historians believe that it predates most classical mythology and was first told more than 5,000 years ago, when Western and Eastern Indo-European languages split. Even though Jack and the Beanstalk is not a story that carries as much heroism or social commentary, it offers a different sort of importance for English culture in that it targets English children specifically. By offering moral lessons, some that predate England itself, it implores that English children grow up with a foundation of honesty, trustworthiness, and humility. Though children's tales may not garner as much attention as those that adults tend to favor, it is the children's tales that, arguably, create the most impact.

Religions

England's connection to religion today is most obviously represented by the monarchy. In modern news and tabloids, the traditions and customs of the monarchy are often coupled with the traditions of the Catholic Church. And while this isn't incorrect, in that the monarchy itself is a traditionally Catholic institution, the representations of the English monarchy are not the sole encompassing of religious customs in England.

England has remained predominantly Christian from its inception, though the denominations have changed slightly. While in its origins England was mostly Roman Catholic and Anglican (after the establishment of the Church of England in the sixth century), now there are more members of the Methodist denomination as well as Islam in England.

According to a 2001 study, almost five million people have been baptized in the Catholic Church, making it the second largest religious following still in England. It falls second only to the Church of England, which has 26 million people within its following ("How many Catholics," 2010). Now, considering the date of these statistics, it's probably a safe assumption that they have increased, but with religion becoming increasingly unpopular and more of a private aspect of people's lives rather than a public following, there are fewer published reports to consult.

Currently, Islam is the fastest growing religion in England, with Judaism behind it, though they are paltry percentages compared to those of the Christian following in the country. As a whole, England is a relatively religious country. It remains tied to its roots, and while it currently advertises the freedom of religion for its citizens, the connections that it still holds to the past are evident in daily life.

Fast Facts

Before diving into the past, having a firm idea of contemporary England may be helpful. England boasts a proud age of over 800,000 years. It has survived countless wars, a long line of colonial control, and successful relationships with powerful nations that still exist today, bolstering the country and providing vital support for other countries around the world. Its government is a combination of the British monarchy and a parliamentary system. It is ruled by both a monarch (either a king or a queen) and a prime minister. While today the monarchy functions as more of a figurehead for the country, its citizens carry a strong sense of pride for their king or queen, as is evident by their withstanding presence in media and culture. The prime minister, on the other hand, now does most of the governmental functions that dictate the direction of the country itself. As a modern country, it is a proud country, one that has a lengthy history and a population of 55 million, as of 2016 ("Population of England 2016," n.d.). It was the first industrialized nation in the world (a story that will be detailed further in the coming chapters) and is still considered one of the world's leading powers.

Truth vs Media Portrayals

Despite being a world power in both history and the contemporary world, England has a problematic relationship with its media portrayals. It has made appearances in many different films and television shows, many of which are period dramas. While this is entertaining to viewers, it paints an unrealistic picture of England as a country. For instance, the television show Downton Abbey was immensely popular on an international scale. It followed an upper-class family in the early 18th century, documenting their trials as well as the stories of their servants. It was a portrayal of how the English upper echelon changed as England entered the modern era. It was inarguably a media sensation; however, when television shows like Downton Abbey or Call the Midwife are coupled with countless period films (most of which take place during the Elizabethan era), it shows that England has stagnated in a culture of the past. If all that is shown of England in the media is of England's history, then it's only natural for viewers to assume that there is nothing of contemporary interest in England today. Their culture is no more, in essence. Viewers might also assume that social customs and cultural expectations are aligned with antiquated ideals when of course this is not the case.

The reader is encouraged to understand that as they learn about England's past, it does not negate where England is today. It is not a representation of contemporary England, but rather an explanation of how it came to be what it is now.

CHAPTER 2

THE TIMELINE BEGINS, 410-1066 AD, THE ANGLO-SAXONS PERIOD

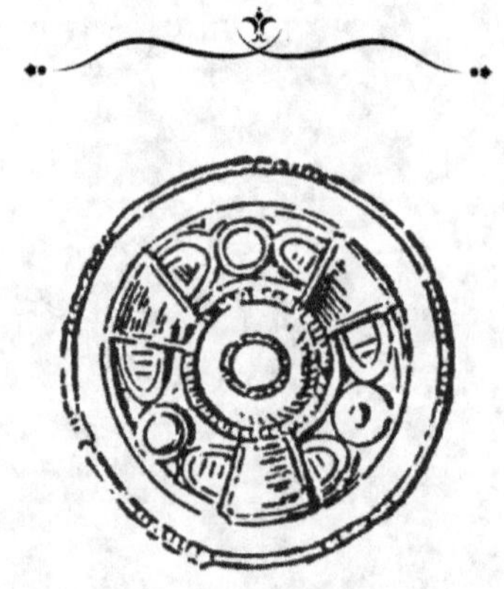

The Anglo-Saxon period in England began in the 5th century when the first settlers came to the land that would become the United Kingdom. The first settlers to arrive in the land were actually invited by the King himself, as defenders of the area from nearby Scots and Picts. Those who came to defend the land were from three tribes—the Angles, the Saxons, and the Jutes—thus giving way to the name of the era in which England was entering. The tribes that came to England would help to define the next few centuries, laying the foundation of the country that would become one of the most powerful and influential in the world. Despite England being founded upon a group of people brought together from different tribes, it would find several unifying forces to create a stable and formative country on its journey to become "the nation of the English." Though the tribes succeeded in defending the territory from the Scots and Picts, it wasn't exempt from further division among its people. The England of the fifth century was a collection of kingdoms that did not recognize a single ruler until the ninth century when the southern regions acknowledged a single lordship as responsible for them. But recognizing lordships and accepting temporary communions was just the start of England becoming a cohesive kingdom.

Religion, Christianity specifically, was introduced to England as a way to unify the nation. By the end of the 5th century, England was still divided into separate countries, but they had all recognized Christianity as a single ruling ideology that governed their systems. It should be recognized that at this time in history, there was no chance of a separation between church and state. In fact, this far back in history, the Church acted in place of a single governing state and helped to initiate the laws and social and cultural rules that would eventually be taken up by the state (or the centralized governments). It was from here that England officially entered what is known as the Anglo-Saxon period, during which the Church and the group of settlers first to arrive in England laid the groundwork for the country to come.

Anglo-Saxons

With the fall of the Roman empire in the early fifth century, a power vacuum surged and competing tribes began fighting over the territory of England. After many battles, the tribes that became collectively known as the Anglo-Saxons won out, obtaining power over England. As the Anglo-Saxons, or the governing unit of the English kingdoms, took power, they began to institute customs and rules for the new kingdoms that would come together to form England. Furthermore, the Anglo-Saxon period, previously known as the Dark Ages, in England's history was tumultuous and riddled with invasions. Nations were new and unstable, but the recent group of settlers was determined to create a new kingdom for themselves. The Anglo-Saxons established early farms, trading concepts, and a language. They spoke what we now term "Old English" and brought literacy to the area. While the knowledge pertaining to them is limited, considering the time frame of their existence, their presence was pertinent to the development of England. Their occupation in England marks the transformative period between Roman rule and the Norman conquest, denoting the end of the Anglo-Saxon period.

It was during the time of the Anglo-Saxons that England was at its most perilous concerning invasions from Vikings. While there are many competing narratives about the Vikings, simply put, they were the second group of settlers that migrated to the area now known as England alongside the Anglo-Saxons. Much like the Anglo-Saxons, the Vikings were made up of three nations of people who, over time and colloquialisms, became merged into two groups of Vikings. Originally, Vikings were classified as either Danish or Swedish Vikings. Not much is known about Swedish Vikings, but it is worthy of note that they were part of the groups that helped to conquer parts of England, even if they were a group that fell to the wayside over time. Eventually, the Danish Vikings, or the Danes, would become what is now commonly referred to as, simply, the Vikings.

Compared to the Anglo-Saxons, the Vikings were considered barbaric pirates, a seafaring population that concerned itself more with warfare than developing settlements. When both tribes claimed territories of England from the Romans, the Vikings and the Anglo-Saxons became neighbors. The main difference between the two neighbor tribes was that of culture. The Anglo-Saxons were overwhelmingly more literate than the Vikings and brought with them the foundations for the English language, much of which is still used today in England. The Anglo-Saxons were also practitioners of the Anglo-Saxon Church, which was the

Roman Catholic Church at the time. With their devout following, they practiced "morally righteous" behaviors, compared to those of Vikings. Since warfare was less of a priority in comparison to piety, the Anglo-Saxons could also devote more time and resources to infrastructure. As a result, they built many of the first churches in England, some of which are still standing today, including Westminster Abbey. Ultimately, as time went on, the Anglo-Saxons won over the Viking territory, pushing their neighbor tribe into near obsoletion.

The Norman Conquest

The Norman conquest marks the end of the Anglo-Saxon period. At the start of the 11th century, the previous King Edward had chosen a son of a nobleman, Harold Godwinson, to be the next king of England. William, the Duke of nearby Normandy, decided to launch an invasion of England. What began as a personal slight against the Duke, who had been promised the title King of England, soon became the most influential invasion in England's history, changing England's social, cultural, and economic spheres forever. Alongside William's endeavors to take the throne were other challengers to the English crown. It was a new nation, but many leaders recognized it as a valuable asset. Both Harald III of Norway and his brother, Tostig, launched attacks to obtain the title of the King of England. Though William, the Duke of Normandy, wasn't directly impacted by these other challengers, the additional conflict helped to destabilize King Harold Godwinson, allowing him to win the conflict.

In 1066, at the famous Battle of Hastings, William successfully conquered England, marking it the last successful conquest of England. His lineage would officially begin the monarchy that would remain through current times.

Throughout his rule, King William survived many attacks on his crown, but he held his kingdom fast and maintained rule over England. Though King William would contribute much to the country of England, on a moral note, he would establish a reputation for victory. England would face many enemies over the long span of its history, but by the strength of itself as a nation, it would continue to prevail.

The long-term effects of the Norman conquest would be tenfold for England. As both a king and a military general, King William instituted new military strategies in England. He built castles within his territory as battle defense stations. These castles would remain standing and in use for hundreds of years. It was also under King William that construction for the Tower of London and Oxford University began. On a cultural level, the  Norman conquest was immensely propulsive for English culture. Since King William was from Normandy, and not from England, he brought with him a new social structure. He introduced Norman landowners to England, replacing the English landowning elite and laying the groundwork for feudalism, the economic and social system that would remain in England for the next 600 years. Citizens could now own land in exchange for military service, changing how people obtained land and how they thought about military service. The hallowed Anglo-Saxon Church changed as well under King William's rule after he brought Norman clergy into the Church. On an international level, King William's conquest brought England closer to France. His ruling introduced the French language to England, marrying some of their vocabularies, and connected England to France with economic and political ties. These ties would remain for the duration of England's existence and is still a relationship maintained today.

CHAPTER 3
1066-1450 AD, ENGLAND'S MEDIEVAL AND MIDDLE AGES

The Late or High Middle Ages began after William the Conqueror's formative reign in England, spanning from approximately 1100–1450 AD. If the Anglo-Saxon period was tumultuous in the sense that every country's beginning is tumultuous, then the Middle Ages were tumultuous in the same sense of a country's childhood. There were a thousand questions to be answered, and England was still discovering itself as a country. Socially speaking, this is the period in which it is perhaps easiest to imagine England. It was a structure of serfdom and monarchy, with feudalism (the system of hierarchy with lords controlling the lands of the public, obtaining labor, funds, and goods from those who lived on it) in full force. After Henry I died in 1135, King William's grandson, Stephen, took the throne and led England into a civil war that would last for the next twenty years. When Henry II took control of England after Stephen, England found a temporary period of peace, until King John (the acclaimed King John of the Robin Hood tales) assumed power and plunged the country into strife once more. He was a ruthless king, with little moral compass. At this time, the Church acted parallel to the monarchy, helping to enact decrees while simultaneously attempting to offer the common people some sort of hope and salvation. The monarchy was the sole governance of England, leaving little room for interpretation or independence. There was no such thing as representation, and the king's orders were the only orders (with the exception of religious standards) that controlled people's lives. If England was going to continue to evolve as a modern country, things would need to change.

Magna Carta

Finally, with the succession of Henry III, England took a turn for social and political advancement with the establishment of Parliament in the momentous passing of the Magna Carta. The public had grown tired of kings ruling as tyrants, and the country was on the verge of rebellion after facing years of abuse under King John's rule. Though it was technically during King Henry III's rule when the Magna Carta took effect, it was not King Henry III himself who signed it. When his father, King John, died when Henry was just nine years old, the young king had no concept of the turmoil he was inheriting. The Magna Carta saw its first drafts in 1215 and 1216, during King John's last years alive as ruler. He served as a tumultuous king, one of the only to be excommunicated and deeply hated by his subjects. It was a pope under his rule that suggested the Magna Carta take effect. If King John signed it into ruling, then the document would restrict all sovereign leaders to a series of laws, designed to limit the oppression of subjects. It was, unsurprisingly, very unpopular with King John, and it took his death for the document to become successful. After King John died and Henry III took the throne, his advisors pushed him to reissue it. The young king took out some of the most controversial amendments that his father had required to be added in order to gain favor as a new king. The Magna Carta went through another round of revision in 1225, but all versions after that would herald back to the 1225 revision as the "final copy."

The Magna Carta was a groundbreaking document, not just for England but for all other emerging countries. Never before had rulers been held accountable, tyranny abounding and oppression forming the backbone of progress. Furthermore, England was taking a step toward recognizing its people as individuals. This idea would not fully be grasped or utilized until the English Renaissance and then again in the Modern eras, in which individualism would birth social reform. With England passing the Magna Carta, they were taking the first step toward a more evolved and civilized empire. England would continue to take such steps throughout its history, often being the first to revolutionize political ideas. It would repeat this again with the Paris Treaty, the Acts of Union, and the United Nations. England would soon be known as the brainchild of many of the most important governmental documents that the world still knows today. Perhaps it can be attributed to the emphasis placed on intellect, or perhaps it is simply a reflection of the country's ability to adapt with the times. Either way, England would continue to propel politics and government bodies forward toward the future. Five hundred years later, with a burgeoning new rebellion on the other side of the Atlantic Ocean, the colonies that would become the United States of America would point to this very document as evidence of one's right to personal freedom from a sovereign leader.

The Black Death

While King Henry III's rule was predominantly one of peace, ushering in new laws to protect the people against their sovereign leaders and implementing Parliament to further institute representation in the law-making process, it was a short-lived period before English citizens found themselves in yet another period of strife. The Black Death, or the Plague, was the deadliest virus to sweep the nation of England in its entire history. It was a bubonic plague that spread across Europe and Asia from 1346–1353, though it also included several surges in later years. While it is difficult to estimate exactly the toll that the Black Death took on England, due to inaccurate records of the time, it's believed that over 200 million people died throughout Europe, 1.5 million of them hailing from England. The virus is said to have originated in Asia; a parasite carried by rats brought to England. With poor living standards and any sort of personal-hygiene rules nonexistent, the virus turned into a pandemic that raged throughout England. The Black Death, though devastating to the English people, also played a vital role in shaping the world. It would act as a sort of reset for the population, forcing people to re-evaluate labor, living situations, economics, art, and social structures. With such a drastically reduced population, England would be required to reassess everything they thought they had decided upon in the past thousand years.

Economically speaking, the Black Death took an immense toll on England. With the major

port cities along the Mediterranean hit the hardest due to the highest populations, trade suffered for England. As a result, trade and economic prosperity all but stagnated during the worst years of the Black Death. The Black Death also affected political spheres, though this is perhaps more oblique than the economic and social effects. Since the plague affected the young, old, poor, and rich, all populations were impacted detrimentally. The monarchs who did survive the Black Death were strained at this time, as is the case for any political structure during times of strife. People looked for answers, for assistance as their lives and the people that they loved fell apart around them. They looked to their government for that help, but with little knowledge about the Black Death, monarchs were at a loss for what to do to support their kingdoms.

The Peasants' Revolt

The reasons for the Peasants' Revolt of 1381 are many, as most disagreements in history tend to be. After the Black Death killed half of the population in England, the remaining workers discovered that they could demand higher wages for their labor. Employers had a smaller population to pull from, leaving them with fewer choices when it came to giving in to workers' stipulations. This lasted for a while, but eventually employers had enough and turned to the government for some sort of regulation to be passed to return the peasants to their place. In 1351, Parliament passed the Statute of Laborers, which lowered wages to the levels before the Black Death wiped out half of the working population. This angered the workers, who felt they deserved more substantial compensation for their labor. John Ball, a radical preacher who had been excommunicated by the Church and traveled England urging peasants to break from the feudal system, was a second catalyst for the Peasants' Revolt. His preachings inspired citizens to rebel, giving them another incentive to strike back. In 1377, two final events pushed the peasants of England toward revolt. With England at war with France, Parliament passed a new poll tax on English citizens to pay for the war. This set the common people back financially, placing yet another stressor on their lives. Finally, in the same year, King Edward III died, leaving his ten-year-old son, King Richard II, in power. Peasants decided to seize the moment to pressure a new king to make changes that might benefit their lives.

Led by a man named Wat Tyler, peasants marched on London in May 1381. English citizens were joined by others from Norfolk and Suffolk, burning buildings and freeing prisoners as signs to the sovereignty that they had had enough and would no longer play as pawns in their chess game. Eventually, they convinced King Richard to meet with them, demanding that he abolish serfdom. Though young, King Richard was not fooled by the revolt and promised to abolish serfdom as their new king. The peasants relinquished their challenge to the king and returned to their lives. While King Richard did not actually abolish serfdom, the Peasants' Revolt of 1381 would prove to be a vital example of England's lower class taking a stand for themselves against the sovereignty. England's resilience and persistence against oppression would not dim as the country continued to develop.

The Hundred Years' War: 1337–1453

History does not occur in a vacuum. While historians and scholars discuss events individually so that students have a chance to best understand the complexity of each occurrence in history, they do not happen in isolation. Events overlap, many occurring simultaneously. It's important to remember this as one progresses through the timeline of England's history and each event is detailed. They are not happening independently but rather impacting one another simultaneously. While the Black Death was raging across Europe and Asia, the Hundred Years' War had already begun between England and France. Due to the early ties of William the Conqueror, England and France had already been tethered as trade and political partners.

The Hundred Years' War that occurred during the late Middle Ages had many driving factors, including years of prior tension between England and France's monarchies. In the immediate years leading up to it, the main events that drove England and France to conflict were those concerning the French crown and the territory known as the duchy of Guyenne. The territory was technically owned by England but had long been recognized as belonging to the French crown. As England grew as a kingdom, they wanted the territory back from France's claim. Secondly, in 1328, France's Charles IV died, with the last known living relatives living in the English monarchy, giving the English reason to claim the French crown.

France was unwilling to acquiesce to England, ensuing a hundred years' worth of conflict. Now, considering the length of the war, the Hundred Years' War was not as constant as other wars in history. It was more a series of battles that paused and began again over a span of a hundred years. The war went on several hiatuses, being picked up by several English kings as the years progressed. What occurred during the Hundred Years' War was an advancement of military developments and a sign of England's power.

When Henry V renewed the war in 1415, the English proved victorious with their superior military techniques and equipment at the famous battle of Normandy. He tried to claim political power in France at the time, too, crowning himself the king of France as well as the king of England. France would have no way with him, though, and surged against him, Joan of Arc leading the way in the siege of Orleans. The French army regathered and reorganized itself, coming back with fresh forces and military tactics. They reclaimed both Burgundy and the duchy of Guyenne, proving military prowess. Though the war never ended formally in a treaty, the English accepted that the French had grown their military and political powers to protect their own kingdom and no longer laid siege to them.

The time would come again when England and France would go to war with one another, becoming a common thread along English history and making the Hundred Years' War only the spark in a fire of conflicts between the two countries.

CHAPTER 4
THE HOUSE OF TUDOR AND BEYOND

The Tudor dynasty has become the object of many historians' interest and media representations alike. The popular television show Tudors capitalized upon the reputation of Henry VIII and his sensational lineage

. Entertainment has turned the House of Tudor into a romanticized and embellished family of shockingly lewd behaviors, but the Tudors were a lasting dynasty for a reason. They did not endure simply because their behaviors were questionable according to the Church. They were methodical and made great social and political changes that had a lasting impact on England.

Under the famous Tudor dynasty, England would most notably undergo religious changes that would both upset the public and the Church. Though it resulted in many conflicts on the civilian level, it would also spark a new idea in England's public and political leaders. The idea of the separation of church and state would be planted during this time. With the tumultuous changes, the separation would seem inevitable and almost an easier option than keeping the two tethered. Of course, the true separation would not actually occur until much later in England's history, but with the leaders of the Tudor dynasty making drastic and modern changes to the religion of the country, it showed people that religion was not as rigid as they might have once believed but, in fact, a flexible and adaptable part of life. This would prove challenging with the Church but would also be a revolutionary idea crucial for the development and evolution of England as a modern nation. Again, this was only proving that England was a nation ahead of its time. For the next several hundred years in England's history, this characteristic would hold true.

The War of the Roses

If it were not for the War of the Roses, then it could be asserted that the House of Tudor, the most famous and last royal dynasty of England before the country became a republic, would not have come to power. In 1455, a 32-year conflict between English noblemen and the English monarchy began. There are some people who believe that the ever-popular television show and book series Game of Thrones was based upon the War of the Roses, and while there were no dragons or fantastical white walkers in the real War of the Roses, there is a grain of truth in the foundation of both of these narratives. Both are concerning families feuding for a single crown; in the true historical case, this was the English crown. For years before the war officially began, two noble families had been in conflict regarding who was the most deserving of the English crown. The House of Lancaster and the House of York both claimed a direct descendant of the prior king of England, King Edward II, since both of them had come from King Edward II's sons.

Though the War of the Roses was initiated by the two families feuding for the English crown, it also set off a chain of events between other noble families who sided with either the House of York or the House of Lancaster. To recall from the earlier chapters, England was at war with France prior to and during the time of the War of the Roses. With funds being sent to the government to help supply the English military to fight against France, noble families were particularly invested in the best strategies to end the war. Since Richard of York, heading the House of York, and the House of Lancaster, headed by King Henry VI at the start of the War of the Roses, disagreed on tactics to end the war, other noble families joined the conflict based on their preferred strategy for the war with France. Throughout the 32 years that followed, the two families fought many brutal battles and performed a series of political manipulations on one another.

In 1455 at the Battle of St. Albans, one of the most famous battles of the war, the House of York took Henry VI prisoner, inciting a rebellion and retaliation from the House of Lancaster and giving temporary control of the crown over to Richard Neville of the House of York. King Richard maintained a fragile hand over the English crown while Henry VI's wife, Queen Margaret, worked secretly to secure her son's rightful place as the future heir. She built a remarkably well-equipped army in her husband's name and eventually sent them to battle with King Richard's army. The House of York won the battle, as well as the next several, capturing King Henry VI once again, while Queen Margaret continued to escape.

In 1460, with Henry under King Richard's bondage once more, King Richard convinced Henry to hand over the crown and end the fighting. Henry obliged, with the condition that he retain the crown until his death, at which point he would relinquish the English crown to the House of York. They signed the Act of Accord, but Queen Margaret was relentless in her desire to secure the throne. She prepared her army and sent it to fight King Richard's in retaliation for the Accord, killing Richard. When Richard's son, Edward, succeeded him, the bloodiest battle in the War of the Roses ensued at the battle of Towton, with 28,000 deaths recorded. As the Yorks won the battle and gained control of the crown, King Henry and Queen Margaret with their son ran to safety in Scotland.

While away, Queen Margaret garnered support from France and eventually ousted King Edward, restoring her husband to the throne in 1470. Soon after, with the death of King Henry, Queen Margaret, and their only son, King Edward returned to the throne. For several years, it appeared that the House of York had won, that is until  Henry Tudor of the Lancastrian house saw his moment to take back the crown. Richard III, the king of England at the time of Henry Tudor's rebellion, was rumored to have been illegitimate and, therefore, unworthy of the crown. Henry Tudor seized his chance and gained assistance from France once more in fighting for the throne. He won and secured the English crown for the House of Lancaster, which quickly became the House of Tudors. The War of the Roses would find an organic and peaceful ending with the marriage of Henry and Elizabeth of York, ending the long conflict. With Henry's arrival to the throne, the Tudor Dynasty had begun.

The Tudors

The Tudor dynasty brought many changes to England, including a restructuring of the monarchy, the Church, and religious and social customs. In totality, the Tudors would rule England for 118 years, through five monarchs, including the famous King Henry VIII and Queen Mary I, the first female monarch in English history. King Henry VII did not last long on the throne, his marriage with Elizabeth bearing eight children, including his only surviving son Henry VIII.

When Henry VIII took the throne in 1509, England was officially entering a new era of unprecedented change. The second son in the Tudor family, Henry VIII was originally destined for a life in the clergy, but after being called to the throne out of necessity, the young king seemed born to rule and took to the newfound power quite naturally and willingly. Henry VIII brought a slew of changes to England, the first and perhaps most famous one being that of the Church. Up until the 16th century, England had long been a Catholic country. The Church was a governing body all on its own and worked in tandem with the monarchy to devise the social and cultural structures of England. Henry VIII sought to change this, though, when his first wife, Catherine of Aragon, only bore him a daughter and no heir to the throne. Per the Catholic decrees, a man is to only take one wife, but Henry VIII created a loophole where there wasn't one before. With the supreme power of the English monarchy, Henry VIII rejected the Catholic Church and declared the Church of England, his own creation, the official religion of England. In this new religion, he was the overseeing power, not the Pope, and marriage was seen through a more flexible lens. Henry VIII annulled his marriage to Catherine of Aragon, a custom not recognized in Catholic traditions, and found himself a new wife in the venture to find an heir. After six other marriages, Henry VIII finally had himself a male heir.

While Henry VIII's creation of the Church of England allowed him to more freely make personal choices, benefiting him as an individual, it also altered England as a country on a broader spectrum. The Church of England, which would later be termed the Anglican Church, would eventually become the most popularly observed religion in England. It would also spread beyond Europe, reaching other countries, though none so completely as England itself. The religious change also altered the lives of common citizens. With the introduction of another church, suddenly religion was not quite as rigid as they'd initially believed it to be. The Church of England shared many values and customs with the Roman Catholic Church but differed, in that it adopted some of the ideals from the Protestant Reformation. It's considered more liberal in its beliefs and customs, allowing people more freedom within the customarily restrictive confines of religion.

Henry VIII also emphasized the importance of military prowess and introduced changes to the English Navy. He is colloquially termed "the Father of the English Navy," birthing the acclaimed navy that would prove nearly unstoppable in future conflicts and wars. When Henry VIII took the throne, he inherited a nearly nonexistent navy with only six ships. By the end of his reign, the Royal Navy had 60 ships, equipped and docked along England's shoreline, prepared for any imminent battle. Today, the British Navy is regarded as one of the most formidable military organizations, next to the United States Military.

Henry VIII is perhaps one of the most famous Tudors, but he is only the first in the lineage of the Tudor dynasty that brought change to England. Henry VIII's only son, Edward, was king for only a brief time before he died, leaving the Tudor monarchy scrambling for a solution. Henry VIII left behind only daughters—Mary, his first daughter, and Elizabeth, his second—to take the throne. Henry VIII's firstborn, Mary, won her right to the throne, making history as the first female monarch.

As her first decree as queen, she reverted England back to Catholicism, disregarding her father's more democratic religion. If King Henry VIII's reign was shockingly progressive, then Queen Mary's reign was perilous in the name of tradition. A religious zealot, Queen Mary launched a campaign of religious persecution, executing over 300 Protestants (or as she termed them "heretics") during her reign and fracturing the religious sectors of England. It was through this crusade, known as the Marian persecutions, that Queen Mary earned her nickname "Bloody Mary," and rightly so. Even if Queen Mary had not been a religious tyrant, she would have unfortunately still been disliked by the majority of the population, strictly on the basis of her gender. England was hesitant to embrace a female leader and, therefore, placed a greater emphasis on her marriage than they had on previous male monarchs. Upon Queen Mary's death, with no heirs to her name, she elected her younger sister, Elizabeth, as the new Queen of England, continuing the Tudor dynasty and enacting a kind of normalcy in recognizing a female as a possible monarch.

Queen Elizabeth I is heralded as one of the most successful monarchs in England's history, despite her rough introduction to the crown. A queen for 45 years, she was not welcomed as a new queen, facing similar discrimination as her sister had before her, with the addition of the scorched name of her mother, Anne Boleyn. Previous to King Henry VIII, children of anyone but the first wife were not considered prospects for the crown but rather "bastard children" who were not given any title or possibility of excelling in social spheres. Furthermore, Anne was also considered distanced from the crown and illegitimate due to Henry and Anne's divorce. With all of that being said, Queen Elizabeth I was the first to deny this tradition and slowly earned a great deal of respect from her subjects by turning England again toward prosperity. She returned England to its Protestant roots and welcomed a more free population. It was under her reign that the English Renaissance occurred, leaving citizens with an overwhelmingly positive perception of Queen Elizabeth I. Having watched the criticism her sister had endured as a female monarch, Queen Elizabeth I won a reputation as the "Virgin Queen" due to her reluctance to marriage, fearing that she would lose her power if she married a man into the monarchy.

It was under Queen Elizabeth I's rule that England became a colonial power. Queen Elizabeth. I saw the importance of conquest and wanted to strengthen England's hold as an international power. Using the Royal Navy that her father created before her, Queen Elizabeth brought England into the conquest game. Sir Walter Raleigh was a favorite sailor and soldier of Queen Elizabeth I, making him an excellent candidate for the conquest missions she was devising. The Queen saw how the Spanish were beginning to sail out to new lands, claiming new colonies for their own, and how this might become a threat to England. Not one to be shown up, Queen Elizabeth sent her own ships out to discover new lands, one of the most famous and successful being Sir Walter Raleigh's. If the name sounds familiar, it is most likely because it is tied to the colony of Roanoke, the "Lost colony." Though it has a rather disconcerting history, Roanoke was crucial in England's path to becoming a colonial power, marking it one of England's first (comparatively) successful colonies and paving the way for other conquests to come.

Since she never married, Queen Elizabeth I didn't have any heirs to her name. When she died after her long reign, the Tudor dynasty officially ended. With the closing of the Tudor dynasty, England would find itself turning toward a new age once again.

The Renaissance

Among all of the topics discussed in this book, the Renaissance is one of the most deserving of additional study. Entire college courses, entire tomes, are devoted to the Renaissance, making a brief introduction in a book of the entirety of English history fairly insubstantial in terms of understanding the Renaissance. As an overview of the period, it was commonly believed to be the era that ended the Middle Ages in England. The beginning of the Renaissance is debated, either starting with the Tudor dynasty or with the succession of Henry VIII to the English throne. Regardless, the height of the Renaissance took place during Elizabeth I's reign. Most of what people commonly learn about the Renaissance is actually specific to the Italian Renaissance. It's often identified as a time of artistic and scientific flourishing. When people think of the Renaissance, images of intricate paintings, inventions, and architectural feats come to mind. While this isn't untrue of the Renaissance, the English were having their own Renaissance in their own country.

While Italy flourished in terms of visual art, the English Renaissance saw a rebirth in terms of music and literature, giving way to famous writers such as John Donne, William Shakespeare, and John Milton. On the other end of the literary spectrum, William Tyndale published his new version of the Holy Bible,  releasing the copy that would influence the King James Version, which is still the most widely used version of the Holy Bible to date.

Similar to the Italian Renaissance, the English Renaissance saw an emphasis on humanism, the belief in individuality and personal expression. This left room for English citizens to begin reimagining their lives as citizens, not just as English subjects. In terms of England's growth, it could be asserted that the Renaissance was the nation's last hurrah in the era of childhood before entering adolescence. As people grew more satisfied with their personal lives and embraced the new morals of humanism, they also sought to better all other areas of their lives. Merchants began expanding trade routes, causing the English economy to flourish. With new inventions came new manufacturing systems, allowing for more efficient production and exportation. Political leaders began to reach out to other countries and attempt to make new alliances in the name of humanism.

Despite the prosperity that the English Renaissance brought, the era came to an end for a number of reasons. Some historians believe that the Counter-Reformation, or the Catholic Reformation, is to blame for ending the Renaissance, and in a country as traditionally Catholic as England, it is not such a feat to believe this. Coming out of the Renaissance, the Catholic Church sought to regain control, seeing humanism as a sinful rejection of the selfless nature of true, devout Christians. The Church began censoring artists again and preaching more widely about limiting one's self-expression in the name of piety. In 1545, the Council of Trent issued the Roman Inquisition, further pushing Renaissance ideals out of the picture. By the Church's decree, anyone exhibiting humanist ideals was punishable by death. Though there were also economic complications, with wars waging across the Italian peninsula throughout the 15th century, creating political instability at the end of the Renaissance, it was truly the Age of Enlightenment and the return to the Catholic Church's values that brought the Renaissance to an end. England would shift, yet again, as it entered the 17th century, finding new ways to fortify its growing kingdom and challenge itself as it continued to discover its place in the Western world.

CHAPTER 5
ENGLAND AND THE "AGE OF MODERNITY"

As England moved into the 17th century, it was quickly becoming a kingdom proving itself as a modern and political power. They had begun colonies in the "New World," garnered a reputation for an unparalleled navy, and established a sense of stability under Queen Elizabeth I. They had made great advancements during their own Renaissance, where they flourished as an independent and humanist country, embracing what seemed to be the morals of the new modern world. But, as the Tudor dynasty ended, England was faced with a new monarchy, and with a new monarchy came new changes that brought civil unrest to the seemingly calm and United Kingdom of England.

This era would also hold many changes for the neighboring countries of Scotland and Ireland. For the foreseeable future, the history of both these nations was considered within the collective history of England, proving another unique quality of England. No other country considers another country's history also their history, but as time progressed, it would become more and more difficult to draw clear boundaries between the unified nations. In the 17th century, Ireland, Scotland, and England saw wars that led to direct impacts on the common people. Lands were confiscated from the poor, disease spread, and taxes skyrocketed. As it would come to pass, England's journey into the modern age was not one of peace or tranquility but of brutality and war. Though, it could be claimed that no passage, for a nation or an individual, into modernity is any other way.

English Civil Wars

After the death of Queen Elizabeth I, her cousin James Stuart, King James VI of Scotland, became the king of England and Ireland. The three kingdoms were united under one ruler for the first time in history, but the new rule would create a false sense of stability. While King James maintained some semblance of stability under his rule, it was when his son, Charles, took the throne that England would plunge into its first civil war. Charles wanted to use his sovereignty over Ireland, England, and Scotland to create a sort of uniformity among the nations. He began by instituting English religious doctrine in Scotland, which was met with resistance due to Scotland's Presbyterian population. Scotland met King Charles with their own forces, pushing him out of their country. King Charles turned to Parliament to supply him with the funds to retaliate against Scotland and pressure them into submitting to their rightful king. Parliament had been wary of King Charles since his assumption of the throne, though, and denied King Charles' request for funds, restricting the king's powers immediately. The disagreements between King Charles and Parliament continued when Ireland, currently under English rule, rebelled against England's Protestant population in Ireland, claiming that Ireland was traditionally a Catholic country and should remain as such. Parliament and King Charles disagreed, unsurprisingly, on how to react to the Catholics in Ireland, and King Charles eventually attempted to arrest five members of Parliament to prove his control over them. When Parliament discovered his power-hungry actions, King Charles feared that they would respond, and he fled to Northern England, signaling the official separation of Parliament and the monarchy for the first time since their alignment in England's early years. The civil war between those who aligned with Parliament and those who aligned with King Charles had begun.

In 1642, civil war broke out between the Royalist forces in the North and West and the Parliamentarians in the South and East. Initially, it appeared that the Royalists would win out in the first civil war, but when the Parliamentarians capitalized upon Scotland's rift with King Charles and allied with them, they gained invaluable support in the next wars to come. The Parliamentarians created what was called the New Model Army, with the help of their allies, and soon became unstoppable for the Royalists. In 1649, they captured, tried, and executed King Charles. For a time, England was under a Republican regime, but with King Charles' living son, Charles II, taking the throne of Scotland, he soon garnered military support to reclaim his father's English throne, resuming the civil war for himself.

The third civil war did not last long, considering the power that the Parliamentary forces had acquired over the years. King Charles II did not succeed in taking power away from Parliament and disbanding them, as his father had sought to do. Instead, Parliamentary forces defeated him, and King Charles II was forced to reconcile with Parliament, ending the third civil war and beginning the English Restoration.

Though the English civil wars did not end in significant

political changes, as other wars had and would in the future, they left a hole in the population. By the end of the three civil wars, a total of 200,000 English civilians and soldiers had died, which, proportionate to the population of the time, is the equivalent of English lives lost in WWI. The English civil wars also showed England that while Parliament and the monarchy would work together to govern their kingdom, it was not always a cohesive relationship.

In 1660, with the return of King Charles II to the English throne, England began a gradual system of repairs to their political structures that had been damaged during the previous three civil wars. At this point in history, the three kingdoms—Ireland, England, and Scotland—were precariously linked and fragile in their political, economic, and social ties. Under King Charles II, Ireland, Scotland, and England were all united once more. To help sustain the newly united kingdoms, England expanded its trade once more and instituted a strict Anglican religious following, seeing it as the least divisive of the religions that had created a schism between the countries over the past several years. Unfortunately, the feelings of mistrust between Parliament and the English monarchy would not disappear but rather resurface again, less than 20 years later.

The Glorious Revolution: 1688–1689

The Glorious Revolution is termed such because technically no lives were lost and no physical battles fought during the conflict. It was, instead, a battle of manipulation and persistence between Parliament and the English crown to each gain more control

over the other in the governance of England. King James II was crowned King of England in 1685, reigniting tensions between Parliament and the monarchy due to his staunch Catholic beliefs. Furthermore, he encouraged a general sense of freedom among the English population, suspended powers from Parliament, and appointed Catholic members to positions of great power in both political and military offices. King James continued to push his boundaries with Parliament when he married a Catholic woman, ensuring that the royal bloodline would remain Catholic even after King James passed. Parliament was disgruntled by this but sought to keep the peace with the monarchy. They invited King James for dinner to discuss a solution to their quarreling. The two came to an agreement that would forever change the governance of England.

Though a relatively short revolution, when compared to other wars in which England was involved, the Glorious Revolution had one of the most impactful endings of any war. Through the Glorious Revolution, England adopted the English Bill of Rights in 1689, which required that Parliament and the monarchy rule in a partnership while also placing some limitations on the crown. This was an invaluable change to England, and an unforeseen, but no less crucial, addition to the modern world. England was the first country to recognize that the ruling and governing powers needed limitations. Prior to this point in history, all rulers had governed their kingdoms with absolute oversight and unrestrained power. After the Glorious Revolution and the introduction of the English Bill of Rights, this pattern would change. The Glorious Revolution resulted in the cohesive partnership that is recognized today between Parliament and the English crown, a relationship that few countries have been able to replicate since. Even in modern times, countries would still be attempting to strike the balance between power and control of their governing bodies.

Age of Enlightenment

Perhaps it could be asserted that Queen Elizabeth I's famous intellect and emphasis on education helped spur the Age of Enlightenment in England. She was venerated as a highly intelligent queen and strived to make a conscious and modern society that was not restricted by religious rules or hampered by past beliefs. She pointed England toward the future, and toward the future they moved. The Age of Enlightenment, also known as the "Age of Reason," spanned the 17th and 18th centuries in England, ushering in immense philosophical and intellectual developments that changed the country for the better. As the Renaissance had placed an emphasis on humanism, the Enlightenment encouraged people to seek out reason and structure. With the return to a stronger government, people started to shift their attention toward organization and understanding the smartest courses of action in all aspects of their lives. The unrest in their political and social spheres pushed people to consider solutions for themselves. Thinkers emerged out of the common population, eager to question and critique the systems in which they lived.

John Locke was one of the most famous thinkers to come from the English Enlightenment. Locke published many works during this time, all proclaiming that embracing human consciousness and reason was the only way for humans to truly be happy. He also wrote about the importance of the separation of church and state, which at the time, was a revolutionary way of thinking. Other thinkers also wrote during this time, such as Thomas Hobbes, who published his most famous work, Leviathan, which established some of the foundations of modern philosophy.

Outside of philosophy and political theory, England made significant scientific advancements under the new thinking. Education and logic were at the forefront of England's collective consciousness now, and famous scientists and inventors such as Nicholas Copernicus and Isaac Newton (not to mention Galileo, though he was not directly related to the English Enlightenment but rather the Italian one) were finally explaining how the universe worked. They were establishing the laws of the natural world, answering questions to which the Church had long been the only authority able to offer any explanation.

Out of the English Enlightenment, people began to realize that their questions could have answers and their world was vast but understandable, at least. With logic and education, people could finally understand what had once seemed so unreachable, it was supernatural or divine in its vastness. Without the Enlightenment, areas of study such as chemistry, astronomy, and the social sciences would not exist. Prior to the Enlightenment, there had not been a reason to study one's past or question one's present. As a kingdom, England was taking steps toward its place as the leader of the modern world.

CHAPTER 6
GEORGIAN ENGLAND

The 18th century in England was one predominantly of transition. The English crown was passing from one monarchy to the other, starting the long line of Georges on the English throne. Political parties within England were strengthening their holds and even extending overseas. As England had devoted much of the 17th century to spreading its roots and becoming a colonial power, they would pay the price for their endeavors in the 18th century. Their colonies would gather confidence and rise up against the now-great British empire, resulting in one of the most successful revolutions in the world: The American Revolution. Unsurprisingly, the famous King George of the revolution is part of this era, which left a permanent stamp on the culture and history of England. The 18th century would force England to test its new boundaries as a kingdom and as a powerful empire with seemingly limitless boundaries. By the end of the century, there would be no question that England was a powerful player in the modern world, having sown the very seeds that would grow into the United States.

On a moral and social level, the Georgian era for England would sew new oats of nationalism and patriotism. The English would continue to hone their pride for their country. The acclaimed Encyclopedia Britannica, a resource that is digitized now and still in use today, saw its first publication during the Georgian era and introduced to citizens and scholars alike the first glimpse of what their country really had to offer to the world. During this time, England maintained what is perhaps its most famous culture and society. It was a unique combination of brutality (both military and civilian) and classical literature, art, and customs. The English would continue this balance of strict civility and organic barbarism for the next several hundred years.

Jacobite Rebellion

Following on the heels of the Glorious Revolution, in the early days of the 18th century, a new rebellion would begin in England. The common people predominantly of Scotland were displeased with the current English monarchy and the outcome of the Glorious Revolution. The Jacobite Rebellion of the 18th century was actually the second Jacobite rebellion, but of the two it was the more successful one in achieving the united goals of both movements. When the first Jacobite rebellion broke out in 1689, it was following the newly appointed English monarchs, William and Mary. William of Orange and Mary II had been selected by the English to serve on the throne instead of James II, who had originally been in line to rule. James II was a Catholic, and the English (ever the wary travelers of the realm of religion) were concerned that his ruling might lead to another Catholic uprising. Thus, they removed him from the throne and promptly replaced him with William and Mary, who were Protestants. But England did not take into account that they were now united with Scotland, an overwhelmingly Catholic country. Those who supported James II and wanted him, or at least the Stuart dynasty, restored to the throne termed themselves the Jacobites and rose up against the monarchy.

The first Jacobite uprising was fairly unsuccessful, ending in flaccid battles, James II's return to France, and a failed renewal of his status as the English and Scottish monarch. Starting in the 1690s and continuing on through 1715, the second Jacobite uprising was built on a continued dissatisfaction with King William and poor living conditions for those in Scotland. They wanted change, and they believed a new monarch would be the answer to their Catholic prayers. This rebellion would end with the return of Anne Stuart to the throne as well as Hanoverian armies beating the Jacobites.

The Jacobites would have two more uprisings. The third would be instigated by the Spanish in the hopes that civil unrest would help them reclaim land they had lost to the English in the War of Spanish Succession. This attempt to overthrow the English crown would falter as well, resulting in thousands of lost Spanish soldiers and no movement on the English crown. The final uprising was not a victory for the Jacobites, but it did result in political changes to protect the English government against them. The Jacobites had earned such a name for themselves across Europe as ruthless, power-hungry rebels who would stop at nothing to attain victory. Unfortunately, it also contributed to a long-standing hatred for the Gaelic culture and any people living in the Scottish Highlands. The English Parliament instituted several precautions to act against possible or confirmed Jacobites. In 1746, Parliament passed the Disarming Acts, which outlawed any representation of Gaelic culture. In addition, they passed a forfeiture of land owned by any Jacobite, robbing them of all livelihood after the rebellions.

The Jacobite Rebellions eventually had a negative effect on the very Scottish Highlanders who had started it in the first place. By the time their rebellions had been stamped out, their entire way of life was snuffed out with it. It would also create a reputation for the Scottish people that would stain the country as a whole. That being said, the minor success of the Jacobite Rebellions was in aiding the future restoration of the Stuart dynasty to the English crown. Their success would swing wide the doors of the 18th century in England.

Acts of Union

To be clear, England had been endeavoring to unite itself with other countries prior to the 16th century. In fact, all the way back in 1284, the English crown annexed Wales, which in effect, gave England power over Wales but didn't necessarily incorporate Wales into the kingdom as a whole. This more complete incorporation of Wales into England wouldn't happen until 1536 with King Henry VIII's Act of Union. Once this was passed, the Welsh people would be given the same rights and laws as those in England. Wales was also granted positions in Parliament, expanding the idea of equal representation and taking the first step of many toward turning England into the United Kingdom. In 1603, with Queen Elizabeth's death and her cousin James I's ascension to the throne, England and Scotland became unified under the same crown, as King James had already been the king of Scotland since 1567. Though it was his goal to unify the two nations, he only accomplished this in a symbolic sense. England created a new flag featuring both the English and Scottish crosses, more commonly known as the "Union Jack." The flag was the forerunner to the flag of the United Kingdom, which would come with the next Act of Union.

In 1702, Anne Stuart, the sister of the last king and queen, inherited the English throne, temporarily returning England to the Stuart dynasty. Queen Anne's rule was short but crucial in forming the political sphere of modern England. At the beginning of the century, Scotland was in dire need of economic assistance. In return, England was concerned that Scotland might serve as a neutral pass-through for France to launch attacks on England. The two sought a symbiotic solution, and unification seemed to be the simplest answer. Scotland was forced to reconcile its parliament but remained able to maintain its system of laws. This would prove problematic in the future, but for the time being, the two countries saw a manageable agreement. In May 1707, a new Act of Union was passed, combining England and Scotland into the United Kingdom. Anne Stuart would serve as monarch for both countries, and Parliament would be the governing body for them as well. As time went on, the United Kingdom would grow more, but the first step had at least been taken. England was nurturing a new side of itself with this decision. Not only was the nation willing to maintain strong trade and political relationships with other countries, but England was also finally prospering enough to, in essence, take another country under its wing and consider it part of its own kingdom.

Political Parties

With England evolving as a kingdom, its political sphere was expanding with it. Within England, two predominant political parties were emerging, an idea that perhaps had existed for centuries but had yet to gain enough strength and commitment to earn a structural shift. It was during the Georgian period that the Whigs and the Tories, the political parties that would

eventually follow to America, emerged in England. During the previous disagreements concerning James II's rise to the throne, the names came as derogatory labels for the opposing sides. In a sense, then, we have the Jacobite Rebellion to thank, too, for England's most prominent political parties. Those who supported James II were given the name "Tory," an Irish term for "papist outlaw," due to their belief in James' lineage as a Roman Catholic on the throne. On the opposing side were the "Whigs," a Gaelic name that indicates thievery. The term was applied to the Scottish Presbyterians for their attempts to steal the throne, as the English considered it.

Though the names were applied to indicate groups that supported or were against the monarchy, they remained even after the conflicts between the Jacobites and the English. It was under Queen Anne's rule that the political parties developed their own connotations. The Whigs became associated with the resistance, a group of people who were in support of Anglicanism and the nobles. They were against the monarchy and were often associated with religious dissent. Tories, on the other hand, were linked to aristocracy. They were more traditional and in support of maintaining the customs that England had established over the past centuries. They were opposed to religious toleration and any foreign affairs that challenged the current state of England.

The impact of these parties would prove especially resounding in the coming years as England faced its most formidable ally and enemy yet. Their own colony, America, would rise up against them to earn its independence, and it was partially these original political groups that would be to blame for the arguments that spurred the revolution. Both the Whigs and the Tories would make it across the Atlantic to the new colony, bringing with them the opinions of their past parties as well as evolving within the political and social climates of their new environment.

The American Revolution

Overwhelmingly, it is the American War of Independence, or the American Revolution, that served as the most altering event of the 18th century, both in England and America. In the 17th and 18th centuries, England had devoted itself to leading the colonization movement in which Spain, Portugal, and France were all involved. While Spain and France soon pulled ahead with England, as the 18th century progressed, it was clear that these three would reign supreme in the efforts to conquer foreign lands. Spain and France had an ulterior motive for conquering lands though: Profit. They conquered lands for the exports that would lend themselves to their respective countries, giving them valuable trade materials that other countries didn't have. As a result, their territories were less colonies and more business franchises. England had more domestic aspirations for their conquests, hoping to spread their kingdom as widely as possible across the quickly expanding "known" world. They claimed land and quickly set to colonizing it, establishing homes and businesses. They looked at colonies as extensions of themselves and less as business ventures. It is true that they took many valuable assets from their new-world colonies, but at the heart of their colonization effort was a desire to have English touchstones across the globe: In essence, to make the country of England borderless and their presence ubiquitous. This strategy, while proving beneficial, would eventually backfire for the English. Their colonists were too self-sufficient, their establishments too successful. In an effort to create lives outside of England, the English soon found that the extension of themselves wanted a severing, and the amputation would be bloody.

Similar to the Renaissance, entire tomes and college

courses have been devoted to the American Revolution. It is a complex war that involved a litany of battles and pivotal events on both sides of the conflict. To begin, the main incentive for the revolution could be clearly seen as the independence of England's 13 colonies grew. Colonists were developing a disinterest in and distaste for England. They felt distanced from the country, both culturally and physically, and were angered by the continued governance of their affairs by an authority to which they no longer felt connected. Tensions had been building between the colonies and England for years before war broke out in 1775. England had gained new territories in the French and Indian War, but with new territories came new expenses. England enforced new taxes on the colonists to help pay for their future plans of expansion and colonization. With the Stamp Act, Townshend Act, and infamous Tea Act, colonists were feeling economically strapped by a country they were growing to detest. England sensed their unease and stationed British soldiers in the colonies to help enforce the tax collections and keep the peace. With tensions rising, it took only a single match to light the fire at the Boston Massacre in 1770, the first of many conflicts between the two sides.

Both the colonists and the English knew that they could not simply shrug off the Boston Massacre, and England sent more troops to the colonies. The colonists responded by creating more conflict. The famous Boston Tea Party was yet another act against the English, followed shortly after in 1774 by the first Continental Congress meeting. American leaders, such as George Washington, John Adams, and Samuel Adams, as well as many others, met to discuss a formal disintegration of the bonds between England and the colonies. England, a powerful kingdom that had fought hard for its borders to extend across the sea would not stand for this insurrection, though, and sent troops to stop the war of independence before it could begin. With the acclaimed "shot heard round the world," when British troops landed and fought the first battle against waiting American troops, the American Revolution began.

Several more battles would ensue in the first years of the revolution, but it was the political game that America played that cost England their most successful colonies. The American Revolution would further capitalize on the discrepancies and history of unease between England and France. Being former English subjects themselves, or at least descendants of them, the American colonists were well aware of the tumultuous history that England had with France. The two were constantly at odds, and the colonists sought to use this to their advantage by allying with the French, a military and political decision that would help to solidify their eventual victory. Americans also drew from England's history of historical documents and its people's own pleas for independence in order to create the Declaration of Independence, inspired by England's Magna Carta as well as its integration of the parliamentary system to establish more equal representation by the nation's own people.

After eight years of battles and political manipulation, England had to formally recognize America's status as a free country with the signing of the Treaty of Paris in 1783. England also had to sign peace treaties with Spain and France, who had entered the war to support the Americans, though more so to see the English finally defeated. While the American Revolution was heralded as a victory for America, it signaled a change in England. It showed the English that in their effort to create an expansive kingdom, they would have to monitor their colonies closely. Ownership, they saw, was not permanent. Their people had minds of their own, and England could not act as an overbearing parent forever, as they would later see with other colonies.

CHAPTER 7
VICTORIAN ENGLAND

The Victorian era in England's history is overwhelmingly recognized as its most prosperous and overall productive period. England made leaps and bounds in terms of economic prosperity and political gain. It extended its colonial powers, asserting itself as the head of international colonial efforts. It expanded its boundaries, became the parent of the greatest success story that colonies would look to for generations, and was in a solid place to build cultural and intellectual progress. The Victorian era only earned its name from the era's monarch, Queen Victoria, who played a major part in shaping England's future. It was during the Victorian era that England saw some of the most intellectual and academic advancements that the world had ever seen since ancient Greece. It was a time for English citizens to prosper, but it was also a tipping point for England. They were at a crossroads, politically speaking, and they were entering the age of Imperialism. As a country with a longstanding history of being an imperial power, England had a reputation to uphold as more countries entered the race to colonize the globe. They also had learned valuable lessons from the American Revolution and would take these into the new century. England would undergo yet more change during the Victorian era, emerging, as they hoped, stronger and more prepared for what the 20th century would bring.

The Victorian era was also characterized by a class-based society. This meant that England was modernizing in a way that it hadn't before. In previous centuries, feudalism had either reigned supreme as the governing societal structure, or it had hung on, enduring longer than most would have preferred. Entering the Victorian era, power was organized differently. Power was no longer based strictly on titles but corresponded to wealth, meaning the more wealth and property someone had, the more power they had. This opened the doors for the majority of the English population who had previously been barred from advancing in society. This idea of freedom for every man would ring true in many different areas of people's lives. More people would earn the right to vote in this era, and cultural restrictions would break as well, giving people an overall less restrictive way of life.

The English Government in Victorian Times

Prior to Queen Victoria taking the throne at the age of only 18, the longest-reigning monarch was King George III. King George III had reigned as ruler of England, Ireland, and eventually the United Kingdom from 1760 to 1820. Today, he is still the longest-reigning king of England. But Queen Victoria was not one to be shown up. She assumed the throne after King George IV and King William IV. When she took the throne in 1837, the kingdom bwas at a political tipping point. They had recovered from the American Revolution but now turned their sights inward to build a strong country from within. In 1837, Queen Victoria inherited the first year of the smallpox epidemic in England. This would only be the first bump in the road of her 63-year reign of England.

Queen Victoria was incredibly popular among the common people, and this would bode well for her as the position of the English monarchy changed drastically during her reign. Political parties were shifting during Queen Victoria's era. The two original parties, the Whigs and the Tories, still maintained their statuses in England, but as the culture was changing, so did they. The parties wanted to shed their old values and names for new, evolved characteristics and classifications. As such, the Tories became the Liberals and the Whigs eventually became the Conservatives, though still favoring aristocratic ideals. The change was made in an effort to survive throughout the rest of the political changes that would take place during the Victorian era. Perhaps it was an assertion of their expectation that they would need to appeal more directly to Parliament in the coming years. Those associated with political parties recognized early that the attachment to the English monarchy and the real power that Parliament held was shifting; showing direct ties to the old monarchy and the old ways might not serve them in the future.

Despite Queen Victoria's appeal to the common man during her reign, the House of the Lords (the English monarchy) was overshadowed by the House of Commons (Parliament). It was at this point that England was turning toward an even more modernized country, one that was beginning to recognize the old ways of a governing monarch less and less. Suddenly, Queen Victoria turned into a symbol of the country, rather than a sole governing head. At this time, Parliament held immense power, also reflecting the social changes in England that emphasized representation more and more. It included 600 members who had been elected by the public to represent England, Ireland, Wales, and Scotland.

Victorian England may have been named after its monarch, but it earned much of its political progress through the strengthening of its parliament.

Imperial Era

The English people had developed a sense of pride over the imperial nature of their country. England was not simply a kingdom strong within itself. It expanded across the globe, and by the 20th century, it would cover over one fifth of the earth's land surface. The British people acknowledged that they were superior to other countries in their political and cultural advancements. Though it could be argued that all citizens feel this way about their country, the English had a certain level of responsibility to this emotion. They were entitled to a feeling of superiority since their country had proven itself, again and again, as a kingdom that would continue to rise, despite each challenge they faced. Coming out of the 18th century, England was eager to continue in the race to conquer the rest of the globe and discover new territories.

At the start of the 19th century, England won victory against France in the Napoleonic wars, resulting in a strengthening of their Navy and an assertion that they were a superior empire. With their newfound strength, they went on to colonize areas in Asia, Africa, and the Pacific Islands. They experienced a period of peace in which, although they were fighting other countries in an arms race, so to speak, they weren't necessarily in any wars. Once islands in the Pacific and countries in Africa were conquered, England's trade exploded. England was at the peak of an indefatigable economy, pushing out more goods and balancing more wealth than it ever had before. The first World's Fair in 1851 was a celebration of this prosperity, showcasing all of the foreign goods that England had obtained and been trading with the world. Upon conquering India, England obtained what was often referred to as "the jewel in the kingdom's crown," as it served to be one of their most profitable sources of exports. When England, Spain, and France turned to Africa, they divided up the continent for each country. This opened wide the slave trade for  England, expanding it from what it already had been generations prior. England also overtook areas in South America, Australia, the Caribbean, and China.

Industrial Revolution

England's working class and their sources of industry were areas that changed the most during this era. Though that may seem like an extreme evaluation, it is true when considering that it was England who arrived at the Industrial Revolution first. England's industrial revolution would serve as an inspiration and a foundation on which America would build theirs 50 years later. Though the end result of the Industrial Revolution served to benefit England tenfold, the events preceding it, which necessitated the industrialization of the country's economy, were incredibly taxing on the people.

In the early part of the 19th century, England and its longtime partner, Ireland, saw great famines sweep the nations. In England, the 1840s were known as "The Hungry Forties," during which poverty and famine skyrocketed in England. Despite the overall prosperity in England's Victorian period, in 1839, they suffered a dip in economic trade, which put a strain on the economy that had grown accustomed to prospering over the past several years. With trade down, there was less money circulating in the economy, and all areas were affected. England suffered poor harvests for the next several years, which coupled with the increasing population (as a result of the initial success of England's new era) were a recipe for economic disaster. In 1845, a potato blight came to England and Scotland, further intensifying the costs of famine across both countries. Then, in the following year it spread to Ireland, ultimately leading to the Great Potato Famine, one of Ireland's most defining historical events.

When England emerged out of these hard times, the people knew that they needed to re-evaluate their economy. Coupled with the developing feelings of independence, freedom, and personal ingenuity among the social classes, the English took it upon themselves to industrialize their economy. Railroads and steamships expanded their routes, spreading farther than they ever had before. With an increase in transportation options, England could not only increase their imports, protecting them from any future famines that would limit them to their own resources, but they could also increase the customers available to them for their own exports. This brought new money into the economy, re-invigorating it. The electric telegraph had been invented in 1837, and soon England began to implement that as well, drawing the borders of their large world closer.

The most recognizable additions of industrialization were also prevalent in England. They shifted from incremental, worker-based economies to industries based out of factories. They changed the training of workers from teaching them trades to teaching them a single aspect of a trade. No more were there cobblers but, instead, 50 people who knew how to make the shoelaces and another 50 who could make the soles. Their economy exploded, but their living standards failed to catch up. America would face the same challenges in the next century with its own industrial revolution, in which economy and capitalism were placed over the well-being of the worker. Furthermore, England's population was increasing exponentially during the Victorian era, going from 13 million to 32 million, and these numbers didn't include immigrants who were coming to England themselves in hopes of having a better life. The population sought jobs in factories, earning very little, but providing the backbone for a booming economy that bolstered elites at the top of society who were becoming increasingly wealthy in this new era.

Intellectual Accomplishments

Britain was the capital of the English-speaking world, making it the center of culture during the Victorian era. England, or at least its citizens, seemed to be well aware of this and did not fail to take leaps and bounds in the literary world. The Victorian era saw a revolution within itself within the world of the humanities and the arts. England brought forth new types of poetry, music, theater, and fiction and nonfiction prose. In the intellectual realm, it would be sufficient to claim that England did not suffer during the Victorian era. It was during this era that England earned its most prominent writer, short of Shakespeare: Charles Dickens. Dickens had such a lasting impact on England, and the world at large, that England would earn its own nickname for the era in which he wrote and the portrayals that he painted of his country: Dickensian England. Charles Dickens wrote incredibly long novels, later termed "Victorian novels" that relied more on common stories of people's lives rather than fables or religious tales of the past. It was his novels that popularized the form of serial publication that other Victorian novels would rely on later.

The Victorian era brought an increase in education and general intellect, and with the booming economy, more people had more money to gain access to what they had previously been restricted from. Literacy rates improved in this era, and now that more money was circulating, nearly every person in Britain could afford to read. What had once been a luxury for only the elite was now becoming knowledge afforded to the common man. Publishers caught on to this and tried to popularize reading, capitalizing on the wider population now available to them. They began printing serial publications, monthly installments of full-length novels, that were more widely distributed and cheaper for the common public. Dickens' novels, a popular favorite of the time, paved the way for other authors, like William Thackeray and Lewis Carroll, to publish in such a way. Other writers began publishing novels that fell into a different category, a new one altogether: Gothic novels. Along with Edward Hyde and Dracula, we also have the Victorian Age to thank for Sherlock Holmes.

Soon, the English population was not only widely literate, but they were also actively engaged in the support of their own modern culture through literature. England was bringing the arts out of the elite and into the popular sphere, creating a more equal and all-around enlightened population.

In addition to fiction prose, there was a change in poetry as well. Poets relied less on the rising literacy rates and more on the shifting political and moral beliefs of the majority. The Victorian era gave rise to the first wave of modern poetry. Poets began writing with an emphasis on the senses, publishing more passionate poems than had populated the canon previous to the Victorian era. Poets also began taking more risks with the style and content of their poems. One of the most famous poets of this period, who capitalized on these characteristics of the changing genre, was Alfred, Lord Tennyson.

Nonfiction writers in the Victorian era were not to be left out. There are two areas within the concentration that perhaps left the most lasting impact on not only English culture but the cultures of all countries: Journalism and science writing. The Victorian era saw the wave of "New Journalism" come crashing in, drawing on the sensational qualities of news reporting. Journalists were quickly becoming entertainers and not just informers of the truth. In fact, it was at this time that England paved the way for all journalism to come that would no longer simply report the facts but would attempt to tell a story that would make people want to continue reading. Furthermore, one of the most widely read books, a lifelong project that still continues today, was first started in the Victorian era: The Oxford English Dictionary.

Last, but not least, it would be a cataclysmic oversight to omit Charles Darwin and his On the Origin of Species from this overview of Victorian history. Darwin released his most famous book in 1859, though he had been a scientist and travel writer for 20 years prior to that. Darwin published his book during the Victorian era, hoping that with the influx of intellectual thought and academic emphasis, it might be more welcomed. People were embracing the necessity of understanding one's world and welcomed the new ways of the artistic and political environments with open arms. Science, however, has always been an area of hesitance and concern. His book questioned the very origin of our human race, staking his claim on years of studying evolution, both of humans and apes, finches, and other mammals that helped him to devise revolutionary theories. He posed the evolution theory, throwing a wrench not only in the common person's assumptions of their origins but in the Church's theories about humans' existence. Darwin's book set off a chain of reactions from both scientific and religious leaders. People were reluctant to believe his theories, though today they are heralded as revolutionary. It is perhaps fair to assume that, despite the progressive ideals of the Victorian era, Darwin's On the Origin of Species was ahead of its time, becoming the most influential academic book in 2015.

CHAPTER 8
THE WORLD AT WAR

Despite everyone's best efforts, no country was quite prepared for the 20th century. Nor was any country quite prepared for just the first half of the 20th century. England entered the 20th century as a declining empire. It had reached its peak during its imperial era, mostly overlapping with the Victorian era, and was now facing the challenges of coexisting with other modern countries in a modern world. England was not the only one on the map anymore, and other countries like France, Germany, and the United States were vying for supreme power. England would be underprepared in terms of military development as it entered the 20th century. Though the English had spent the last 50 years dominating the colonization scene, they had overlooked military advancements, leaving themselves with a scant number of military troops.

Socially speaking, they were amending some of the wrongs that they had sewn during the Industrial Revolution. England was instituting social reforms to improve the quality of life of the common population, who were predominantly overworked and underpaid for their labor. England worked to institute work reforms to improve conditions and give their workers' rights. They were also implementing education changes to improve the overall quality of their intellectual population. The Victorian era had set the stage for a well-educated and enlightened English population, and the 20th century would build on this foundation.

Politically, England was struggling with the steady reduction of the power of its traditional monarchy. In 1909, the Liberal Party passed the Parliament Act, denying monarchs the right to veto any financial bills. This was further emphasizing the changing role of the English monarch. The modern world was one fit for a parliament, not a single power, and England was slowly embracing it. Women were vying for the right to vote, latching onto the growing sense for equal representation that seemed to be spreading across the country. Their efforts, along with any and all social reform, would be halted in 1914 with the start of World War I.

As the world left behind the Victorian era, countries moved toward progress. Economic, social, and cultural shifts abounded. The Industrial Revolution in England established a new society, one driven by progress and permanently linked to other countries. Trade and colonial ties had always been intrinsic to England as a country, but as they entered the new 20th century, they began to realize that it was not simply trade that connected countries. International relationships were quickly becoming dictating factors within each country. It would eventually become more and more apparent that a single country's actions did not occur within a vacuum. As the world grew, the magnetism between each border and the relationships among each nation grew tighter and tighter.

Though there are many different theories as to just how

the First World War began, there is no argument regarding England's involvement in its development. England would prove its military and social prowess during the war years. Its economic and social systems would be tested, but throughout the next 40 years of England's history, the nation would be challenged and emerge as one of the world's key power players.

The First World War: 1914–1918

The Beginning

Germany was England's unforeseen enemy as they entered the 20th century. In the 19th century, England had focused on a political policy known as "splendid isolation" in which it placed its efforts on strengthening its European kingdom. The English had their sights set on an unstoppable United Kingdom and were striving to make this a reality. Unfortunately, as England realized at the beginning of the 20th century, this left them exposed and vulnerable to other countries outside of Europe. In the first 10 years of the 20th century, England laid the groundwork to repair this misstep. They signed the Anglo-Japanese Alliance in 1902 and the 1904 Entente Cordial with France; in 1907, they attended the Anglo-Russian Convention that allowed England to expand their navy and other military efforts. It also established a cordial relationship with Russia, who seemed to be the closest with Germany, the rising threat in the early 20th century.

Germany was expanding their navy, which attracted England's attention immediately. England had an established, centuries-long reputation for having the strongest navy, so when Germany began building more ships and adding to their naval reserves, England's concern was sparked. England watched as Germany was quickly becoming a military powerhouse. They had a history of choosing military conquest before moral appeals when dealing with other countries, and England was well aware of this. In 1911, after the Agadir Crisis involving French and German troops and naval ships, England and France began secret negotiations to discuss the possibility of Germany beginning a war in Europe. Their once age-old rivalry would prove to become the most lasting and vital partnership in the wars to come.

Some historians believe that it was England's apprehension concerning Germany's military expansion that caused them to enter the war. Others are more convinced that it was actually Germany's booming economy that England saw as a threat that should be expelled. Others still believe that it was actually England's loyalty to France that brought them into World War I. When Germany invaded Belgium in 1914, England was afraid of history repeating itself. In 1870, German and Prussian states obliterated France, and their military had only strengthened since then. England was afraid that if the Germans continued to push across France, they would reach the English Channel, gaining control of one of their most vital trade routes. England couldn't let France be defeated again and place itself in an economically vulnerable position that would require its involvement in a new war.

The reasons for World War I beginning—in other words, the spark that lit the fire—are still undecided and debated among academic circles constantly. The most popular and widely circulated story of the beginning of WWI is told through the lens of the assassination of Archduke Ferdinand by a Serbian rebel, causing a schism in Austria-Hungary and Serbian relations. Russia and Germany came to the aid of each region as support split down party lines. Russia supported Austria-Hungary, and Germany supported Serbia. Here entered the concern about the state of France as Germany was escalating its military presence, along with England's concern about looking overly self-centered or too concerned with its own problems within its own borders. The theory of England wanting to come to France's aid and getting caught in the crossfire was true, but what also weighed heavily on Britain's government was the consequences of its previous century of isolation. The world was not one of isolation anymore but one of support and integration, and England needed to show that it was willing to support this turn of the modern world. Furthermore, on a more selfish and economic note, England needed to protect its oil investments in Iran. If Germany gained too much power, they could overthrow the British presence in Iran and take the oil supplies for themselves.

When Germany invaded Belgium, England officially declared war on August 4, 1914, claiming that its entrance into the war was due to the protections required of the nation by the Treaty of London, while safeguarding its more political incentives. The declaration of war on Germany required the support of every dominion, colony, and protection of the United Kingdom, meaning that even though Britain declared war, it was certainly more than just English citizens and the English government that were involved in this first world war.

War, Terrible War

Again, World War I is another topic to which entire books, college courses, and scholars' lives are devoted to studying. World War I was monumental in bringing the world, including England, into the modern violence and political games of the 20th century. It ushered in a new kind of world, one that required the kind of strength, on the political and civilian level, that countries had never had to supply. It introduced modern warfare, tactics that soldiers had never used before. Coming off the heels of the Industrial Revolution, many countries were utilizing technology that they themselves didn't understand. With a combination of modern technology and outdated tactics, World War I was one of the deadliest conflicts in history and, in fact, the deadliest war the world had seen thus far. It would not be surpassed until World War II, though in some ways it was more gruesome even than that.

England's involvement in World War I was fairly absolute. They ran political games as well as contributed soldiers to the fronts that sprang up all across France. With the start of the war, countries chose sides, falling into either the Central powers (mainly comprised of Germany and Austria-Hungary) or the Allied powers (the United Kingdom, Japan, Italy, Russia, and the United States). Immediately facing Germany's unparalleled military powers, England realized that it needed to re-evaluate its military. World War I brought many changes to England, but the most obvious military advancement was the creation of the British Air Force. Airplanes were an innovation from the last century, but with the new type of warfare of the 20th century, they were now being utilized for military conquest. As British and French forces fought German forces in the early years of the war, England strived to continue to make advancements with their military technology. They were engaged in trench warfare, the well-known stalemate tactic of the First World War. Both sides had found themselves at a stalemate for months before England took another step forward in modern warfare and introduced the first tank to the battlefield. The first tanks were dangerous and difficult to maneuver, but it was, at least, a step in the direction of military evolution on England's part. It would continue to advance as years went by, the First World War being only a rough introduction.

World War I was the first time that England had ever been truly affected on its home front by a war. Previously, it had been successful in keeping wars in other countries or maintaining a stronghold at its borders, but with the integration of aerial warfare, the English found themselves in what was called "total warfare." Civilians were being bombed in their home country, transforming how the British people began to think about war. No more was it something that occurred outside of their homes, and even their country. In the new world, it was a matter of daily concern and fear, invading every aspect of people's lives. In this same vein, the newspapers that had been revamped during the Victorian age sought to help the war effort as well. Wartime propaganda was a major asset during World War I and would remain a tool for governments during wartime for every war following it. Under total warfare, all avenues were geared toward supporting the war effort, especially the manufacturing and factory businesses. The workforce turned toward the war, changing what they manufactured, how they manufactured, and who was allowed to work. As the war went on and the number of

casualties continued to steadily rise, English men began enlisting to replenish the troop numbers and to fulfill their duty to their country. But with all of the men going off to war, someone had to maintain industries on the homefront. In this way, World War I is sometimes credited with letting women into the mainstream workforce, changing the standards that the British held for equality concerning gendered careers. Women earned jobs wherever they could to help support the war effort, keeping the country running while their men fought in the terrible war. Eventually, World War I became too consuming to keep women on the home front. Though it took some political shifting, by the end of the war almost 80,000 women had joined the armed forces as nurses or cooks, breaking the staunch barrier between them and the military. Both civilians and troops were heavily impacted by the war. By the end of World War I, military deaths were said to have risen above 850,000, while the civilian death rate surpassed that of both the Spanish flu and previous famines. It was by no means a low number though, considering that while civilians died of malnutrition from war rationing, they were also hit with the Spanish flu in 1918 and lost the lives of more innocent people.

Though it may appear on the surface that England was a united front at home, such was not the case. In the Victorian era, while England experienced immense wealth and prosperity, it drew thousands of immigrants to the country. Previously, it had been a sign of England's success as a nation to stabilize itself enough to attract citizens of other countries. But when World War I broke out, it was soon seen as a threat by many English citizens. In August of the first year of the war, Parliament passed the Aliens Restriction Act, which required all foreign immigrants who had come to England to register with the police and the government. By the next year, almost

70,000 German, Hungarian, and Austrian immigrants had registered. England claimed it was a way to keep track of the immigrant population, but really it was a reflection of their mistrust of the "enemy" in their own country. Registered citizens of other countries were restricted on their travel plans and what merchandise they could purchase, and their homes could be searched at any time. As anti-German sentiment rose across the nation, England soon started interning foreign citizens. Although, by 1915 with the sinking of the Lusitania, such attitudes had peaked and would only decrease as the war went on.

The Aftermath

The first turning point in World War I that swung the war in the direction of the Allied powers was the arrival of American troops to Europe. After the sinking of the Lusitania, America arrived in Europe in 1917 to join the Allied powers. Though America's contribution during WWI on the ground was actually quite minimal, their presence gave the appearance to the German forces that the Allied powers had infinite troops who could be mobilized at any time and transported anywhere. This was understandably intimidating to Germany and helped to sink their morale. The second turning point of the war was in 1918 when German forces attacked too quickly, depleting their forces substantially in the Battle of the Marne. Finally, when Allied forces finally crossed the Hindenburg Line on the Western Front, forcing German troops to retreat, it was only a short time until November when Germany, depleted of goods and troops, had to call an armistice to end the war.

The impact of World War I on England and the world at large is undeniable. Germany's territory was minimized exponentially, and its economy was quickly depleted with the enforcement of reparations to France for the war. This would eventually impact England as Germany turned back to them in WWII for supporting the peace treaty that required reparations. England's economy was also heavily taxed from the war. They had gone from being the leading economy of the world to one of the largest debtors. It had also led to political changes, as many people turned to support the Labour Party, replacing the previously established Liberal Party, which had been strong going into the war. However, the largest impact on England was by far a psychological one. The English had believed themselves a proud, unstoppable country, but by the end of World War I, they had been extremely humbled. With their social structures shaky and their economy on the mend, they would turn to the only standing country that had emerged from World War I on the upside: The United States.

The Interwar Years: 1918–1939

Between the two world wars, England attempted to catch its breath. England would undergo more political changes within its bodies of government. They would undergo the same Great Depression that crushed other countries around the world, and although it would not have the same detrimental effects on England as other places, England  would no doubt be affected. What categorized the interwar years as crucial for England was a transformation after the Great War. England took the time after World War I not only to recover from its losses in all areas of life but, in a sense, to start anew. Activism for women's rights as well as the treatment of the working class would see an influx of energy and dedication. England would begin an era of social reform that it would turn to, once again, after the Second World War.

In the political realm, there was conflict between the Conservative and Liberal parties, but with Prime Minister Lloyd George, a controversial Conservative of the time, the government steered toward providing benefits for its war heroes after the Great War. The rise of the Labour Party, a political party of social democrats and unionists dedicated to standing for the common man and working class, took place during the interwar years. The Labour Party would lead much of the political change in these years, as well as after World War II a few decades later. They assisted in changing policies that benefited workers and restored a national industry of development and manufacturing to England. Again, it was their work that would be built upon in later years, after World War II, during Thatcherism. The Labour Party soon became so influential that, during the interwar years, England's government was termed the Labour government, and all decisions were controlled by the majority party. This led to an increase in funding for low-income housing. The Labour Party also extended conversations with the Soviet Union, being one of the first nations to recognize them as such. This would serve them in the war to come. Where the Labour Party faltered was in 1923 when their anti-communist sentiments got the better of them, and they authorized the search and seizure of the Workers' Weekly newspaper office, setting off a negative reaction from both the Liberal and Conservative parties. After being tried, the Labour Party was overthrown by the Conservative Party once more. The two parties would argue throughout the next 10 years, alternating between the controlling party in office until 1931, when England finally settled on having a national government. It's important to note, though, that even today the influence of the Labour Party in England is immense, often controlling many of the political decisions for the country as a whole.

On the international stage, the English were watching Germany rebuild its economy and military presence, and they were concerned that they might be headed toward war. In preparation for such an event, they strengthened their ties with Arab nations, securing their oil reserves and trade routes. In 1919, after World War I, the victorious Allied powers had created the League of Nations. This created a new kind of union among the nations of the new world. It created a series of requirements that all of the nations involved would follow, including a reduced arms presence and open conversation between all nations regarding security and military decisions. In short, the League of Nations supplied accountability to the countries involved after the war, ensuring that no country could go undetected and all were considered represented in the world. As one of the leading countries that were part of the League of Nations, England was committed to its relationship throughout the next several years.

England also underwent social changes in the interwar years. For instance, there was a general decline of religious values and traditions throughout these years. Some historians attribute this to the aftermath of the war. The age-old argument that God cannot be real if there is so much suffering on Earth rose again following the Great War. But more than that, people began viewing the Church and its customs and beliefs as outdated. The Church of England needed a substantial re-evaluation in order to keep up with the modern world, and when they didn't undergo this, Brits reacted. Sunday school attendance dropped, as did missionary work, volunteerism, and overall membership. The decline of boarding schools also contributed to this change in England. Though the tradition of boarding schools would continue to persist for the next several decades, attendance to the specifically religious boarding schools declined, shifting toward nondenominational boarding schools. As a historically religious country, built on the culture of the Church, this was a startling, though no doubt unsurprising, shift in England's culture. The decline in religion also heralded positive changes for women.

Once society was freed from the traditions of the Church and its views on gender, women saw their chance to begin the suffrage movement once more. Women had gained a foothold in the world of work during the Great War, and they saw this as an opportunity to expand upon the image of equality that they had begun to build out of necessity. During the interwar period, women would finally obtain the right to vote, though their wages would no longer be equal to those of men, as they had been during the war. This would prove to be a continuous battle for women in the modern age.

As the 1930s drew to a close, the area of concern at the forefront of England's radar was the triple threat that seemed to be emerging on the international stage: Germany, Japan, and Italy. Though Germany's economy had been crippled from the reparations forced on it after World War I, the nation had returned with a vengeance under the leadership of Adolf Hitler, a war hero from the First World War. Germany had been building its military technology and presence. Furthermore, Italy had been following suit under Benito Mussolini, and Japan, in the Pacific, under the emperor Hirohito, had also built a substantial military presence. It appeared that the 20th century was quickly becoming one defined by dictatorships. England would feel a mounting sense of pressure from all nations as it attempted to discern which nation posed the greatest threat moving into the rest of the 20th century.

The Second World War: 1939–1945

England's Prime Minister Winston Churchill was famous for many things; an articulate and graceful way of speaking was one of them. He would say of World War II, "This is not the end. But it is perhaps the end of the beginning." This was right in many ways, all of which pointed toward how drastically WWII would change not only the nation of England but also the world at large. World War II would span only six years, and yet it was one of the most formative periods of England's history to date. It was a period of unprecedented violence, destruction, and peril for many countries, but particularly so for England. Its people would be tested again, after having survived World War I only to be thrust once more into the grievances of war.

In truth, the English had been preparing for war with Germany prior to the official start of the war. They had been watching Germany progress toward military prowess, as well as its relations with the Soviet Union improve, and preparing themselves for the possibility that the German beast was no longer slumbering. On September 1, 1939, Germany made its first move in the Second World War, mobilizing its troops and invading Poland. According to the Anglo-Polish military alliance that England had signed with Poland, they were contractually obligated to come to Poland's aid in the event of invasion. Furthermore, England was already concerned about Germany's growing presence in Singapore, a vital territory of England. If the Germans gained too much power, they would encroach on the British presence there, depriving England of vital resources. Joining with France, its longtime ally from the First World War, England declared war on Germany on September 3, beginning the world war. Other countries would soon follow suit, many of whom had originally been colonies of Great Britain. Australia, South Africa, New Zealand, and Canada each declared war on Germany in support of England in the days following England's declaration.

As Germany pushed forward, invading Poland, Denmark, France, Norway, and Belgium (to name a few), it was England's military that stood as the primary force against Germany. England quickly mobilized troops, having learned from its mistakes in the First World War, and instantly reignited its wartime industries. In 1940, Italy merged with Germany in the war, forming the Axis powers. They had a dangerous presence in southern Europe and began to attack Britain from the Mediterranean side. England's allies in New Zealand, South Africa, and Australia provided ships and troops to aid Britain in defending the southern borders and Mediterranean territories. England's history of colonialism and longstanding relationships with other countries were finally coming to benefit them once more. Many people are well aware of the attack that the Japanese launched in December 1941 on the American military base, Pearl Harbor. But what many are unaware of is that the date was also shared by the attack that the Japanese launched on Malaya, a territory that England had occupied for several decades in an attempt to secure control of China. With Japan's attack on British troops in Malaya, England was officially fighting all three Axis powers and at war on three different fronts.

Winston Churchill

Winston Churchill was certainly not the first Churchill to join British politics. A descendant of the First Duke of Marlborough, and his father, a Tory politician, Winston Churchill had practically been born into England's state government. He served in England's House of the Commons as both a Conservative and a Liberal, an unusual change in politics and one that would serve him well later in life when he needed to appeal to both political parties as prime minister. During World War I, he had been integral in guiding the government toward military advancement. It was Churchill who established the Royal Naval Air Service and helped invent the first tank. In the years leading up to the war, Churchill warned his fellow politicians of the rising nationalism in Germany. He warned that it should not be overlooked and that England should be preparing at the very least, if not subduing Germany immediately before it became a problem of international concern. His fellow Parliament members disregarded him, though, choosing to try and keep England off of Hitler's radar as a solution, obviously to no avail and much to Churchill's disdain.

When Churchill became prime minister in 1940, he inherited an office tainted by poor decisions from the previous prime minister, Neville Chamberlain. In early 1938, Chamberlain had given Germany a piece of Czechoslovakia, a strategy that he hoped would calm Germany and render England an ally instead of an enemy to be attacked. If Germany was given territories, then perhaps it would not wage a war to conquer them. When Germany invaded Poland, the people saw that Chamberlain was not a prime minister fit for wartime, and they replaced him with Churchill. Immediately, Churchill showed the British people that this war would be long and grueling and would demand everything of them. In July 1940, Germany began a  three-month-long air raid campaign on England, bringing the war back to the home front. As the war waged, Churchill would not only become a highly respected prime minister, but he would also bring a sense of moral direction and comfort to the British people. He was famous for his speeches, both in Parliament and on the radio. Churchill also worked closely with United States President Franklin D. Roosevelt to create a unified front against the Axis powers. Churchill is heralded as being the leader of the Allied victory in World War II, and yet it was only a few months after their victory that he was ousted. Though this is no reflection on Churchill's leadership or dedication to his country, it was instead further confirmation that he was the prime minister for the war, a man cut of the cloth needed to get England through one of its most trying times.

The Home Front

England had been here before. It had learned in World War I that a world war could not simply be fought on the battlefield, in the trenches, or on the fronts. It was fought from home and outward: An epicenter and its rings of impact. If the English were going to make it through the Second World War, they were going to need to do it with the strength and success of their home front first. Without a home, what were their soldiers fighting for? Beginning in 1938, when England saw Germany, Italy, and Japan all seemingly preparing to attack, it began bolstering its home front for the possibility of war.

Food was one of the paramount concerns for England. After having survived several famines surrounding World War I, the country was resolute in its plans to avoid this as it entered the second war. Building even more on what they had done in World War I, propaganda and the media were massive proponents of the home front effort. They kept civilians focused on what was important during these trying times, and they spread information as the government rolled out new initiatives for the war effort. In 1939, Britain launched the "Dig for Victory" campaign that encouraged civilians on the home front to plant "victory gardens." The idea was simple: if everyone on the home front was supplying gardens for themselves and their immediate family, then the agricultural and farming industry could be devoted to supplying food for the troops. Furthermore, it wouldn't place as much stress on those industries as more and more men were called away to serve in the war. In urban areas, victory gardens were even more popular. The government planted these to help bolster city food supplies, taking the pressure off of the ration system, and it helped to build morale among the people. With victory gardens, they had a common goal and a common source of fulfillment. Victory gardens would help to keep the British people fed and their spirits high, even as England instituted rationing, one of the hallmarks of wartime.

Rationing was necessary for several reasons, though it comes with only negative connotations. Images of cookbooks teaching young women how to cook a meal with only water, flour, and a mushroom come to mind, as well as soup lines and ragged faces. Rationing was crucial for England during wartime, and for all countries during the Second World War. Rationing on the home front limited people to the bare essentials in order to reduce waste. It also reduced the need for the import and export industries, freeing up the harbors and ships for military use. England was predominantly an import state: It imported 20 million tons of food each year to feed its ever-growing population. This included fruits, vegetables, cheeses, and grains. Germany knew this and sought to target England's shipping routes for attacks, hoping to starve its citizens. To reduce their shipping needs and combat some of the attacks that did still happen, the Ministry of Food instituted rationing in response to the shortages. Citizens were given an allotment of each type of food that they were allowed to buy on a weekly basis, limiting each household's consumption. In truth, it's difficult to tell how much this aided England, given the rationing horror stories alone, but it's equally difficult to say how many more people would have died from starvation had rationing not been in place. At the heart of the effort was England's dedication to its country at large, proving once again that the British were a benevolent people, willing to stand strong for their country's efforts. This, too, would hold true in the work industries.

England didn't have Rosie, who was the United States' inspiration, but it's quite possible that they didn't really need her. Though England still worked closely with the United States, and Winston Churchill had instituted an agreement with the States to supply them with munitions and other military supplies, England knew that it couldn't accept all of its materials from the United States. Importing everything put England at risk for attacks and being left with nothing with which to face the Germans. England ramped up productions, converting all of their factories into munitions production sites to increase its inventory. The nation began building aircraft, seeing that this was the new way of warfare. They built more tanks and ammunition, attempting to prepare for the unforeseeable future. Though Churchill warned the

British people that the war would be long, it would go on even longer than they had anticipated, demanding more of them with each year that passed.

The Theaters

One of the most difficult challenges for England during World War II was juggling all of the different theaters. England was quickly coming to regret their colonial past as they entered the war, with British presence all over the globe. The British Empire had not yet fallen, and England was still very present in multiple territories outside of its own. Unfortunately for them, there was not just one enemy in World War II but four. The Axis powers knew about England's claims in different areas of the world and divided themselves among England's stakes to weaken it from each side. As a result, there were not simply the Western and Eastern Fronts of the war, as there had been in World War I. World War II elevated what the world knew of warfare in the previous world war, bringing it to an extent no one had seen before. The war became so big that it expanded beyond fronts and, instead, ushered in an age of theaters.

The world broke up into the European Theater, the Pacific Theater, and the Mediterranean and Middle East Theater. Most of England's fighting took place in the Middle East and European Theaters, though in the early days of the war, it also had troops in the Pacific Theater as well. While other countries were typically involved in only one or two theaters, England had stakes in them all from its colonial pasts. The Japanese were the enemy heading the Pacific Theater while Italy headed the Middle East, and Germany headed the European Theater.

To begin, Italy, led by dictator Benito Mussolini, hoped to create the next Roman Empire by conquering the surrounding lands. The Italians attacked Greece and Yugoslavia, countries that England had previously controlled, and were met with British forces, holding them off. But Germany realized that they needed allies, and when Hitler allied with Mussolini, he sent troops to Greece and Yugoslavia, successfully defeating the British. As the war progressed, both German and Italian forces would continue to creep into the Middle Eastern and Northern African countries, where England had maintained sovereign control and regulations over the oil production there. Germany was a militarized state, though, and, heading the Axis powers, declared that the Middle East and Southern Africa were the places that they needed in order to win this world war. The Germans divided their resources among the two theaters, keeping British forces spread thin. For much of the war, the territories would appear to be headed toward German control, though England would keep its forces there for the duration of the war. It wouldn't be until the United States entered the war with fresh reserves and military equipment that the Allied powers would see victory in the Middle Eastern and African theaters.

The Pacific Theater involved the countries of Australia,

New Zealand, China, Japan, and the Philippines, along with other islands surrounding the larger countries. It began in 1941 when Japan declared war and invaded Hong Kong, Borneo, and Malaya. England had holds in all three areas, previously controlling Hong Kong as a withstanding colony inside of China. They had oil reserves in Borneo and Malaya, making Japan's declaration especially threatening. The two countries would wage war for the next four years, eventually resulting in an Allied victory when the United States joined the fight and helped to defeat the Japanese military, which didn't have the same military reserves, and Germany, who proved harder to defeat. Though there would be animosity between England and Japan for the next several decades, in modern England today, Japan is recognized as one of England's closest allies.

The European Theater is by and large the most commonly spoken of and well-known theater in World War II. It saw the creation of concentration camps, housed the Holocaust, witnessed the first use of atomic weapons, and eventually the defeat of the most powerful dictators in history to date. It was within the European Theater that the world saw the Axis powers first break. When the war first broke out, the Axis powers were comprised of the Soviet Union, Italy, and Germany. But Hitler betrayed Stalin, the dictator of the Soviet Union, and launched an invasion of the Soviet Union from the southern side. Stalin then became an Allied power, aiding in the defeat of Hitler by the end of the war. Early in the war, in 1940, Germany overtook both France and Belgium so quickly and with so much force that awaiting British troops retreated to Dunkirk, one of the most famous retreats of the war due to the sheer number of British troops lost in a single battle. With France under Germany's control, the Germans turned their attention to England next. Germany launched a barrage of air raids and attacks in what Winston Churchill would call "The Battle of Britain." Though it depleted British forces and resources, they did not resign England to Germany, proving a vital victory for the Allied powers.

It was at this point that Germany turned on the Soviet Union, seeking to expand its territory east if it couldn't be expanded west. German troops easily breached the Soviet Union's borders, pushing all the way to the major city of Stalingrad. Once there, though, Germany met its match with the overwhelming number of troops on the Soviet side. The Battle of Stalingrad would be one of the bloodiest battles of the entire war, completely wiping out Germany's sixth company. After this battle, Germany would never recover and would spend the remainder of the war slowly being pushed back to Berlin on this front.

In 1941, after Japan bombed Pearl Harbor, the United States entered the war and sent troops to Normandy to liberate France. After discussing strategies with Woodrow Wilson, the president at the time, he and Winston Churchill decided that this would be the most successful course of action. England was still closely allied with France and obligated to protect and defend its neighbor country, but since France had been overthrown by German troops at the start of the war, in order to uphold their relationship, the English needed to regain France. As another  major player in the Allied powers, England needed France to regain its strength and home front if they were going to win the war. The Battle of Normandy, also known as "the storming of the beaches," was another turning point for the Allied forces. With British troops storming a cluster of beaches occupied by Nazi soldiers and U.S. troops storming another series of beaches, the two Allied powers soon defeated the Nazi presence on the French coastline and began pushing inward, slowly liberating all of France. The final push in the French region was the Battle of the Bulge in 1944, one of the last battles in the war and the European Theater. Though this was technically an American victory, it allowed British troops to push into Nazi forces from the south and west, leaving only the Eastern Front for the Soviet Union to press into Berlin. Through the collective tactics of the Allied forces, they were able to defeat the Nazi forces in 1945, ending the Nazi regime.

The End of the War

More than 25% of Europe's overall economy had been consumed by the end of the war in 1945 ("United Kingdom home front," 2022). Britain had placed 55% of its labor force into the war effort ("United Kingdom home front," 2022), leaving the country with a stunted economy and workforce, which had likewise shrunk considering the casualties that England suffered in the war. The United Kingdom had lost over 450,000 people in World War II, including those from the crown's colonies who had died fighting. Coming from this set of circumstances and moving forward, England would try to greet its new society in a world that was attempting to repair itself as well. Coming out of World War II, the only country that could be leaned on for financial assistance and that had not been touched culturally and detrimentally on the home front was the United States. They were fortunate, in that the war had never touched their own borders, outside of Hawaii with the bombing of Pearl Harbor. England, as well as the other countries in Europe, was not so fortunate. England was faced with rebuilding itself once more and, arguably, more comprehensively than it had before in the aftermath of World War I.

Before countries could begin rebuilding themselves on an independent basis, they each knew that there was reconciliation to be done on an international level. England was familiar with the way of the new world, in that it could not practice isolation and think it could remain a strong kingdom. Politics were played through relationships and accountabilities, and the world had failed this responsibility in the buildup to World War II. Nations had ignored warning signs and did not have the political infrastructure in place to act as a single, strong unit, even once they accepted the signs of impending war and potentially dangerous dictatorships. What had previously been known as the League of Nations, the collective agency of protection and alliances among nations after World War I, would evolve into the United Nations after World War II. While the initial plans for the organization were actually formed between Franklin D. Roosevelt, the then-current President of the United States, and Prime Minister Winston Churchill, it was perfected and put into place after World War II.

In the middle of the war, after the United States had entered the conflict, Churchill and Roosevelt both knew that they needed a new organization to help ensure peace across the globe. They knew that something needed to be improved upon so that this wouldn't happen again. Roosevelt had already discussed the idea with Stalin during the war, and with the three largest Allied powers on board with the idea, plans for the United Nations were solidified. In 1944 at the end of the war, China, England, the USSR, and the United States all met to discuss the details of the organization. They wanted something more solid than the League of Nations, and the powers needed to be less abstract in this new collective. At the meeting, they agreed upon four key principles of the United Nations: to obtain and agree upon international peace, to keep the relationships between countries cordial in order to avoid conflict, to achieve cohesive cooperation among nations, and to discuss possibilities and events that would make the previous principles a reality, instead of stagnated ideals. In other words, where the League of Nations had simply stood for international peace, the United Nations would strive for and achieve it, creating a world of prosperity, equality, and justice. As they continued to meet, these principles would only be the first in a series of articles that the UN would uphold. In 1945, the United Nations held its first official meeting, solidifying a new headway into the modern world.

England, following World War II, would undergo many changes. It would continue to strengthen its relationship with the United States. This would only become more fruitful an allyship as England continued into the 20th century with Thatcherism and its mirror image, Reaganism. The end of the war also signaled a change in morality and society. There was no more gray area when it came to personal or national freedoms, and some of England's last colonies would realize this. World War II had been a breach of freedoms in every way. The Holocaust had shown to religious and national cultures that to be discriminated against, in any way, was a violation of one's human rights and that this discrimination could escalate quickly and rampantly. Furthermore, the liberation of the Jewish people, those most affected by the Holocaust, showed people all over the world that a community could come back from persecution, no matter the scale. The modern world would not be one of control but one of independence. England would be most directly affected by this as it sought to repair its economy while steadily losing some of its oldest and most reliable sources of income: Its colonies.

CHAPTER 9
MODERN ENGLAND

While it's true that the world wars were not all that happened in the 20th century, they did impact England for the entirety of it. The previous chapter is not called "The World at War" simply because the entire world fought for 100 years. It is called this because the world faced consequences for the duration of the century for the wars that were fought. Even though both world wars had drawn to a close by the halfway mark of the 20th century, their events would continue to dictate England's actions for the rest of the century, and arguably even beyond. A world war is nothing to scoff at. Two world wars are certainly not to be disregarded for their weight, and England would be bearing this weight for the time to come.

The Decline of the British Empire

Britain's colonies had long been a signal of its wealth and success. They offered England valuable income, materials for exports and imports, and areas of allied support, which had proven especially valuable in the past 50 years. But the world had survived wars and witnessed the consequences of one country controlling the fate of another, and Britain's colonies began seizing their own independence. In 1947, India, previously "the crown jewel" of the empire, would be the first to declare its own independence in the era of what would later be termed England's decolonization. The prime minister of India at the time called on Gandhi, who had advocated for Indians to pull away from Britain back in the 1920s, as inspiration for their resistance. Tensions with Britain rose at the close of WWII, and after the economic strains of the war, England quite frankly didn't have the money to combat India's resistance. Furthermore, Japan was pushing into Southeast Asia, creating yet another risk factor for England to weigh. As a result, England's Prime Minister Clement Attlee resigned control of India that year, granting them their freedom.

Once India broke free of colonialism, other colonial powers saw this as their time to move into the modern age as well. On a social and cultural level, the world was moving away from accepting and embracing the concept of having colonies at all. In 1932, Time Magazine had recognized Gandhi as the Man of the Year, creating the lasting image of heroes as those who pushed against colonialism. This shifting mindset of the general public was dangerous for England and meant that its empire could no longer stand as the modern age progressed. The media portrayed Britain negatively as it tried to contain its colonies, placing extra pressure on them to relinquish control. In 1957, Ghana became the first of many African countries to overthrow British rule, declaring themselves a free nation. Seeing this as the end of the British Empire as they knew it, in 1960, Prime Minister Harold Macmillan gave the famous "Wind of Change" speech that expressed to the British public and government at large that decolonization was the way of the new world, and they would have to accept it.

Though England tried to regain some of its colonies in the

Soviet Union during the Cold War, a conflict that strained the Soviet Union due to problems with the United States, England failed in this as well. In 1997, when Hong Kong was given back to China, Britain had essentially lost all colonial control short of Australia. By the end of the 20th century, what England had known as its untouchable empire, the most powerful kingdom that the world had known since the Roman Empire, had disintegrated.

The Welfare State: 1945–1979

After the war, the social issues of England were glaringly apparent. When politician William Beveridge wrote "The Beveridge Report," he identified five "Giant Evils" that England had to tackle coming out of the war. According to the report, if the English were going to recover from the first half of the 20th century, they would have to focus their energy, finances, and politics on five areas of social reform: squalor, ignorance, want, idleness, and disease. England was in need of desperate and comprehensive social reform, and for the next 30 years, its government would institute a litany of acts that completely revitalized England's education, healthcare, and labor systems.

In 1944, England passed the Butler Act, which freed education for all British citizens. This education act abolished fees for secondary school and did away with the age restrictions for sectors within schools that broke up children by age, rather than ability, making the minimum amount of years that a child was required to be in school much longer than before. It also provided school meals and education for adults through community colleges and for younger children through nursery schools. In June 1946, England passed the National Insurance Act, which created the British equivalent of America's Social Security system. It required all working adults to pay a contribution toward receiving sick, unemployment, and retirement benefits as well as other allowances. This act would be improved upon in 1951 when the Butler Act's list of contributions would become more specific and inclusive of those who benefited. In 1966, it would be replaced entirely by the Social Security Act. The criticism that the National Insurance Act received for its disregard for mothers, specifically, was solved with the passing of this next

act in August, which provided family allowances for mothers in the UK. The year 1948 saw a slew of social reform bills passed, including the Children's Act, the National Health Service Act, and the National Assistance Act. Through these three new reforms, England readdressed the Poor Laws, which provided welfare for the homeless and had been in effect since Medieval times. They also provided free basic healthcare for British citizens and, under the Children's Act, created a social-care system for orphaned or abused children. By 1979, England's social system was entirely modernized and finally strong enough to support the new modern nation that it had created. Though it appears, on paper, as an overwhelming amount of change in a short amount of time, it would prepare the British citizens for the next 20 years under one of their most influential prime ministers yet.

Thatcherism: 1979–1990

Margaret Thatcher is notorious for a reason, and it is not simply because she was the first female prime minister of Britain. Margaret Thatcher had earned her seat as Prime Minister through an early life in both law and politics. She served as the secretary of state under the returned

Conservative government in 1970, earning a reputation as a ruthless and strict conservative. England had nearly bankrupted itself in the previous years with its fervent institution of social reform, and Thatcher would set her sights on repairing this and restoring England's economy once and for all. In 1979 when she was appointed Prime Minister, she brought England into an era of staunch conservative politics, which would later be termed "Thatcherism." In her first term, Thatcher sought to undo some of the social reforms that England had instituted in the previous 30 years. She limited some of the school reforms, including free lunch. She was also faced with a brief war against Argentina, to which she reacted quickly, ending it before her first term was up. Thatcher also turned her attention toward battling the inflation that had risen substantially in the past decades. She limited the funds distributed to housing, healthcare, and other social reform organizations. Though her efforts actually led to rising unemployment, the British citizens saw hope in her strategies to fix England's economy and elected her for a second term.

In Thatcher's second term, her conservatism rang loud and true as she shifted Britain's economy back to a centralized model. She returned industries to England, privatizing state-owned companies that controlled transportation, oil, and other extremely fiscally beneficial industries. She encouraged supply-side economics and a free market, structures that she was sure would reignite the economy. Thatcherism also became defined by the more cultural characteristics of independence and freedom. As Thatcher limited the involvement of the state government, citizens began to see that this was less a political game and more a way of life and cultural shift for England. Though England had started as an independent country, in the past centuries, its government had preached the ideals of collectivism and colonialism. It had formed relationships with other countries and sought to protect the insurance of all its citizens with social reform, but this had cost England its strength as an independent country. It was under Margaret Thatcher that the country tried to regain this strength.

Unfortunately, Thatcher's strategies were fairly unsuccessful. Though her ideals mirrored those of Ronald Reagan in the United States, the two countries' successes were not equal in terms of their economies. Under Thatcher, unemployment did not decrease, and though she reduced funds sent to social reform organizations, she did not decrease government spending substantially. In addition, England's inflation rate was not lower than it was when she took office in 1979. Still, though, she is heralded as a monumental prime minister in England's history for the steps that she took to try and institute change. She has become known as "the Iron Lady" for her fierce determination and her willingness to face every challenge she inherited during her terms.

Brexit

In 1975, the President of the United States, Gerald Ford stated that Europe's economy as well as the Western world at large was stronger for England's involvement in the European Union/United Kingdom conglomerations. In truth, they were a key player in the union, as one of the oldest countries in Europe. Despite challenges over the years, England had the strongest economy and the most established forms of trade, which bolstered everyone's economies. The English were also vital in supporting the development of other countries that later joined the European Union. This was, at its heart, a symbiotic relationship. So then, why, in 2016, would England begin the formal process of leaving the European Union?

Since its inception after World War II, the European

Union had been the social and political collection of 27 nations, mostly from the European region. It sought to maintain peace and economic prosperity after the war, collectivizing European nations under one jurisdiction and market. It was supposed to unify the strength of each country's economy as well as strengthen the relationships each country had with one another. As a result, the European Union was, in itself, its own governing body that acted as an umbrella government for all of the countries within the union. If the EU passed legislation, then each country had the option of implementing it. For the most part, many of the countries were content with this system, but as the years went by and England regained its footing after WWII, the English were eager to become completely independent again. Eventually, its relationship with the EU placed more stress on England than it did to ensure its peace and success as a country.

One of the largest contributing factors to England leaving the EU was its policies toward immigration and foreigners. As you well know by now, England had a complicated relationship with immigrants over its centuries of existence.

But as England continued through the 20th century, and even moving into the 21st century, the sheer amount of immigrants coming into England would prove a discomfort for many Brits. The EU had a welcoming immigration policy for foreigners from the Middle East and North Africa, but since England had historically established itself as a safe territory for immigrants, it was being flooded with the immigrants coming into Europe and choosing to take refuge in England rather than other EU countries. Some politicians in Britain hoped to amend this and saw that leaving the EU might be a solution.

Economically speaking, England also had issues with how the European Union was handling the financial challenges of the 21st century. With the recession in 2008 and a 20% unemployment rate across southern Europe (Mauldin, 2016), England was displeased with the lack of solutions the EU provided as a collective. Comparing itself to Germany, which enjoyed a 4% unemployment rate at the same time (Mauldin, 2016), England felt itself at a disservice due to its economic responsibilities with the European Union. Many believed that staying in the EU would stagnate their economy, leaving them in a system of the past while other countries were free to move forward.

A second reason for England leaving the EU could be owed to Margaret Thatcher and the rise of nationalism that she encouraged during her terms as prime minister. One of the resounding qualities of Thatcherism was a sense of self-sufficiency and independence, supported by the return of industry to England and the reduced power of the state. It was this nationalism that encouraged some Brits to support Brexit. Though organizations such as the EU, NATO, and the IMF were created with countries' security and insurance in mind, England began to view them as antiquated and only applicable to the problems they had faced immediately after WWII. In the modern world, it behooved England to stay within the contractual obligations of organizations such as the EU, seeing the connection as a restriction rather than a benefit to England as a whole. After 2008, the English felt they had no other choice besides breaking from the EU in order to reclaim their own control of the country.

Thirdly, when it came to voting for Brexit, there were three parties deciding on the end result. Both the Conservative and Liberal parties were in support of remaining within the European Union, but a third party, which had broken from both of them, was for formal separation. The party that broke from the two established parties was one working against the elite. The common people had lost faith in their government, feeling that the politicians who had supported the union from the start had lost their right to control the fate of the country. As a result, when the third party won a majority over the established two, passing the "leave" vote from the EU, it signaled a change yet again in England's history. The people had won, once more, exerting pressure over the English elite and exhibiting the weight that their votes and their representation carried in political policies. Once and for all, England was a country of the people.

CONCLUSION

To say that England's history is rich is to call a perfect gelato delicious. It is an oversight, a gross underappreciation, and an insignificant evaluation. But there is no other way to say it. There is no other way to express the sheer vast nature of England's history in a single sentence. Perhaps it is better to say that England's history is complex, or, perhaps still, that it is as endless as the river Nile. Though, even the river Nile meets an ocean. Even complexity knows its limits. England knows neither end nor true limit.

England has been around for over 800,000 years, a value that is quite nearly unparalleled; what else is this old? What else has withstood as much and continued living, thriving, and growing for this many years? In that time, England has established quite possibly one of the most influential and powerful nations in the world. It began, as any true beginning should, with immigrants, people who were each an unknown to one another. It was born out of warfare, in all truth, and it would wage wars true to its form for many years to come. England created itself, created a system, where there was previously nothing. A group of immigrants and foreigners, people who were not wanted in other regions, came to England and created a kingdom. In all honesty, England created the American dream before there was an America.

England laid the groundwork for political systems that other modern countries sought to recreate and that countries that have yet to establish themselves are still trying to mimic today. England is credited with being the birthplace of some of the most important art of the modern world. Without England, there would be no Shakespeare, who is credited with many of the tropes and ideas of modern literature. Without England, there would not have been Charles Darwin, and without the brave embrace of intellect and logic during England's Age of Enlightenment, the theory of evolution would never have been shared for the world to know.

England is the mother of colonialism, plain and simple. Though it is a marred history and a lineage of corrupt power and overt control over innocent people, it is a crucial part of history and the construction of empires. England's colonies became lasting, independent nations. They became strong and integral parts of the international trade and political spheres. It's possible to claim that without England's influence to begin with, they might not have been introduced as seriously to other countries. This is sad but quite possibly true. England as a country, as a nation, and as a kingdom carries weight. Its name as a nation—and the British people themselves—carries influence.

Without England's influence, Winston Churchill, a man famous for his bravery, his headstrong nature, and his pride for his own country, would never have been able to play such a key role in World War II, the worst war that the world has known to date. England would remain a haven for immigrants, opening its borders to people from all over Europe and, eventually, all over the world. It would redefine what it meant to be a nation, what it meant to be a kingdom. Though it would not be until Benito Mussolini rose to power in Italy in the early 20th century that someone would speak of building the next Roman Empire again, it is safe to say that it was, in fact, England who came the closest to this endeavor.

Today, England is no longer a colonial powerhouse. It is a vital trade partner, an ally to many nations, and the head (even still) of Europe. When one thinks of Europe, one likely still thinks of Rome, but mostly it is England that comes to mind. It takes a truly strong nation to build a kingdom so famous and powerful as the United Kingdom, only to break from it and remain intact. England is solitary now, perhaps more than it has been in centuries. But moving forward, one need only look to the past to predict England's future. The nation will not only survive; it will thrive. It will continue to influence the world. England will continue to lead the world in many spheres, lighting the way for things to come.

APPENDIX:
KINGS, QUEENS, AND PRIME MINISTERS OF ENGLAND

What follows in this chapter is less a narrative and more of a reference table. In your continued studies of England's history, it will be difficult to keep all of the monarchs and Parliament heads straight throughout the years. This book is a tool, one that can be used throughout your studies. This chapter is meant to benefit you throughout this book and beyond, as you continue to track England's robust history. You will find that you recognize quite a few of these monarchs and prime ministers from the previous chapters. Many of them had received credit and substantial ink to their names and their reigns throughout history. Others have not garnered such a reputation and will not seem familiar. Let it be known that this is not to indicate the insignificance of some rulers and prime ministers but is, rather, an unfortunate effect of an abbreviated book of English history. Simply put, there isn't enough time and space to discuss every single one of England's monarchs and prime ministers. You, the reader, would be here for the rest of time, and that's only if the book itself was ever finished (a highly unlikely feat in itself). All of the following monarchs and prime ministers have contributed, in some way, to the development of England's history. They are included here to act as a comprehensive list so that you can, perhaps, pursue your own studies on one or several in the future.

Norman Kings

- William I (The Conqueror), 1066–1087

- William II (Rufus), 1087–1100

- Henry I, 1100–1135

- Stephen, 1135–1154

Plantagenet Kings

- Henry II, 1154–1189

- Richard I (The Lionheart), 1189–1199

- John I, 1199–1216

- Henry III, 1216–1272

- Edward I, 1272–1307

- Edward II, 1307–1327 (deposed)

- Edward III, 1327–1377

- Richard II, 1377–1399 (deposed)

The House of Lancaster

- Henry IV, 1399–1413

- Henry V, 1413–1422

- Henry VI, 1422–1461 (deposed)

The House of York

- Edward IV, 1461–1483

- Edward V, 1483–1483

- Richard III, 1483–1485

The Tudors

- Henry VII, 1485–1509

- Henry VIII, 1509–1547

- Edward VI, 1547–1553

- Mary I (Bloody Mary), 1553–1558

- Elizabeth I, 1558–1603

The Stuarts

- James I, 1603–1625

- Charles I, 1625–1649

Lord Protectors

- England became a republic for 11 years from 1649 to 1660, and the Commonwealth of England was declared on May 19, 1649.

- Oliver Cromwell, 1653–1658

- Richard Cromwell, 1658–1659

The Restoration

- Charles II, 1660–1685

- James II, 1685–1688

- William III, 1689–1702

- Mary II, 1689–1694

- Anne, 1702–1714

The Hanoverians

- George I, 1714–1727

- George II, 1727–1760

- George III, 1760–1820

- George IV, 1820–1830

- William IV, 1830–1837

- Victoria, 1837–1901

The House of Saxe-Coburg-Gotha

- Edward VII, 1901–1910

The House of Windsor

- name changed in 1917 due to the anti-German feelings in Britain at the time.

- George V, 1910–1936

- Edward VIII, June 1936–December 1936 (abdicated)

- George VI, 1936–1952

- Elizabeth II, 1952–2022

- Charles III, 2022–Present

Prime Ministers

- Lord John Russell, 1846–1852

- Edward Smith Stanley, 1852–1852

- George Hamilton Gordon, 1852–1855

- Henry John Temple, 1855–1858

- Edward Smith Stanley, 1858–1859

- Henry John Temple, 3rd Viscount Palmerston, 1859–1865

- Lord John Russell, 1865–1866

- Edward Smith Stanley, 1866–1868

- Benjamin Disraeli, the Earl of Beaconsfield, 1868–1868

- William Ewart Gladstone, 1868–1874

- Benjamin Disraeli, 1874–1880

- William Ewart Gladstone, 1880–1885

- Robert Gascoyne-Cecil, 1885–1886

- William Ewart Gladstone, 1886–1886

- Robert Gascoyne-Cecil, 1886–1892

- William Ewart Gladstone, 1892–1894

- Archibald Primrose, 5th Earl of Rosebery, 1894–1895

- Robert Gascoyne-Cecil, 3rd Marquess of Salisbury, 1895–1902

- Arthur James Balfour, 1902–1905

- Sir Henry Campbell-Bannerman, 1905–1908

- Herbert Henry Asquith, 1908–1916

- David Lloyd George, 1916–1922

- Andrew Bonar Law, 1922–1923

- Stanley Baldwin, 1923–1924

- James Ramsay MacDonald, 1924–1924

- Stanley Baldwin, 1924–1929

- James Ramsay MacDonald, 1929–1935

- Stanley Baldwin, 1935–1937

- Neville Chamberlain, 1937–1940

- Sir Winston Churchill, 1940–1945

- Clement Attlee, 1945–1951

- Sir Winston Churchill, 1951–1955

- Anthony Eden, 1955–1957

- Harold Macmillan, 1957–1963

- Sir Alec Douglas-Home, 1963–1964

- Harold Wilson, 1964–1970

- Edward Heath, 1970–1974

- Harold Wilson, 1974–1976

- James Callaghan, 1976–1979

- Margaret Thatcher, 1979–1990

- Sir John Major, 1990–1997

- Tony Blair May, 1997–2007

- Gordon Brown, 2007–2010

- David Cameron, 2010–2016

- Theresa May, 2016–2019

- Boris Johnson, 2019–2022

- Liz Truss, September 2022–October 2022

- Rishi Sunak, 2022–Present

IRISH HISTORY & MYTHOLOGY

INTRODUCTION

Ireland is a nation with a storied past. It's a nation that has roots going back 8,000 years—much of it unrecorded. The first written language in Ireland, Ogham, only started being used during the first millennium because the tribes of Ireland believed in the value of oral tradition. Even when the written word started being used, it wasn't an everyday affair as passing down knowledge in the form of stories was still the preferred way to educate. If you were driven to remember the things you were told, then it was believed that your mind would be strong and your capacity for retaining knowledge would be high.

This was effective, looking at the structures that were built and other feats that were achieved based on orally transmitted knowledge. But it does make it difficult for people of the modern era to learn about life during prehistoric and ancient times. Luckily, a lot can be learned from the art, architecture, and other archeological remains that have been left by those that came before. Using this information, we've pieced together a comprehensive history of the island in this book.

A central point of Irish history is the mythology and beliefs that have been passed down from the Gaelic Pagan way of life. These myths have seeped into daily living and are a topic of conversation as common as talking about politics of the nation. Traditions and superstitions have been created around the creatures of myth, and these traditions are abided by without even thinking. In many cases, the myths and their creatures are just stories that we tell children before bed, but they have become integral to the identity of the nation.

This book examines the Pagan belief system, as it was then, and as it is now with Neopaganism. There is also an in-depth catalog of creatures of myth and characters of the supernatural. These sections both engage the mind and excite the imagination. The lives of the ancients were interwoven with the folklore imparted in this book, and it can be awe-inspiring to think that the creatures you read about have been part of the lives of people for hundreds, and sometimes thousands of years.

The last part of the book examines the impact of the history and mythology of Ireland on its two modern nations, The Republic of Ireland and Northern Ireland. The lives of those in modern rural areas and small towns place importance on what has been passed down by preceding generations. The lives of those in the largest urban areas, particularly Dublin, have often been influenced by international trends and lifted people away from their roots. One of the main purposes of this book is to allow you to reacquaint yourself with those roots and to allow you a glimpse into the identity of the Irish nation—a nation with a history stretching back thousands of years.

CHAPTER 1
PREHISTORIC IRELAND

Preliterate Ireland didn't stretch as far back as some other prehistoric cultures. The earliest evidence of people in Ireland dates back to around 7 or 8,000 B.C.E. While there weren't written records of the time, and while written records that might have existed during the later prehistoric periods are lost or destroyed, a lot of information can be gleaned from archeological finds.

Earliest Settlement—The Mesolithic Age

The first settlers seem to have come to the island via the area of Coleraine in Northern Ireland. They seem to have crossed on a land bridge that had been extant at around that time and set up their first hunter-gatherer settlements. Another possibility is that they came to Ireland on wooden boats, landing in the region that now includes Antrim in the north of the island. There's an indication that the people who arrived in Ireland had come from Scotland because there were cultural similarities with the Scottish peoples of the time. It's possible that there was more than one crossing, on both land bridges and in boats. In addition to people crossing over, there's evidence that animals also crossed over on the land bridges of the time. There isn't much evidence of animals on the island before this time.

The era was called the Mesolithic Age. The Mesolithic Age refers to the earlier of the two stretches of the Stone Age; the other period being the Neolithic (or New Stone Age). In Ireland, the Mesolithic stretched from the arrival of the first people around 7 or 8,000 B.C.E., to around 4,000 B.C.E. (while it stretched back almost 200,000 years in some other places on the planet). This era was marked by a hunter-gatherer economy, the use of microliths (small flint pieces used in tools and weapons), and a meat-heavy diet. The population of Ireland mainly occupied coastal regions at first, particularly in the northern parts of the island.

As the period stretched on, they moved along the coast to the east and the south. There are indications that Mesolithic people went inland along some of the rivers, but not too far inland due to the heavily forested landscape of Ireland at the time. The hunter-gatherers moved from location to location, never permanently settling. They formed settlements where they went with wooden huts for each family that formed part of the tribe.

This continued until around 4,000 B.C.E. when the tribes started clearing away trees to make space for farming. Ireland was covered with thick forests at the time, which was ideal for hunting and gathering, but not for domesticated life. When trees were cleared off from an area, animal stock was reared and the ground was cultivated for raising cereal crops. These pastures and cultivated areas of land gradually grew in size, allowing for larger communities. One of the defining characteristics for the early agricultural and hunter-gatherer groups of Ireland were rituals where the body and objects were ceremonially painted. There were clear signs of an identifiable civilization emerging.

Mount Sandel

One settlement, Mount Sandel, is perhaps the earliest settlement of the era that's been uncovered and thoroughly examined by archeologists. The settlement seems to have been occupied for around half a millennium from approximately 7,000 B.C.E. The settlement consisted of round huts in which saplings had been bent and stuck into the ground to form a circle approximately 19 feet across. The saplings were covered with deer hides, thereby allowing protection from the elements.

There was a central hearth for the small community where the food that was caught would have been cooked and eaten communally. The settlement wasn't very large and could house 15 people at the most. The hearth would have been the central point for social interaction of the small community while they stayed warm next to the fire. In terms of food, those early settlers would  have eaten multiple aquatic creatures, including shellfish, mackerel, eels, and the occasional seal. Land creatures would have included wild pig, deer, and game birds. A fish drying rack was found, which indicates that the Mesolithic inhabitants knew about food preservation by drying meat.

It is assumed that the main food eaten during the summer and other warm months was fish. Winter months likely had eel as the main dietary component, providing protein and omega-3 fatty acids. Plant components of the diet consisted of berries, fruit, and hazelnuts. Arrows, spears, and harpoons could be used to hunt fish and to kill other animals when meat was needed. The main land animal used for food would likely have been wild boars due to its prevalence at the time (being particularly useful as a food source in the cold winter months). The skins of animals that had been caught would have been used to clothe people in the village to keep them protected from the plants and creatures they walked past when entering the forest and providing warmth in the cooler parts of the year.

There are other archeological sites dated to the Mesolithic period in Ireland. The information gleaned from them is similar to those of the site at Mount Sandel—a lifestyle that largely consisted of roaming, a meaty diet, and use of small stone tools. The period that followed is the Neolithic Era.

Neolithic Era

This is the "New Stone Age" and stretches from approximately 4,000 to 2,000 B.C.E. in Ireland. The period reached its height around 3,000 B.C.E., with large structures and lots of archaeological evidence left behind from this time.

The period started with waves of immigrants coming from the British Isles and beyond beginning in around 4,000 B.C.E. The native Mesolithic population was still present, but they were absorbed into the Neolithic population groups in some cases and displaced in other instances. The new population wasn't a hunter-gatherer society, but an agrarian one. They chopped and burned down the thinner forest layer close to the top of hills and created farmland on which to base their homesteads.

Along with farming came food security from the larger quantities of food available from farming, and because reserves could be stockpiled. To protect their homes and fields, the Neolithic farmers often built stone walls or other perimeter fencing around their homes and fields. With the introduction of cows, sheep, goats, and cereal grains from Britain, farmers could easily produce food each year within their protected fields. The homestead contained the houses for individual families and central buildings for communal affairs. With the protection in place and the farmland created, the dwellings were designed in a more permanent fashion for their residents. It was common for communities to consist of 20 to 30 people in multiple houses that each contained a family unit.

The houses were large and rectangular wood structures made from branches and trunks that were interwoven, with mud as a binding and insulating agent. Beams leaned against two sides of the structure's roof to provide additional support. The roof itself was made from thatch and reads to protect against the weather. There would often be a small opening in the roof that let out smoke because Neolithic people tended to cook inside their homes, rather than the exclusive use of a communal cooking point by Mesolithic communities. Cooking was done over a fire with meat put on spit and smaller pieces put on a stone in the fire to fry on. Bread was likewise made on a stone placed in the fire using grain that had been ground from the harvest.

The difference between the stone tools of this era and the ones before were that the Neolithic tools were often larger, more detailed, and of a higher quality. Flint was still used, but porcellanite (found in Northern Ireland) was also introduced due to its added toughness. Porcellanite was a useful material that was traded between Ireland and other lands, contributing to the trade and cultural interchange of the time. This included art, clothing styles, and more.

Coiled pottery was one of the forms of art commonly used in households at the time. When decorated, it could be a tool for imparting cultural elements from the tribe and incorporating elements from other tribes from whom ideas and goods had been accepted. This type of pottery was made by coiling clay around until it made the form of a pot, at which point it was smoothed out and decorations were added (using fingers, sticks, or stones as a decorative tool). The pot was then hardened in the fire, after which point it could be used for storage or to make lamps. When used as a lamp, it was filled with fat at the bottom, which was then lit when light was needed.

The security of life as the Neolithic period wore on resulted in a population increase. The population increase required more land for farming and living, thus driving people lower into the dense forests of the lowlands. To add to this, the change in climate and the use of the uplands for farming (with dead organic material forming peat) had resulted in some of the ground becoming bogs. As such, even established communities needed to move into the lower lying lands. They repeated the practice of deforestation in the regions where they needed to farm. As such, the island was now inhabited in the high and low areas, with the hills often becoming points of established, ceremonial importance.

Common cultural structures of Ireland and other European regions at this time were the large buildings that were created for social and burial purposes—also called megaliths—which were mainly found on the hills. Funerals and death were important to the culture of prehistoric Ireland, and these buildings were integral to many of those funerary practices. The next section will cover some of the main types found in Ireland.

Megaliths

Monuments are structures that tie together communities.

They can be used to commemorate a part of the group's history or identity. Representing religious and spiritual beliefs is another purpose behind building monuments. The earliest known monuments in Ireland are more than 5,000 years old. This includes the Hill of Tara and passage of the tomb at Knowth. Both sites were used for burials and respecting the dead, among others.

There are many monuments in Ireland dating from the Stone Age (in excess of 1,500), particularly from the 4th millennium B.C.E. onwards. The cultural aspect that ties many of these monuments together can be seen in some of the art (such as swirling patterns) that occur at multiple locations. There are also similarities of design between some of the monument types. The types of monuments that can be found in Ireland include megaliths, dolmen, burial mounds, ringforts, and ceremonial grounds.

A megalith is a large stone that's placed upright, often with a ritualistic or culture-linked purpose. There are multiple formations that are used, including single standing stones (also called menhirs or gallauns), portal tombs, stone circles, court tombs, passage tombs, and wedge tombs. The purposes for the erection of megaliths are often as burial sites, to honor ancestors or important figures (such as deities, chiefs, or heroes), and to mark major achievements. The simplest of these, standing stones, aren't clear as to their purpose. They may have been used for any purpose ranging from rituals to cattle-rubbing posts to prevent damage to crops and fences. What can be said is that they are often humongous and taller than fully grown people.

Portal tombs, also called dolmen, are monuments that are made of two or more large stones holding up a capstone. The stones used are often extremely large, with the largest capstone in Ireland weighing over 150 tonnes. The dolmen often creates a passage or enclosure in the middle, which seems to have been used for ritualistic purposes in many cases. In some cases, they were used as burial locations, sometimes for many people over a period of hundreds of years. In other cases, it seems that they marked a ceremonial location for things such as feasts (likely feasts that honor ancestors or buried individuals). Then there are some dolmens where the purpose of the sight isn't clear at all. All that can be determined at those sights are that many people expended large amounts of effort to create a monument that's still standing thousands of years later.

Stone circles can be found all over Ireland, particularly near the coast. They are a common feature in many western European ancient societies but are particularly common on the Emerald Isle and in the UK. There is much debate as to their actual purpose because there isn't any written record from the preliterate societies that constructed them. That said, there are a few common assumptions that archeologists use. The first is that they were constructed as time markers or calendars of some sort. This holds credence in that there are many stone circles that mark the passage of the sun and show when it's the summer solstice, one of the two equinoxes, among other dates.

Then there's the hypothesis that they were used for religious and cultural ceremonies. One particular type of indication as to the veracity of this theory is that multiple stone circles have a dolmen in the center that was used as a burial site. It's not too much of a stretch to say that the sites were thus used for worshiping and healing. But the popular idea that stone circles were constructed for the use of druids and their worshiping or healing practices is likely not true, considering that the preponderance of the stone circles were constructed thousands of years before the arrival of the Gaels in Ireland. The earliest ones that we know of were constructed in the 4th millennium B.C.E.—perhaps even earlier.

A final possibility that's commonly advanced is that stone circles were gathering places for their communities. This would have made them centers of trade, as well as sites of social gatherings. The link between the marking of important agricultural events (due to the motion of the moon and sun) would have made the stone circles a useful device for farmers in those communities. Whatever they were actually used for, there's no denying that stone circles still capture the imagination of many thousands of years after they were made.

A court tomb, also known as a court cairn (due to the piles of rocks within the perimeter stones), is a collection of megaliths or stones that forms a court. The structure has four sides (usually with two long sides that are somewhat equivalent in length and two shorter sides that aren't equal in length) and often has more than one chamber inside. There's a semicircular entrance hall or forecourt on the one side of the court (usually at the larger of the two short sides of the structure). To keep the structure in place, there is orthostat (large stone slabs placed on their sides) or dry stone (walls made by stacking stones without adhesive materials) that forms a perimeter around smaller rocks on both the outside of the court and the chambers on the inside of the court. There were roofs on top of the court cairns that were held up by overlapping stones or by forming corbels (stone structures that jut out of a wall to support a roof) to hold up the roof.

Court tomb might have been a misnomer for these buildings because there are few with evidence of burials or human remains. Those that have evidence mainly contain remnants of cremations that were carried out in the court. The preponderance of evidence from the size and formation of these constructions show that they would have made effective locations for gathering people, whether it was to hold weddings, initiations, religious gatherings, or for civic purposes. There are still remains of many court cairns (more than 400) in Ireland—mainly in the northern half of the island.

Passage tombs, also called burial mounds, are made up by a collection of structural elements. There are chambers in the center wherein rites could take place. The chamber is connected to the outside world by a passage. The entrance to the passage is of a sturdy design, sometimes with large stones holding it up. There's a large mound of earth placed over it all. In the central chamber you might find things such as basins and motifs or other designs.

In the Newgrange, there is a high ceiling in the chamber that goes about 13 feet high. It also allows sunlight to pass through the passage on winter solstice for a few minutes, thus illuminating the inner chamber and indicating the approaching new year. These sites are sometimes surrounded by kerb stones (large stones with special designs and patterns etched onto their surface that were used to prop up the earth and grass of the mound) and cairns (man-made piles of stones). The kerb stones are still of keen interest to archeologists who are trying to understand their meaning. In some instances, the designs on the kerb stones seem to change their shape and significance based on variations of light and shadow.

A structure that's more common in the west of Ireland than the other parts of the island is the wedge tomb. This is a type of stone structure where multiple stones are used as walls that hold up a roof of stone slabs—the roof slabs, in turn, being covered with cairns (stacks of smaller stones). The walls and roof  taper to form a wedge-like shape (hence the name). The opening, which is at the larger side of the tapering rock structure, faces the direction of the setting sun—west or south-west. Further, they are mainly found on the sides of hills, normally about two-thirds of the way up their respective hill. They are often used to house remains (sometimes for more than one person), whether cremated or buried, along with tools and pottery. These tombs started being constructed around 2,500 B.C.E., thus they are the newest category of Stone Age monument to be constructed in Ireland, yet this didn't make them any less popular than other Stone Age monuments with around 400–500 of them extant.

Ring forts have been made at different times throughout Irish history and are one of the most common historical structures on the island, with more than 40,000 that are known about. There were ones made during the Stone and Bronze Ages—called fairy forts. Then there are ones that were made during the Middle Ages. Those made during the Middle Ages were mainly the round foundational remnants of wood or stone homes that housed farming families. These homes are called ring forts because they were commonly surrounded by a bank, either of stone or earth, with a ditch directly outside of it. There was an entrance with a gate where inhabitants could enter and exit the home's property.

The older version, fairy forts, served essentially the same purpose. They were the location of prehistoric homes and forts that housed farming families and could be used to protect those families and their stock. There were ridges and ditches, sometimes multiple concentric rings of them, that surrounded the family building or compound. Many of these had an underground storage location, which came to signal entrances to the Otherworld in Irish mythology. The flee of the godlike race, the Tuatha Dé Danann, to the Otherworld in folktales was linked to the ditches that were found in the ground of these fairy forts. A holy significance was thus attached to these sights, resulting in great reverence being directed to them.

The actuality of their original construction was far less glamorous. The fairy forts—also called lios, rath, and cashels—were homes and fortifications of wood, stone, or mud that were surrounded by wooden fences and earthworks. Their purpose was to keep livestock in and to keep out danger in the form of predators and raiders.

A similar structure used for an entirely different purpose was a ring-barrow. These were locations where bodies or cremated remains were buried. They were sites that started to be raised during the Stone Age, but continued to be used until the Iron Age, i.e., were used until around 600 B.C.E. They were made by placing a ditch and raised band of earth around a grave—usually a single grave rather than a grave for multiple people. These vary from barrows (also called tumuli) in that barrows consisted of a pile of earth (or rocks) placed over a body to form a small hill-like structure.

The purpose of a barrow could also be broader than a ring-barrow since a barrow could house multiple bodies or could be a marker for a cemetery. Some barrows had an entrance and most of them had a ditch that formed a ring around the tumulus's mound. There's been some debate, but it is thought that a barrow was an indication of the buried person's social status. This is partly because there are sites with multiple barrows, some being larger than others, as well as other moundless graves (either in the form of cists, stone boxes, or earth-cut graves). As a note, a cist is a hole built in the ground (often lined with wood or stone) in which remains are kept.

The next period, the Copper Age, was a period when there was less construction of large stone tombs and buildings. The focus had shifted to smaller structures and underground places of burial. The same can be said for the Bronze Age, which followed directly after. The next section will give you an overview of life in Ireland during these periods.

The Chalcolithic and Bronze Ages

The Chalcolithic Age, also called the Copper Age, was the transition point between the Stone and Bronze Ages. There were many copper and gold deposits in Ireland during prehistoric times. It was one of the higher yielding copper producers in ancient Europe. The copper was mined, then the ore was transported to be smelted and molded. In earlier times, the techniques to smelt and mold weren't highly developed, which meant that much of the earlier copper tools were made by shaping cooler copper with hammering tools. The Copper Age of Ireland started at around 2,500 B.C.E. and reached its height at around 2,000 B.C.E., relatively on par with the time of the Bronze Age.

The Bronze Age was a further advancement of the developments of implements in the Copper Age. Smiths realized that by making an alloy with tin, they could produce stronger implements—seeing that copper was quite soft. Due to the lack of tin in Ireland, Cornwall became a strong trading partner because of its large tin mining operations—with Ireland trading gold and copper for the tin. The importing made it expensive at first, which is why some parts of Ireland didn't have much of a Bronze Age before the introduction of the Iron Age. The Bronze Age officially lasted from around 2,600 B.C.E. to 2,100 B.C.E., making it a relatively short archaeological period. That said, there were many developments that took place in this time.

Stone tools were still used in some circumstances (e.g., hammers) since it was cheaper to access than metals. That said, the stone tools that were produced were of a higher quality, and in some cases more decorative elements were added. The techniques that had been developed from the start of the Stone Age made it easy to produce high quality stone tools at a low cost. There were, however, a few things that made metal tools more desirable because stone shattered when hit against something too hard while metal didn't. And even if it did get damaged, it could be altered back into shape or re-cast into another usable form. Additionally, copper and bronze tools could be made a lot sharper than stone ones.

Legal System

The legal system of prehistoric Ireland passed along orally due to the lack of a writing system. The legal system was largely carried over into written form when Christianity arrived in Ireland in the 5th century A.C.E. The thousands of years prior to that may have had many alterations to the law, but it can be assumed that much of the legal structure of the communities was the same.

The society of prehistoric Ireland was largely tribalistic, meaning that there were many tribes that owed allegiance to each other and were self-governed. Those tribes had a few officials, such as a king and a judge, that upheld the laws of their people. The tribes around them would have had their own judges and kings and officials. Remedies for legal problems were mainly imposing fines or compensating the victim or their families, whatever the cause of the legal situation. There wasn't a distinction between civil and criminal law, so whatever the type of situation where the wrongdoing occurred, the victim or their family would approach the relevant official to have the dispute adjudicated. An appropriate fine or other form of compensation would then be levied against the wrongdoer.

The person who heard the case would make an independent decision as to the relevant compensation. The judge, or king or other official holding court, would hear out the case presented to them and make a decision they deemed fair based on the laws they were taught orally. There wasn't interference from other individuals and there wasn't a jury. The king or judge was seen as holding the authority of the law. They were the embodiment of the law, which meant they were neither above it nor subject to it. In addition to the protection that law offered, religion was also important as a guidance in matters of survival and morals.

The Iron Age

The Iron Age was the period when iron started being used in larger quantities. It had been used in multiple locations around the world during the Bronze Age, but it wasn't particularly harder than bronze, so there wasn't any reason to incorporate it into society on a large scale yet. The innovation of adding carbon and other ingredients to make steel is when it started becoming more popular because steel was harder than bronze. When you put it through the process of quenching (rapidly cooling it from a heated state by dunking it in things such as water or oil), the steel becomes even harder. Add to this the fact that you can cast iron (and steel) and that iron is the fourth most abundant element in the Earth's crust, then you have a winning combination that made this the material for tools of the day. It's still one of the most popular materials for tools to this day.

The Iron Age in Ireland was dominated by the Celts, to whom the next chapter will be dedicated.

CHAPTER 2
GAELIC IRELAND

The Celts were an ethnic, linguistic, and socio-economic group that stretched across much of northern Europe and Asia Minor during the last parts of the Bronze Age and through the Iron Age. The Celts had a rapid period of expansion during their height in the 5th to 1st centuries B.C.E. Before we look at how they relate to the Gaels of Ireland and how they were involved with Irish development, first we're going to look at a few key characteristics of Celtic culture and lifestyle.

The Celts wore clothes made of natural fibers (usually linen and wool, but sometimes silk or hemp). They also used leather and fur for the durability and protection against the elements offered by both. The clothing worn by people of Celtic communities were matters of great pride, sometimes taking more than a month to make a single article of clothing. The clothes were usually in the forms of robes, dresses, tunics, and skirts for both men and women. These items were often brightly colored with the natural colorants available at the time (even stale urine in some cases for its yellow color). Adorning yourself with jewelry, headbands, and feathers was also popular as it showed wealth and status in addition to acknowledging religious beliefs in some cases.

The society of the Celts was male dominated, yet women could hold positions of importance in both official and social capacities. These positions included things like ambassadorship, warriors, and kings. Social standing often had to do with the wealth of the individual woman concerned, which she could get from inheriting, work, or as gifts from her husband. Jewelry such as necklaces, rings, and bracelets were the prime way to show your wealth and cement your social standing, along with embroidery.

The religion of the time varied from Celtic tribe to Celtic tribe. While there was much similarity in the religious beliefs of the tribes (such as pantheistic worship and acknowledgement of the importance of nature or natural features), each tribe had its own gods and variations for popular rites. The religious beliefs of the tribes influenced how they created art, with much of the art being in the form of patterns and shapes, but some of it showing humanoid figures (often with animal parts). These figures were normally deities that were honored as both a sign of respect and as a way to show wealth. Art came in the form of jewelry, stonework, embroidery, goldsmithing, and designs on household objects (such as clay lamps).

The government of the Celts was fractured in much the same way as their religion. While there were kings that held authority over large numbers of people, a better description would be to say that the Celts were a mixture of tribes that had authority over themselves. Each tribe had its own ruler and structure to protect the population and levy tax. Things that brought multiple tribes together included hunting, defense against opposing ethnic groups, trading, and religious worship or major festivals. Thus, despite each tribe being self-governing to some extent (even if there was an external king that had higher authority than their local chief), they were still incorporated with other Celtic tribes that might have been very distant from their own location.

The Celtic population groups that are found in the British Isles include the Gaels and the Brythonic. The Gaels were the Celts that had originally landed in Ireland and occupied it during the Iron Age, while the Brythonic were the Celts who had originally settled Britain during the same era. There was warfare between these two subsections of the Celts since that era, resulting in migration of both population groups. The Celtic populations of Ireland, Scotland, and the Isle of Man are the descendants of the original Gaels; and the Celtic populations of Wales, Cornwall, and Brittany are the descendants of the Brythonic. The rest of the Celtic tribes and population groups have majorly been absorbed into other cultures and population groups since the invasions of the Ancient Romans into the rest of Europe.

Arrival in Ireland

The Celts arrived in Ireland around 500 B.C.E. It's assumed that they arrived over a period of hundreds of years, gradually spreading throughout the island and mixing in with the native population of the Bronze, Copper, and Stone Ages. Celtic language and culture spread with them, as it had done throughout northern Europe, Britain, and

beyond. The language was used in oral form and written records weren't really made use of until the 4th century A.C.E., although some examples have been found originating in the first century A.C.E.

The Language of the Gaels

Oral tradition was used to pass down cultural knowledge and history, medicinal and craft knowledge, and anything else of significance to the Gaels at the time. It was said that some druids were able to keep entire catalogs of medicinal plants in their mind, thereby providing professional care to the ill that came to them for aid.

When the written language came into use, it wasn't used for long texts, but rather for short inscriptions on a number of signs and monuments (such as tombs). The written language of the Gaels was called Ogham, and it consisted of lines and nicks cut into a surface, with 1 to 5 lines for each letter. Ogham was used in Ireland until around the 8th century A.C.E., when the Roman language, as used in the Christian faith and influences of other languages from trade partners, altered the written language practices.

Political Division

The society was divided into finte, which were communities with a king at their top. Patrilineal descent was the order of the day, so male descendants would inherit land and responsibilities from the deceased king or relatives. The descent could also include fostered children in some cases, meaning you could inherit certain things even if you weren't related by blood, but rather by adoption. The society was further divided beyond the family you came from. It was a hierarchical society with its own caste system. There were the unfree, the free, the doernemed, and the soernemed.

The unfree were slaves. They had to provide work at no cost. They could not own possessions nor land, and they passed on their unfree status to their children.

Freemen was a dual category. There were the free who were poor and owned little to nothing, yet they were treated better than the unfree. There were also the freemen who held possessions and land, thus gaining social and political status in their communities. This higher tier of freemen could qualify as a briugu if they elected to open their homes to others. If they held this role, they would have to provide food and shelter to anyone who came, up to the capacity of their home. This came with benefits on both a social level and in relation to the freeman's political and legal rights.

The doernemed were the professionals of Gaelic society. They were physicians, legal representatives, poets, historians, and craftspeople. These positions required study and practice, and they could be passed on to your descendants. Particularly skilled doernemed were classified as ollam. They were sponsored by wealthy individuals and families, gaining much more financial freedom and personal status than others lower than them on the hierarchy.

Soernemed were the top caste and consisted of chiefs, kings, highly skilled poets, druids, and their families. These individuals had powers to rule and had large collections of resources. Each position had a different role that was essential to the identity and sovereignty of its tribe.

Legal System

The legal system of the Gaels was called Brehon Law, and it remained in influence until more than a thousand years after Ireland had converted to Christianity. In fact, some parts of Brehon Law are still in force to this day, even if in altered form. The main causes of alteration were the introduction of Christianity, Norman rulership, English rule, and modern changes for the law to suit society's needs. Original Brehon Law applied to all parts of life and was uniformly applicable, even to the kings.

One of the main characteristics of the original legal system was that criminal and civil matters were treated and remedied as one—there was no distinction. When a transgression was committed against someone, the main remedy was to provide them (or their dependents) with compensation to take care of any financial needs of the injured party. The focus wasn't on punishing the perpetrator, but on providing for the victim. If the victim had been murdered, for instance, their family would be provided with funds from a fine that was levied against the murder. If the fine couldn't be paid, then the murderer would either be enslaved, waiting until the killer could pay the fine, or killing the murderer.

The situation was similar if you harmed someone physically. In this case, you would consult your victim's attorney or the victim directly and determine how much would be an appropriate payment to compensate for the wound. This needed to include the price of accommodation, food, and care. The fee would vary depending on the part of the body that was wounded (with the highest fines being for body parts that could lead to death), how intensely it was damaged, which would be determined by a doctor upon inspecting the patient. Further, the wrongdoer would need to take care of their victim while they were recovering. The matter of intention when causing the wound held a lot of importance, as well as actions done by the victim that contributed to their injury.

Inheritance was another matter of importance in Brehon Law. It dictated that the property you inherited also came with added responsibilities and expectations, depending on the social standing that it gave you. For instance, if you inherited the family lands, you would also inherit the responsibility that came with maintaining those lands for the benefit of the rest of the family. If a person inherited the status of the head of the family, he would also have to care for the widows of the family

and pay the debts of those he was responsible for if they couldn't pay it themselves. If the person refused to take on the responsibilities due with the inheritance, then they would forfeit the property and position (and would possibly be kicked out of the family altogether). Men could inherit any type of property, depending on their closeness to the deceased (in terms of biological relationship), and the order of their birth. Women, on the other hand, were only able to inherit money.

The law was also concerned with the treatment of women. While men generally held senior positions and could hold more types of property than women, women could still hold high positions (such as queen) and seek justice for wrongs that were committed against them. An example of this was divorce or financial compensation if a woman's husband beat her up too heavily while disciplining her or if he heavily abused her. That said, a husband could beat up his wife to "correct" her behavior. In terms of property, the marriage joined both the husband and wife's possessions, but they could be separated back in some cases.

Finally, Brehon Law regulated the ranks and functions of kings. There were three levels of kings. The bottom level was in charge of a single tuath (or kingdom). The next highest level would hold power over multiple tuaths or tribes. While the final rank was known as the king kings or the high king and had authority over all people in the region. This meant that they would provide governance for all those people, embody the laws of the region, provide judgements, lead ceremonies, and perform other official roles. If they didn't perform their functions properly or were injured (i.e. if they didn't possess the quality of kingliness), then they would be replaced with an alternative king. As such, the king did hold the highest political power in their land, but they were on par with the law, not above it.

Religion in Gaelic Ireland

The Celts in general had different religions from tribe to tribe. This was the same with the Gaels. Each group had their own deities, heroes, and beliefs. That said, there were common denominators among the Gaelic religions, the chief of which was that there were gods in each to embody the most important parts of nature and the most important characteristics of human life, such as love. As such, there were hundreds of gods, but they weren't all uniformly worshiped in Ireland—save a few of the most important and established ones.

Another common denominator of Gaelic religions was the belief in the animation of inanimate objects. Rocks, trees, mountains, and a number of other natural features were all believed to have a soul, and thus to be worthy of respect. Even though things such as rocks were lifeless, their similarities with humans and animals (such as endurance in dealing with environmental stresses) were noted and admired. The nature of those objects (such as rivers) and of animals were carried into the descriptions and identity of the gods in any given religion of the Gaels. This was occasionally carried to the extent where ownership was disallowed of certain natural features due to the divine nature associated with it.

Another aspect of Gaelic religion was that religious tolerance was not only allowed but was encouraged. In other words, the trade partners and the foreigners living in lands owned by the Gaels were allowed to practice their own religions. This didn't only relate to beliefs, but also related to ceremonies and rituals. When Christianity became popular in Ireland, it was easily assimilated into the Gaelic population due to their comfortable acceptance of people of all beliefs. Soon Christianity became the majority religion, once it was figured out how to incorporate some of the core pagan beliefs and practices into the traditional Christian ones. While this was a challenge due to Christianity being monotheistic, it was managed through such practices as making some of the Gaelic gods into saints who had performed miracles and incorporating Gaelic festivals into the Christian calendar, albeit with alterations).

In the next chapter we will explore Ireland during the Early Christian Period in which St. Patrick lived, and the Viking period that followed.

IRELAND
DUBLIN

CHAPTER 3
IRELAND DURING THE MIDDLE AGES

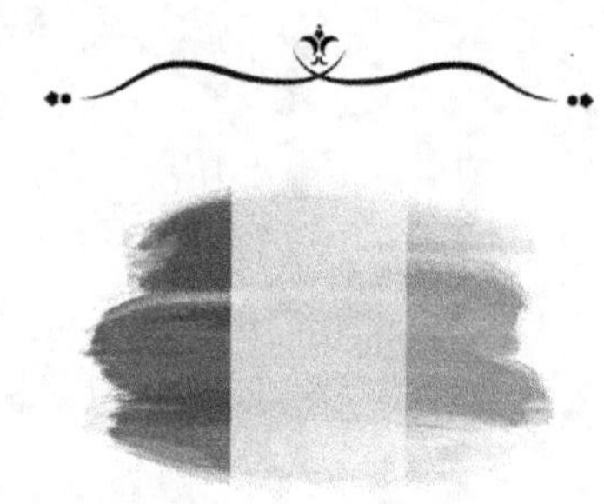

The Middle Ages in Ireland was a period full of changes and invasions. This chapter looks at the most important historical changes of this period, right up to the reign of King Henry VIII.

Early Christian Ireland

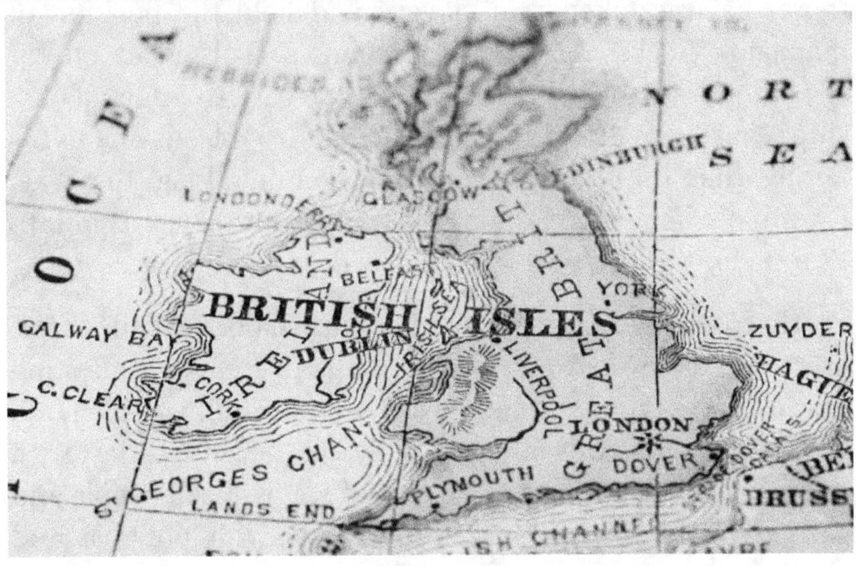

Christianity came to the British Isles with the Roman Empire, which had itself converted to Christianity as the chief religion in the early 300's A.C.E. First it had been accepted with the Edict of Milan, after which it openly became the most important religion of the empire. This spread to the British Isles, where it had become a popular religion with the locals of England. The English locals were often captured by the Irish as slaves, and those slaves are believed to be the first individuals to bring Christianity to Ireland. Those slaves would share the faith with the people they came into contact with, resulting in a basic understanding and burgeoning acceptance of the religion. The first major conversion, however, is said to have been brought about by the patron saint of Ireland, St. Patrick.

St. Patrick

Saint Patrick was born to a family in England that was under the rule of the Roman Empire during the fifth century A.C.E. He lived comfortably until his capture by Irish bandits when he was 16, at which point he was taken to Ireland. While there, he was taken into slavery and held the position of managing flocks and herds of animals. This went on for several years until he secured an escape back to England on a ship. Once he reached England, he had trouble getting to his family due to hunger and incarceration along the way. Eventually he reached them, at which point they sent him to Europe for training as a religious leader.

He completed his training and was ordained. While there, he received letters from the Christians in Ireland requesting that he go to them and help with efforts to convert the land. He later accepted this offer and sailed to the land to start with ministering and converting en masse. He baptized people and carried out confirmations. Interactions with political and royal powers were also important to create goodwill, so he provided gifts to officials and required no gifts in return.

People knew him as a miracle worker, allegedly raising people from the dead, providing provisions using the power of prayer alone, making snakes leave Ireland, and causing a herd of pigs to appear, among other feats. There are also stories in which he battled mythical beasts to protect those of the local population. With the work he did and the miracles he performed, he was one of the most influential early Christians and he is lauded as the individual that converted Ireland to make it a Christian land.

Other Important Figures During This Era

The early Christian era of Ireland lasted from around 400 to 800 A.C.E. (with St. Patrick believed to have lived and worked in Ireland during the 400s).

Saint Brigid of Kildare was one of the other two patron saints of Ireland, along with Saint Columba. She was born to a slave and a noble (in the fifth century A.C.E.), with her dad selling both her and her mom to a druid early on in life. While under the ownership of the druid, she remained devout to her Christian faith, even managing to convert him. He gave her back to her father due to his respect for her, at which point her father tried to sell her to a king in Ulster. She once again showed her devoutness, and the king granted her freedom from parental care and slavery as a sign of respect.

She performed works of devotion and got the attention of a king in Leinster, who provided her with a plain in Kildare to build the first nunnery in Ireland. The nunnery was successful, leading to her establishing more over the succeeding years. All the while she continued with her work of conversion and performing miracles, such as providing enough beer for a colony of lepers from to barrels that had originally been filled with water. Some say she is merely the Christianization of a figure that had originally existed as  a deity in the Pagan faith, while others say she was a born and real woman who became a saint. Whichever the case may be, her legacy has resulted in a permanent mark in Ireland.

Saint Columba, also known as Columcille, was born in 521 A.C.E. and came from an ancestry of royals. He was devout from an early age, studying and becoming an ordained priest. He was an influential figure, founding the towns of Durrow and Derry, and founding Christian communities across

Ireland, Scotland, northern England, the Inner and Outer Hebrides, and the Orkney Islands. He had a storied life that provided guidelines to many. The story started with a squabble over a valuable book of Psalms, a book which he had secretly copied without the approval of its owner.

When the owner found out about it, he brought the matter before their king to adjudicate the dispute. The king declared that both the original book and the copy that had been made (the copy still existing today in the ownership of the O'Donnell clan) would go to the owner, and that St. Columba would be imprisoned. The saint broke out of the prison and caused warfare to break out when he incited his kinsmen and followers with the story of his mistreatment by the king. The warfare was violent and resulted in the death and injury of many people. The saint felt horrible for the destruction that had been created in connection with him, so he voluntarily exiled himself and a group of his followers to the island of Iona as penance.

Not being satisfied with sitting and feeling sorry for himself, the saint was a man of action. He built a church on Iona, and it would become the mother church of all the others he would go on to found in the British Isles. His churches and monasteries were places of learning and of faith. The sheer amount of change he brought about by founding these churches and training others to spread the faith is why he is known as one of the three patron saints of Ireland.

The Early Christian period lasted for a few hundred years. It was a period when many conversions took place, making Christianity the main faith of the island. Religious buildings became centers of religious, social, and commercial life, with some of the monasteries becoming the leaders of scholastic education for the whole European continent. The High Kings converted to Christianity and Paganism was absorbed into the Christian faith.

The era came to an end when the Vikings started invading and establishing themselves as a force to be reckoned with.

Viking and Norman Ireland

The Vikings were seafaring warriors who exerted their influence on much of Europe due to their military prowess. They originated in Scandinavia and were originally thought to be an agricultural people. The combination of their large population (possibly overpopulation in relation to their resources), their superior strength, and their above-average fighting ability led them becoming raiders of the lands surrounding them.

The societal classification system of the Vikings had landowners (the chiefs) at the top, who would provide land to clan heads, freemen, and retainers (the servants or laborers of the other classes). In other words, land ownership was a prime determinant of social standing. But, with the rise of the Viking population, there was demand placed on further expansion and conquering of surrounding regions. The populations of the Viking lands (mainly present- day Scandinavia) had

become too large and powerful to remain complacent with the land they already had. Raiding was the solution to this situation.

Raids would normally entail traveling in a longship to a region with reasonable resources. This would be followed by striking the region, fighting and killing where necessary to subdue the population of the village or town. Once subdued, resources would be plundered, then buildings, trees, lands, or infrastructure would be burned. This whole process would be quite fast due to the strategy being to strike, take, and leave. This earned the Vikings a reputation of piracy, hence them being given the name víkingr, which meant "pirate" in a few historical Scandinavian languages.

Early Vikings in Ireland

During the 700's A.D., the Vikings started successfully raiding the Irish coast and up its rivers. Their main targets were monasteries and religious buildings where high value goods were held with minimum protection. They established strongholds on the Irish coast from where they could maintain their fleets and establish trade routes within and outside of Ireland. The strongholds were the towns of Cork, Dublin, Limerick, Waterford, and Wexford—all of which were fortified by the Vikings for their protection against the locals. In addition to the valuables, materials, and food they obtained on their raids, the Vikings established a slave trade where they would capture native Irish and sell them for financial gain.

Despite the power of the Vikings and their influence on the trade routes of Ireland, they weren't able to capture kingdoms, despite the political landscape of the island being highly fragmented. This was mainly because there was a large ruling class due to the decentralized nature of the kingdoms, and because there could be multiple successors for each king. In other words, when a king was killed (or even their entire family), they could just be replaced by the next most eligible native successor, thereby leaving no power vacuums and preventing anarchy. As such, the Irish were able to maintain their independence everywhere except for the Viking coastal strongholds, and even these would come to fall under Irish control once again.

In the late 900's, the high king Brian Boru led forces against the strongholds of the Vikings. Unlike previous attempts to take control of the Viking-controlled parts of Ireland, Brian Boru's attempts were successful. First his forces captured Limerick, followed by the capture of Cork, Wexford, and Waterford. The most powerful stronghold, Dublin, would come under his control, which briefly caused the Viking population of the town to retreat. The high king was killed shortly after the retreat took place, but the effects of the warfare were permanent. The Vikings who had been incorporated into the Irish landscape could no longer take what they wanted without backlash. Rather, they were allowed to continue trade and to participate in the civil affairs of the Irish (even intermarrying and having children), but in a capacity similar to fellow countrymen.

Norman Ireland

The Normans were the Vikings who had raided and taken over the land that resides around northwestern France at present. The area had been raided by Vikings, who subjugated much of the local Frankish-Celtic people. The king of West Francia (a kingdom that occupied much of what is today the western third of

France) formed a treaty with the leader of the Viking invaders, Rolo, in which they would take control of part of West Francia (in the region that is today known as Normandy), in exchange for protecting the local population and converting to Christianity. Rolo and his Viking subjects kept their promise, mixing with the Frankish-Celtic population of the region during the 10th and 11th centuries C.E. and becoming known as the Normans.

During the 11th century C.E., William the Conqueror (a Norman leader) expanded the power of his nation by taking the English throne. This made the Normans the most powerful political force in the British Isles, leading to incursions on Ireland soon after. The final blow was in 1169 when the Norman crown in England took control over large parts of Ireland under the approval of the Pope of Rome. The Pope disagreed with the way Christianity was practiced in Ireland, thus consenting to the island's subjugation by the Normans in return for stricter compliance with Roman Catholic practices among the island's population.

The result was the Angevin Empire, which consisted of half of France, all of England, and parts of both Wales and Ireland. Irish politics were brought under the control of the Lordship of Ireland. The Lordship continued even when the French took control of the regions falling under the Angevin Empire from the Normans over the 13th and 14th centuries. Ireland thus remained officially under English control for centuries, despite political changes that happened in the larger nation during that time.

At the start of this period, there was a big focus on expanding the agricultural and commercial sectors of Ireland. This was sped along by the establishment of many towns, hundreds of churches, and plenty of castles around the island.

While the Normans held strict control in parts of Ireland, they couldn't maintain their command. This was partly due to a lack of direct involvement from the kings in England, but perhaps more because the governing system incorporated in Ireland was disorganized. The local Irish didn't need the organized structures of the Normans to be successful, thus they held their own without the need for assistance from a strict governing structure. The Normans were absorbed into the Irish population by intermarriage as a result, at least in the areas beyond the Pale.

The 13th century marked the real turning point of real power of the island. During the 13th century, many of the local Irish lords started conflicts with pure Norman-backed lords. A strategy that was particularly effective was surprise attacks to take resources and cause havoc. Further, some of the Norman lords started getting greedy or strapped for resources, resulting in infighting, which made it easier for the Irish to overpower them. The Irish and Irish-Normans were thus able to take control back from many of the less significant English nobles.

The 14th century had even more of a power shift with the occurrence of the Black Death and the distraction of English monarchs by the War of the Roses. The Irish populations of the island were able to withstand the dire effects of the Black Death better due to a more spread-out rural population than the loyal English living on the island. The close living of the English in towns such as Dublin resulted in the plague both spreading faster in those areas and taking longer to stop affecting those areas. As such, the population of towns was more heavily reduced than that of rural areas.

As for the lack of financial and military support from the English crown due to their concern with the War of the Roses, the result was that Irish lords and those loyal to their cause were more capable of attacking and taking control of areas that they previously weren't able to—particularly since the lordship of Ireland had been delegated to a powerful family that had resided in England for more than a century (the Fitzgeralds of Kildare). In the end, there were very few areas outside of Dublin where real control was in the hands of the English. This all changed after the rule of Henry VIII.

CHAPTER 4
IRELAND FROM THE RULE OF HENRY VIII

The control of the English monarchs had waned until the 16th century, with the little control that remained being centered around Dublin and surrounding areas in the Pale. When Henry VIII was crowned and made general and king, he gradually took more steps to take control of the island nation. The first was to appoint Gerald Fitzgerald (the Earl of Kildare at the time) as his deputy to hold the lordship of Ireland. Gerald had shown that he was a powerful man and he had great ambition.

The appointment proved to be problematic in the long run because both Fitzgerald and other members of his family participated in rebellions against the Crown and its interests. This included signing treaties with foreign powers that had an interest in taking Ireland away from the control of the English. One of these was the Pope, and another was Emperor Charles the V of the Holy Roman Empire. Both had vested interests in keeping the Irish population from being converted to Protestantism to the same degree the English population had since the start of Henry's reign. When the disloyalty became too severe, Henry executed several prominent members of the Fitzgerald family and instilled Edward Poynings (a capable soldier and administrator) to take over the Lordship of Ireland.

Edward had been integral in incorporating a new legal system wherein the legislation that was passed to control Ireland wasn't fully under Irish control. The legislation was created in England and the Irish parliament would then get to accept or reject it as it was (in other words, they weren't able to draw up their own legislation to handle the problems they faced). This created a legal system that was out of touch with the population that it was created to protect and control.

Another one of Edward's priorities to change the legal system was the reduction of the number of monopolies on the island as they held too much power. This didn't only refer to the reduction of monopolies controlled by the Irish, but also those controlled by individuals loyal to England. Couple the reduction of monopolistic power with an increased number of military resources, and Ireland was gradually brought more under English rule.

Henry had seen the importance of ruling the island, thereby converting his title from "lord" of Ireland to "king" of Ireland, which no other English monarchs had done before him.

All these developments resulted in a lot more interference into the lives of the Gaelic and Gaelic-Norse lords than they'd been accustomed to over the previous two centuries. The lords already waged private wars between each other, but now the new English government was putting its fingers into these conflicts as well. An example of this is intervention into the inheritance matters of multiple lords and their successors, ultimately changing succession laws to male primogeniture.

There were also instances of English soldiers and officials violating their mandate by killing lords and locals, as well as taking their land.

Many of the Gaelic and Gaelic-Norse lords rose up against the newly rekindled English power. The king and his deputy didn't take kindly to this, with the result that lords who rose up had their lands confiscated for the benefit of the Crown. This practice continued during the reigns of Queen Mary and Queen Elizabeth I following Henry's death. Both these queens granted the use of the confiscated lands to people they had shipped from England to Ireland to make a more loyal population and workforce on the island. The people taken from England were mainly lower classed individuals and laborers who could make a useful labor force for those in charge of the new plantations that were created under the behest of the queens.

Another development that happened during the reigns of Queen Mary and Elizabeth was that martial law was implemented in many areas. The martial law allowed the English soldiers and people in power to execute individuals without the need for a trial by jury. The executions were largely carried out to reduce the amount of 

raiding by the locals. The Irish lords started getting fed up by the new rules being implemented because it prevented them from having private armies (in exchange for not needing to pay tax and getting their rental income entitlements formalized as statutes), forcing them to take responsibility for masterless men in their regions (to prevent those men from being executed), and they were being forced to do things in compliance with the ways of the English.

Insurrection was a result of this. The Pope declared Queen Elizabeth a heretic for her enforcement of Protestantism. He sent troops to assist the Irish in their attempt to overthrow the Crown's control of Ireland. The period of unrest lasted for the rest of the 16th century, with the most powerful Irish lord, Aodh Mór Ó Néil, forming a coalition with other Irish lords and getting the Spanish army involved in an attempt to oust the English. In the end, the English won and the Irish lords either accepted their lands back under strict rules or left the country in what's now called the Flight of the Earls in 1607.

The lands that had been confiscated were used as plantations and the English government invited many of its subjects to relocate to Ireland. The plantation that left the most lasting effect was the Plantation of Ulster in Northern Ireland. The plantation became home to many Scottish Presbyterians, English Protestants, and Welsh settlers, entrenching a firm cultural identity in the north of the island that's felt to the present day. This is one of the contributions to the political division between the present Republic of Ireland and Northern Ireland.

Along with the continued conflict between the Catholic and Protestant religious affiliations, there was also a cultural revolution that took place. The culture, laws, and language of the Irish were frowned upon by the new inhabitants of the island and the centralized government in Dublin, resulting in the government Anglicizing them. Thus, English common law and the legislation passed by the Irish Parliament (under the authority of the English government) became the law of the day. For all intents and purposes, the powerful lords of the Irish had been relegated to powerlessness by the removal of their hereditary rights, the incorporation of the English legal system, the influx of other ethnic groups that didn't accept the Irish lords' power, and the Protestant Ascendency.

The Protestant Ascendency refers to the gradual transition of power into the hands of Protestant elites and clergymen during the 17th century. This was particularly seen after the support of Irish Catholics for James II as he attempted to keep the Crown during the Glorious Revolution. After James was defeated in 1690, several steps were taken to give more power to the Protestants in Ireland and to limit the rights of the Catholics. One of these was that any individual who was Catholic would be kept from holding office; while another was that property and power would be kept out of the hands of the Catholic elites in accordance with the new penal law implemented by English powers.

The situation became difficult for many living in Ireland, especially when some of the steps taken by the English government affected the whole country, not just the Catholics—mainly trade policy discrimination. As a result, many emigrated from Ireland to other nations, especially the United States. This would continue for centuries as life remained difficult for many due to the laws being implemented by the English-backed Parliament in Ireland. Parliament would only gain independence in the late 18th century, by which time tens of thousands of people had abandoned the country.

The undesirable living conditions led both the Protestants and the Catholics to rise up against the English monarchy's presence in Ireland. They had been inspired by the developments of the French Revolution and the new democratic system of government that had been established there, along with the personal liberties that had been granted to the French as a result. The English government intervened swiftly in both the military and legal arenas, resulting in the abolition of the Irish Parliament and the acceptance of the English Parliament as the official lawmaking body for the entirety of the United Kingdom of Great Britain and Ireland. For all intents and purposes, the rebellion had failed, yet there were some freedoms granted to the Irish citizens as a result of the English government realizing its position was untenable if it kept on violating the personal dignities of Irish citizens.

The 19th century was marked by a lot of subsistence living due to the low amount of resources and trade opportunities allowed for the Irish population. Feudalism had taken hold over the preceding centuries and with the help of the new legal system that had been incorporated by the English government over the preceding century. Tenants would provide income from their harvests to the landlord in exchange for the land they lived on. And if they weren't able to provide income from harvests, then they would provide labor in exchange for lodging. The order of the day was small farms in most of the country outside of the largest towns and cities. The need to export much of the plant and animal output to keep their financial affairs afloat, much of the population had to rely on potatoes (and many a time only on potatoes) for food.

The Potato Famine of the 1840s (which resulted in the death of more than a million people) pushed the population's exodus from the island even further. About 2,000,000 Irish and Scottish settlers in Ireland fled for the United States and other countries. While abroad, those that managed to build up positions of prominence and financial success sent resources back to those in Ireland that were resisting English control. They also managed to get the support of prominent individuals in other nations towards Irish independence. The buildup of support contributed to the Fenian Movement of the 1860s, which was an unsuccessful revolution followed by a decade's-long resistance effort that eventually contributed to success in the 20th century.

Nationalism had been a hot topic for hundreds of years, but finally came to fruition in the early 1900s after the Easter Rising. The Easter Rising took place in 1916 when rebels occupied important buildings in London and put up resistance against the English military that was stationed there. When the rebellion had been subdued after a week (in which about 2,000 people were injured and killed), the English government executed the heads of the resistance. Their execution swayed public opinion in favor of the revolutionaries and their cause, with sustained unrest over the next 2 years.

In 1919, the Irish Republican Army started launching guerilla attacks against English forces all over the island. These were successful a lot of the time, necessitating the declaration of a ceasefire in 1921. The ceasefire was followed by the signing of a peace treaty by some of the Irish republican representatives, which stated that the violence would come to an end on the condition that the Irish were granted home-rule

in all but 6 of the northern counties (although the independent counties would still remain a member of the British Commonwealth of Nations). While this was a step ahead, it wasn't good enough for other factions of the republican movement (especially the Irish Republican Army), thereby resulting in a civil war starting before the declaration of independence for the Irish Free State was even passed at the end of 1922.

In 1923, the Irish Free State's forces won against the Irish Republican Army, with the resultant end of the civil war. There was still some unrest, but this was majorly reduced. In 1937 a constitution was passed that emphasized the sovereignty of the new nation, which was to be renamed from the Irish Free State to Eire. Eire continued gradually unlinking itself with the UK, stating that it was a neutral party during the second world war. In 1949, true independence was gained when the Republic of Ireland Act was passed and all ties with the Commonwealth were severed—with Eire changing its name to the Republic of Ireland.

A further step that was taken to emphasize independence and enforce peace was to outlaw the Irish Republican Army in the Republic of Ireland, which was still fighting to make the six northern counties independent. All this managed to do, however, was to drive the Irish Republican Army underground, where it continued to do its work. In the 1970s, further violence built due to the tension between the Catholics and Protestants in Northern Ireland. The two Christian factions have yet to come to a real state of peace, with more than 3,000 people having died in the period of unrest that's existed since the 1970s.

Perhaps the most memorable and least peaceful incident of this violent period (also called the Troubles of Northern Ireland) was Bloody Sunday in 1972. There were protesters in Northern Ireland that wanted equal rights for the Catholic minority. There was inequality between the two factions on both a legal and an actual level. The British soldiers present open-fired on the protesters, killing 14 unarmed marchers in the process. This violation of human rights caught the attention of the world, resulting in negotiations that were held in the presence of neutral third parties (particularly the White House of the United States). The result was an agreement (signed in 1998) that reduced the amount of political and economic tension and determined a way forward for the nations.

Despite the violence of the Troubles and other recent historical events, the people of Ireland are still one nation. The

pain and struggle in the nation's history is a shared experience by all on the island and is largely due to outside influences over the last few hundred years. The people of Ireland still have a strong unity in relation to the beliefs and mythology of the past, and this can be a binding foundation for growth towards one another in terms of acceptance. The next three chapters detail the mythology of Ireland for a good understanding of that foundation.

CHAPTER 5
IRISH PAGANISM

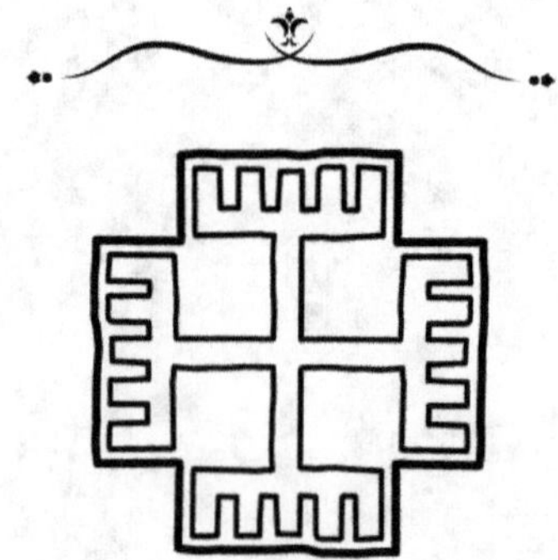

Gaelic paganism was the religion of the ancient Irish people, particularly the Gaels. There were many deities and multiple forms of worship. Paganism refers to religious beliefs prior to Christianity, thus Gaelic paganism mainly refers to the religious beliefs held before the conversion of Ireland by Saint Patrick and the other early Irish saints. The Irish system of belief was so dear to the hearts and culture of its people that even when Christianity became the main religion of the island, many of the pagan practices formed a part of Irish Christianity. The main beliefs of Irish pagans were in a pantheon of deities, specifically the Tuatha Dé Danann, and the belief in the spiritual nature of all things, whether animate or inanimate.

Lebor Gabála

The Lebor Gabála, translated to the Book of Invasions, was written in the 12th century A.C.E. by scribes of the Christian church. It sought to integrate the Bible with the folklore and history of Ireland. It wrote of the multiple stages of human contact with Ireland and has come to be held as an authority on the cultural folklore of the nation.

The first human contact with Ireland was said to be one of Noah's granddaughters before the Great Flood. She had fled to the island with a group of just over 50 individuals when she was denied passage on the Ark. All the members of her party (including herself) died while protecting a man named Fintan from death. His survival during the flood was followed by him preserving himself by various transitions between animal forms and his human form until the next group of humans arrived on the island.

The next group was led by a great grandson of Noah named Partholan. This group came from a community that had been established after the flood. That community had broken out in widespread disease, so Partholan and his people fled in an attempt to keep alive. Upon their arrival to Ireland, all of them died within a week due to infection from the disease they'd carried with them.

Nemed, another descendant of Noah, came with the third group of people who were said to inhabit Ireland. The group (called the Nemedians) came from Scythia, which roughly equates to modern day Iran. While they journeyed to the island and upon their arrival they were attacked by the Fomorians. The Fomorians were sea pirates that were led by a king named Balor the Cyclop. The onslaught of the Fomorians proved to be too hostile for the Nemedians, leading them to flee the island and settle all over the known world.

Nobody inhabited Ireland over the next 200 years. The Fir Bolg were the first people to attempt habitation of the island after the 200-year period of desertion. They were the descendants of the Nemedians who had settled in Greece. Forts and homes were built as the Fir Bolg established themselves. They managed to create a thriving group until the arrival of the Tuatha Dé Dannan.

When the Tuatha Dé Dannan arrived, they first burned their ships. This meant that they wouldn't be able to return to their ancestral home and would be forced to make Ireland their new home. When they burned their ships, the whole of Ireland was covered in clouds and mist for three days and three nights. The sun couldn't get in, and all was difficult to see. Once the mists and clouds cleared, the Tuatha Dé Danann remained.

The Tuatha Dé Dannan were said to also descend from the Nemedians, albeit from Nemedians that had settled in northern Europe after being driven out of Ireland. The Tuatha Dé Danann had learned magic and, as such, were menacing foes for the Fir Bolg. The friction came to a head in the Battle of Moytura wherein the Tuatha Dé Danann emerged victorious. The Fir Bolg would go on to serve the Tuatha Dé Dannan following their defeat.

The story of how the Gaels and Gaelic got their names and how the Irish language came to be was also described in the Book of Invasions. It was said that one of Noah's descendants, Fenius, had been at the Tower of Babel. He had heard many languages and understood much of each. When  he left, he chose Ireland as his destination. From all the best parts of the best languages he'd heard at the Tower, he created the Irish language.

One of Fenius' descendants, Goidil, gave his name to the language Fenius had created—Gaelic. He also gave his name to the people who spoke it—the Gaels. Goidil's mom had the important role of founding Scotland. Her name was Scotta and she was the daughter of a Pharaoh. The similarity between her name and the name of Scotland is evident.

Another prominent member of Goidil's family was his grandson, Eber Scott. He was reputed to have conquered the whole of Spain, where he established himself as ruler. They were known as the Milesians while ruling the nation. Despite having a flourishing kingdom in Spain, the family didn't abandon Ireland. Eber Scott's son, Miledh, saw Ireland floating in the sky from one of the towers of his castle. He sent three of his sons, Meremon, Heber, and Ir, to Ireland where they in turn conquered the Tuatha Dé Danann. The Tuatha Dé Danann were driven into the Otherworld where they're said to still reside to this day.

Three of the Tuatha Dé Danann got the agreement of their conquerors that Ireland would be named after them in perpetuity. They were Erin, Banba, and Fodla—all daughters of the goddess Ernmas who was known as the mother goddess. The Milesians agreed to this and upheld the promise they gave. Eire is the local name for Ireland and means "plentiful land." To honor the other two sisters, both Banba (as the embodiment as the power of the land) and Fódhla (originally the name of the territories that included the Hill of Tara) are used as poetic and honorary names for the country.

With the Tuatha Dé Dannan subdued, the Milesians went on to form a powerful culture and civilization in Ireland.

Now that we've looked at the invasions that were presented as the history and part of the mythology of Ireland, we're going to take a deeper dive into its mythology.

The Four Mythological Cycles

There are four mythological cycles of importance in Gaelic

paganism and mythology. These are the integral eras of stories and myths that define the Irish pre-Christian culture and that are still of importance when imparting Irish culture to this day.

The first is the mythological cycle. This covers the myths about when the Tuatha Dé Danann arrived in Ireland and the causes for them leaving Ireland for their underground homes in the sidhe. Further, the descendants (or in some cases, the altered manifestations) of the Tuatha Dé Danann, called the Aos Sí, are described largely in this cycle. The Aos Sí refers to the fairy and mythological creatures that are still celebrated in stories nationally and internationally to this day.

The second—the Ulster cycle—refers to the time around the first century A.C.E. It revolves around heroes of the time and the feats they accomplished. Most of the myths in this cycle take place in Ulster (the north of the island) and Leinster (the east of the island). These stories are tales of bravery and achievement, providing morals for listeners to live by.

The Fenian cycle is the third cycle. The most famous of all

Irish heroes, Fionn mac Cumhaill, is the central point of this cycle, along with the other warriors that were a part of his team, the Fianna. The Fianna were the elite fighting force of the High King of Ireland, and they were the aspiration of many young men and women. This cycle provides tales of their most famous figures and their accomplishments over both human and mythological foes.

The fourth and final cycle is called the historical cycle. This part of Irish mythology describes the lives and interactions of the royals as told by court poets. As such, it is also often called the cycle of the kings. The kings, particularly the High King, held a lot of sway in ancient Irish society. Thus, this cycle provides a look into the personal lives of the most elite of the ancient Gaelic society.

The cycles were passed down from person to person and poet to poet using oral tradition. As was the style with the ancient Gaels, things weren't written down, rather favoring the sharp memories of the top poets of the land to keep the nation's memories and mythology alive. It was first written down (to our knowledge) in the 11th century A.C.E. by Christian monks who altered some of the material they were told to put it in a light that suits the Bible and Christian traditions more. That said, a lot can still be gleaned from those written works, despite alterations that were made to the stories they were told.

The Otherworld

The Otherworld is also called Mag Mell, which means "the plain of delights." It's hidden from the human world and consists of multiple locations. The sidhe is the first location, in which the faeries and mythical creatures of Irish lore reside. Life in the sidhe across Ireland is similar to human life, with fighting and power struggles being a part of daily life. Parts of the Otherworld similar to this can also be found in natural locations around Ireland, such as under lakes and in caves. Other parts of the Otherworld are peaceful and paradisiacal—the islands beyond the west of Ireland.

If you wanted to get to one of the paradises, you would have to undertake difficult journeys full of feats of the body and mind. You couldn't just stumble upon these places, and if you got access, you would be able to stay for eternity. You could also go to one of these paradises if a deity or faerie invited you, normally for the purpose of teaching you something or because they were romantically interested in you. Sometimes you would end up in one of these paradises when you passed away and if you hadn't been reincarnated yet. Some of the most well-known paradise lands follow.

The Plain of Apples was an island that was the home of the Manannán mac Lir, the ocean and death god. His daughters lived there with him, and he raised his foster son Lugh there according to some accounts. It was one of the 150 Otherworld islands that were free of sickness, fighting, and lack of provision. The symbol of the island was a silver branch  with golden apples on it. If you shook the branch, you could produce music that would induce relaxation, sleep, and healing.

The Isle of Joy, also called Moy Mael, was a land on which you would forget all your concerns. You wouldn't age while you were there, but if you left it, you would gain back many years, growing old or turning to dust if you stepped on other land—a few days on the island were equivalent to hundreds of years in the human world. While you were there, you would forget your life and the people in it, along with your cares and concerns. You would laugh heartily at most things, and you would be in a state of joy.

Another pleasant place without treachery or grief was the Land of Women. It was the home to many women and no men. A year there would translate to hundreds of years in the human realm, but you wouldn't notice as you didn't age on the island. The island was inhabited by beautiful women who would provide you with lodging, food, and comfort. You could stay there as long as you liked, and you didn't have to leave if you didn't want to.

The Land Beneath the Waves was a realm that was under the water. It consisted of orchards, grassy plains, and flowery meadows. It was inhabited by warriors and royal households. It was a place of peace and comfort that was shielded from the rest of the world. As with the other lands of Tír na nÓg, it was under the rule of Manannán mac Lir.

Tír na nÓg was the "Land of Youth," and was the home of the remaining Tuatha Dé Danann after they left the realms of Ireland. It was variously described as an island of the Otherworld, or as all of the Otherworld islands together. Manannán mac Lir was its ruler. With godly duties over the ocean and death, he was able to control his realm to have calm seas and to negate death for his inhabitants.

As a land free from want, and as somewhere that could only be entered upon by invitation, the Otherworld was a place for people of Ireland to strive to reach. It gave them motivation to be the best they could and to represent the ideals of behavior prescribed by the tales passed down to them.

The Wheel of the Year

The Wheel of the Year was, and still is, used to determine the phases of the seasons and the sun. The god Taranis was associated with the Wheel in that he was both the head of the gods in many Celtic religions, and he was the protector of the gods. As the head god, he wielded thunder and had control over storms and unpredictable weather. The association between weather changes and the passage of the year inevitably meant that he was linked with the cycle of the year as a whole. The Wheel was often used in depictions of him and symbolized more than just the passage of time, but also his strength and mobility as the protector of the other gods, and how fast a storm can catch you without you having expected it.

The Wheel of the Year consists of eight festivals at present. There were four during ancient times, but Neopagans have added four other festivals with ancient roots to the Wheel of the Year to mark some of the important changes during the year. For our purposes, we're going to examine all eight, with the ancient ones being referred to as the major ones and the more modern ones referred to as the minor ones. The four ancient ones were called the Imbolc, Beltane, Lughnasa, and Samhain. Due to the heavy reliance of the ancient Irish on the year's farming crops, these festivals were just as relevant to the food harvests as to the passage of time. The four more modern festivals are the Ostara, Litha, Mabon, and Yule.

Imbolc

The Imbolc is the first of the four major festivals in the year. The term can be given a literal translation of "in the Belly" due to it showing that spring is starting and winter's ending. In other words, it symbolizes the start of the agricultural year and the growth of the food that will later fill our bellies. The festival takes place on the first of February as

the year transitions out of winter. During ancient times it was a momentous occasion because there was almost nothing to do and no way to get food during the winter months due to their harshness. Not only would plants start growing, but animal breeding would also commence for the year.

The festival was associated with the goddess Brigid. She was a goddess of the sun who was associated with motherhood, smithing, healing, poetry, cows and ewes (as life-giving motherly animals), cockerels (who signified the starting of the new day), and snakes (as a symbol of renewal). Her name is translated to "exalted" or "powerful," which closely relates to her ability to generate growth with the rays of the sun, and to inspire with the inner healing and vitality she can bring about in all of us. A common theme in the stories about Brigid throughout the various Celtic cultures that worshiped her is that she is to be seen as an embodiment of fire and all the qualities related to it (whether it be light, heat, inspiration, punishment and justice, or otherwise).

Fire is an integral part of the festival. Bonfires are lit and kept going throughout the festival as they invite the sun back after a long winter of cold and shorter days. It's a time of jubilation that symbolizes rebirth and purification. People use well-water to purify themselves for the start of the new agricultural year. While maidens and young men used to meet for ritual mating in ancient times to mark this period of renewed fertility in the year. In essence, this festival is about the coming of new life after the lifeless period of winter.

Beltane

This festival is celebrated at the start of the summer when the weather warms up. It's held on the first of May, resulting in its alternative name, May Day. As with Imbolc, it's also linked with fertility—due to plants becoming greener and growing stronger. Another name for Beltane is the Fire Festival as the translation of the word Beltane is "bright fire." As with the Imbolc, fire is seen as a cleansing element that purifies and heals. To celebrate this aspect of the festival's significance, bonfires are lit for people to sing, dance, eat, and generally be merry around. Like in prehistoric times, the central fires are seen as a way for people to come together and be protected while remaining social with one another.

This festival is one of the more popular times for people to get married because of the fertility connotation with the festival and time period. In fact, it was believed that this festival marked when the gods and goddesses of the Celtic pantheon got married to one another. A superstition that developed over the years was to jump over a broomstick to mark transitions into a new life as a married couple. The couple also needed to wear a special wedding ring, called a claddagh ring, which signified their union.

Lughnasa

Lughnasa usually takes place on the first of August each year, marking the start of the year's harvest season. To commemorate the occasion, it was common for participants to make corn dollies with the final sheaf of grain of the harvest. It's a time of abundance like no other in the year, and as such is a period when much celebration takes place. There are typically many stalls piled with the harvest of the year, along with foodstuffs that have been prepared for the occasion. One of the more interactive activities of the festival is when young men and women forage for bilberries to make

bilberry cake with. Bilberries are a traditional sign of affection and are thus used in matchmaking gifts.

The festival is held in honor of the god Lugh and was believed to represent the time when he returned as a grown man to Ireland from the Tír na nÓg (the land of paradise and youth). He had been taken there as a baby and grew up under the guidance of his foster father. When his foster father saw that the Tuatha Dé Danann were in trouble, he knew that he needed to take Lugh back to bring him to their aid. Before he did this, however, he gave Lugh the Fragarach, a sword that could compel others to tell the truth. Upon his return, Lugh was able to help inspire the Tuatha Dé Danann to overcome the Fomorians in battle.

In association with the festival, Lugh dedicated the Tailteann Games to be held in honor of his foster mother (Tailtiu) each year. They were held from approximately 1600 B.C.E. to 1171 A.C.E. The games were a hub of interaction, with people participating in sport, trade, dating, and feasts.

Samhain

Samhain is the last of the four major festivals during the year. This is the festival that marks the official end of the harvest period. It takes place from the 31st of October to the 1st of November. The festival was perhaps the most important of the four major ones and was participated in by all citizens during ancient times. It would last three days and three nights (or in some cases, six days) in early periods, with all members of a king or chief's population needing to present themselves as present to the leader. It was believed that you would be cursed if you didn't present yourself.

As with the other major festivals, fire was a key component of the festivities. First, a druid would light a community fire. Community members would then light torches to take home and light their own hearths with the fire the druid had lit initially. This was partly because it was thought that the barrier to the Otherworld thinned at this time of the year, so the fire would keep you and your family safe. Dressing up as monsters or animals was another approach taken to keep inhabitants from the Otherworld from kidnapping you or your children. That said, not all spiritual and fantastical matters were believed to pose danger to participants of the festival. The ancestors of members of the community were believed to visit their families during the festival, allowing the families to update them about the year's events and for the children to play games with their ancestors.

Sacrifices and offerings were also important when participating in this festival so that spirits and creatures from the Otherworld wouldn't curse you or your community. Safety and security were a priority at Samhain. When the festival commenced, commanders and soldiers sat on thrones that had been prepared for the occasion. Further, it wasn't uncommon for the death penalty to be doled out for any civil disobedience that had taken place during the festivities. Cattle were sacrificed, and offerings were made in the form of food, drink, or smaller sacrifices. That said, the food and drink wasn't all for the purpose of offerings; in fact, it was common for all the days of the festival to be rife with feasting and drinking alcohol to excess.

Samhain was absorbed into Christian festivities due to its popularity. Later in time it came to be known as All Souls's Day, then All Hallow's Eve, and finally as Halloween—the popular holiday we celebrate annually today. The trick-or-treating we see today is a spin-off of some of the aspects of the celebration from earlier times.

Ostara

This festival takes place on the spring equinox in April of each year. It serves to symbolize the middle of spring, which is why it was named after the spring goddess, Eostre. Due to the connotation of spring with fertility and growth, the symbols of the hare and the egg are synonymous with this festival. Both of these are symbols related to the Eostre and had connotations with growth. A hare was believed to die each night and get reborn in the morning when it emerged from its burrow, hence the connection with the idea of rebirth and growth.

Eggs were similarly seen as sources of rebirth and growth, with the added nuance that the yolk and egg white were seen as an example of the symmetry of the world (with the yolk being the sun and the white being the sky). The balance of the egg also ties in with the balance of the equinox due to the day and the night being of equal length. The legend behind the festival is that Eostre found a frozen bird while wandering and took pity on it. She gave it life by turning it into a hare, but the hare retained the ability to lay eggs. This myth gave further credence to the concept of renewal associated with both the hare and the egg.

This festival is newer than the four original ones in that it was first celebrated starting in the eighth century A.C.E. It was a festival that was a combination of Christian, Celtic, and Germanic traditions revolving around spring, fertility, and planting of crops. Birds and flowers are both symbolic of the celebration in that birds are the signal for a new day and the return of the sun, while flowers bring to mind the idea of fertility. Easter possibly got its name from this festival and the goddess associated with it, considering the similarity between the terms Eostre and Easter.

Litha

Litha is an important festival that celebrates the middle of the summer, also known as the summer solstice (the longest day of the year). As such, it's a day that's commonly spent outdoors appreciating the daylight that's representative of the mythological Oak King—a deity of daylight. On this day, you celebrate the inner strength and light you have, often meditating if you practice Neopaganism. The light of the day is commonly celebrated with a fire, whether it be a large bonfire or a small fire you make in a pot at home.

The ancients (both of Celtic and other cultures) celebrated  this day with various traditions. The Celts in particular held bonfires where people could dance and enjoy themselves. If they were brave enough, they could jump through the bonfire for good luck. It was also a good time to get married or to build on the fire of your romantic life by practicing love magic—or at least, that's what's practiced by many Neopagans today.

The key myth underlying this holiday was the triumph of the Holly King over the Oak King. The Oak King represented daylight, whereas the Holly King represented the night, thus the lengthening of the nights after the summer solstice. This would be rebalanced after Yule when the Oak King won out against the Holly King, resulting in the increased length of the day between the winter and summer solstices.

Mabon

Mabon takes place on the fall equinox, near the end of September. It's to acknowledge the dark times to come in the winter ahead, and to emphasize balance in life. It takes place after much of the year's difficult farming and harvest work was completed, thus allowing families to put up their feet and enjoy the fruits of their labors. The day is marked by completing tasks that have been left unfinished, cleaning out the house, and to get rid of things that you don't need in the house. This allows you to enjoy the period more so that you can reflect on the things you've accomplished in the year and reward yourself with some leisure.

The festival was often three days long, which was the period of the abduction of the god who the festival was named after. Mabon was a sun god who was the son of the Great Goddess of the Earth. When he was newly born, he was stolen for three days, in which time the world went dark. There's an undercurrent of understanding that winter is coming soon after the festival and that we need to be thankful for the sun and the light as it's contributed to our lives over the period leading up to the harvest.

Some of the celebrations involved pouring of libations on the trees of the forest. This was to pay homage to the Green Man, who was the god of the forest in some Celtic cultures. Other offerings made to him included fertilizer, wine, ciders, and herbs. In general, the festival was a period of giving thanks and appreciating what you've been given and what you've worked for.

Yule

Yule happens in the middle of winter, from the 20th to the 23rd of December (which is why some call it midwinter). It's a celebration that takes place on the winter solstice when the day is the shortest of any in the year, and the night is the longest. It's steeped in mythology, with the belief that the Oak King beats the Holly King on this day, thereby allowing the days to get longer for the rest of the year. As such, it's a period of hope and revitalization of the world.

The rebirth of light is an underlying concept to the celebration. In some Celtic tribes it was believed that the God of Light or the Sun Child is given birth in the interval of the festival. To celebrate the return of light and the sun, bonfires are held at home and in public places. Bonfires have different significance during different festivals—in this festival it's a way of welcoming the increase of sunlight back. It's also a time of community and family spirit, with people drinking and feasting for the whole night.

The eight festivals above are important aspects of the Gaelic Pagan religions. They were a way for communities to come together and to provide them with hope and purpose throughout the four seasons of the year.

In the next chapter we're going to explore another central theme of Gaelic Paganism—mythological creatures and figures.

mystery

CHAPTER 6
MYTHOLOGICAL CREATURES

Oythological creatures are an important part of most cultures around the world. No more so than the Irish, with an influence from the Gaels and other prehistoric people. Due to the metropolitan nature of the Irish over the last few millennia, many of the mythological creatures have been introduced from other cultures or have been exported to other cultures. As such, we are familiar with them on an international pop culture level (such as mermaids), albeit in a glamorized form. This chapter will delve into the creatures that make Irish mythology tick.

The Aos Sí

The Aos Sí are also known as the sidhe. They are the faerie creatures that the modern Irish sometimes refer to as "the folk," "the good neighbors," or "the gentry." They are said to live in the thousands of earthen mounds scattered around Ireland, which is why the term "sidhe," translated to "the people of the mounds," was chosen to describe them. There are two main beliefs about how they came to be. The one is that they are the Tuatha Dé Danann who settled underground in the Otherworld after they were defeated by the Milesians. The other belief is that the Aos Sí are their descendants and have gradually changed shape and size over the millennia. What is generally agreed upon is that there are many types of Aos Sí, and that they have different abilities and dispositions towards humans.

Faeries

Faeries aren't the stereotypical fairy that we see in Disney movies and series. While they serve as the inspiration for those portrayals, there are actually many types of faeries. Some are beautiful and elvish in nature, while others are akin to hags. They are more often than not believed to be smaller than the average human and they are almost always attributed with magical abilities. They don't normally have wings (although some do), but many of them can fly or travel at high speeds.

The life of a faerie can be quite pleasant. They enjoy their time in the Otherworld by singing, dancing, feasting, playing games, making love, and fighting. The lives of high-born faeries are very comfortable, and they have power over many lower-born faeries in their sidhe. But even the lowest born of the faeries are powerful. They sometimes use it for malicious purposes, in which case it's called black magic, but it's normally used for helpful or naughty reasons. They love playing annoying tricks on humans, which is why some of us are thought of as having bad luck. There are also many that enjoy helping humans, in which case you may believe you have good luck.

Leprechauns

Leprechauns are popularly shown as very small older men with green clothes and a hat. They're often described as having a short fuse and being a bit too fond of the bottle. Leprechauns are known for being capable cobblers and being very good with money. The history of the leprechaun is that they're descended from the luchorpán (water sprites) of the eighth century A.C.E. These water sprites mated with household faeries that stole into cellars and drank all your alcohol at night. Their offspring were the leprechauns who kept the mischievous ways of their ancestors.

They're so fond of money that they might just trick you out of yours. When you make a deal with a leprechaun, the silver they give you from their pouch will likely return to it once the transaction is completed; and gold they give you from the pouch will turn to leaves or to ashes. What's more is they likely won't feel guilt for tricking you out of your money because most leprechauns see humans as silly creatures that are too greedy for their own good. Despite their tricky behavior and fondness of money, they aren't fond of get-rich-quick schemes. Leprechauns work to make their money and don't have a problem with putting in effort. They will trick you to teach you to think in the same way.

In other words, while they are mischievous, it's with the purpose of making you comfortable with the idea of working hard and not taking the quick route to wealth. That said, you might still be in luck to get rich quick if you catch one or get ahold of their magical token (usually their enchanted ring or an enchanted amulet). They'll either give you their treasure or  they'll grant you three wishes in order to buy their freedom. So, if you're in for the chase, the telltale sign of a leprechaun being in your vicinity is the tap-tap-tapping sound of their small hammer while they're making shoes.

Clurichaun

The Clurichaun is a type of leprechaun, but with a whole extra level of mischievousness. They look similar, with small bodies and an old male appearance. But they're a bit more on the rough side, taking chances to steal and borrow wherever they go. If one asks you for money, don't be surprised if you end up with nothing; the same goes for a business agreement or a trade.

Their mischief extends beyond monetary matters. They love breaking into houses and stealing from your cellar—much like their ancestors did. If you have pets or livestock, they might just steal them too. Clurichaun have been spotted riding dogs, goats, fowl, and sheep across the countryside. So, don't fall into the trap of offering one a place to stay for the night or letting them watch your pets while you're getting something—you might just end up never being able to find them again.

Far Darrig

These are a type of leprechaun of a very disheveled and dirty appearance. There's one type, called rat boys, that have an appearance almost like a humanoid rat. They have a long snout, a skinny tail, skin that's dark and hairy, and a staff of blackthorn wood and a human skull as a topper. They tend to be sociable and like to hang around with humans. You'll find them around rivers, under bridges, close to sewers, in landfills, or on the coast. They often enter people's homes without invitation, taking advantage of their hospitality by lighting a fire and sponging off of your food, drink, and tobacco or cigarettes. The conversation will flow freely and engage you but will be full of contradictions. The rat boys are also fond of playing pranks on you, albeit lighthearted ones that don't lead to real harm.

Another type of far darrig, the red men, are more malicious. It's not so much that they wish to do harm, but their addiction to gnarly mischief leads to inevitable damage. Their favorite pastime is to kidnap people (adults and babies) and to plot different traps to kidnap people. If they capture a child, they'll swap it with a changeling to bring bad luck to your household. If you're an adult, they'll lock you up in a dark room in their house and spook you by letting out their evil-sounding cackle outside in their lair. You'll only be let out on the odd occasion when they want you to make them a meal of skewered hag, after which you'll be taken back to the dark room. Eventually they'll let you free so that you can return home, but not until after they've sufficiently demoralized you.

The red cap is a slight variation from the red men. They are normally found in old forts or churches, especially when these are abandoned. The sound of barley being ground against stone is characteristic of them, and if this becomes louder or longer to an excessive extent, then it's an omen of death. The red cap has no problem with committing murder when you

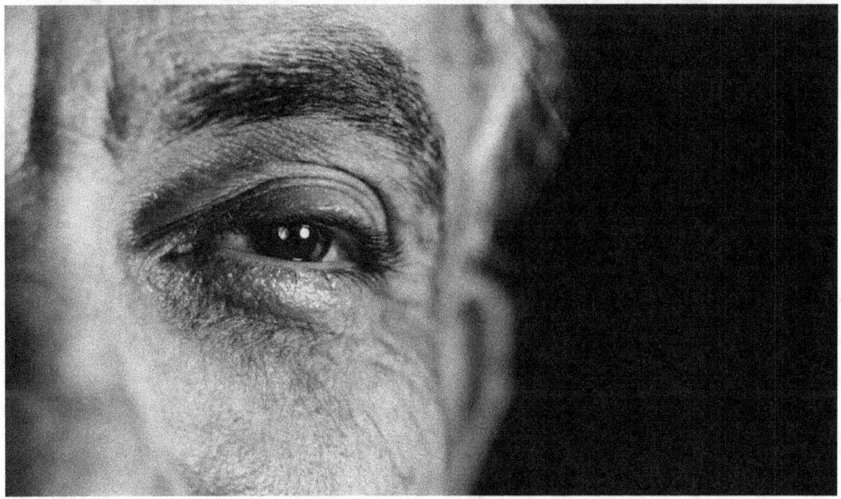

enter their home, using either stones that it throws at you or its trusty pike. If it manages to kill you, it'll use your blood to keep its cap's dye bright—with their life force being strengthened when the cap is brighter and saturated with fresh blood. The red cap is recognized by its stature as a stocky and short old man with long teeth, fingers and nails, iron boots, and red eyes. The way to vanquish them is to recite Christian scripture in their presence, in which case they'll vanish and leave behind one of their teeth.

Pooka

This is a type of goblin that can cause a lot of problems in your daily life. It's a shapeshifter, so you might spot it in any number of forms. The major forms are as a rabbit, goat, dog, bull, donkey, or horse—with a horse being the main form. If you see it in horse form, it will likely have a penchant for trampling all over your garden or crops. Humanoid forms include young men or beautiful women. But, in all of the forms, it'll likely have red or golden eyes that betray its faerie nature.

In all its forms, it might try to do annoying things to get a kick out of you. This includes mild annoyances such as stealing the vegetables you've grown to violent and dangerous things such as causing buildings to collapse. There have also been stories of pookas being in a particularly foul temperament, leading them to sink ships with their crews. But this is a severe case and most pookas wouldn't sink to that level. In fact, some are downright well-intentioned, with it being willing to provide you with advice on problems you're facing.

An average pooka, however, is neither highly evil nor kind-hearted. They're in an unpleasant middle ground of enjoying playing with our lives as if we're toys for their enjoyment. A favorite pastime is for them to call your name so that you come outside your home to meet them. If you come outside, they'll kidnap you; while if you stay inside, they'll damage your home and land. If they kidnap you, don't freak out too much because they'll likely give you a wild ride that leaves you disoriented and forgetful of the experience. This is especially true if you're drunk and on your way back home after a night out.

Banshee

A banshee is a female figure who is often described as beautiful, but with red eyes from crying. She dons a green dress and gray coat. When she senses your death or the death of someone in your family is coming, she'll cry in your vicinity. It's a heart-wrenching tune that'll fill you with grief, although in many cases the crying is overwhelming and leads to your ears hurting. It's been said by many that if you manage to catch a banshee, she'll tell you how you're going to die. So, if you think you're ready to find out about your death, a banshee is your best bet.

One of the best-known tales of a banshee was one in which the banshee wasn't a harbinger of death, but a woman in love. She had appeared to Connla the Fair and told him that she was of the sidhe and all who resided there lived eternally without need or conflict. The realm of which she spoke was the Otherworld (also known as Mag Mell), and she intended for him to come with her and be happy there. His father, Conn the Hundred-Fighter, heard her and called his druid to intervene by preventing her voice from being heard.

She threw an apple to nourish Conn while she was away so that he would be sustained without her presence. The apple was all he could eat and all he wanted to eat for the month following her disappearance—a self-replenishing apple. She returned

after the month with the druid's spell worn-off, thus being audible to all. She warned Connla against using the services of his druid again and she reiterated the pleasures waiting for Conn if he came with her. Conn took a leap of faith into her crystal boat, and they sailed away—a journey to the Otherworld.

Dullahan

The dullahan is likely one of the scariest creatures anywhere. It's a headless horseman that carries a human spine as a whip and his head under his arm as a lantern. The head glows allowing him to cast his fearful light around for people to see. The horse he sits on is always a black stallion—sometimes headless too. If you see the dullahan, then you know that someone is going to die where he stops. Unlike the banshee who warns that someone is going to die, the dullahan brings death with him like a cloak to the unsuspecting individual when he arrives. If you see the dullahan, just hope that he doesn't stop in front of you...or that you won't die of fright.

Leanan Sídhe

These are sometimes also called a faerie sweetheart. If it's a woman, it will be an attractive and enticing individual; while if it's a man, it'll be handsome, but vampiric in appearance. They're slightly elvish when you look at them, but in an enticing way. The Leanan sídhe are fairies that provide you with a burning passion that can inspire you and bring success into your life, so long as you make them happy in the bedroom. If you displease them, however, don't be surprised if you wind up dead soon after—they don't take well to offense. So, it's up to you whether you allow one into your life, but just know that as much as they can bring you to greater heights than you might have expected, they can take away all you have just as fast.

Changelings

If you have a newborn, it's important to watch out for changelings. These are the deformed or mentally incapacitated offspring of faeries that they swap out for human children. The human child will be raised as if they were a faerie and will likely be unaware of their real parents' existence. Likewise, the changeling will now be raised by you and will, for all intents and purposes, your child. There were initially believed to be two ways to get rid of a changeling and get your child back. The first was to torture it, and the second was to get it to laugh.

The first method was cruel and resulted in many cases of scarring child abuse in parents who had mistakenly thought their child was a changeling. Many people didn't realize that a changeling is incapable of doing anything other than singing or making music, hence someone who only has a form of disability is certainly not a changeling. It's not only cruel and illegal to do this, but ineffective. The other method works far better because even if the child isn't a changeling, you'll have made their day better by making them laugh.

Similar to a changeling, you occasionally find a stock, whose an adult that's been swapped out for a wooden carving that looks and acts like a human. At first it will sound and act well, but soon it will become bedridden and absent-minded. Finally, it will start dying, resulting in the smell of decomposing wood and a wooden skin texture and color. Meanwhile, the human is in the Otherworld—either under their own choice or from being taken as a slave or worker.

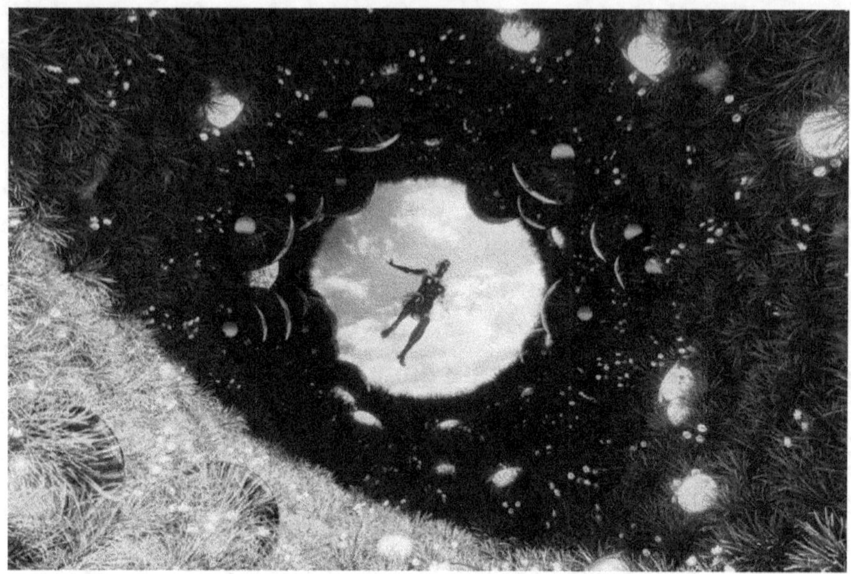

Fachan

Also called Peg Leg Jack, this a giant-like creature that has caused many deaths by scaring the observer out of their wits. In addition to a fondness for attacking humans unawares (with a mace), their appearance is such an assault on your senses that you can't help but be frightened beyond belief. They have a giant-like size, a tuft or mane of hard hair or black feathers, one eye, a warped arm coming out of their chest, and a single leg. Their leg has an immense amount of strength allowing them to bound with great speeds and letting them appear seemingly out of nowhere, which only contributes to the alarm you get when you see them.

Cú Sidhe

These are also known as hounds of rage. They're large, black or dark green dogs that hunt for the faeries. They might kidnap human women and they lead people that have passed on to the afterlife. Further, they nurse faerie babies, thus providing them with strength. It's considered an omen of death if you see one, almost like the association between the

Grim and death in Harry Potter and the Prisoner of Azkaban. Tell-tale signs that differ it from other large, black dogs are its fiery eyes (sometimes one normal and one fiery one), its size (the size of a small horse), and its brutish nature. In some cases, they're snow white with one red eye and one red ear. You're not likely to find them far from bogs, moors, earthen mounds, or rocky outcrops.

Cait Sí

The cait sí is a cat of the sidhe that's larger than normal and of ghostly appearance. They have black fur and a white patch on their chest. The cat is actually a witch that has the ability to transfigure, although she might still walk on two legs when in cat form if she knows nobody is watching. She can't transfigure back and forth more than nine times, which is potentially where the phrase "a cat has nine lives" originated. Although they're more common in Scotland than Ireland, they can still be found in the Green Isle. The reason to guard against them is that they like to steal away the souls of the dead, thus denying them peace. If you need to protect against this, know that they'll avoid cold—hence them almost never entering morgues.

Wyrm

A wyrm is a reptilian worm of great size. It's the Irish form of a dragon, albeit without wings and only rarely with fire-breathing abilities. In some cases, they might have clawed feet, but this isn't a given. Wyrms like to rest at the bottom of water bodies, in caves, or in swamps. When they occupy a marsh or swamp, you'll notice there's a slight tinge of disease in the air. This is because they're toxic creatures that poison their environments—with their blood being especially toxic.

The creatures are extremely powerful and have been included in many of Ireland's greatest myths. They are so powerful that when a hero tries to overpower one, they might create lakes and rivers in their wake while getting away. The most impressive wyrm was likely Caoránach, the mother of all demons and wyrms—the epitome of evil. She was so powerful that it was said Saint Patrick himself had to slay her.

Saint Patrick was also said to have gotten rid of Ollipheist, another legendary wyrm of Ireland who wasn't known to be violent. The wyrm had heard that the saint was on a journey to vanquish him, so he became angrier and angrier. He grew so angry that he gobbled up a bagpipe player that was passing by. The piper, however, was drunk and didn't even notice he'd been swallowed up, so he kept on  playing. This nauseated Ollipheist to the extent that he vomited up the piper, and fearing for the danger of the approaching saint, he fled the island. In the process, he created Ireland's greatest river—the Shannon.

Demna Aeoir

Also called demons of the air, these are flocking creatures that roam the skies. They have wicked intentions and drag people to hell, whether it be from funerals or the battlefield. Their demonic shape is somewhat similar to that of spectral black birds. They are believed to be the cause of much of the stormy weather that keeps us up at night. Their shrieks crescendo into the loud, awful sound of the wind in the worst storms. They'll flock through the air, moving like schools of fish move through the ocean.

Sluagh

The sluagh are somewhat similar to the demna aeoir in

that they also have the appearance of shadow-like black birds. Further, they also travel in great numbers that form writing clouds of dark smoke. Individual sluagh are found to have gnarly taloned hands and feet and they have a slightly humanoid form, but with a darkened gray skin and beaklike face. These creatures have the cruel desire of taking people who have found love and getting them to do heinous acts that can't be forgiven (such as maiming and killing people). In the process, they snatch up the soul of the now-damned person and have their nasty way with it, but only after abusing the person by dragging their body through the mud and pools until the body can't stand it any longer.

Fear Gorta

The fear gorta is also known as the hungry man. He's an emaciated figure that shows up with a begging bowl and dirty appearance. He looks like he's on the verge of death from starvation and he'll have a green tinge to his skin. If you provide him with nourishment or good hospitality of some nature, he'll bless you with good luck. But, if you mock him, scorn him, or otherwise mistreat him, he'll punish you with an unending hunger. No matter how much you eat, you'll remain hungry—from now until the day you die. He'll also bring you illness and bad luck to compound the trouble you'll face from hunger.

The power of the fear gorta is such that he can make you a wealthy ruler if you're a poor person; and he will make you into a vagabond if you treat him badly, even if you're a business magnate. The nature of a fear gorta is embedded in his creation. If a person dies of starvation next to a sidhe, this is their fate—they will be a bringer of disease, famine, and gloom.

Alp Lauchra

This is a newt-like parasite that can make your life a living hell. Also called a joint eater or just halver, this creature is a lover of food, especially good food. You get this parasite by spending time in streams or rivers where there's a lot of green life in the water (i.e. algae, spores, seeds, and microbes, among others). You might not notice it's entered your body, but if it has it will sit comfortably in your belly while you slowly degenerate. It eats everything you eat, especially the tastiest bits of the good or the parts of the food that contain the most nutrition.

You'll start getting ill from the lack of nutrition flowing into your body, requiring you to take drastic action to get rid of the hunger and to start building up your body's food reserves again. The easiest method is to eat a lot of salty beef and to not drink any water, resulting in you feeling parched. Don't drink water at this stage but lay down next to a stream or other body of water with your mouth open. The creature will eventually scramble out of your mouth so that it can rehydrate, at which point you should make sure to close your mouth and to avoid touching it. If you do happen to touch it with your skin, you'll end up with a numbness in the part of your body where you came into contact with it.

The second option is to get someone to sit on your belly, while another person dangles a tasty morsel above your mouth. Eventually the hunger and the temptation will become too much for the alp lauchra, leading it to abandon the safety of your belly to try and snatch up the food. At this point you need to close your mouth and move fast to get away from the creature, so it doesn't re-enter your body.

Hags

Hags were old women who looked weak but were actually strong. The mother of all the other gods and goddesses was a hag, which shows the amount of power that could be wielded and imparted by one of these beings. Hags were known to be wise and to have magical control of the elements and the weather. If they were angry, they could create storms, and when they walked the lands, they made them barren. They had a nasty sense of humor, often sitting on people's chests at night to give them nightmares, and then putting the person into a state of sleep paralysis if they woke up in the middle of the nightmare. The person would be unable to move until the morning, no matter their level of discomfort or fear.

The Storm Hag

She is often called the Cailleach or the Queen of the Winter. Her strength thrives in winter, particularly nearer the end when the days start getting longer again. She holds a lot of power in her hands of blue-green fire. Not a particularly beautiful hag, she's described as ogreish, tall, and warped with a glowing face. Her main influence on human life is when she generates great storms that wipe out ships, towns, and crops.

In the ocean water, she is known to have the ability to create waves that tower dozens of feet high.

Water Horse

You might have heard of a film with this name, although the creature isn't exactly the same as in the film. The water horse is, in fact, a long creature with the tail of a whale, the body and head of a horse, short and stumpy legs with large feet or large fins in the place of legs. A water horse is covered in a black hide and has a flowing mane on its neck. When you look into their eyes, there's a distinctive glint that shines back at you. They are bothersome creatures that will eat your animals and your crops. They might even have an evil nature on occasion where they trick passers-by to approach while they're in the shallows, only to put the traveler on their back and pull them down to a watery death.

Man-Wolves of Ossory

The Kingdom of Ossory was situated in the southeastern part of Ireland from around the first to the 11th centuries A.C.E. Although it was a part of Leinster, it remained independently controlled for much of its existence.

It was believed there were people in Ossory who could transform into wolves, with the body, temperament, and appetite of a wild wolf while in the transformed state; although you wouldn't develop an appetite for human flesh,

no matter how long you were in the form. If they elected to change into wolf form, they would have to leave their human body behind at home, which could be problematic. Your body looked dead while you were in wolf form, and if someone chose to remove it, you wouldn't be able to change back into human form. Thus, it was best practice for friends to be warned when you were going to change into your wolf form, otherwise you might have to stay in the form forevermore.

Another nuance of the transformation was that you would transfer any physical changes to your human body that you had experienced while being a wolf. An example of this would be if you had a large meal and you got covered in blood—your human form would be covered in blood when you returned to it later on. Another example was if you were stabbed by a farmer as a wolf, in which case your human body would have a stab wound that needs medical attention when you re-transfigure.

Dwarves

The dwarves of Ireland aren't the benign little creatures we know from Snow White. They're small creatures that are related to water sprites, much like leprechauns are. The realm of the dwarves is in the Otherworld, under the lakes and seas of this world. They're group creatures, much like those in the Lord of the Rings franchise, albeit less stoic and severe. Further, they're not obsessive on the matters of treasure and making shoes...at least not in the Irish strains of dwarves. Rather, they live similar to humans under lords and kings who command and protect them while they carry on with lives much like ours.

Abhartach

The abhartach is a type of vampire that once plagued the Irish countryside. He was originally a chief that had a penchant for commanding his people in a way that was much like a dictator. His people wanted to be treated better, so they beseeched another chief to come and slay him, which the other chief did. What nobody expected was that he climbed back out of his grave with a taste for human blood. He demanded a bowl of fresh blood for his consumption from the villagers, so the chief who had killed him originally came to the villagers's salvation once more.

Once more, the abhartach got up from his grave with a desire for blood, so the chief who killed him consulted the druid for advice. The druid told him to bury the abhartach upside down and to lay a stone upon the grave after killing him with a wooden sword. This was done, and finally the villagers were free from his tyranny. The abhartach is thus a vampiric dwarf whose grave should not be disturbed, lest you want to release his evil upon the Irish countryside once more.

Dearg Due

The dearg due is another vampire of Irish origin. She was created through neglect and loneliness. Originally a beautiful woman from Waterford, she was married off to a chief that soon showed he had no interest in her at all. He neglected giving her attention and she soon got so lonely that she left the castle to go die by herself. Upon her death she was resurrected as an undead version of herself with a taste for revenge. She found the chief who had rejected her so severely and she unleashed her wrath upon him. Once she was done, however, she had grown fond of the taste for blood, leading her to become a vampiric undead shell of herself.

The Questing Beast

This creature's mother was a princess who lusted after her own brother. She made a deal with a demon that she would have sex with him if he made the brother fall in love with her. When she slept with the demon, she was impregnated, and she blamed the pregnancy on her brother. The king, her father, had her brother sentenced to death by having a pack of dogs tear him up as punishment for the crime she falsely accused him of. He cursed her before his death by saying she would give birth to a demon who made the same sound as a pack of dogs.

She later gave birth to such a demon—a demon with the head and neck of a snake, the body of a leopard, the thighs of a lion, and the feet of a male deer. In other renditions of the story, the creature was small, soft, and beautiful. Whichever rendition you accept, the creature made the frightful sound of a pack of dogs, either by itself, or by the offspring in its belly that were clamoring to get out. Eventually, the questing beast gave birth to its children, who then promptly tore her up as her uncle had been.

Selkie

These were creatures that could transform between the shape of a seal and human, although preferring the shape of a seal. They had a skin for each form, and if you were to get ahold of their seal skin, you would be able to entrap them. They would live normal human lives in this case, but always looking for their skin and seeking their life in the waves, even when they had full human families. If they found the skin, they would run away and resume their life as a seal, only returning once every year to see their children.

Female selkies were beautiful women in human form, and male ones came in the form of handsome men. The male selkies would use their good looks to seduce human women, having a particular taste for dissatisfied women, especially those whose husbands had been away for long. Some claim that selkies were condemned souls who had been punished with the life of a seal for their actions.

Merrow

The merrow was an Irish mermaid, creatures that were much less glamorous than what we see now in films and series. The females were beautiful women who were irresistible when they brushed their hair. They swam with the tail of a fish, but could come onto land if they put on a special cap. She would come on land to take human lovers, but if one of those lovers took her cap, they could force her to remain in human form while they had their way with her. If she wasn't trapped, however, she would bring her lovers back to the water with her, where she would kill them and trap their souls.

Male merrow were frightful looking creatures who the females refused to mate with. They had green hair and scales, and their arms were stubby. The refusal of female merrows to mate with them because they preferred to mate with human men made many male merrows hate sailors and capture them from their ships or the water. The men who were captured would have their souls imprisoned beneath the water, preventing them from escape and peace.

Dobhar Chú

This was a monster that inhabited lakes, rivers, or the sea.

Its name was translated to "the hound of the deep," and it looked like an otter with flippers. They were large at seven feet long, and their flippers were often bright orange. These creatures were said to be the children of the Loch Ness monster in Scotland but had traveled to Ireland to exact revenge on its population because of Saint Columba rescuing a man from the Loch Ness monster. They had a taste for humans and would exact their bloodthirsty desires without a moment's hesitation. Their shape and size allowed them to travel vast distances quickly, with some reported sightings as far away as North America.

Ellén Trechend

This was a giant three-headed vulture-like bird who could breathe fire. It appeared from a cave along with goblins and copper-colored birds to cause devastation to Ireland. With the help of the birds and goblins, it was able to do exactly that, ruining the lives of many people in the process. Its reign of terror could only be ended once the poet warrior, Amergin, killed it to bring order back to Ireland.

Ghille Dhu

You're very unlikely to ever see a ghille dhu as they're known for being secretive to the point of paranoia when it comes to human presence. They're almost solely found in the forest, so you're very unlikely to find them in or around human settlements. If you're in the forest and they feel like you might be looking at them, they might just get the forest's undergrowth to grow around your limbs and bind you in place so that they have enough time to flee. It might be very difficult to get out of the foliage they've grown around you, so be prepared when you go into the woods so that you're safe in the case of a survival situation. In contrast, the ghille dhu is much more comfortable with children than adults, leading them to ensure children find their way safely out of the undergrowth if they get lost in the forest.

Féár Fortach

This was a type of hungry patch of land near a Sidhe that was covered by grass. It would be created when vile acts took place around the holy areas around the Sidhe. When stepped on, the grass would impart an unending hunger that you could never satiate. If you ate what would have been your fill at every meal thereafter, you would still starve to death, or at the very least turn into a physical husk. The only way to protect against these patches was to put a crust of bread in your pocket or to scatter oat bread crumbs on it. Alternatively, you could scatter salt on the patch and burn it.

This chapter included many of the creatures you may have encountered in Irish mythology. They ranged from the benign and beautiful to the ugly and vengeful. In the next chapter we will explore figures that were integral to the nation's mythology and folklore—particularly deities, the Fianna, and giants.

CHAPTER 7
MYTHOLOGICAL FIGURES

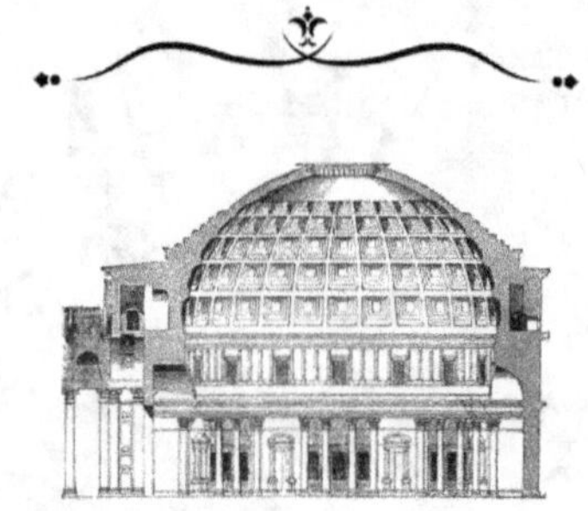

The mythological figures of Irish Paganism were practically innumerable due to each tribe having their own deities and version of the Pagan religion. That said, there were some deities that were found in almost all the tribes and who were integral to the mythological cycles that were formalized in writing by Catholic monks from the 11th century A.C.E. onwards. In this chapter, we will explore these figures and other figures that may have become important in Irish mythology after Paganism became a minority belief system.

The Tuatha Dé Danann

The clan of Nemed were the predecessors of the Tuatha Dé Danann. Their founder, Nemed, had come from a region beside the Black Sea with his wife and thousands of followers. They traveled to lush Ireland and established homes and villages there. He hired four Fomorians (giant pirates) to build a castle for him in each quarter of the island. Once they had built the castles, he killed them, thus exacting revenge on the rest of the Fomorians.

The Fomorians sent forces to wage battle with the Nemedians, with the conflict being violent and persistent. Some Nemedians were swept away by the sea during the warfare and carried to the lands that make up Denmark and its islands today. Other Nemedians could see their defeat coming and abandoned Ireland to travel and find a new home—which they established in the mountains of Greece. The Fomorians, as the victors, left a group of their own to control the land, while the bulk of their forces returned to their home beneath the waves to the north of Ireland.

The Nemedians who established their home in Greece, who had become known as the Fir Bolg, worked as manual laborers for generations. They grew tired of eking out an existence, deciding to steal the ships and head back to their ancestral home. Once there, they established themselves at the mouths of five Irish rivers and moved inland, taking back control of the island from the weak Fomorians who had been left to control the island.

After settling in the Danish lands, the other group learned about the occult from poet teachers in the four cities of Fálias, Foirias, Fionnias, and Muirias. The poet teachers were Mórfheasa (in Fálias), Easras (from Foirias), Uiscias (from Fionnias), and Séimhias (from Muirias). The four poets taught the Tuatha Dé Danann all they knew, until they were better at the arts of pagan cunning than their teachers). The arts were druidism, magic, devilry, knowledge, and prophecy. There were also tokens from each city that were provided to the Nemedian group. The tokens became the four treasures of the Tuatha Dé Danann (as they were known when they left back to Ireland) and were important to their identity as a nation once they re-established their presence in Ireland— now as a race with magical abilities and heightened strength. Tuatha Dé Danann is translated to the "people of the goddess Danu." They had become a supernatural, magic-wielding race through their training.

The four treasures were the Lia Fáil, on which the kings of Ireland would later be proclaimed. It would cry out whenever a new king took over the rule of Ireland. It is currently on the Hill of Tara where the ancient High Kings were inaugurated. The Claiomh Solais, translated to the "Sword of Light," was wielded by the first king of the Tuatha Dé Danann, Nuada. When he used it, no opponent he faced could escape its wrath. The Cauldron of the Dagda was the third of these tokens. It could never be depleted and would provide food for the massive feasts of the god of hospitality and abundance. The final token was the Spear of Lugh, Sleá Lúgh, that was wielded by the god of light, Lugh. It would always hit its target and was an indomitable force in battle.

When the Tuatha Dé Danann landed in what is now Leitrim in Ireland, there was a fog that lasted for days. They burned their ships so that they could not return to the lands of their learning, and when the smoke and fog lifted, they sent out a party of representatives who met with representatives of the Fir Bolg. The Tuatha Dé Danann wanted half the island, which the Fir Bold was not prepared to offer. Thus, the First Battle of the Mag Tuired commenced. Ultimately the Tuatha Dé Danann won and gave the Fir Bolg Connaught, taking the rest of Ireland for themselves.

Ultimately the Tuatha Dé Danann ruled Ireland successfully for many generations. They held power until the Milesians invaded and beat them after the Second Battle of Mag Tuired. At the point of victory, the Milesians offered the Tuatha Dé Danann a contract in which the latter would refrain from living in the human world of Ireland and would retreat their populations to the Otherworld. A list will follow of the most prominent Tuatha Dé Danann from before, during, and after the height of their control over the nation.

Danu

Danu was the mother goddess of the divine beings of the Tuatha Dé Danann race. She gave birth to the generation of deities that would later go on to expand the race. Thus, she was the mother of her nation. As such, she was the goddess of fertility, femininity, and motherhood. She  suckled the babies of the gods to provide them with her power. She was skilled with magic and was particularly good at controlling water and wind.

Dagda

The Dagda was one of the most important gods of the Gaelic pantheon. He was the father of many of the other gods and of many warriors. His main realm was agriculture and fertility in relation to food and plenty. He was the custodian of the Cauldron of Plenty and would host large feasts where all could eat their fill. As such, he was also a god of hospitality and generosity, within limits. If someone abused the hospitality that was provided to them, he would punish them.

One of his neighbors took advantage of his hospitality at a time by eating the same amount of food that would come from three boars each day. To teach him a lesson, the Dagda put gold coins in his food and the man died when his stomach couldn't process it. While the Dagda was almost killed as a result for violating hospitality rules (since he was accused of poisoning a guest), he proved it was gold that had killed the man—and in the process he taught the valuable lesson of appreciating the hospitality you're provided with.

This tied in with his duty as a god of natural law and order. He was considered a fair god, but he would dole out death when he deemed it necessary. His capacity for delivering death was potent, with him making a potent fiend on the battlefield. He was a warrior of great wisdom and strength, and the added capacity of good control over magic. His magical capability was far above the others as he was the head of all druids.

He was described as being large, but with clothes that were too small, thus having an unkempt appearance. His hair and beard were messy, and he looked foolish. Despite this, he was described as being friendly, welcoming, and powerful.

Brigid

Brigid was a daughter of the Dagda and Danu. She was a goddess of fire and the sun, thus she had bright red hair. As a sun goddess, she had power over fertility, particularly in relation to agriculture. Spring was her realm of power, which put her in the favor of the later Irish population—hence her reputation as a kind-hearted and motherly deity. Her powers included capability with art, crafts, and poetry, which meant that she was a vital power in the pursuits of many of the working-class Irish.

Despite being kind-hearted, she could also be violent when it came to protecting what was important. She taught people to stand on their own two feet and was a capable warrior who led by example. Due to the dual nature of her power, she had a beautiful half to her face representing her roles in relation to spring and motherhood, while she also had an ugly half that showed the violent nature of her warrior spirit. Her ugly side warned of death in the same way the appearance of a banshee did.

Neit

Neit was one of the sons of the Dagda and Danu. He was a husband of two of the goddesses who made up the Morrigan. Just like the Morrigan, he was a war deity. In battle, his ferocity and passion were characteristic of his fighting style. The violence inherent in his nature was appropriate as he was originally a Fomorian. After fathering multiple other Fomorians, he changed his allegiance to the Tuatha Dé Danann.

Midir

He was a son of the Dagda and Danu who was responsible for forming many of the lakes and rivers of the countryside. He was a capable magician who displayed intelligence in the things he did and created. He was of noble appearance, with a circlet of gold in his blonde hair and gem-encrusted shield. The story of his pursuit of Étain has cemented him into the culture of the Irish, showing the lengths a man would go through if he genuinely loved a woman.

Ainé

Ainé was a goddess of wealth who was born to the Dagda and Dany. She was the goddess of summer, thus making her a goddess of the sun and fertility as well. She was a goddess of plenty in relation to harvests and crops, as well as a goddess of love. In a myth of the king of Munster, Ailill, raping her, she bit off his ear and made him ineligible to continue holding the kingship as a result. At this point, she became a goddess of sovereignty because was now able to influence the rulership of the nation.

Cermait

Cermait was a son of the Dagda and Danu who was best known for having an affair with Lugh's wife. When Lugh found out, he killed the god, leaving the three children of his affair fatherless. When the three children—mac Ceacht, mac Gréine, and mac Cuill—grew up, they slew Lugh. They took over his role as king of the Tuatha Dé Danann and became the last kings before the race agreed to migrate to the Otherworld. The three cycled the kingship, holding the position for one year each over a period of 29 years until the Second Battle of Mag Tuired.

Nechtan

Nechtan was a god who held custody of the Well of Wisdom. The well was situated under nine chestnut trees who imparted wisdom with their fruit. In the well was the Salmon of Wisdom which ate all the chestnuts as they fell in the water. It was a sacred place from where Fionn mac Cumhail ate the salmon and became the wisest warrior in Irish history. When Nechtan's wife violated the sanctity of the well by walking around it clockwise, the well spat out the water that carved the River Boyne into the countryside. In the process she lost an eye and limbs, eventually dying in the river's flow to the ocean.

Nuada

Nuada (also called Elcmar) was the first king of the Tuatha Dé Danann and led his people when they arrived in their ships. In the First Battle of Mag Tuired, he lost his hand, which made him ineligible to hold the title of king. A hand of silver was made for him by Dian Cécht, but this only aided his capacity as a warrior, not his eligibility as a king. Dian Cécht's son then used magic to reattach his original hand, which made him whole and allowed him to claim back his title from the tyrant Fomorian king, Bres. His second reign was a period of generous and fair rule—a period in stark contrast with the rule of Bres. Nuada was also known as a god of hunting and fishing, contributing to his capacity of being generous.

Boann

Boann was the goddess of the River Boyne. She provided fertility with her waters, and she was an individual of great knowledge and poetic ability. When she was the wife of Nuada, she had an affair with the Dagda and didn't want her husband to find out. The Dagda grabbed the sun and made a single day that was nine months long so that she would have their child after a single day of pregnancy. As such, Nuada didn't notice the affair as he wasn't aware the pregnancy took place on that day.

The child, Aengus Óg, was put in the care of Midir, who raised him to prevent Aengus finding out about the infidelity and taking out his anger on the child. Boann later became the wife of Nechtan, the custodian of the Well of Wisdom. When she failed to respect her husband's warnings, she disrespected the well and lost her life in the process. In the process she created the River Boyne, which was imbued with her essence.

Aengus Óg

Aengus Óg was the son of the Dagda and Boann. He was the god of youthful love who, as such, had mastery of poetry and cunning use of words to woo his lovers. He was a god of youth who had powers over life and death. He could resurrect the dead and provide youth to those he deemed fit. Further, his power over youth gave him the good looks of a young man. However, being human wasn't his only form, as illustrated in the myth of the dream of Aengus.

In this myth, he dreamed of a beautiful woman who he fell in love with instantly. He couldn't find this girl anywhere, so he employed the help of other deities. He found her after two years with the help of a king who located her whereabouts. She was in a group of 150 women who were chained to turn into swans on a lakeshore for a festival. They would remain swans for a whole year. Aengus made a deal with the captors that he could keep her if he identified her in swan form. When all the women turned into swans, he transfigured himself too, calling out to find her. When they located each other, they flew off while singing a song that was so beautiful that it put the captors to sleep for three days.

Morrigan

Morrigan was the goddess of death and destiny. She was a warrior goddess made up of three sisters (Badb, Macha, and Nemain) in one form. Her powers extended to being a provider of prophecies that would show people their fate. In battle she would circle the warriors as a crow and eat the remains of the dead. As a human, she was beautiful and could seduce men easily. She could hold many forms, being a shapeshifter, with the four main forms being that of a maiden, a fierce warrior queen, a crone, and a raven. On occasion she would appear as an old washerwoman that scrubbed the bloody clothes clean of those who had fallen in battle.

Her first personage, Badb, was a war goddess who had the human appearance of a crone. She would make men on the battlefield confused and frightened if they opposed those she favored. She was known as a death bringer, killing men with terror when she cried out as a crow.

The second personage was Macha, who was also a war goddess. Her powers extended to being an earth goddess, and a goddess of horses and cows. Maternal reproductivity, agrarian fruitfulness, and sexual fertility were all associated with her. Her most famous myth revolves around her giving the men of Ulster a curse of falling asleep and feeling menstrual cramps because they didn't intervene when a king put her and her unborn children in danger. The danger was caused by forcing her to run a race against the king's prized horse while she was pregnant and not allowing her to stop when she went into labor with twins.

The third personage of Morrigan was Nemain, the goddess of madness in battle. She would fly above battlefields and terrorize warriors. Her monstrous shriek was akin to that of a banshee and signaled the death of many people. She used her power over fear to debilitate the enemies of warriors and forces she favored.

Manaanán mac Lir

Also known as Lir, he was a sea god who ruled the island paradises of the Otherworld. He protected sailors and provided abundant crops to those under his custodianship. He used his swine to give immortality to those who ate them, even bringing gods back to life with them. He had a magnificent chariot that he could ride across the water and a suit of armor that was impenetrable.

When Badb was chosen as the king of the Tuatha Dé Danann after their defeat by the Milesians, he was displeased. As such, he didn't join with the rest of them, but created his own sidhe away on his islands. Áeb, a moon goddess associated with the growth of flowers and plants, was offered to him as a wife by Badb as a gesture of goodwill. They were happy and had four children, but she died giving birth to a pair of their twins. Badb offered him another wife, Aoife, who became the stepmother of the children.

She wasn't happy with the attention the children were given by their father, so she carried out a plan that turned the four children into swans. Lir followed his children and formed a settlement around the lake where they lived. Badb joined him at the lake, where they all lived for 300 years. The swan-children flew away and lived on a sea for 300 years, and a different lake for a further 300 years. When they flew back over their father's settlement after 600 years away, they saw he wasn't there any longer—the Tuatha Dé Danann had settled in other parts of the Otherworld.

Lugh

Lugh was the second king of the Tuatha Dé Danann, despite being half-Fomorian himself. He held the all-powerful abilities of controlling storms and the sun and was powerful beyond comprehension. He helped incite the revolt against the Fomorian king of the Tuatha Dé Danann, Bres, when he ruled with tyranny after king Nuada lost his hand. Lugh managed to kill Balor of the Evil Eye to avenge his killing of king Nuada.

Lugh was a god of nobility who was expert in the matters of rulership. He held people to their contracts and gave swift judgment to anyone that broke their oaths or the law. Further, he was an impressive warrior of vitality who wielded the Spear of Assal. None could stand against him if he was their foe in a conflict as he was willing to lie and cheat to win in fights he deemed important. His expertise extended from fighting to matters of language and craft, making him a skilled artisan and poet.

Sovereignty

Sovereignty was the spirit of the Earth. She could decide who should be the ruler of Ireland. When a king met her expectations, the land would be fertile, and the nation would win at war. But should he fall short, she would punish the land with failed crops and losses. New kings were symbolically married to her when they were crowned. During the ceremony, he would be expected to promise that he would protect and maintain the land and his people. Fertility and abundance were her gifts for his loyalty to this oath. Holy wells and horses were both associated with her.

Étain

She was originally a princess of Ulster in her first life. She was in love with the god Midir, who was already married. His wife took offense to their affair and transfigured her into multiple forms, eventually settling on a fly. The fly was blown away and swallowed by a distant queen. After swallowing the fly, the queen grew pregnant and gave birth nine months later. Reborn, Étain had no recollection of her first life, so she was married off to the High King. She was found by Midir in her new life, who pursued her once more. She fell in love with him again but remained faithful to the king.

Midir challenged the High King to a game of fidchell, with a kiss from Étain being the prize should he win. The High King agreed, but he lost and the time came for the kiss, he reneged and brought in military forces to seize Midir. The god changed both him and Étain into swans and they went into hiding while the High King went on a rampage in which he destroyed many sidhe while looking for his wife. He found them eventually, and Midir said he would give her back if the king chose her correctly from 50 versions that had been created of his queen. The king chose incorrectly, at which point he agreed to leave Midir and Étain alone to live a life together.

Through this process she became a goddess of transformation, rebirth, and love. Dawn, rain, and the sun are some of the important associations with her, especially in relation to their ability to produce or highlight transformation. Her role extended to responsibility for healing people when they were ill and transporting their souls to the afterlife when they died.

The (Potentially) Sacrificial Trio: Taranis, Teutates, and Esus

The sacred triad consisted of three Gaelic gods: Taranis, Teutates, and Esus. They are currently believed to have been the three gods to whom human sacrifice was approved of, with each requiring a different form of sacrifice.

Taranis was the god of thunder, storms, and bad weather. This meant that powers could directly impact the lives of farmers, making it important to keep him appeased. His symbols were his thunderbolt and a wheel. Tuetates was a god of the people. In other words, he was the god believed to hold the tribe together as a community. Esus was the god of mastery and lordship, particularly in relation to a skill or zone of influence in your life. He was associated with egrets, cranes, and sacred bulls.

Dian Cécht

He was the gods' physician. He was able to cure anyone by throwing them in a well and pulling them back out. He helped make the silver hand of Nuada but was jealous of his son's ingenuity when he managed to reattach Nuada's original hand using magic. The jealousy drove Dian Cécht to murder his own son.

Bodach

The bodach is the storm hag's husband, and he holds just as much power. He might look like an old, poor farmer, but he is in fact the king of Mag Mell (the realm of paradise where you don't age). Together, he and the storm hag parented the banshees of the world. The capabilities of the banshees likely come from his capacity to foresee when disaster and death will take place. Despite his large responsibility as the king of Mag Mell and his power as the consort of the storm hag, he still enjoys moments of trivial mischief.

Climbing down chimneys to poke you awake while you sleep is a favorite pastime of the bodach. If he can't get in

through the chimney, he'll come in through open windows or a crack in the walls. You might not realize why you're having such a distressing night of no sleep because he appears in the form of a shadow that can flit back and forth throughout the house. In his eyes, we are silly creatures and the trivial games he plays aren't of much consequence because he's privy to far more important matters, namely the deaths that people will face one day.

The Fianna

The Fianna were a fierce group of warriors who provided for themselves by hunting and trading things from the wild. They had a high moral standard and demanded competence from their members. The position you held was a lifelong commitment, with intense criteria to meet if you wanted to join. Most of the stories in the Fenian Cycle were made up of their exploits.

Near the end of their existence, they started losing sight of their values of honor and started getting too high an opinion of themselves. This is represented in the story of how they were wiped out. The band of warriors were supposed to get a tribute when the granddaughter of the high king married her fiancé. He was killed before the wedding took place, making the tribute unnecessary. The Fianna refused to leave without their tribute and created a commotion with the princess and her family.

The High King's son then raised an army and waged war with the warriors. They fought as well as they could, but the sheer numbers they faced overpowered them, thus wiping out the greatest fighters Ireland had ever seen.

Fionn mac Cumhail

Fionn mac Cumhail, also known as Fionn MacCool, was a

warrior and hunter who held the final position of leadership of the Fianna. He was strong and clever, with his wisdom being enhanced when he ate the Salmon of knowledge. In addition to being a warrior, he could also transform into a giant. The story of how he created the Giant's Causeway is the most famous detailing his dual life as a giant.

As the story goes, he created the causeway so that he could reach another giant named Benandonner in Scotland to fight with him. When he got there, he saw the other giant fast asleep, and he realized how much bigger the Scottish giant was. He thus ran back to Ireland, where his wife came up with a plan to keep the other giant from causing problems.

His wife, Oona, was also a giant, so she wrapped up her husband in a blanket and made it as if Fionn was her baby. When Benandonner arrived in Ireland, he saw the "baby" and immediately grew frightened of how large the father must be. Thus, he ran back to Scotland, tearing up the middle part of the causeway as he went.

Giants

There were many giants in Irish mythology. Most of them were humans with the ability to transform into giants, while a few were permanently giants. Some of the most famous ones are noted below.

Amergin mac Eccit

He was a giant who had grown mad at the men of Erin. As such, he decided to attack them by throwing boulders and lumps of earth at them. His supernatural strength made it possible for him to pick up rocks that far outweighed any of the men he was 

facing. His career was as a warrior poet, and he is known as the individual who slayed the three-headed monster Ellén Trechen.

Iliach

Iliach was Amergin mac Eccit's brother. He also attacked the men of Errin. First, he threw weapons until all the weapons he could lay hands upon were exhausted. He then threw boulders and clumps of earth at them. When he couldn't lay his hands on anything else, he even pulverized the bodies of those he had killed and threw balls of human flesh at his enemy.

Dryantore

Dryantore was both a giant and a magician. He is known to have been one of the few individuals who managed to capture the Fianna.

In the myth of their capture, his two sons and brother-in-law had been killed by Fionn mac Cumhail in battle. His sister, Ailna, was also a giant and she had come to her brother so they could exact revenge for the deaths. To do this, he caught Fionn mac Cumhail and some of his companions using magical music that made them powerless. Once powerless and asleep, he imprisoned them in a cell.

Fionn and his companions escaped using trickery, and when Alina saw they escaped, she died of chagrin. With her out of the picture, the warriors killed Dryantore and feasted in his castle. After their meals and a good night's rest, they were returned to the realms of men.

Cú Chulainn

He was the best warrior of the Red Branch, the elite military wing of the king of Ulster. They were loyal to the king, but not necessarily to the High King of all Ireland. Cú Chulainn was a son of Lugh, the god of light and the sun and Dechtire, the daughter of a druid. His mom got pregnant with Laugh after leaving her wedding with another man in the shape of a bird. She had Cú Chulainn and raised him for three years before returning to her home.

He grew up to be very large and with great strength. He had seven pupils per eye, seven fingers per hand, and seven toes per foot. The other men of Ulster were occasionally struck with a curse where they would fall asleep and experience menstrual pains for nine days at a time because of their lack of intervention when the goddess Macha had been forced to race against the king's horse while she was in the advanced stages of pregnancy. The Gaelic deities like Cú Chulainn and the competence he showed as a warrior so much that they exempted him from this curse.

He performed feats of strength and good character. In battles, he would go into fits of rage and berserk hordes of enemies. He single-handedly defended Ulster against the forces of the queen of Connaught at age 17. We can confidently say that he is one of the best-known warriors of Irish mythology.

Cú Roí mac Dáire

Cú Roí was a human king who had supernatural powers. One of them was to increase in height and to become beefier, making him a giant. One day he transformed into a commoner, and then into a giant form of this commoner. Three nights were prompted to cut his head off in this form and eagerly went for the opportunity because he disgusted them in this form. Cú Chulainn defended the vagabond-looking giant, teaching the moral that there's more to things than your status and looks; there's also goodness.

Fomorians

This was a race of supernatural giants. They were one of the earliest races to settle Ireland. Known to be monstrous, deformed, and ugly, they yet held power over the forces of nature—especially destructive ones like plagues. They came from a land under the sea to the north of Ireland.

Normally bloodthirsty and fond of war, they enslaved those they conquered where they went. Their biggest foes were the Tuatha Dé Danann, who waged war against them. Bres, one of the Femorians, became the king of the Tuatha Dé Danann when their king lost his hand. When the tyranny of Bres was put to a stop by ousting him, the Fomorians took offense, leading to the Second Battle of Mag Tuired.

Some of the most famous ones are listed below.

Bres

Bres was an exception to the norm of ugliness. Be was beautiful beyond compare, but the beauty was skin deep. He took over the role of the king of the Tuatha Dé Danann in an attempt to repair the relationship between the two races. But his suppression using unfair taxation created famine and strife for those under his rule because they couldn't keep enough resources together to live comfortably. This led to the Tuatha Dé Danann ousting him when Angus Oh gave them the courage needed to revolt.

Domnu

She was one of the evilest Fomorians. Her supernatural role was to oppose light and goodness. In carrying out this role, she gave birth to many of the Fomorians who would later fight against the Tuatha Dé Danann.

Balor

Perhaps one of the best-known Fomorians, Balor had an eye that was altered by a potion that generated evil while he was a child. The eye gained the ability to kill or poison anything it looked at, thus making it the embodiment of evil. He was a supernatural figure who represented darkness and wickedness.

Ethniu

She was a daughter of Balor. It was foretold that she would give birth to a child that would overthrow him, so he imprisoned her in a tower so that she wouldn't get pregnant. Balor made the mistake of stealing the cow of the deity Cian, so Cian broke Ethniu out of the tower. He then impregnated her, so she gave birth to triplets, but Balor killed two of them by drowning to keep his kingship safe. The third, Lugh, survived and eventually fulfilled the prophecy that had led his grandfather to kill his siblings.

The figures in this chapter lead storied lives that gave us lessons we can live by. Whether they were cruel or kind, their message impacted on those who listened, leading to inspiration and warning. In the next chapter, we will explore how the collection of Irish history, beliefs, and mythology have impacted the Ireland of today.

CONCLUSION

In this book, we first looked at the lives of the prehistoric people of Ireland. They may have been simple, but the ingenuity they had in facing the problems of their lives with the tools at their disposal was astounding. First, they developed tools of stone, then copper, bronze, and finally iron. Throughout this, they developed international trade routes and intricate belief systems based on oral tradition. A characteristic body of art was developed during this period that's still characteristic of Ireland today. During the Iron Age, the Gaels settled alongside the prehistoric people of Ireland, forming a complex society that still intrigues us today.

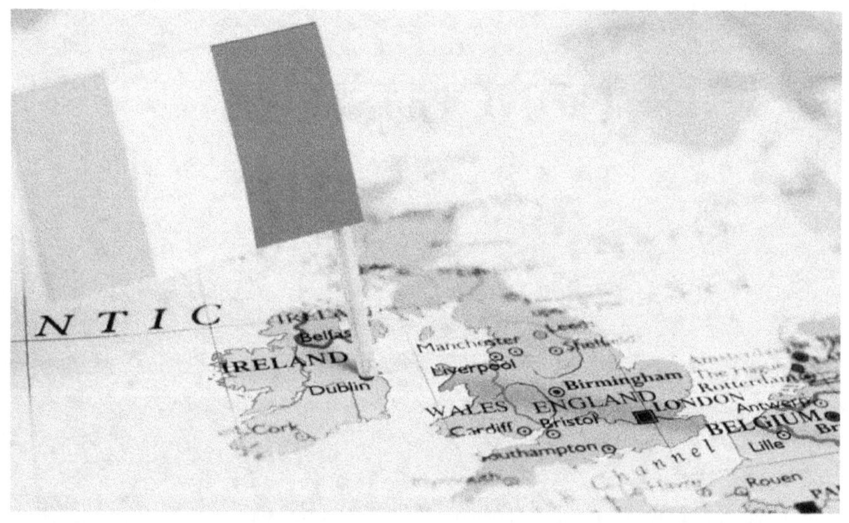

They were the first race of Irish settlers to leave a written mark—a mark that provided insight into their beliefs and what they held important. They also advanced the art, architecture, religion, and government of the ancient nations of the island. The ideas and beliefs they developed were mainly written down by later Christian settlers who created centers of learning in their monasteries. As such, there were some alterations to those teachings. But, when read with a pinch of salt, those alterations can be bypassed, leading to an interpretation of the underlying Gaelic convictions. Yet, myths weren't restricted to those earlier Gaelic times. There are famous myths that stem from the early Christian period as well.

One such was that the goddess Brigid was believed to have converted to Christianity, thus becoming the patron saint that's now celebrated throughout Ireland. Another was that St. Patrick was said to have vanquished multiple giant wyrms, along with the other snakes that lived on the island. These myths were later incorporated into the Lebor Gabála alongside earlier Gaelic myths. The earlier Gaelic myths were incorporated into the Four Mythological Cycles that you can use today to systematically study Irish mythology.

The first of the four cycles revolves around the Tuatha Dé Danann and their exploits. Many of the most impressive figures of Irish mythology are included here, such as Nuada (the first king of the gods). The second was the Ulster cycle, which detailed heroic tales of the first century in Ulster and Leinster. The Fenian cycle was the third, which described the exploits of Fionn mac Cumhaill and his legendary band of warriors, the Fianna. Impressive myths recounting battles with giants and all types of creatures that the Fianna had to face and overcome were chronicled in this cycle. The final cycle described the lives of the High Kings of Ireland and their families as told by court poets for generations.

The Gaelic people further left Ireland with its most important Pagan festivals. These were the Imbolc, Beltane, Lughnasa, and Samhain, which concerned important times during the agricultural year. More specifically, they marked changes of the seasons and the significance those seasons had or would have on the harvests of farmers. The Ostara, Litha, Mabon, and Yule festivals are also ancient festivals, but with more significance in relation to the cycle of the sun through the year. These festivals take place on the two solstices and equinoxes of the year.

The early Christian period was followed by continuous invasions and attempts at subjugation by the Vikings, then the Normans, and finally the English Crown. The period when the English Crown was directly in control of Ireland (since the rule of King Henry VIII was perhaps the most difficult period of Irish history, especially for Catholics and individuals of Gaelic descent. Under Queen Mary and Queen Elizabeth I the plantations in which Scottish, English, and Welsh people were moved to displace many of the local Irish. The displacements and the usage of the land in the Pale by the English-controlled government and their loyal subjects relegated the Irish to lower quality lands.

Things became more difficult for the native population due to the lack of care by their British overlords, leading to untold harm in the following centuries. The Potato Famine was the breaking point of negligence, leading to the deaths of more than a million people. An exodus of people from Ireland followed as a result, with most emigrants leaving for the United States. While the suppression and negligence of the Irish nation led to many deaths and people abandoning their homeland, it also led to the spread of Irish ideas and beliefs to the rest of the world.

Those ideas included the mythology and the Pagan beliefs that had been with the Irish nation from before the times of the Celts. It's a body of stories that imparted lessons that still positively impact and unify the Irish today.

Use the knowledge you now have of Irish history and mythology to raise respect for the identity of this nation. It's a worldwide nation sharing its history, beliefs, and lessons across the globe.

SCOTLAND

INTRODUCTION

The history of Scotland is nuanced. There are more complexities to this nation's past than many are first led to believe. The Scottish people are sometimes shown to be rough or unsophisticated, and there are stereotypes about their culture. To break away from these fixed ideas, a deeper understanding of who they are as a people is required. Delving into their background is the best way to gain a solid foundation about their national identity.

Looking at the past of this nation makes many historians present their history with a nationalistic twist. In other words, they tend to make the Scots seem like downtrodden examples of virtue. Others might make them seem like a bullied people who have had to deal with a constant threat to their sovereignty on their southern border. While there may be truth to some of this, it's more helpful to gain an objective perspective upon which to base further understanding. Productive dialogue will be the result.

With objectivity in mind, this book presents the history of the Scottish people in a neutral fashion. Where events in other countries are provided, it's to place local Scottish developments into better perspective. The mention of independence of the country at multiple points of the book should be interpreted as providing information as to the country's level of autonomy, not to advocate for or against higher levels of self-rule. The priority of the book will be to provide an overview of the adventures, battles, people, and periods that came to define the Scots.

With the aim of proper understanding in mind, this book is broken into five chapters that each cover a different era. The first covers prehistory, the Roman conquests, and the kingdoms of the Britons, Picts, and Scotti tribes. Information that's devoid of myth as much as possible to debunk misconceptions is provided. The purpose of this is to give an accurate prehistorical picture. This is followed by the era of the Scottish kingdom in the second chapter.

The unification of the Scotti, Picts, and Britons into the kingdom of Alba is examined in depth. This kingdom was the predecessor of the kingdom of Scotland and as such is a necessity for historical education. The progression of the kingdom of Scotland's rulers along with the events that provide context to their rule is then examined in the third chapter. The Renaissance and Scottish Reformation are two such events. The final chapters of the book will give you an overview of the unification of the crowns and parliaments of England and Scotland, followed by the developments of a modernizing Scotland from the start of the Industrial Revolution to present.

Books published by History Brought Alive are well written and thoroughly researched. The resources used are reliable and will provide you with accurate information. We have a large catalogue of books that are loved and read by many. This book is no different. You will be provided with information that is interesting, detailed, and well-rounded about the periods of this nation's history. This includes prehistory, ancient history, the Medieval periods, and the modern era. Don't waste your time and energy on confusing and ineffective books. You have the answers you need right here.

CHAPTER 1
THE EARLY HISTORY OF SCOTLAND

The history of Scotland stretches back before written records. There are archeological records stretching back thousands of years. In this chapter, we're going to explore Scotland from its earliest prehistory right up to the birth of the kingdoms of the Picts and Britons at the start of the Early Middle Ages.

Prehistoric scotland

It's assumed that people crossed the English Channel during the Paleolithic period (between 12,000 and 10,800 B.C.E.). The channel wasn't filled with water because the Ice Age had stored enough of the water in ice sheets for the sea level to drop. The crossings were believed to have been made from France. No structures from this period are available to study, likely due to the inhabitants having been hunter-gatherers who only settled temporarily in different locations.

With the ending of the Ice Age around 10,000–9,500 B.C.E., Scotland was heavily wooded, making it ideal for hunting small animals and foraging. Flints have been found by rivers, along the coast, and in caves, indicative of their hunting practices.

The Mesolithic period, or Middle Stone Age, ranged from around 10,800 to 4,100 B.C.E. in Scotland. Therefore, there was a slight overlap between the Mesolithic and the later Paleolithic periods. The Middle Stone Age is distinguished by stone tools that were slightly less crude and the use of microliths (small flints used to make arrowheads, spearheads, and tool attachments). The tools used also expanded to other substances, such as antlers, bone, and wood. Structures of the time were typically made with a wooden frame and weren't very large.

People's diets included a variety of foods, ranging from fish and animals to berries and nuts. The people of the Mesolithic period also started farming on a very small scale by making small clearings in the trees. Fishing became more common with the introduction of hooks. This combined with their predominantly hunter-gatherer lifestyle to make a more well-rounded diet, as evidenced by archeological finds of camp waste. The waste includes charred hazelnut shells, fish bones, and burnt wood. These waste dump sites are called middens and contain a wealth of information about the prehistoric peoples' way of life, even if the organic material present in the middens has long since deteriorated.

The earliest settlement in Scotland that we know about was at Cramond. The site is dated back to around 8,500 B.C.E. and can be found outside the village of Echline. The firepit in the middle runs 23 ft long and 1.6 ft deep. It's surrounded by hearths on which inhabitants could relax to absorb the warmth of the flames at night or during cold days.

Holes in the earth around the location indicate that upright posts were present to make walls. The walls were likely covered with animal skins and the roof made from turf. The community was hunted for at least some of its food sources, as shown by flint arrowheads that were found by archeologists.

The Neolithic people (people of the New Stone Age) brought the development of farming with them. This period stretched from around 4,100 to 2,500 B.C.E. in Scotland. One of the most distinctive characteristics of this period is that permanent structures and settlements were much more common than before. Instituting farming was likely the cause because individuals could rely on the same pieces of land for their food sources over periods lasting years. Large forest areas were cleared around 3,000 B.C.E. to make space for the farmland of locals following this new way of life.

Some believe that the farming was developed by people locally, but a large number of historians state that the farmers traveled from Europe to settle among the people already present from the earlier Stone Ages. The immigration combined with better food security resulted in a population increase. Hoe blades and other agricultural tools made farming more effective, resulting in even higher levels of food security.

There were multiple villages in Scotland that were established during this period. Skara Brae in Orkney is one such settlement. Another one that's perhaps better known is Calanais on the Isle of Lewis. Maeshowe is a third. These sites teach us a lot about the lives of those who lived thousands of years before us.

Further sites of interest are the permanent stone structures that the Neolithic people of Scotland made. This includes stone circles, tombs and cairns, megaliths, henges, and rock art panels. Archeological finds from this period show that stone was used for a large variety of purposes in addition to making structures. Things like axe heads, attachments to weapons, and carved stone balls have all been found. The purpose of these balls is not yet known; thus, we assume they were used for decorative purposes. They are unique to the British Isles, and a number of them were found in Scotland.

The next period in prehistoric development was the Bronze Age, which lasted from around 2,500 to 800 B.C.E. in Scotland. Metalworking arrived from the European mainland, altering multiple facets of life. Copper, bronze (combination of tin and copper), and gold were some of the first metals used. This is not to say that nonmetal substances weren't used for a variety of purposes. It's just that the introduction of metalwork was a game-changer that was widely incorporated.

Other materials used were amber, bone, wood, stone, antlers, clay, and a range of other natural substances. Metal, however, was used for a variety of functions in short order, as evidenced by hoards that have been found in Scotland. Hoards included jewelry, weapons, and tools.

Another characteristic of the Bronze Age was the change to the method of handling the dead. Both cremation and burial were used. However, burials took place both in groups and individually (often with personal trinkets), and the structures used for burials seemed to become simpler (such as the use of cists).

Other stone structures were also simplified and made more practical. This included hillforts and brochs (circular stone towers). Brochs are widespread in Scotland, with around 500 still remaining, even if just as foundations. Although brochs are sometimes called Pictish towers, the era of the Picts only comes much later in prehistory.

The Bronze Age also showed an increase in warfare. This was possibly because of the ease and speed with which weapons could be produced. There may be other reasons that will never be known.

The Iron Age followed the Bronze Age, from around 800 B.C.E. to 400. During this age, weapons and tools became more effective due to iron being stronger than copper (and stronger than bronze when alloyed with other metals). The methods of processing iron would also have a large effect on the material's strength, with these methodologies being perfected as time progressed. In Scotland, the Iron Age also saw the arrival of the Celts and their way of life.

The Celts were a people who had spread all over Europe and in some of the Middle East. They were a collection of many tribes with individual identities. That said, even though each tribe was distinctive, there were similarities between them all. These included their pagan belief systems, their agricultural lifestyle, and often a hierarchical social structure. There seems to have been less of a hierarchical society in the early Celtic tribes of Scotland, as evidenced by communities with similar household styles and lack of a high degree of ornamentation. Some of the structures that abounded from the Celtic period of the Scottish Iron Age included wheelhouses, souterrains (underground storage chambers), forts, and ordinary stone houses.

The Romans arrived in the middle of this Celtic period—around 43. They were a warring empire set on conquering as much land and as many people as they could. The tribes of Scotland and those from lower in Britain who had fled to Scotland put up too much of a challenge for the Romans. While the Romans did manage to conquer large parts of northern Britain, they weren't able to subdue the tribes for long periods of time.

To make matters simpler, Hadrian's Wall and the Antonine wall were built across the Central Belt. These kept the tribes that were too much trouble to conquer on the one side and the "civilized" conquered peoples on the other. The Central Belt had long been a point of transition between different Celtic peoples. Thus, the walls were erected along a convenient neck of the island that would solidify these location divides.

The Romans brought many things with them. Things such as board games, wine, glass vessels, and coins were all incorporated into the societies they had conquered. Through trade and other relations, the hardy tribes of Scotland gradually incorporated some of these Roman articles into their living, including the strong tribes of the Picts, Scotti, and Britons that gradually thrived to the north. That said, perhaps the biggest impact the Romans had on these tribes was the introduction of Christianity and Latin, both of which would increase in prominence after the end of the Iron Age.

The next section will take a deeper look at the Celts of the early and middle periods of the Iron Age.

The Arrival of the Celts in Scotland

The Celts were a grouping of multiple peoples of the prehistoric world. They stretched across much of Europe, including the British Isles. The people were united by the similarity of their languages and their tribal nature, use of an economy that was based mainly on agriculture (or sometimes mining and artisanry alongside farming), and social hierarchies.

The society of the Celts in Scotland during the Iron Age was arranged as farmsteads, villages, or hamlets with multiple family households. The society seemed to be more flat than that in other Celtic regions, that is, their hierarchy was less prominent. This is due to multiple homesteads of a similar nature often being built close to one another, as assumed by historians. The society would likely have been competitive, and there was little to no need for an overarching governmental or ruler class from around the sixth to first centuries B.C.E.

The amount of farming during the last few centuries B.C.E. was higher than before. Financial wealth was an effect of this, resulting in families forming powerful dynasties. An artifact—

silver chains weighing multiple pounds—was indicative of this dynastic power. Other signs of an increase in wealth were that jewelry had become highly ornamental and seemed to be accessible to a large percentage of the population. The assumption is thus that there was a period of general affluence at the time.

During the conquest by the Roman Empire during the first century, the writer Ptolemy noted there were nine tribes who occupied the region. The following section expounds on them.

Caledones

This tribe consisted of people who were described as being red-haired and having large limbs. They were described as being fast and fierce, which resulted in the Romans never fully conquering them. The name of the tribe translates to "possessing hard feet," which could have alluded to their endurance or to the rocky land they lived on. The tribe was located in the tract of land that stretched from modern-day Fort William to Inverness.

A warlike people, the Caledones built hillforts and farmsteads fortified with earthworks. Their economy was largely made up by farming, and the settlements they lived in were scattered.

Smaller tribes that were included in the Caledones were the Carnonacae, Creones, and Smertae. The Smertae were believed to smear themselves with blood, either from sacrifices or from their enemies. Whether these tribes were all separate peoples who came together when mutual defense was needed or whether they shared a mutual leader is unknown. That said, they were a strong opponent for the invading Romans, and they even overcame part of Hadrian's Wall during the 180s. A peace treaty was signed with them, but they didn't keep to it, attacking Roman soldiers on multiple occasions.

Emperor Septimius Severus tried to gain dominance over them around 209, which turned out to be a success for him. After being defeated, the Caledones gave up part of their land to the Romans, which was then razed and made unusable. Even after defeat, the Caledones continued fighting, gradually eroding Roman troops with surprise attacks and help from other tribes. When Septimius Severus's son was sent to destroy them once and for all in 211, his own troops refused as they refused to acknowledge him as their emperor. The outcome of the intended destruction thus turned around, resulting in a peace treaty in which the Caledones gained back their lands. A century later, the Romans again campaigned into the north.

The Caledones were described as having red hair, just like the Picts. This has led some to believe that the Picts were a tribe that developed from the earlier Caledones.

Damnonii

Damnonii translates to "the masters." Very little is known about this tribe other than their location. They were said to occupy parts of south-central Scotland and sections of the west coast. The Romans claimed to have conquered them and occupied their land during the invasions.

Epidii

The region occupied by the Epidii was rocky and mountainous. Their name originates from a word for "horse," which links up with the presence of ponies and horses in the Highlands that are suited to rocky terrain. They were thought to have originated on the Islay and then to spread into northwest Scotland. A low population was a natural result of tough lands and living conditions, with the tribe being described as not having large numbers. The combination of the low population and irregular landscape meant that it wasn't worth it for the Romans to try to send troops to overcome, control, and tax the people of this tribe—there wouldn't have been a good return on investment.

Novantae

The Novantae lived in what is today Dumfries and Galloway when the Romans first invaded. The lack of archeological finds of Roman military installations in the area denotes that there was likely a peaceable relationship between the tribe and the empire. Further marks of a peaceful relationship are the lack of tribal defense structures, despite two centuries of Roman occupation. The people of the Novantae were mainly herders and farmers.

Selgovae

This tribe occupied the south-central Highlands. Their name means "the hunters," and they were thought to be part of the Brythonic class of Celts. Their settlements were commonly made up of small forts with stone or wooden walls. The capital was a fortified hill town, but it was abandoned in 79 due to the presence of a Roman installation nearby. Several other towns and settlements were abandoned at the time, likely due to the intense combat that took place because of Roman troops being stationed throughout their lands. Despite the ever-present threat, the tribe grew in strength, reaching its height in the second century.

Taexali

The east of Scotland was occupied by this tribe. They lived on farms and hamlets that had few defenses. The way of life of the Taexali was peaceful and consisted of farming their fertile lands. The lack of defense made them a soft target, resulting in Roman conquest in 84. When the Roman forces retreated to the south of the Antonine Wall, the Taexali were once again able to take control of their lands to continue their pastoral way of life.

Vacomagi

The Vacomagi tribe was located in what is today Moray, which is a mountainous area. Their name translates to "inhabitants of the curved fields," which shows that they were an agricultural tribe—much like their southerly neighbors, the Taexali. Very little is known about them.

Venicones

This tribe was located in and around Fife, just south of the Taexali. This region was the best location from which the Romans could quell the attacks of other tribes, which meant the Venicones were soon dislocated so their land could be occupied more permanently by the Romans. The Venicones were perhaps a tribe who had fled north during the conquests of the regions that now make up England. Unique practices of the tribe were the use of bronze armlets that could weigh up to 3 lbs and burial in stone graves.

Votadini (Also Otadini)

Archeological evidence at the Traprain Law hillfort establishes them as extant from at least the eighth century B.C.E., and the Traprain Treasures are attributed to the tribe. They occupied southeast Scotland and northeast England, living in hillforts and villages. Hadrian's Wall was built across the southernmost parts of their lands, while the Antonine Wall was erected across their northernmost territories. Some of the Votadini settlements and forts were incorporated as a support structure for the troops that manned the walls. It seems that the relationship between the tribe and the Romans was mainly peaceful, with the tribe continuing to occupy their own lands.

They became a powerful people, with one of their fifth-century kings (Cunedda) having aided the people of Wales in warfare. They also occupied the kingdom of Lothian from the third to seventh centuries, keeping their power strong until invasions by the Angles wore them down. The Angles overtook the lands of Lothian until Kenneth I MacAlpin regained the territory in the tenth century. The Gododdin were said to be the descendants of the Votadini.

Now that we've examined the nine tribes, we're going to look at the actions of the Romans. The next section dives into the invasion that took place and any effects it had on the people of the tribes over the long term.

The Roman Invasion and Its Impact on Scotland

The Romans invaded and successfully conquered the peoples of England between the first century B.C.E. and the second century. They permanently left their mark on the people, including cultural, architectural, artistic, and commercial aspects. Commercial aspects included a continent-wide trade route that brought both goods and people from other parts of the empire. This allowed those living in the southern parts of Britain to build wealth and to take on a Romanized way of life. The same cannot be said about the tribes occupying what is now Scotland.

Many of the tribes of northern Britain made good soldiers. They were hardy people who knew the land they lived on and were willing to put up protracted opposition. The Romans saw them as uncivilized, and they saw the Romans as unnecessarily violent. During the first century, attempts were made to conquer the northern tribes. The Battle of Mons Graupius of 83 or 84 was the breakthrough the Romans were looking for.

Julius Agricola was a general at the time who personally participated in the attacks. He sent a fleet of ships as well as infantry to attack the opposition. The tribal forces who had previously always fled when conflict arose were now forced into a position where they had to attack or submit—they couldn't run away. This was because the Romans threatened the main food stocks of the Caledonian tribe, which could have left its people starving if left undefended. The forces faced the Romans, who closed in on them and forced them to flee to the trees.

The forces of the Romans followed them into the trees, and the result was the death of a third of the tribal forces—10,000 people. The remaining 20,000 people couldn't be found the following day, and the general was lauded for having subdued the whole isle of Britain. That said, further campaigns were held into Scotland. The area was far removed from the heart of the Roman Empire.

The tribes renewed their vigor after the Battle of Mons Graupius, standing their own against the Romans. The Romans managed to gain control of many regions of the area, including islands off the coast of the Scottish mainland and parts of the Highlands. The cost of sustaining power over the region, however, was too high.

It was more economical to separate the savage northerly tribes from the subdued ones. A major contribution to this was likely the nonhierarchical structure of the tribes of the region. They could elect replacements for dead chiefs quickly, which meant that power vacuums didn't destabilize the tribes. The new chief would rekindle his forces, and the Romans had to continue providing manpower to sustain victories over the area. It was just too costly in relation to the benefits reaped.

The solutions were Hadrian's Wall (built in 122) and the Antonine Wall (built around 142). The walls were manned, and fortifications were put up along them. There were very few attempts at conflict other than some clashes along the border regions of the empire and tribal lands.

The tribes to the north unified to form a nation called the Picts, meaning "painted people" (due to the blue tattoos and paint they put on themselves). In 306, a campaign was held to strengthen protection against the tribes who were coming down to attack the wall. The campaign was led by the emperor Constantius Chlorus. Once the border was reaffirmed along Hadrian's Wall, the troops needed to return to the heart of the empire to protect it from growing threats.

The continued troubles in the empire meant that a growing threat of the Picts couldn't be combatted properly. The Picts broke past Hadrian's Wall in around 360, and the troops who were sent by Emperor Julian couldn't quash them fully. The Picts increased their power and were capable of asserting themselves further into the Roman territories of England. Things were getting more heated close to home for the Roman Empire, resulting in withdrawal of its troops altogether around 411.

The tribes of Scotland maintained their own cultural beliefs and practices throughout the Roman occupancy. There might have been some trade and other forms of interaction besides warfare, but Roman culture only started being adopted by the people of Scotland once the Roman soldiers left. The main cultural aspect that had been maintained was Christianity, use of Latin (such as on stone carvings), and incorporation of a more hierarchical cultural structure than before. These Roman legacies were partly due to the invasions the tribes were now making south into Romanized areas of England.

To protect themselves from these invasions, the people who lived in the south of Britain hired the Angles to protect them. This backfired, with the Angles soon taking the opportunity to overcome the people they had been hired to protect. Further, they also invaded the areas of the Scottish tribes in an attempt to increase their power there. This was successful in some areas.

To understand the full context of what was happening at the time, it's necessary to look at parallel developments. The tribes of the Scotti, the Picts, and the Britons will be examined in the following sections. They formed before the arrival of the Angles and would go on to develop into the Scottish kingdom over the next half millennium.

The Scotti and Dalriada

The Scotti were a Gaelic-speaking people. The term Scotti was used by the Romans to describe the people of Ireland, where the Scotti were believed to originate from. This is based on myth, however, and little evidence has been found to state that the Scotti weren't descended from people who had been living in Scotland before their time. There are some structures and objects that are similar on both islands from the time period (the early first millennium), but this could be due to trade, alliances, or marriage offerings.

The first records of the Scotti show that they emerged around the fourth century. They continued existing until the ninth century, after which they merged with the Picts and some of the Britons to form the kingdom of Alba. Alba later changed into the kingdom of Scotland. In the first century they were recorded, the Scotti seem to have established long-distance trade routes. They had goods from the Mediterranean and Gaul, among other areas. If the myth of the crossing of a whole people from Ireland is based on fact, then some of these trade routes would have been well-established.

This kingdom was called Dalriada. Eventually the Scottish regions of Dalriada gained power, while the Irish regions lost theirs. There would have been a ruling class that controlled what is now County Antrim and Northern Ireland, as well as the Inner Hebrides and Argyll. The main stronghold of this kingdom was said to have moved from Ireland to Scotland during this period. Dalriada flourished for centuries. St. Columba is described as having brought Christianity to the kingdom and granted King Aidan his right to rule during the sixth century.

During the later part of the sixth century and the early part of the seventh, battles between rivals for the Scotti throne caused turmoil in the kingdom. Other battling and warfare were also common at the time. The Picts often attacked the Scotti, especially when they were encroaching on their territory. The Angles also brought conflict with them. The Scotti remained strong throughout this, gradually expanding east, further into the territory of the Picts.

The power of the kingdom started faltering in the middle of the seventh century. To prevent it from becoming too weak, Oswy (an English king) consolidated Dalriada as a part of his kingdom. Part of his justification was the religious right to rule. The monastery of Iona, which was the most influential at the time, had led some to believe that previous kings of Dalriada had been placed on the throne as unnatural leaders. As a result, the ruling family's authority lost some of its status, allowing another family dynasty to take its place.

The new dynasty grew its power strategically. Marriage alliances with the Picts were one of the ways in which the power of the family was consolidated. Irish Dalriada was eventually wiped out, possibly by the Vikings during the next two centuries. This consolidated the power of the kingdom even more with the central family dynasty. There might have been a colony of some of the remaining Dalriada kingdom who established themselves in Pictland. Coupling this with the regime of intermarriage, the two kingdoms started influencing each other more and more.

The power consolidation and the allied position with the Picts (some of the time) meant that the Scotti were able to expand their zone of power. The Britons, Angles, Irish, and Vikings exerted pressure on the kingdom, but its heightened strength meant that it was able to stand firm. Eventually, the kingdoms of the Picts and the Scotti merged under Kenneth I MacAlpin during the ninth century. This was the birth of Alba.

The next section will give a better understanding of the Picts as the second major ethnic group that formed the kingdom.

The Picts

The origin of the Picts is unsure, but it's likely that they were established during the Iron Age. There's a possibility that they were the aboriginal people of Scotland or that they formed from Celtic tribes in Scotland already or that they were a Celtic people who had sailed from Scythia beyond the Black Sea. If the latter is to be believed, they sailed to Ireland, where they were refused, resulting in them sailing across the Irish Sea and settling to the north of the Britons.

The Picts were a strong tribe, and they raided the Britons to their south. One of the kings of the Britons, Marius, beat them in battle. After the battle he allowed them to settle in the far northeast of the island, where Caithness is now located. They didn't have women with them, however, so an agreement was made with the Scotti to their west that they be given women to marry. The condition of this agreement was that succession disputes would be resolved by referring to the female line. While all this might or might not be myth, a fact is that the Picts did use the matrilineal line when resolving succession matters.

The tribe started flourishing in the fourth century, a period of success that would last for centuries. The kingdom of the Picts at the time was made up of multiple subkingdoms or tribes that were loosely linked together. The tribes were made up of family groups who lived close to one another. These family groups and tribes would unite to protect the loose federation from opposing peoples during times of unrest. Gradual consolidation took place over time, with two dominant kingdoms resulting—the Dicalydones and the Verturiones (another name for Fortriu).

The kingdom of Fortriu (under King Bridei) expanded its borders and started subjugating other Picts, until a united nation was formed. This nation came to be known as Pictland. During the same century, the Anglo-Saxons started throwing their weight around and establishing power throughout Britain. The kingdom of Northumbria was such an Anglo-Saxon region and became the dominant force of southern Scotland.

Northumbria was too powerful for the Picts to resist, resulting in it becoming a vassal kingdom during the seventh century. This wasn't a permanent state of affairs, with the success of the Picts at the Battle of Dun Nechtain in 685. The result of the battle included more independence from Northumbria for the Picts.

Over the next century, the Picts did a lot of battle with the Scotti to their west. This continued to the end of the eighth century, when a Pictish prince was put on the throne of Dalriada. They weren't yet fully united as a kingdom, but relations became better, allowing both kingdoms to positively interact with each other.

When Kenneth I MacAlpin eventually unified the kingdoms in the ninth century, the term Pict started fading from use. Some myths say he slaughtered all of the Picts, but a far more likely reason is that the Picts were assimilated into the Scotti. The nobles of both kingdoms used customs that were more uniformly Scotti in nature, and the use of the Pictish language reduced, particularly with the focus on using Scots and Gaelic dialects in churches.

The Britons

The Britons were initially a Celtic grouping from the regions of prehistoric England. They lost much of their land during the invasions of the Romans. Some of them stayed behind and became Romanized, while others settled in different regions of the island. One of the regions they were displaced to was to the north in what is now Scotland. They established kingdoms and tribes there, some of which would become strong and others fail.

With the invasions of the Anglo-Saxons starting in the fifth century, more warfare and displacement took place. One of the more powerful Briton kingdoms that was established in the process of this relocation was Dumbarton, which originally meant "the fortress of the Britons." Dumbarton was a place that allowed the Briton culture to boom, with the creation of art such as poetry, tales, and ballads. Distinctive jewelry, pottery, and other artifacts were also created at the time.

The next three subsections will give an overview of three of the more powerful Brittonic kingdoms that existed on or within the borders of modern-day Scotland.

Rheged

This kingdom originated before the arrival of the Romans. It occupied northeast England, bordering on the region that Hadrian's Wall would be built on later. It remained intact through the Roman occupation and was powerful when the Romans left. It finally fell after the Anglo-Saxon invasions, with the Viking conquests having erased what remnants might have remained.

The kingdom consisted of an alliance of multiple Celtic tribes called the Brigantes. The location that's today the city of Carlisle is possibly attributable to this kingdom during the Iron Age. That said, there were few heavily populated settlements in the kingdom. This was largely due to the poor quality of the soil combined with the rocky and moored regions within it.

During the period leading up to the Anglo-Saxon invasions, Rheged split up into two kingdoms, North and South Rheged. The northern kingdom was able to expand its borders, annexing territory in what is today Dumfries and Galloway. The kingdom remained strong and, with the cushion of the southern kingdom, managed to remain strong for a long period during the Anglo-Saxon invasions, only falling in the seventh century.

Dumbarton

Dumbarton was the only Brittonic kingdom that didn't fall when the Anglo-Saxons invaded. The Anglo-Saxons were positioned to its south, while the Picts were to its north. The kingdom retained its independence despite these two rival peoples being right on its doorstep. It even managed to remain intact during the Viking invasions.

The Viking invasions started around 866. They were composed of forces from the king of Dublin, Olaf the White, and his wife, Aud, who was the ruler of the Hebrides. The stronghold of Dumbarton was sacked during this time, with riches and people being taken to be sold in Ireland. In spite of this and the death of their king at the hands of the Picts, the Britons of Dumbarton remained extant, eventually being absorbed into other kingdoms.

Kingdom of Strathclyde

This kingdom was founded around 450 and took up parts of northern England and southern Scotland. Its original name was Ystrad Clud, which was used until it changed to Strathclyde in the ninth century. The Damnonii were the main early constituent tribe of this kingdom, and its earliest rulers (that we know of) were Tudwal and Rhydderch.

More is known about this kingdom than some others of the time. Famous artifacts from the kingdom include Dyrnwyn (a magical sword), the Govan Stones, and the Govan Sarcophagus. The religion of Strathclyde was Christianity, likely under the influence of the mother church in Iona. They followed the Leges inter Brettos et Scottos (the Laws of the Britons and Scots) and were the home to the majority of the Britons after the destruction of Dumbarton.

The kingdom of Northumbria posed continual problems to Strathclyde as it was the dominant kingdom in the region surrounding Strathclyde. It was not, however, the Northumbrians who brought down Strathclyde, but the Vikings, who destroyed its capital in 870. The remnants of the kingdom were absorbed into other Anglo-Saxon kingdoms in the tenth century and then leased to the Scots king Malcolm I in 945. When the Scots defeated the Anglo-Saxons at Carham

during the eleventh century, the region was absorbed into the Scottish kingdom.

With a thorough foundation about the earliest periods of Scottish history, you are now ready to look into the developments of the Middle Ages. The next chapter will be dedicated to developments of the Medieval times, including the invasions of the Angles and Vikings and the rise of Alba and Scotland.

CHAPTER 2
THE MEDIEVAL PERIOD

The Middle Ages lasted from around 400 to 1500. This period is split into three main parts: the Early Medieval Period (around 400–1000), the High Medieval Period (1000–1300), and the Late Medieval Period (1300–1500). The Early Medieval Period is sometimes called the Dark Ages because of a lack of written sources that have lasted from that period, not because of a lack of development or a backward way of life. This means that we mainly use archaeological evidence or sources written during the later periods for information from this time.

The invasions of the Anglo-Saxons and the Vikings took place during the Early Medieval Period, while the Roman invasions withdrew from Britain. Many churches, hillforts, Pictish stones, and castles were erected during this era. Christianity gained prevalence, while paganism lost much of its presence. The kingdoms of the Scotti and Picts became more prominent, and they united during the latter part of this period.

The High Middle Ages were when the kingdom of Scotland went through much of its initial growth. It stopped being called Alba and formed a union of multiple cultures into one identity. The monarchy gained power, and the First War of Scottish Independence took place.

The Late Middle Ages were marked by an increase in the number of monasteries and cathedrals being built, as well as its first university. Central control of the government was firmly established, including tax and trade. Burghs were established and answerable to the monarchy. The end of the Late Middle Ages was when the Scottish Renaissance started to flourish.

The Anglo-Saxons

When the Romans left Britain, it left the people to the south open to attacks and raids from the Picts, Scots, and other northern tribes. The Angles were asked to provide protection so that those in the south of Britain could retain the comfortable lifestyle they held when the Romans provided protection. The Angles were a Germanic people from the border region of modern Denmark and Germany. They had a militant nature and could be powerful foes. Thus, instead of providing protection to those in southern Britain, the Angles invaded to claim Britain for their own benefit.

They went ahead to conquer the southern regions (Roman Britannia) and then formulated seven kingdoms to their benefit. This arrangement was called the Heptarchy, that is, "rule of seven." These kingdoms were formed during the fifth century, and they remained extant until the invasions of the Vikings in the ninth century, when a majority of them were destroyed or rearranged.

Two of the northernmost kingdoms of the Heptarchy were Bernicia to the north of Hadrian's Wall and Deira directly to the south of Bernicia. The placement of Bernicia was right on the border of multiple tribes of Celtic origin, with contest over the territory during the sixth and seventh centuries. It managed to annex multiple areas from the Britons, including Dun Eideann. It also took possession of Deira along with parts of Mercia (located in the center of modern England) to form the kingdom of Northumbria. Northumbria became the preeminent kingdom of its area.

This power was finally checked with the invasion of the Vikings. They lost much of their influence, eventually being captured. During this time, Alba captured Dun Eideann.

Eventually Alba took most of Northumberland in 1018 after conflict with the Vikings and the remaining Anglo-Saxons.

Viking Invasions

The Vikings first raided the coast of Scotland around 793, including the raid of the monastery of Iona in 795. They established strongholds in the northwest regions of Scotland and on multiple islands surrounding Britain. They were a formidable sea people, and as such, they were able to take towns and land on the coast and claim said towns for themselves. Resources were taken from conquered lands or raided areas to be traded all over Europe. Vikings largely left their Northern European homes for reasons such as increased population and a lack of desired local resources.

Churches and castles were thus prime candidates for raids. Churches weren't always heavily protected, and they contained lots of valuable objects. Castles, while sometimes more difficult to access, contained many valuables and were a good source of animals and people to trade. Not all these raids were recorded, and archeological evidence isn't always easy to find as raids could sometimes be fast and often resulted in minimal destruction to fixed property. As the threat of the Vikings grew, people started preparing. They were willing to protect their assets, even if it came to violence or even if it meant that they would be placed in hidden hoards.

The British Isles were one of the nearer areas available for conquest and raiding to the Vikings. It was easily accessible by boat, and there was a wealth of natural and man-made resources available. The lands they took in northern Britain were mainly in the west, which left the Picts relatively undisturbed. Although they were both strong groups of people with military capacity, they were able to coexist to some extent.

The Rise of the Scottish Kingdom

When the Scotti and Picts came together under the rule of Kenneth I MacAlpin in 843, the kingdom of Alba was born. At first it wasn't very large, occupying northeast Scotland. That said, the combination of the strengths of the Picts and the Scotti meant that not even the Vikings could subdue the newly unified kingdom. When the Vikings started withdrawing from the region, Alba expanded. Multiple surrounding territories were conquered in battles, such as during the Battle of Carham of 1018. King Malcolm II stopped English forces from the south and annexed the province of Lothian to the kingdom.

Malcolm II's successor was Duncan I, who took power in 1034. His reign resulted in massive expansions of the kingdom. Cumbria and Strathclyde were officially absorbed into Alba. After this unification, the name Scotland started being used more and more for the kingdom, while Alba was used less and less. Even though the term Alba was still sometimes used to describe Scotland, after the eleventh century, this name was used much less.

When William the Conqueror took England, this posed a threat to Alba. The new English kingdom had robust military capacity and a lot of wealth. However, this danger was largely reduced after signing the Treaty of Falaise, which was ratified in 1175. The treaty stated that the English king would be seen as the overlord of Scotland. This meant that Scotland would have to pay him certain amounts for the use of the land it was on in line with the feudal system.

The feudal system consisted of a king or overlord granting management of land to nobles in return for their allegiance, and the nobles would in turn grant use of that land and protection to tenants. In return for this use, the tenants would provide rent, labor, and farmed goods, among other things, to the noble. With the ratification of this treaty, the king of England was the feudal overlord, and the king of Scotland was one of the subjects to whom he granted management of land.

One of the implications of this treaty was that Scotland was no longer preoccupied with protecting itself from England. It could focus on agriculture, commerce, and its own affairs—so long as it provided military support and other defined benefits to England. As such, the economy of Scotland grew, which in turn increased the power of the church. The church was directly involved in the lives of its members, providing both a commercial and social center, along with religious guidance. People donated to the church and paid tithes, which was one of the reasons it became so important as an institution in later times. It worked hand in hand with the government (i.e., the monarchy) to manage Scottish society.

The next section will give summaries of the lives and impacts of the first kings of Alba up to the start of the tenth century. This will provide a better context of the lives of the Scottish people and the events they were confronted with during the last parts of the Early Middle Ages.

Kings of Alba

Kenneth I MacAlpin

The king to unify a nation, Kenneth I MacAlpin was the son of a king of the Scots clans of the Gaels. His father had military success against the Picts. Kenneth took on the position of ruler of the Picts, establishing himself firmly as their leader over a period of more than 15 years. He expanded his Pictish territory through conquest and possibly with marriage.

The unification of the Pictish and Scotti territories over a protracted period gradually formed the beginning of a joint identity. Both the Picti and the Scotti were tribes that were descended from the Celts. Kenneth died around 850, leaving his brother to take over his position to consolidate the regions Kenneth had conquered.

Donald I

Following the founder of a kingdom is never easy. Donald I was in the tough position of succeeding his brother, who had founded Alba and fought to establish its power. He wasn't as popular as his brother because he had a slightly blithe personality and his mother was foreign. That said, he consolidated the power of the kingdom and prevented it from splitting into parts (as many kingdoms did soon after being founded).

He established the use of tanistry (election of a king or chief by their extended eligible family) to ensure certainty about the process for appointing new successors. This would mean not only that the best of the possible candidates was chosen (i.e., the most persuasive and powerful) but also that there wouldn't be a shortage of replacements when a king died. A monarch didn't need to have children to ensure a successor was in place, and the crown wouldn't be given to someone too feeble to protect the nation.

Constantine I

Not much of Constantine's period as king of the Picts and Scots (from 863 to 877) was recorded in writing. The majority of what we know consists of legend. The period was a turbulent one, with the Dublin-based Danish king instigating raids into Pictland and the land of the Scots each year. The southern areas of Northumberland and Galloway were also under constant attack, with the commander of the Great Heathen Army (Halfdan Ragnarsson) perpetrating the attacks. The king was constantly on the lines of battle, eventually dying while combating raiders to the north.

Aed

Aed, who was one of the sons of Kenneth I McAlpin, became the king of Picts. He assumed the throne in 877 and was killed in 878. He was a feeble king who had failed to protect Pictland from the Viking invasions, resulting in widespread loss of wealth and anarchy. The commoner, Giric, was a refugee of the Viking invasions and managed to gain favor with Aed. With Eochaid as his accomplice, Giric got rid of Aed, and they took on the throne of Pictland together.

Eochaid and Giric

These joint monarchs ruled from 878 to 889. The relationship between the two is unclear, but it is clear that Giric played an integral part in making it possible for Eochaid to take the throne and that the period of their rule wasn't the most peaceable of times. Eochaid was the son of the king of Strathclyde and the nephew of King Aed. They managed to get rid of Aed and took the crown for themselves.

During the early part of their reign, Giric got rid of any Picts in the court who could pose a threat to their rule. In their stead, Giric installed loyal Scotti in the court. He could not, however, dispatch the two biggest threats to the throne—the two Pictish sons of Aed. They were safely in exile under the protection of their aunt, who had married an Irish king. The sons were Donald and Constantine, who both would go on to rule the nation after Giric and Eochaid.

At that point in time, there was still a clear delineation between the Scots and the Picts, with the crown serving as joint rule over both Celtic groups. Their reign came to an end when Eochaid enlisted the help of his nephew Donald to dispose of Giric. After disposing of him, Donald realized that he could seize the crown for himself, so he drove Eochaid out of the kingdom.

Donald II

Donald was the king of the Scots whose reign lasted from 889 to 900. He reigned during a turbulent period wherein the Danes and some tribes of the Highlands raided the kingdom. Not much is known about his death, but what is known is that his brother, Constantine II, was his successor. What makes his reign most notable, however, is that the Picts stopped being mentioned during this time. This was likely due to their assimilation into the national identity of the Scots, but history is unclear on this fact.

Monarchs of Scotland Until the First War of Scottish Independence

While Scotland was still sometimes called Alba, there was a gradual transition to the use of the word Scotland, or the kingdom of the Scots, starting around the end of Donald II's reign. This next section summarizes the lives of Scottish kings from this time to the end of the High Middle Ages.

Constantine II

The rule of Constantine II was the longest of any Scottish king during the tenth century. He reigned from 900 to 943 and retired to the position of monk until his death in 954. When he assumed the throne, the largest threat to the kingdom seemed to be the Norse, who had invaded and caused a lot of destruction throughout Alba during the first few years of his reign. He managed to drive them out during his fourth year as king. This drew the attention of the Danish king of Dublin (Rognvald), who laid waste to the town of Dunblane.

Constantine II was able to muster and strengthen his forces to face Rognvald and his allies, resulting in victory for the Scots at the River Tyne a few years later. After this the Norse were no longer a persistent threat to the kingdom, and he was able to focus his forces on the West Saxon kingdom in the south. To deal with the threat that was steadily encroaching on Scottish lands, he enlisted the help of other kingdoms in Britain. They were, however, solidly defeated by their powerful southern foe, with four of the kings dying, as well as one of Constantine II's sons.

When he returned to Scotland after the defeat, he abdicated, and the crown moved to Malcolm I. His reign included nonmilitary changes, the major one being the incorporation of the Church of Scotland, which had not been allowed to form by the earlier Pictish kings of Alba. Further, he managed to install his brother as the king of Strathclyde, thus resulting in a closer tie between the kingdoms, bringing the Britons of that kingdom closer to the kingdom of the Scots. As such, while his reign ended with a defeat from the West Saxons, he managed to secure his kingdom from Norse attacks, to gain allegiance with other kingdoms around the Scots, and to establish a national church.

Malcolm I

When Constantine II abdicated to become a monk in 943, Malcolm (who was his cousin) was elected to be king. His reign resulted in the expulsion of the Danes from York (which was under Scots authority at that point), obtaining Cumbria in the north. Northern parts of the kingdom were lost to the kingdom of West Saxony, which occupied parts of what is today England

and the islands to the west of Britain. During the same year when Malcolm lost the northern territories of his kingdom (954), he was killed during a rebellion in Moray.

Indulf

His reign lasted for eight years from 954 to 962. He was the successor of Malcolm I and the son of Constantine II. He was a strong leader in warding off the Vikings, protecting his people from incursions both from the sea and over land. His military prowess led to the capture of Edinburgh and Lothian in what is now southern Scotland. He then went on to defeat the king of the Danes, Eric of the Bloody Axe, in battle. He intended to abdicate the throne and become a monk, but it's unsure whether this happened or whether he died before carrying out his intentions.

Dub

Dub was the son of Malcolm I and the successor of Indulf. He ruled from 962 to 967. His reign was during a time with very little record keeping and a lot of mythological twists to events; thus, not much can be said about him for certain. He was the brother of Kenneth II and the father of Kenneth III. During his reign there was some warfare, in which it is possible that he gained lands in central Scotland. It's thought that he was killed on the orders of Culen, his successor.

Culen

Not a king to make any particularly lasting progress for the nation, Culen held the throne from 967 to 971. He was the son of Indulf, yet Dub was elected to the position of king instead of him. He contested this through conflict with Dub and the (assumed) orders to kill him. When he became king after Dub's death, he occupied himself with attempts to overcome the kingdom of Strathclyde for the purpose of subjugation. This was, however, unsuccessful. The king of Strathclyde (Riderch) went on to kill Culen in 971, likely as revenge for Culen killing Riderch's brother and raping his daughter.

Kenneth II

One of the longest periods of rule of the tenth century was that of Kenneth II. He reigned from 971 to his death in 995. The early part of his rule was characterized by a lot of warfare. Strathclyde and Northumbria were two of his main areas of conquest, with the aim being to obtain as much land as possible between the rivers Tweed and Forth for the Scots. He is believed to have acknowledged the English king Edgar as the Scottish overlord. In exchange, it is believed he received all the land between the two rivers—the land was called Lothian at the time.

He married an Irish princess with whom he had Malcolm II. His marital tie to Ireland served to strengthen his kingdom's position in Great Britain, which was composed of multiple kingdoms at the time. The later years of his rule were greatly concerned with expanding the kingdom northward, with attempts at obtaining lands in Orkney and Moray. These attempts were largely unsuccessful at the time of his murder, but the southern possessions of the kingdom were secure.

Constantine III

Constantine III had been elected to the throne when his predecessor had been killed in 995. His predecessor (Kenneth II) was his cousin. He reigned for two years, after which he, too, was killed.

Kenneth III

Kenneth held the throne for around eight years. He is thought to have obtained it by killing his predecessor. He was not entirely a usurper, being the son of Dub, who had been the king of Alba. His descendants were believed to include the mother of Macbeth. As he had done with his predecessor, his successor had him killed before taking the throne.

Malcolm II

Obtaining the throne by force in 1005, Malcolm II killed Kenneth III to take his place. He was a ruler who made use of military force, obtaining victory over Northumbria in 1016 to extend the domination of the Scottish kingdom. He also managed to gain control of Strathclyde, which he gave to his grandson (Duncan I) to rule. He tried to get around the succession process for his successor so that the throne would go to his grandson as well. He succeeded, but in doing so, it laid the groundwork for the violence that ensued with Macbeth and Duncan's son, Malcolm III Canmore. Other than the violence that would come, Malcolm II was known for his long reign (lasting until 1034) and for expanding the Scottish borders to a size that almost corresponds with the Scotland of today.

Duncan I

Having a relatively short reign of only six years, Duncan had the favor of his grandfather (King Malcolm II). Strathclyde had been a region that had been outside the power of the Scottish kingdom before the reign of Malcolm II. Upon gaining power of the region, the king granted it to Duncan to rule, which was against the custom of the time.

Further, when Malcolm II died, he nominated Duncan as his heir, which further violated custom. The system in place at the time would have given the rule to someone in an alternate branch of the royal family, which is one of the reasons Macbeth rose up against Duncan within the first few years of his rule—Macbeth being from the other branch. To protect his power, Duncan went on the offensive and laid siege to Macbeth's lands. This didn't deter Macbeth, who killed Duncan a year later in 1040 and took the crown.

Macbeth

Macbeth started his years of rule as the chief of Moray after inheriting the position from his father. He is believed to have been a descendant of Kenneth II of Scotland, while his wife was a descendent of Kenneth III. He had a claim to the Scottish throne when Malcolm II died, but his cousin (Duncan I) inherited it instead due to breaking the customs that were in place about who should get the throne. As a result, conflict broke out between the two factions of the family (Macbeth and his supporters on the one side and Duncan with his supporters on the other).

Macbeth's forces killed Duncan in battle in 1040, following which Macbeth took the throne. There was some warfare with the rebels and nobles during the following years. During the last few years of his reign, Macbeth had to cede parts of southern Scotland to Malcolm III Canmore, the eldest son of Duncan I, due to pressure from opposing forces. Malcolm III proved to be a strong enemy, eventually overcoming and killing Macbeth in battle with the help of the English in 1057. The story of Macbeth's life was formed into a play by Shakespeare, albeit with some alterations from fact.

Lulach

Lulach was the stepson of Macbeth and reigned a period of mere months from 1057 to 1058. His claim came mainly from his mother, who had been a relative of Malcolm II. His uncle was likely the strongest claimant to the throne when Duncan I was put on the throne. His biological father had been the king of Moray, which was a separate kingdom from Scotland at the time. To obtain the crown for Moray, his father had killed Macbeth's father, who had been the reigning Moravian king.

After a short period of exile, Macbeth returned to Moray where he killed Lulach's father and took back the throne that had belonged to his own father. Lulach's mother married Macbeth, and he took Lulach in as his heir. He was thus to inherit both the thrones of Moray and Scotland. Macbeth chose to abdicate in favor of Lulach as he was a younger man who could better handle the threats of Duncan I's sons and their supporters. Lulach was killed in battle a few months into his reign, which paved the way for Malcolm III Canmore to take the throne.

Malcolm III Canmore

After his father had been murdered by MacBeth, Malcolm III remained in exile for more than a decade. He gathered supporters and military forces, killing MacBeth in 1057, after which he took over as ruler. St. Margaret of Scotland was to become his second wife. She was the sister of Edgar Aetheling, who would have been king of England had William the Conqueror's invasion not been so successful.

This was after he had given refuge to Edgar and his sisters while they were in exile from England. Later, Malcolm went on to acknowledge William the Conqueror as the overlord of Scotland in 1072, and Edgar went on to live in France. In the end Malcolm violated the fealty agreement by raiding England multiple times, finally resulting in his death on a raid in 1093. Three of his sons succeeded him on the throne.

Donald Bane

This was the one king who held the throne twice. First, he held it for half a year during 1093 and 1094 and then for three years from later in 1094 to 1097. His brother, Malcolm III, had been king of Scotland for many years. He obtained the crown by laying siege to the castle in Edinburgh and getting elected to the position of king by the lords who were eligible to vote.

Duncan II, Malcolm III's son, took the crown with outside support. He had the support of the English, the Normans, and the Saxons.

After having Duncan II killed, Donald retook the throne. The English backed forces to overthrow Donald, which they did successfully after the three years of his second reign. Edgar, a son of Malcolm III, was installed into the position of king after Donald's defeat. With his removal, so went the Celtic customs for electing their king (called tanistry), and a more Norman and Anglo-Saxon style of monarchy was introduced.

Duncan II

Duncan II was the son of Malcolm III who was only on the throne for a few months. He was not accustomed to the Celtic way of life as much as Donald Bane, who was the elected king of Scotland at the time of his assumption of the throne. Growing up as a hostage in the Norman court of England, he was accustomed to the rule of William the Conqueror and was largely under the influence of the new English government. With their backing, he gained the throne, but he wasn't capable of holding the throne in a country where he was essentially a foreigner. Donald Bane and his supporters killed Duncan, allowing Donald to take back the throne.

Sons of Malcolm III Canmore

Edgar, Malcolm III's eldest son, reigned for a decade from 1097 to 1107. Due to his descent from both a Scottish and an English king, he was a uniting force for the Anglo-Saxon and Celtic-descent peoples of the nation. The fealty agreement his father had made to William the Conqueror remained in force, and he was selected to depose his anti-English uncle (Donald Bane) who had taken the throne after his father's death. He was not able to hold the protection Scotland held over the Hebrides from Norwegian raids. As such, he gave the islands to Norway. He left no heir as he had been a devout, unmarried individual, thus leaving the throne to his brother.

His younger brother, Alexander I, reigned over northern Scotland for 17 years from 1107 to 1124. Edgar had specified their younger brother, David I, was to rule over southern Scotland. To keep the peace and honor Scotland's fealty to England, Alexander married an illegitimate daughter (Sibylla) of the English king. Further, he assisted the English king in warfare against Welsh elements, committing to his status as an ally of the English crown. Even though he was an ally of the English and acted in accordance with overlordship, he was committed to keeping the Scottish church independent and under the control of the Scottish monarch.

The youngest of the brothers who reigned (they had three other brothers who didn't rule) was David I. He was the ruler of southern Scotland during the reign of Alexander I, in accordance with their eldest brother's will. When Alexander died, David became the king of the whole of Scotland.

As the king, he was an agent of change. He issued the first Scottish royal coins and established many castles around which some of the most notable Scottish settlements today are located (Edinburgh, Stirling, Roxburgh, and Berwick, among others). Further, he introduced cultural change by bringing in many Anglo-Normans to intermarry and live in Scotland (including the Oliphant, Bruce, Comyn, and Stewart families), so long as those new settlers provided monetary support or military service to the Scottish crown.

He had been present in the English court during the earlier years of his life, thus exposing him to a foreign way of life and Norman sympathies. He married an English noblewoman and went on to hold lands in Huntingdon and Northamptonshire. Part of the reason he succeeded in ruling southern parts of

Scotland was because he obtained the help of Normans in England to force his brother Alexander to give him rule in those parts.

The power of David had the effect of influencing the line of succession to the English throne. His recognition of Holy Roman Empress Matilda as heir contributed to her taking the English throne. In order to back her better, he combatted the forces of the man who had been crowned the ruler of England (Stephen) instead of the empress. His support went back and forth between Stephen and Matilda, with the main intention of obtaining more control for himself over Northumberland. Eventually he took power over Northumberland after Matilda's son (whom he had knighted) became the king of England (King Henry II). David remained in power until his death in 1153.

Malcolm IV

King David's firstborn was Malcolm IV, who reigned from 1153 to 1165. He rose to the throne as a child (around age 11), which meant that he didn't have much experience or competence as a ruler. His early death also meant that he couldn't effect much change as an adult, thus putting him at the effect of others' decisions or influence for much of his reign. Before he rose to the position of king of Scotland, however, he had inherited the earldoms of Northumberland and Cumbria, in exchange for the English king's recognition of his earldom of Huntingdon. When he died in his early twenties, the Scottish crown moved to his brother, William I.

William the Lion

William inherited the throne in his early twenties, meaning he was already an adult with full legal capacity at the time. He had also inherited the earldom of Northumberland, which he gave up to the English king in the 1150s—as his older brother did. When he inherited the Scottish throne, William went on the offensive and started attacking the sons of King Henry II of England, the king whom he'd renounced his earldom for. The purpose of the attacks was to gain back the county. Unfortunately, he was captured during a raid he held in 1174 and could only obtain his release by recognizing the English king as overlord of Scotland.

This meant that Scotland was once again under the power of the English king, thereby striking at its independence. Further, the English church was to be recognized as taking superiority over the Scottish church. During the years that followed, William established one of the most affluent abbeys in Scotland.

The years that followed included a lot of back and forth with the church in Rome in an attempt to remove the Church of England as the "middleman." In proceedings with the Pope, William was able to overturn this arrangement in favor of Scotland being under no other churches other than the church in Rome. William was also able to get out of the overlordship arrangement by paying large sums to the English king starting in 1189. The one issue that could not be resolved, however, was that of Northumberland.

The English king forced William to abandon his claim to the county in 1209. This came after years of conflict between the two. Despite the issues of the overlordship, the church, and Northumberland, William had managed to consolidate the power of Scotland into a central authority. The central bureaucracy's officials were able to manage the affairs of the whole nation under the authority and approval of the king. During this period, King William established many of the burghs that are still extant in Scotland. These burghs served to make the central government's work more efficient and effective.

Alexander II

When his father died, Alexander II took over the throne in 1214. His father had been an agent of stability through the process of regaining Scottish dependence with money and getting the church out of the control of the English church. Alexander II took the progress his father had made and built on it by improving relations with England. At first he was on the side of rebel lords who were against the English king John, as he intended to gain English territory for Scotland. However, after John's death and the accession to the throne of Henry III, he both gave public honor to the new king and married his sister to strengthen their ties.

Just over 20 years into the reign of King Henry III, Alexander II signed a peace treaty with him. The effect of the treaty was that Alexander II would have no claim to the English throne, but that he would be granted lands in England. The border between the two nations was set (and is approximately in the same location today). Alexander was concerned not only with the Scottish relations with England but also with interior relations between the crown and the lords of Scotland. He fostered genuine support from lords who had previously only supported the monarchy in formality. Further, he conquered Argyll and brought it under the firm control of the kingdom.

Alexander III

Alexander III had ascended to the throne when he was a boy (in 1249). He had been married to the daughter of the king of England, who was also underage at the time. His father in law wanted to take over control of Scotland to the advantage of himself and England, trying to take control of Alexander III.

The result was a political party that advocated for English interests seized the young king. The Scottish took control of the situation by controlling the government under the authority of parties who were against the English. They remained in control until Alexander was of age at 21.

Under Alexander III's reign, the Normans were combatted, and their invasion of Scotland was brought to an end. The Normans already controlled islands off the west coast of Scotland, and they wanted to expand their power to the Scottish mainland. As a result of their defeat, however, the Normans gave control of the Hebrides islands and the Isle of Man to the Scottish. The rule of Alexander III was known to be a period of political and economic stability, with little governing interference from other nations.

His children had all died before him, leaving his granddaughter to inherit the crown after his untimely death in 1286 (he fell off a cliff while riding a horse). The death of his granddaughter before she came of age or had children was the main contributor to the Wars of Scottish Independence.

The First War of Scottish Independence

King Alexander III had managed the country during a time of relative peace. He had managed to expand the kingdom of the Scots by fostering the Treaty of Perth. As a result of the treaty, Scotland grew to include the Isle of Man and the Outer Hebrides. This happened as the result of warfare between Scotland and the Norwegians, in which the Scottish ultimately gained the winning hand.

Trade was good, and people were able to build up personal wealth. This was about to come to an end. When he died (in 1286), none of his living children remained. His granddaughter, Margaret, was due to inherit the throne after his death. She was the child of his daughter, also named Margaret, and King Eric II of Norway. Unfortunately, she died a mere four years after her grandfather in 1290, leaving Scotland without a leader.

The result was that there were many claimants to the throne. The risk of civil war seemed imminent with factions supporting different claimants. The two largest factions were those who believed the Balliol family should get the crown and those who believed the Bruces should. The king of England (Edward I) was invited to assist in calming the disputes, which he eventually did in 1292 in what is now known as the Great Cause.

Edward eventually decided that John Balliol was to become the Scottish king, but he wanted him to acknowledge Edward's overlordship in return for deciding the matter. John agreed to grant Edward overlordship, but this incited unrest in Scotland. To calm down the situation, John agreed to the Auld Alliance with France in 1295, which served to pacify many of the Scottish. That said, it also had the effect of inciting Edward I to raise an army, which he marched on Scotland in 1296.

Multiple campaigns were led against Edward, such as those of the Scottish Guardians from 1297 to 1304. Another campaign was that of William Wallace, who managed to garner a lot of support, resulting in the success of the Scottish at the Battle of Stirling Bridge. He managed to retain a lot of support until his deciding defeat at the Battle of Falkirk in 1298. All the while, infighting continued throughout Scotland, particularly between the supporters of the Bruce family and the Balliol family.

Robert the Bruce was crowned in 1306, and he campaigned until 1314, gradually driving the English out of the country. In 1314, at the Battle of Bannockburn, the final victory of the First

War of Independence was won against the English force of King Edward II. After this, the Scottish started raiding into England itself, and they also helped the Irish in their campaigns against England.

The friction between the two countries gradually reduced, but proper peace was only brought into being after the ratification of the Treaty of Northampton in 1328. Robert Bruce died a year later.

The Great Cause: 1292

The predictability of the successor to the crown had ended with the death of Margaret the Maid of Norway when she was eight years old. Her grandfather, King Alexander III, had ruled for almost four decades when he passed. He had three children who would have been eligible for the throne, but all of them passed away before Alexander III died. His only grandchild was Margaret, who was also the daughter of the king of Norway. She was four years old when her grandfather died, thus leaving her as his successor (due to a lack of other living descendants).

This was the cause of confusion, which led to many claimants for the throne. The claimants were members of the greater family tree of the previous kings of Scotland. Many of the claimants had support of powerful individuals and families throughout the nation, thus making for a splintered situation that could have resulted in civil war. A few of the most powerful lords of Scotland, later called the Guardians, asked the king of England (Edward I) to help decide whose claim was the most legitimate. Their intention was to resolve the situation as peacefully as possible.

However, in exchange for Edward's intervention, the Guardians were asked to promise to make him overlord of

Scotland. The Guardians stated that they did not have the authority to make such a decision and that he could only discuss such terms with the future king of Scotland once he'd helped with the selection.

Edward thus went ahead to make his selection. He looked at the line of kings who had held the crown over the previous few generations. King David I, who had died in 1153, was the last king to leave surviving descendants. The oldest male descendant was Robert the Bruce's grandfather (who had the same name). The grandfather, however, died in 1295 before any coronation had taken place. The next eldest descendant was John Balliol, who was the son of a Scottish noblewoman and an English nobleman.

Robert the Bruce was younger than John Balliol, thus making John the heir in terms of the law of primogeniture (where the oldest living descendant inherits). To further improve John's claim, the eldest daughter of his common ancestor with Robert was his grandmother, while the second eldest daughter of the common ancestor was Robert's great-grandmother. This meant that John came from the elder existing line of descent of the claims from himself and Robert.

Following the crowing of John, tensions intensified rather than subsided. This was because John's family, who were a powerful family who originated in France and held a lot of property in England, didn't get along with the Scottish nobles and were only eligible for the crown through marriage with Devorgilla, who was a noblewoman whose family held power in Galloway. Thus, the Balliols might have been seen as imposters or as having gotten the crown through luck, whereas the Bruce clan (which Robert was part of) was a powerful and wealthy clan in Scotland (and thus not seen as outsiders). The straw that broke the camel's back was when John accepted Edward I as the overlord of Scotland.

Inauguration of John Balliol: 1292

When Edward I selected John Balliol for the throne, he pressured the new king to recognize him as lord paramount of Scotland. This meant that he would be the full title holder of the land of Scotland under feudal law—there would be nobody with a superior title to him over Scotland. John agreed to this, which meant that he would have to provide military support to Edward when told to provide it. This occurred soon after, in 1294 when Edward demanded troops for a war against France.

The Scots people didn't agree with this, and unrest occurred. To pacify them, John agreed to the Auld Alliance, which was ratified as the Treaty of Paris in 1295. Edward retaliated by going to war with Scotland for violating their duties to him as lord paramount of Scotland. This was the start of the Scottish Wars of Independence.

The trading port of Berwick was the first location where the English struck. It was a port of economic value to Scotland. To further incite the Scottish, he took up residence in Berwick Castle for a month.

He then went on a campaign where he struck multiple towns and settlements, including Dunbar, where the Scottish were subject to a bloodbath. Multiple nobles were captured and sent back to England in captivity in the aftermath of the Battle of Dunbar. Edward rolled on, destroying or taking possession of multiple places, including Jedburgh, Roxburgh, Stirling, and Linlithgow. John Balliol and his nobles submitted to Edward to stop the destructive progression. Edward took John's crown, his royal insignia, the Black Rood of St. Margaret, and the Stone of Destiny. The submission wasn't enough, however, with Edward continuing to pillage and destroy.

Auld Alliance: 1295

The Auld Alliance was the agreement that drew the nations of France and Scotland together. It was ratified in 1295 with the purpose of preventing England's expansion of its borders. The alliance would bring diplomatic and military benefits to both parties, and it would provide the Scots with jobs in the form of being mercenaries for France. It was a valued alliance between the two countries, which brought economic benefits for more than a century.

Likely the most notable use of the alliance was in 1415 after England won a massive victory against France at the Battle of Agincourt. The Scots were asked for aid, in response to which they sent 12,000 troops. The combined troops of France and

Scotland beat the English in their first joint battle at the Battle of Baugé in 1421. The Scots troops were rewarded with titles, food, and wine. The next major battle was the Battle of Verneuil in 1424. The forces experienced a heavy loss at the hands of the English, but the cushion of the Scottish soldiers allowed the French enough time to prepare themselves against total domination from the English.

Those Scots that remained in France gained permanent residence. They were able to trade with other Scots back home, with French wine being a particularly hot commodity. A good relationship would continue between the two countries for many centuries. The major turning point for the alliance was after the Scottish Reformation, when the core religion of the two countries differed. The Scottish Reformation also brought a slightly closer relationship between England and Scotland.

William Wallace

In the friction that followed Edward I's enforced recognition as lord paramount of Scotland and raising troops against the Scots for violating that recognition, sentiment grew among the common folk for incitement of a rebellion. William Wallace was one such individual. He killed a sheriff of England and inspired Scottish people to join him as his troops. He managed to gain the support of the Bishop of Glasgow, who lent him enough credibility to gain even more supporters.

Robert the Bruce was one of Edward I's allies at the start of this period of unrest. He was sent by Edward to bring down Wallace and his allies. Robert started carrying out this command, but at the same time started questioning Edward's intentions. He would later change sides and join the rebellion against Edward.

The Battle of Stirling Bridge in 1297 brought a major blow to Edward's campaign of domination. The rebel forces, under the command of Wallace, were able to beat a large English army that was composed largely of cavalry. They did this by allowing the English onto Stirling Bridge, which wasn't very wide, and then pushing back with their spears once there were enough English soldiers on the bridge. With the combination of the narrow bridge, boggy ground, and use of cavalry rather than infantry, the English lost and had to retreat. Wallace was promoted to Guardian of Scotland after this clash.

Skirmishes continued between the sides, but the Battle of Falkirk in 1298 was the major confrontation. The Scots lost this battle and multiple other battles over the next six years. Eventually the Scottish nobles had to submit to Edward, both as a result of atrophied forces and because of infighting among the Bruces and the Balliols (along with their supporters). The submission resulted in the rebellion being outlawed and Wallace becoming a wanted man. When Wallace was captured, Edward directed that he wanted him executed—in return for which he would reduce the intensity of his onslaught.

The execution was gruesome. First, he was pulled to his place of execution by a horse while he was naked. Then he was hung, and his genitals were cut off while he was still alive, only to be burned in front of him. This was followed by being cut open before he died so that his innards could be removed, including his heart. After this, the body was cut into four parts, and his head was chopped off. The parts were sent all over England and Scotland as a display of victory over the leader of the revolutionary forces.

Robert the Bruce

Robert was from the powerful Bruce clan. His family was related to the royal family of Scotland through marriage. His grandfather had claimed the throne when it was vacant in 1290. His grandfather died before he could rule properly, leaving the throne empty. Using primogeniture (where the oldest living descendant inherits), Edward I awarded John Balliol the crown, not Robert the Bruce. Robert, however, wanted the crown, so he assisted in the insurrection against John Balliol.

Robert remained an ally of Edward I for a few years, but this changed in 1299 when he was made Co-guardian of Scotland with John Comyn. He even assisted William Wallace in his revolts against the English. These two Guardians held a lot of power, both being the head of two of the most influential families of Scotland. The main problem was that the two Guardians didn't get along very well. This came to a head in 1306 when Robert killed John Comyn in Greyfriars Kirk in Dumfries.

Killing him gave Robert the chance he needed to take the position of king as John had been his only real opposition at the time (seeing that Edward I had stripped John Balliol of his crown and royal insignia). However, it also brought renewed vigor in Edward's campaign against Scotland, seeing as John Comyn was married to a cousin of Edward. Nevertheless, Robert was crowned (without Papal approval) and started ruling the Scots.

Reign as King: 1306–1314

The English tried to quash Robert and his forces, with Robert experiencing two big defeats during his first half year as king. The aftermath of the defeat included executions of his siblings, the imprisonment of his wife, and going on the run (out of Scotland) to escape Scottish allies of England. Legend says watching a spider spin a web gave him the inspiration he needed to be patient and have hope for success. Upon this inspiration, he traveled to the south of Scotland in 1307 to garner support and win minor victories.

The minor victories helped him gain more supporters. The death of Edward I in 1307 helped him gain even more supporters as Edward II wasn't yet as experienced an opponent as his father. The rebel forces thus gained traction and started pushing the English out of Scotland over the next few years. The final victory came at the Battle of Bannockburn in 1314.

Battle of Bannockburn: 1314

The Battle of Bannockburn took place in 1314 when the Scottish had overcome all the English strongholds in Scotland other than the castle at Stirling. Edward II had assembled large forces at the castle with the intention of protecting the interests of all those loyal to him in Scotland. While Robert had a lower number of forces, his troops laid proper groundworks, and they used the surrounding forest tactically.

Once the battle started, there was some back and forth between the forces. It seemed like the Scots were retreating after a seeming stalemate between the forces. This wasn't the case because the Scots were merely altering their position to cut off the English forces. In the clash that followed, Robert and an English night faced each other in personal combat for most members of both armies to see. Robert cut off the knight's head, after which the English troops retreated.

That night the Scots were in a celebratory mood, while the English had a rough night. The following day the Scots started off with prayer and a religious service, followed by meeting the English troops in battle. The earthworks they laid proved to be disastrous for the English, and the Scots eventually won. Edward II fled with his life.

In the aftermath of the battle, the Scots considered that they had won their freedom from overlordship. This, however, wasn't formalized until 14 years later with the signing of the Treaty of Northampton.

Declaration of Arbroath: 1320

In the 1290s, the Pope directed the Scots to seek a peace agreement with the English. This wasn't done as the Scots wanted to break out of the yoke of the English king. When Robert the Bruce incited further rebellion, this went directly against the Pope's direction. Then in 1306, when he killed John Comyn, the murder took place in Greyfriars Kirk, thus violating the laws of the church. Robert confessed to the crime, and the Bishop of Glasgow absolved him. Despite this, Edward I outlawed Robert, and the Pope excommunicated him.

The excommunication was ignored, and Robert was crowned by Scottish bishops a month after the murder. The bishops went against the excommunication with the intention of advocating for the autonomy of Scotland. Thus, while he was crowned, the coronation wasn't sanctioned by the Pope and would not be recognized by all internationally. A letter of excommunication was resent in 1308.

When they were invited to the Council of Vienne in 1310, the Scottish clergy requested that the Pope recognize Robert as king. They wanted him to absolve Robert of the murder that took place in Greyfriars Kirk. Absolution was granted, but not by the Pope, rather by a cardinal. The absolution letter granted him absolution for the murder, but didn't grant him approval to be king. In fact, the letter referred to him as a layman.

The Scottish nobles wanted to receive proper recognition for their independence and their king. They sent the Declaration of Arbroath to the Pope with this intention. The declaration was given the seal of 8 earls and 40 barons of Scotland. The letter showed a unification in the nobles of Scotland and indicated that all they wanted was freedom as a nation.

As a result of the declaration, the Pope sent a letter to Edward II stating that he wanted Edward to make peace with the Scots. Further, Robert was recognized by the Pope as lawful king of Scotland in 1324. Eventually the English caved and recognized Scotland's independence in 1328.

The Last Years of His Reign

Edward II was deposed in 1327. His successor was Edward III, but a regent was put in place until the boy king could take on full responsibility for daily affairs. The regent wanted to maintain peace with the Scots, resulting in the Treaty of Northampton in 1328. This was partly with the intention of reducing the amount of raids that the Scottish had continually been taking into the north of England since the success at the Battle of Bannockburn in 1314. The kingdom of Scotland itself had been relatively free of infighting over the last decade of Robert's reign, largely with him being perceived as the uniting figure of the nation who had overcome the English.

The Treaty of Northampton: 1328

This treaty brought final peace between the two nations since the start of conflict with Edward I in the 1290s. The treaty stated that the English agreed that the Scottish could govern themselves under their own king and that Robert I (the formal title for Robert the Bruce) was acknowledged as rightfully holding the crown. The treaty further agreed that the kings and their nations would be allies that would provide each other with mutual assistance.

Further, provisions were made to take the Auld Alliance into account. If the Scots were to assist the French in warfare against the English, then the English would be allowed to retaliate against the Scottish. In exchange for the concessions from England, the Scottish would have to pay a large sum of silver. They would also have to conclude a marriage contract between the son of Robert the Bruce and the sister of Edward III.

In the next chapter, we will look at the reign of the Stewart monarchs of Scotland. This will start with the reign of David II, the last non-Stewart monarch, so as to provide context. The Second War of Scottish Independence, the Scottish Renaissance, and the Scottish Reformation will also be included as major events immediately preceding or happening during the Stewart line's reign.

CHAPTER 3
THE REIGN OF THE STEWART KINGS

The Stewart monarchs descended from Robert the Bruce. His daughter had married a man called Walter the Steward, hence the surname Stewart. Their reign over Scotland spanned through the Late Middle Ages, the Renaissance, and the unification with England. In this chapter we will explore their reigns and important developments that took place during these times.

The Second War of Independence

The Second War of Scottish Independence started in 1332—four years after signing the Treaty of Northampton. The instigation of this was likely resumption of the conflict between the Bruce and Balliol factions for the throne when Robert the Bruce died. The four-year-old David II (Robert's son) was the selected successor, but his guardian died while he was young, and he was married to the sister of Edward III, which complicated matters. Further, the Balliols were disinherited by Robert the Bruce, inciting them and those loyal to them to join with Edward III in an attempt to take the crown.

The Battle of Mar, which was part of the ensuing conflict, resulted in the death of the lord of Mar, who was the regent of David II. The lord of Liddesdale, who was an illegitimate son of Robert the Bruce, was also killed in battle. This left no protection for the young king, resulting in Edward Balliol (son of John Balliol) being crowned a few weeks later. He ruled over some parts of Scotland while David II was growing up, with his chief point of operations being in Galloway.

David II was sent to be cared for by the king of France, Philip VI, in 1334 to keep him safe. Control of the parts of Scotland that weren't under the control of Edward Balliol was handed over to the newly chosen Guardians of the kingdom. The unrest between the Balliol and Bruce factions continued, with neither party gaining full control of the kingdom. David returned to Scotland in 1341, at the age of 17.

Edward III resumed warfare with France in 1346, at which point the king of France asked Scotland for aid in return for acting as guardian to David II and also in line with the Auld Alliance. The Scots thus invaded England, while the English invaded France. English forces met the Scots at the Battle of Neville's Cross, in which David II was captured and a former regent, the earl of Moray, was killed. David was imprisoned in London for 12 years, and he wasn't allowed to contact any of his citizens from Scotland. Eventually a truce was concluded under the Treaty of Berwick, which allowed David to be released in return for a large ransom. The treaty signaled the end of the Second War of Scottish Independence.

Early Stewart Kings

To gain context, we will look at the last non-Stewart king of Scotland (David II), including the entwined reign of Edward Balliol. This will be followed by the Stewart kings up to the reign of Mary, Queen of Scots.

David II

The period during which David II ruled was a turbulent one. When his father died, he was just a child, and Edward Balliol (John Balliol's son) was given the throne by the English. He was the de facto ruler of Scotland while David II grew up, with the lords of Scotland splintering and the sense of unity under Robert the Bruce being lost.

Edward obtained the crown by invading Scotland with a French army, getting the backing of English lords who had their Scottish lands removed during the reign of Robert the Bruce. As such, he started off his reign by undoing a lot of the unification that had taken place over the previous decades. First, Edward ruled for three months, but he was forced out later in the year of his inauguration (1332). The English king had assisted in getting Edward back on the throne to continue his rule, for which Edward gave away parts of southern Scotland.

He took it back the following year, but did so after agreeing that the king of England was to be the overlord of Scotland. This struck back at the independence that had been fought for during his predecessor's reign. He had a lot of ties to the French and English, having spent much of his earlier life there. Thus, his loyalties were not necessarily with his own people. He ended up giving all his Scottish lands and titles to the English king, thus striking hard against the independence of Scotland.

David II was a much better liked candidate for the throne by the Scottish people as his father had brought a lot of the country together. Further, David II had more loyalties to the Scottish than the English or French, being from a prominent clan that had established themselves in the region over the previous two centuries. His main connection with England was the marriage that had taken place between him and the sister of Edward III of England (he was four at the time and she was seven). That said, the marriage was arranged as part of the terms of the Treaty of Northampton, and David wasn't raised in England or with English guardians.

David II would have taken the throne as a boy, but the forces of the English king were too powerful, and his regent had to throw in the towel. David II thus went into exile and grew up in the court of the French king (as his descendant Mary, Queen of Scots, would 200 years later). As his teenage years came to a close, he assisted in fighting battles with the French against the English. He was able to enter Scotland and gain his authority of king in multiple regions in 1341.

While on the throne, his attention remained preoccupied with fighting his English counterpart. In one of these conflicts, David II was injured and taken prisoner. The English let him go, on the condition that Scotland would pay a large fee for his release. The fee was too much, so David II agreed that the son of the English king would take the Scottish throne when he died (which happened in 1371). This agreement, combined with a closer friendship with the English king and financial wastefulness, served to alienate his kingdom from him. Parliament took control and voted against the agreement he'd made with the English regarding his succession, giving the crown to his nephew Robert II instead.

Robert II

Robert II was already old when he took the throne, or at least by the standards of the time (age 55). He had some experience with power when he took the throne in 1372 due to his prior position as earl of Strathearn. He was the first Stewart king, with Walter the Steward being his father. With the assistance of Parliament, he took control of the situation when David II tried to make the English king's son his heir in exchange for canceling his outstanding ransom payments. As a result, Scotland's relationship with England deteriorated, and war broke out again four years after Robert II's reign started. He didn't make any large reforms or bring major improvements during his rule.

During the last few years of his period as king, his sons administered the nation on his behalf. Robert II's sex life contributed to later stability of the kingdom. He had nine children from his first wife (with their marriage taking place after the births), thus giving rise to questions about their legitimacy. He also had eight illegitimate sons (that we know of). His second marriage produced four legitimate children, but strife ensued between them and the children from his first marriage—some of his first wife's children feeling they should have been eligible for the crown. His reign ended with his death in 1390.

Robert III

A child from his father's first marriage, Robert III was the regent of Scotland during the four of the later years of his father's reign (1384–1388) due to his father's old age. In 1388 he was injured, leaving him incapable of effectively holding power until his death in 1406. Nevertheless, he was crowned king in 1390 when his father died. Almost all of his reign was governed by regents.

Robert Stewart, First Duke of Albany

The third son of Robert II and a brother to Robert III, Robert Stewart was never formally crowned the king of Scotland. That said, he was the regent of Scotland for the last two years of his father's life (1388–1390) and for the first eight years of his brother's reign (1390–1398), after which the eldest son of Robert III took over the role of regent. When the son started being too much at odds with Robert Stewart, he was locked up and eventually died, paving the way for Robert Stewart to be chosen to resume the position of regent after the death of Robert III in 1406.

The new king, James I, was unable to govern due to being held prisoner in London. Despite the king being held by the English, Robert Stewart continued waging war with them. He held the position of regent until his death in 1420, most of which time the main priority was warring with the English. His son took over both his dukedom and the regency, but lasted only five years before being executed on the commands of James I.

The Renaissance in Scotland

The Scottish Renaissance started later than in many other countries. It started in the fifteenth century with the advent of the printing press as an instigator. The printing press allowed literature to be spread around more freely, and it encouraged the use of the written word in everyday life. This section will look at the major aspects of the Renaissance and the effect it had.

Politics

The royal court was the instigator of the social revolution that took place during the Scottish Renaissance. It brought ideas of sophistication and reform from foreign nations due to the intermarriage that took place between the French and

English royal families, among other non-royal families of money and influence. James IV was perhaps the most influential royal proponent for the Renaissance. He was an advocate for better education and improved literacy, both in Latin and in the vernacular of Scotland.

Use of Latin improved the population's interchange of ideas with the continent. People of the continent used Latin as their lingua franca at the time. Use of the Scottish written language also meant that classical literature and the history of Scotland could be disseminated better to the common masses. The introduction and support for the use of the printing press were a contributor to this exchange of ideas and the elevation of the population's literacy, especially since it ensured that written language wasn't something only available to the wealthy or those working for the church.

A prominent political idea that spread as a result of the increased literacy and interchange of ideas was that the ruler had to rule for the well-being of the commoners, not just their own interests. During this period, Parliament of Scotland gained traction, resulting in seniority being given to the law over the king. The advance in demand for a more active government resulted in a permanent navy and armed force to protect the people and taxes becoming more orderly.

Religion

Exposure to Protestant ideas was one of the effects of the Renaissance. Restructuring of the church was taking place in many countries on the continent, as well as England. The printing press also meant that Bibles were easier to obtain, resulting in people being able to gain its knowledge for themselves, rather than through someone else's interpretation. Faith became more important to the Scots, and they could better emulate what was written by gaining a personal understanding. People were also exposed to other fields like theology, philosophy, and science. They could thus gain alternate perspectives that either altered or enhanced their religious beliefs.

Other developments

Development of the arts was one of the main outcomes of the Renaissance. Painting and crafts took on new knowledge, as well as literature and architecture. The manners a person used to conduct themselves started showing their level of sophistication. Further, displays of power became more important as people cared more about the impression they gave others. This contributed to bringing about a social revolution.

The social revolution placed more value on personal usefulness than before. In earlier times, people's families and their connections were everything. However, with the Renaissance, the desirable skills and knowledge someone held would determine the amount of wealth they could amass.

Even the royal family's status shifted from their right to rule to their capacity to hold the ruling position. While their position had elevated because of the Renaissance, the use of mathematics to get better weapons was of more importance. The royals were able to amass better weapons to protect themselves, thus making it much more difficult for other nobles to try to overcome them. The shift was thus from connections to capacity to hold their own.

Kings of the Renaissance

James I

James was the king of Scotland from 1406 until his death in 1437. That said, he only assumed the role of king in 1424 due to being held prisoner for more than a decade in London (from the very start of his reign). Despite being unable to govern directly for his first years as king, he still managed to get his uncle (Robert Stewart) imprisoned and later (likely as a result of his orders) executed in 1420. The years from 1420 to 1424 were ruled by a regency of Robert Stewart's son, until the king of England released James in that final year. During James's reign, control was taken of the war with England, and the priority became governing Scotland and its people.

He started his period of direct reign by having multiple lords, including the son of Robert Stewart, taken into custody. Some of them were executed for crimes such as treason. Relations with the Highland lords were also strengthened, with attempts made at improving their loyalty to the crown. He was a well-educated man who wrote a long poetry book, The King's Book.

He was driven in cleaning out the governing system of the country. Financial matters in the kingdom were brought under his direct supervision. There was a crackdown on bribery and corruption. Payments from the church to Rome were reduced in an attempt to bolster the nation's financial wealth. There was also a push to improve the administration of justice to the common people. When he was assassinated in 1437, his assassin and conspirators were captured and executed on the orders of his widow (Joan Beaufort).

James II

The start of his reign was turbulent. He was inaugurated at the age of six when his dad passed away. The kingdom grew in instability because families of power tried to gain control of the regency and raising of the adolescent king. Some of the advancements that James I brought fell away due to the friction between the factions, thereby taking away focus from the common people and governing.

James II officially took over his duties in 1449 at the age of 19. As his father had done, he confiscated the property of lords who had caused trouble for the monarchy. He used their lands to generate income to fund various expenses and campaigns of the kingdom. The main reforms he made were to re-establish the central government and improve administration of justice through all strata of society.

England once again started asserting that it had the authority to rule Scotland. Conflict thus resumed more substantially with England, with multiple raids being made by James II and his forces. He died in a siege in 1460.

James III

James III ruled for 28 years from 1460 to 1488, starting at the age of eight. The first six years of his reign were ruled by regents, including his mother. He was kidnapped after this (age 14) by a collection of Scottish lords. These lords effectively took control of his upbringing and ruling of the country for the next three years.

The rest of his reign after he took back control from the lords wasn't any less tumultuous. The problem was partly that he was out of touch with many of his nobles by championing the arts and being less driven by their interests or concerns. Things got worse.

He arrested two of his brothers on suspicion of treason. The one brother, the duke of Albany, was able to escape and fled to England. Meanwhile, James III had confiscated both brothers' lands and property. The duke of Albany enlisted the help of English armed forces to march back to Scotland and demand back his lands. They were successful in pressuring the king to do so, but the king managed to push his brother back out a year later.

Many of the nobles were alienated during this period, resulting in them jumping on the bandwagon when the English soldiers entered the country. They tried to rebel against the king, which he was able to quash on multiple occasions. During the rebellions, some of James III's best supporters were killed by the rebels, resulting in reduced support for the king. In the end the revolts proved to be successful. James III's son and successor was won over to the cause of the rebels, and James III himself was killed after being captured in 1488.

James IV

James IV was a king who was actively involved in the internal affairs of Scotland. He reigned from the age of 15 in 1488 until his death while fighting on foot in the Battle of

Flodden in 1513. When the nobles of Scotland rose up against his father in rebellion, James IV sympathized with their concerns. This would be shown during his reign.

His inauguration after the death of his father was followed by five years of actively interacting with the lords of Scotland. He did not only try to build relations with those in the south but pursue stronger relations with those in the Highlands as well. All the lords of Scotland were brought under his authority in one way or another, including conquest.

When James IV had the whole kingdom under his control, he focused on upgrading the power of the central government. Financial matters of the kingdom were included in this new central authority. The royal household was brought to a high standard of education and refinement, and political discourse was elevated. The result was that the finances of Scotland were improved and the nation started being seen as a refined one among the other powers of the continent.

He was a champion of the arts and learning. This was quite appropriate for the time as the Renaissance had been taking the world by storm for more than a century. The nation itself had entered the Renaissance during the reign of his father, and the concepts of artistic, political, and economic improvements were relevant issues of the day. In line with this, Janes IV vigorously supported improvements in education, the introduction of printing presses to Scotland, and patronage of art (specifically literature).

The relationship between Scotland and England was to become an issue during the seventh year of James IV's reign. He had supported a pretender to the English throne, resulting in breakage of a brief period of calm between the nations. As a result, conflict broke out between the nations. Multiple invasions and raids took place.

The situation was pacified when James IV married Margaret Tudor, the eldest daughter of the new English king (Henry VII). He had his successor and only legitimate child with Margaret (although he had many illegitimate children too). A peace agreement was brought into place as a result of their marriage, relationship, and successors.

The behavior that dishonored the agreement was continued skirmishes and raids across the mutual border of the nations. These skirmishes didn't cause serious national problems, but things would change when Henry VIII took power in England. Friction between the two nations was largely due to mounting tension between France and England. Scotland was a major ally of France and backed it in the warfare that would follow between France, England, and other European nations.

The end came soon after England invaded France. While the English forces were occupied with the French, the Scottish troops invaded England. Multiple raids were carried out, but James IV would die in the process. At the Battle of Flodden in Northumberland, he died while fighting on foot, leaving the kingdom to his son with Margaret Tudor.

Margaret Tudor

Margaret married James IV when she was 14 years old in 1489. She was the oldest daughter of the English king Henry VII. Henry VIII was her little brother. While her husband was alive, she was loyal to Scotland and its interests. And when he died, she took over the regency for her son, the infant king James V.

Her behavior during this time would contribute to military and political difficulties later on. She would shift her allegiances back and forth between France and England, largely dependent on her financial interests. While she was a daughter to an English monarch, her loyalty wasn't necessarily very strong as her father had provided a small dowry when she married James IV.

She married Archibald Douglas, a pro-English man, the year after James IV's death. Parliament didn't look kindly on her quick remarriage, and they also didn't approve of her shifting back and forth between her allegiances. They replaced her as the regent and sent her into exile. She lived her exile out in England, during which time she and her husband became estranged. As such, she had their marriage annulled to allow her to remarry in 1527.

Her third husband was Henry Stewart, who would go on to have a beneficial relationship with his stepson, King James V. James V had taken the role of king directly into his hands by that time. He made his stepfather Lord Malvern and took both him and Margaret on as two of his closest advisors. The relationship of advisors continued for many years until it was discovered that Margaret was betraying both her country and her son.

She had been sending confidential information to her brother, King Henry VIII, in England. Betrayal of state secrets was a major crime, as it is today. As such, James sent her away so that she couldn't participate in political affairs. She remained out of the political sphere until her death in 1541.

James V

He came into power when he was less than a year old in 1513. During his first year, his mother served as his regent. This was followed by John Stewart, the duke of Albany, serving as his regent from 1514 to 1524. His mother was his regent once more from 1524 to 1525. His stepfather, Archibald Douglas, imprisoned the young king from 1526 to 1528 after a brief period of guardianship had lapsed. He did this with the intention of consolidating power for his own benefit.

James escaped the imprisonment and forced Archibald to flee to England. He then took on rule directly, starting with consolidation of the kingdom under his central authority. In 1534 he ratified the Treaty of Perpetual Peace with Henry VIII of England, which had the intention of bringing a truce between the two countries. Four years later he married Mary of Lorraine (also called Mary de Guise), who was a noblewoman from a noble family.

The last few years of his reign, James became more demanding with his taxes. He was strict regarding religious devotion and showed himself to be a harsh individual. In 1542, Henry VIII attacked Scotland, and his nobles didn't support his army. They despised his cruelty and weren't willing to respond to his call to arms, resulting in an easy victory for Henry VIII. He had a mental breakdown and died later that year. His daughter, Mary, Queen of Scots, was born six days after his death.

The Reformation in Scotland

The writings of Martin Luther regarding religious reform started appearing in the 1520s. They didn't gain much traction with the Scots at first because they were a devout Catholic nation and the effects of the Renaissance were only just starting to show. The "Act anent heresy" was passed in 1525, which stated that anyone caught importing or reading the ideas about religious reform would have to forfeit their possessions. This gave Scots even less motivation to alter their behavior.

Things started changing in the late 1520s. Patrick Hamilton, a student who returned from Germany in 1527, started sharing Lutheran ideas. He was burned at St.

Salvador's College in 1528, drawing public attention to what was going on.

The small number of people who had started converting to Protestantism now had a martyr to advocate for their stance. They vandalized multiple Catholic buildings from 1528 to 1532, drawing more attention to their message. Another student with Protestant beliefs was tried and executed in 1533 at St. Salvador's College, giving another martyr for the cause. Further executions were performed at the college in 1538 and 1539, drawing more attention.

The seeming reign of terror of James V resulted in more questioning the status quo of the church and the monarchy. To cool the flames of violence, Mary de Guise took on a tolerant frame of mind toward new religious persuasions. She advocated for Catholicism but didn't fully stop people from exploring the ideas of Protestantism. The attempts at bringing unity between England and Scotland during the early 1540s would have negated an open anti-Protestant policy framework. That said, she didn't try to bring about a better understanding between the religious factions or try to understand her Protestant nobles' perspectives better.

When commitments were renewed with France after moving Mary, Queen of Scots, to live with the French king in 1548, a firmer stance was necessitated. The French were an intensely Catholic country, and their royal family swayed Mary de Guise to take a more anti-Protestant perspective. Further, Mary Tudor was instituted as the queen of England in 1553, which briefly put a Catholic ruler on their throne. This meant that Protestants in Scotland couldn't cross the border to live in a more tolerant country. Tensions rose, and skirmishes became more common. While England reverted to a Protestant country in 1558 under Elizabeth I, this couldn't revert the tension that had been formed in Scotland over the previous five years.

Rebellion broke out in Scotland during 1559. The rebellion started when Mary de Guise took control of Perth. Once it was under her control, she imposed martial law and exacted the Catholic way of worship on its citizens. A boy was killed by her troops in this process, providing a show of brutality that the common people and the Protestants could unite behind against the regent. Further, James Stewart (illegitimate son of James V) retaliated by declaring for the reformers.

Once he declared for them, he conquered both Fife and Edinburgh with the intention of bringing religious change. With his allies, the Lords of the Congregation, Protestant power was exerted in multiple parts of Scotland. Further, Parliament outlawed Catholicism in 1560 and renounced both the legal power and spiritual custodianship of the Pope over the kingdom.

A group of Protestant ministers worked out a series of reforms for the churches of Scotland starting in 1561. John Knox was included among their ranks. When Mary, Queen of Scots, returned to Scotland in the same year (after her mother, Mary de Guise, had died), she walked into a highly conflicted environment. She had been brought up Catholic in France and wished to continue practicing her faith accordingly. That said, she didn't want to upset the powerful Protestant powers of the nation. As such, she worked with her half brother, James Stewart, to create a more religiously tolerant policy for Scotland.

With the turmoil at the end of Mary's reign, largely due to smear campaigns about her love life, she wasn't able to hold onto her power any longer. Her half brother thus took over as regent for her son, James VI, who was crowned after her deposition. He was brought up Protestant, with James Buchanan (of radical Calvinist affiliation) being one of his main tutors. Protestantism had become the common religion of Scotland by the time he started ruling directly. He continued James Stewart's pro-Protestant approach and perhaps took it even further.

He contributed to the reform of the Kirk (the Church of Scotland) by introducing the Episcopacy. This meant that he would choose who would hold the position of bishop. The bishops he chose would then go ahead to govern the church, thus making him their formal leader. He also used the development of the printing press to introduce cheaper Bibles so that almost everyone could get their own copy. Training of ministers was a priority, with him opening the University of Edinburgh to cater to the new demand for a large body of educated Protestant clergy.

He introduced a catechism of questions for churchgoers and ballads that were formed into church songs. Courts of church elders were formed, with the intention of disciplining their congregations. Congregations were expected to behave in a manner that was deemed appropriate and to attend church services regularly. They investigated matters under their jurisdiction, such as sexual offenses, and meted out disciplinary measures to counteract behavior that wasn't appropriate to their codes. With these changes, the Reformation came to an end, and the practice of belief was altered permanently in both England and Scotland.

John Knox

John Knox was likely the most well-known proponent of the Scottish Reformation. He was born in 1514 to a family that had little money. He was dissatisfied with the way society was structured and wanted change. The Catholic church was seen as an institution that had built up a position of power and affluence, partly through corruption (mainly from bribery), yet not providing enough care to adherents in need. Morals were seen as lacking in the Catholic church, and the most important clergy were often foreign.

John approved of the writings of early Protestant authors and later grew to become an ardent supporter of John Calvin. He had many Protestant friends from a young age, with more than one of them being executed for heresy due to their beliefs. This further built on his opinion of the Catholic church being made up of persecutors. His views extended to Mary de Guise and other powerful people whom he saw as capable of making change yet weren't willing to.

While in exile in England, he experienced the Protestant reign of Edward VI. He had a high opinion of the young king and became his royal chaplain. Knox contributed to writing the English book of common prayer. The young king passed away before the prayer book could be issued, and his successor was the Catholic queen Mary Tudor. He criticized the new queen and her religious morality, including finding fault because she was a woman in a position of ruling.

When Elizabeth I was instated, however, the prayer book was published, and she reinstituted Protestantism. He returned to Scotland soon after Elizabeth I's reign started and just before Mary, Queen of Scots, came back from France.

He fought to establish a reformed Protestant church and worked closely with James Stewart and his allies. When Mary, Queen of Scots, returned in 1561, he criticized her reign from the very beginning, largely because of her Catholic affiliation. Gradually the Protestant elements of Scotland gained power, while Mary and the Catholic elements lost theirs. When she was in England after her deposition, Protestantism was made the official religion of Scotland. John died five years after Mary's son, James VI, was born. Before he died, however, he played a part in teaching the boy to take on a Protestant outlook in life (seeing as the boy had been baptized a Roman Catholic).

Mary, Queen of Scots

Mary, Queen of Scots, was born in 1542. Multiple persons of power (including Henry VIII) wanted to take control of her upbringing to both influence her outlooks in life and have the power of regent. Her mother ultimately won and was her first regent. At age five, Mary was sent to France to be brought up in the care of the king of France. Mary's mother was of the Valois and Guise families (both being families of money and power in France), which influenced her decision to send the young queen abroad.

Her life in the court of the French king was sheltered, with many luxuries and a good education made available. For all intents and purposes, she had become a French woman and lost touch with her Scottish identity—even her first language was French. She married Francis II of France a year before he became king of France in 1559, but he died a year later due to an ear condition. She thus returned to Scotland in 1561, after both her husband and mother had died.

Upon her return, the situation of the Protestant and Catholic conflict demanded most of her attention. Further, Francis II's father had claimed the English throne on her behalf when she was a girl, resulting in Elizabeth I having a hostile attitude toward Mary from the start. Mary was a threat to Elizabeth's rule. There was thus tension both locally and with Scotland's more powerful southern neighbor. To pacify the situation, she adopted a position of religious tolerance with the help of her half brother, James Stewart (who was a

Protestant noble).

Four years after her return (1565), Mary married Henry Stewart, Lord Darnley. This poured fuel on the fire because he was disliked by many nobles in the Scottish court. Further, due to both him and Mary being Stewarts (also Stuarts), this made the couple more of a threat to Elizabeth I's rule than they had been individually. James Stewart, who had been one of her closest advisors, was also antipathetic to her new husband.

The year after her marriage (1566), both Lord Darnley and James Stewart were involved in a plot to remove Mary from the throne, along with multiple other nobles. She was heavily pregnant at the time. The first step was to kill David Riccio, one of her confidants and friends, in front of Mary. Lord Darnley withdrew from the plot before it came into fruition, likely because of getting ill and because Mary had given birth to their heir. He died in 1567 after an explosion at his home outside of Edinburgh—with strangulation marks being found around his neck.

Those with vested interests against her started sharing the idea that Mary was responsible for Lord Darnley's death. They stated that she had plotted his death with James Hepburn, the fourth earl of Bothwell. She was further accused of having had an affair with Bothwell at the time of the alleged plotting. When Mary married Bothwell three months after Lord Darnley's death, it lent credence to the accusations, and factions that were against her managed to get her deposed. Her one-year-old son was crowned as her replacement.

After the deposition she was kept under house arrest, which she escaped in 1468 in an attempt to reclaim her throne. This didn't go as planned, so she fled to England soon after to seek refuge with Elizabeth I. Due to Mary's earlier claims to the English throne and factions who were against Elizabeth, she imprisoned Mary to keep her throne safe. The imprisonment lasted for 18 years, during which time Mary wrote requests to be relieved many times. Eventually Mary resorted to conspiring an escape.

The conspiracy involved the remaining Catholic individuals of power in England trying to get her to take the throne. It involved the death of Elizabeth I. Mary might not have been an active conspirator in all of the plan, but the risk the plan posed when discovered gave Elizabeth no choice but to have Mary tried for treason. Mary was tried in an English court of law, which sentenced her to death by beheading in 1587.

With Mary dead and James VI in power, the Stewart line took on not only the Scottish throne but also the English throne. The following period resulted in the union of the crowns and the union of Parliaments. The next chapter will cover the unions and the concurrent Jacobite risings.

CHAPTER 4
THE UNION OF THE CROWNS AND THE UNION OF PARLIAMENTS

Scotland had been a nation holding power in the north of Great Britain for more than a thousand years. Although there had been many attempts to conquer it, none permanently succeeded. In the end, it was the Scots who subjugated their neighbors on the island through the unification of the crowns under James VI.

James VI

James VI was the son of Mary, Queen of Scots, and Lord Darnley. He was born in 1566 and crowned as king in 1567. A range of tutors were used to raise him as his father was dead and his mother was imprisoned for most of his life. Four regents ruled on his behalf before he took direct control of the throne. He took direct control after he was captured in 1582 (age 15) in a plot to place his mother back on the throne, after which he gradually took more control of issuing his own policies.

He pursued an alliance with England in 1585, both in an attempt to ensure peaceful relations between the countries and in an attempt to be nominated by Elizabeth I as her heir. The English were a Protestant nation, which made them a better ally for Scotland as a country with a new bulk of Protestant citizens than the long-term ally that was France (seeing that France was strictly Catholic). When his mother was executed in 1587, he didn't provide any strong protest, but rather prioritized the relationship he'd been maintaining with Elizabeth.

He remained largely uninvolved in the affairs of his Protestant and Catholic nobles, allowing them to exhaust their resources against each other so that he could retain absolute rule without opposition. He believed that he was entitled to his rule by God and declared himself to be the head of the Presbyterian Church of Scotland. When Elizabeth I eventually died without children in 1603, he was named her heir. He was a valid claimant, both due to his line of descent and his faith.

When he took on the English crown, both England and Scotland had a joint ruler. This was called the union of the crowns, and James later stylized himself as being the king of Great Britain. He moved to London and had the affairs of Scotland run through a privy council in his name. He corresponded with them using letters to keep abreast of the happenings of the kingdom. He also had a royal commissioner who represented him at the Scottish Parliament.

While he managed to hold onto the affairs of Scotland without too much trouble, he faced a lot of difficulties as the king of England. He was known to be extravagant and wasn't capable of resolving the debt that had been accrued by England during the wars with Spain under Elizabeth I. He also had multiple disagreements with the English Parliament, partly due to employing multiple poorly chosen advisors. There was also the factor that he didn't understand the English people as well on a cultural level. He couldn't remedy this very easily because the English monarch was expected to remain more distant from the common citizens than the Scottish.

During the last year before his death in 1625, his son and heir, Charlies I, and the duke of Buckingham administered his kingship on his behalf. He had become old and didn't have the necessary capacity to wield the power needed to administer the countries under his dominion (England, Ireland, Scotland, and the colonies).

The Union of the Crowns

When James VI inherited the English crown in 1603, the union of the crowns took place. The crowns of Scotland and England had never before been held by the same person. He soon stylized himself the king of Great Britain and had the

Union Jack created from a combination of St. George's Cross and the Cross of St. Andrew. He tried to convince the English Parliament to remove anti-Scottish legislation and to install pro-Scottish laws, which succeeded on a superficial level. The English Parliament agreed to repeal the most hostile of laws against the Scots.

During this time, the laws of both countries were their own, and they each had their own Parliament (until the Acts of Union in 1707). The economy of each country was completely separate, along with their churches. That said, the same ruler dictated what was to be done in the government of both countries. Further, the conduct of both governments was to be carried out in such a way that it didn't have too heavy a detrimental effect on England.

The effect on the Scottish economy was an overall negative one during the first century after the union. France and the Netherlands were two of Scotland's best long-term trading partners. When they went to war with England, Scotland was prevented from backing them, which resulted in embargoes from those countries against Scotland. Religious affairs of Scotland also received a blow. Gradual changes were implemented that aligned the Scottish Kirk with the structure of the Church of England.

The biggest effect, however, was the absence of James VI (and following monarchs) from Scotland on a physical level. This came to a head with James VI's successor, Charles I. The Scots felt like they had no monarch present and caring for or guiding them, while the English felt that they were being led by a foreign king who didn't understand them.

Charles I

Charles I grew up in Scotland while his family moved to England. He was a shy child who stammered. His manners and temper were both good, and he had no known vices. However, he was out of touch with his citizens because he only mixed with the upper classes and he didn't travel much. As an individual living in a near-ivory tower, his method of connecting with the world was through art and religion.

In 1625, at the age of 25, he inherited the role of king. He believed that God had given him the absolute right to rule. This was a problem in England where Parliament had gained a lot of power in the recent past. Frequent clashes occurred between the king and Parliament throughout his rule, mainly over matters relating to taxation. He was known to dissolve Parliament on more than one occasion. At one point he thought that Parliament was taking on a revolutionary tone, after which he refused to call a new Parliament for 11 years (from 1629 to 1640) and imposed his personal rule on the country.

He had alienated himself from his Scottish nobles by enforcing practices of the Anglican church on them (by introducing a new liturgy and ecclesiastical policy). An assembly of ministers and prominent members of the public took place in Glasgow in 1638, resulting in the National Covenant. This cut off much of Charles's power over the Kirk.

The Bishops' Wars started in 1639 when Charles raised an army to overcome the Scots in an attempt to defy the National Covenant. The Scottish forces were called the Covenanters. The Bishops' Wars were part of the Scottish Revolution, which was part of the Wars of the Three Kingdoms. The Irish Confederate Wars and English Civil Wars were also part of the Wars of the Three Kingdoms—all of which started during the reign of Charles.

The Second Bishops' War took place in 1640, during which Charles experienced a major defeat and had to call the English Parliament to get further backing. The events that unfolded with Parliament led to the English Civil Wars from 1642 to 1651. Parliament and its allies were on the one side, while Charles and his allies were on the other. The Covenanters allied themselves with the English Parliament, and eventually Charles had to give himself up in submission.

He broke free from Parliamentary custody after the Covenanters handed him over to them. After fleeing across Britain, he eventually stationed himself on the Isle of Wight, where he negotiated with his army, the Scots, and the English Parliament to try and broker an understanding in 1647. In

1648 the last Scottish supporters of the king were killed, and in 1649 he was tried and executed for multiple offenses.

Charles II

Charles II was born in 1630 and had a comfortable upbringing during the first few years, including a good education. He was sent to France early in life to escape the violence that was taking place under Charles I's reign. When his father was executed in 1649, the Scottish crowned him their king. This was in violation of the sentiment of Cromwell's government in England. He agreed to the Presbyterian Covenant as a condition of his rule, which was a regulation that was anti-Anglican and anti-Catholic.

Oliver Cromwell was a powerful adversary. The Scots faced his New Model Army in 1650, which resulted in a great victory for the English. Charles II instigated an invasion into England in 1651, which also resulted in defeat for the Scots. The invasion left him with no choice but to flee to France where he had few connections, little access to money, and not many friends. His fortunes would change after Cromwell's death in 1658.

When Cromwell died, it left England with the problem of his strongest allies fighting to take over his position. The drastic solution was to place Charles II on the English throne in 1660, in what is now called the Restoration. He was given the crown on the condition that he meet multiple reforms laid out by Parliament. His rule was known for bringing a better compromise between the multiple religious factions of England—mainly Anglican, Catholic, and Nonconformist.

Little heed was paid to ruling the affairs of Scotland in comparison with those of England. He ruled until his death in 1685. He was succeeded by his brother as he had no legitimate children (although he had 14 illegitimate children, possibly many more).

James VII

James VII was Charles II's brother. He was raised mainly in England, from which he fled in 1648 during the civil war. While abroad, he spent time at the Hague in the Netherlands and then in France. He served in both the Spanish and French militaries. Unlike his brother, James VII was a Catholic. This caused some upheaval when he returned to England, resulting in him being sent to live in Brussels in the 1670s to pacify the public.

After Brussels, he was stationed in Edinburgh as the King's High Commissioner—a post he held from 1679 to 1682. When his brother died in 1685, he inherited both the English and Scottish crowns. He instituted a policy of religious tolerance for Catholics and Nonconformists and placed multiple Catholic individuals in official positions of his government. Unrest started breaking out because of the change from the Protestant state they had grown used to during the rules of his brother, father, grandfather, and Elizabeth I over the previous century.

A group of nobles invited William of Orange, who was married to his Protestant cousin (Mary), to invade England and remove James VII from power. William's invasion took place in 1688, which resulted in the Glorious Revolution. No blood was shed, and James VII fled to France. He tried to regain control of the crown in 1690 with forces that he gathered in Ireland. The forces were defeated at the Battle of the Boyne, after which James VII spent the rest of his life in exile in a palace near Paris.

William III

William of Orange was born in 1650, two weeks after his father passed away. He inherited the position of head of the House of Orange. The house had power, connections, and money. When his mother died when he was 10 years old, the Dutch aristocracy and English royal family both tried to get custodianship of William. Ultimately, he remained in the Netherlands for the rest of his upbringing.

When he was a teenager and into his early twenties, the Netherlands were involved in a lot of warfare. The disaster year struck in 1672 when armies from multiple countries invaded the Netherlands, with the French getting right to its heart. Formalities were abandoned in the aftermath, and William was granted the position of stadtholder (ruler of the nation), adding to his existing role of heading the House of Orange. As stadtholder he formed peace arrangements with France and pacified the English by marrying Mary (the Protestant daughter of James VII).

William became a Protestant figurehead of Europe. He took the time to openly criticize the rule of his father-in-law in England as a Catholic king. Being such a figurehead, having Mary's hand in marriage, and being a grandson of Charles I made William a desirable replacement for James VII. A few nobles thus invited William to invade and depose his father-in-law. After the Glorious Revolution, Mary and William were crowned as joint monarchs of England, Scotland, Ireland, and the other realms of the kingdom in 1689. They ruled together until Mary's death in 1694, after which he ruled alone to his own death in 1702.

Queen Anne

Queen Anne succeeded William of Orange as the crown's last Stuart (Stewart) monarch. She was born in 1665 as the second daughter of James VII (Mary of Orange's younger sister). She was a shy and pleasant individual, but of a sickly constitution. She married George, prince of Denmark, in 1683, with whom she had 17 pregnancies (one of which was successful). Their son, however, died at the age of 11.

As the last Protestant member of the line who was eligible for the throne, she was crowned when William of Orange died in 1702. Much of her rule was controlled by a council that governed on her behalf. During her reign, there were multiple major victories against France, and the union of Parliaments took place under the Acts of Union 1707. This period was one of uprising and violence in Scotland, as the majority of the public and nobles weren't in favor of the union. After she passed away in 1714, the crown moved to the Hanover line of monarchs.

The Union of Parliaments

Unifying Parliaments of Scotland and England started being discussed in earnest in 1702 when Queen Anne took power. It was a hotly debated topic, with all sorts of nobles sending out pamphlets to advocate for their vested interests in the matter. Arguments for joining Parliaments were that it would bring Scotland access to England's colonies and it would reduce the amount of warfare they were exposed to. Those against the merge said that it would damage the country's sovereignty and that parliamentarians living in London would be both out of touch and less accountable to their constituents.

Formal negotiations were entered to determine the provisions of the union in 1706. As the provisions were announced, the existing tension in Scotland was exacerbated. Riots broke out, and the government started introducing regulations that outlawed the formation of crowds in some contexts. Parliamentarians and judges were jeered at by upset crowds. In retaliation people were told to keep their households in check, and punishments were meted out for offenders. In the end, negotiations ended, the Acts of Union were passed, and the Scottish Parliament was dissolved in 1707.

Some of the outcomes from the union were that the royal line of succession would have to run through Protestant rulers, the economies of the countries would be tied together, the legal system of courts of each country would remain under their own jurisdiction, and Scotland would regulate its own educational system. Parliaments were ultimately joined, and parliamentarians were sent to represent Scotland in London.

Jacobite Risings

With the Glorious Revolution, James VII was removed from power in 1688. There were, however, multiple factions that still wanted him in power. The major faction was the Catholic church and its adherents. The Scottish Episcopalians were another as they were able to coexist in a less hostile environment under his rule. Some were also those loyal to the traditional line of Stewart kings. These supporters were called the Jacobites (Jacobite referring to an ancient rendition of the name James).

The Jacobites first rose up in 1689 with an army consisting largely of Highlander forces. They won at the Battle of Killiecrankie—their first major conflict. Further battles were waged during 1689 and 1690, resulting in defeat after defeat against the armies of William of Orange's new government. The Jacobites stayed largely subdued for the next 24 years. In 1714, George I of the Hanover line was placed on the throne.

The first major rising was called the Fifteen (due to it taking place in 1715). During the Fifteen, thousands of Jacobite Highlanders formed into an army and marched south. They faced their opponents in support of the Stewart who would have been king if the crown had remained in the family line— James Edward Stewart. The outcome of the conflict was uncertain, with the Jacobites losing the passion they had for the cause. The passion couldn't be rekindled, even when James Edward Stewart landed in Scotland later that year. It would be 30 years before the next Jacobite rising took place.

In 1745, the charismatic son of James Edward Stewart— fondly called Bonnie Prince Charlie—landed at the Outer Hebrides to start building support for claiming the throne. He gathered a Highlander army that he led to victory against the government's army in Edinburgh. They continued south but couldn't manage to gather enough support in England, so they returned to Scotland. At the Battle of Culloden in 1746, the army faced the troops of the duke of Cumberland along with government soldiers. A bloodbath ensued with Bonnie Prince Charlie's fighters being executed after the battle for treason.

He fled to mainland Europe, and the Jacobite cause didn't gather any future momentum. James Edward Stewart died in 1766, while the Bonnie Prince died in 1788. With their deaths, the cause of the Jacobites went cold.

This chapter looked at the end of an age of passion for the Scottish monarchy and fighting for independence. The next chapter shows how the Scottish refocused during the coming periods of the Industrial Revolution and the Modern Era. A lot was accomplished, and a lot of change took place.

CHAPTER 5
THE MODERN ERA

In this chapter three of the most important parts of Scotland's modern history will be examined. The first is the Industrial Revolution and how it benefited the nation. The Highland Clearances will be the second topic we look into, with a subsection covering how Scotland's diaspora has spread across the globe. The final part will examine how Scottish nationalism has become a more relevant topic over the last century and the key events that have taken place along this line.

The Industrial Revolution in Scotland

Prior to the Industrial Revolution, Scotland had a rural and agricultural economy. This was set to change when the Chemical Revolution took place in the 1750s. At the time, a professor of chemistry for the universities of Edinburgh and Glasgow (Joseph Black) had made a discovery. He had isolated carbon dioxide, which he detailed in a thesis he published in 1756. This thesis had the deeper significance of showing that you could isolate elements from a substance to make them purer. The discovery led to a small boom of isolating other elements, specifically oxygen, hydrogen, chlorine, and nitrogen.

Making use of these discoveries, Joseph worked with another professor (William Cullen) to form a substance from chlorine that would speed up the process of linen bleaching. The efficiency of the bleaching process made Scotland a more competitive nation in the linen industry. Soon other developments were incorporated into the process of linen making, advancements that had mainly come from England. They included the water frame, the spinning jenny, and the mule. A resultant rapid increase in the linen production industry made Scotland a global industry leader.

Soon thereafter, the factory system was developed in Scotland. It made use of cheap labor, combined with machine production, to produce large amounts of linen more efficiently. Cotton largely replaced linen as it could be made into finer cloth. Imports of cotton obtained from India and other English colonies were processed in the Scottish factories (mainly by women and child labor at low rates of pay). Final products were then exported to European and American markets, establishing an international trade route in the process.

The next major industry in which Scotland became a leader was tobacco supply. Agents took tools and other developments to the American and West Indies plantations and obtained tobacco in return. The developments and tools led to more efficient production of tobacco and better stockpiles.

Soon a system developed wherein the Scottish agents would pick up slaves in Africa; then take the slaves, tools, and other things to the plantations in the West; and return with tobacco from the stockpiles on the plantations. When the stockpiles reached Scotland, tobacco would be sold to markets in Europe and beyond. In short order, they dominated the tobacco trade due to faster turnaround times than those of other tobacco traders in other nations. The sugar industry soon followed in the same fashion.

Developments took place in the banking industry because of this increase in trade. The banks in Scotland had large amounts of money from the trade and industry taking place. As such, they innovated things such as the bank overdraft. During the same era, a Scotsman named Adam Smith wrote The Wealth of Nations—the book that formed the foundation of capitalism. With the innovations taking place in the Scottish economy and banking sector, he developed the principles that guide free trade up to this day.

A last major Industrial Revolution development from Scotland was attributable to James Watt. He advanced the technology of steam engines, allowing them to work more efficiently. Less water would be required to power engines and factories as a result, while their output became more powerful. Soon the first passenger steamship was made (1812), after which Scotland would later become the world's most productive manufacturer of ships. The first steam train was also innovated, leading to railways, which formed the backbone of cheap transport for the world's developing industries.

The Highland Clearances and the Scottish Diaspora

From the 1750s, large farming estates of the Highlands started undergoing processes to make them more efficient. They were drained and enclosed, crop rotation was implemented on a large scale, and cattle were swapped with sheep. Farm outputs and profits increased, but this would all come at the expense of the comfort and livelihoods of families.

In the 1780s, the populations of farms were relocated to other parts of the estate, usually to small farms called crofts on the seaside. The people were evicted (sometimes by burning down their past homes on the estate) with the expectation that they would make their livelihoods on fishing and kelping. They were to provide rent for the crofts they were allotted.

The developments of the Industrial Revolution contributed to the situation. The mindset that production was everything had taken hold, and land efficiency became more important than ever. Those that got in the way were a necessary sacrifice in return for profit.

Successful urbanization had taken place in lower parts of the country, so many Highland estate owners thought they could produce the same results. The changes in the economic situation of the relocated Highlanders were serious because the crofts could not provide the output they needed to support their food requirements. To make matters worse, the Great Highland Famine took place in the mid-nineteenth century, with blight affecting the potato harvests.

The result was the croft communities couldn't support themselves and needed to rely on charity for survival and they couldn't afford the rent due to estate owners for use of the crofts. The kinder landowners paid for the relocation of their tenants to better lands to the southern areas of Scotland, while more cruel landowners simply evicted them. The lower population, along with other economic factors, meant that croft settlements could sustain themselves for the third quarter of the nineteenth century and could pay their rent. Soon, however, depression hit and weather conditions had a negative impact on their output. The Crofters' War of the 1880s resulted.

The government and general public sympathized with and even supported the crofters, with a solution being demanded. The solution came in the form of a government investigation, followed by passing of the Crofters Holdings (Scotland) Act. It provided holistic interventions that offered some relief. Rental debt from crofters was adjudicated and adjusted, payment plans were worked out, security was provided against eviction, the Crofters Commission was established to judge disputes between landlords and crofters, and crofters were allowed to keep the benefits of extensions to their crofts.

By the end of the nineteenth century, further government provisions were made to alleviate conditions. The government purchased some of the land from their landlords with the intention of benefiting the crofters. Both agricultural and transportation infrastructure were improved. This solution was partly successful, but problems still remained. A definite sense of class division developed, along with the sense that lords of Highland land didn't care about their people. The Highlands are still dotted with the shells of buildings that were evicted in the clearances.

The Spread of the Scottish Diaspora

There had been a spread of Scottish people to other countries throughout the nation's history. A notable example is the settling of Scottish mercenaries in France after the Auld Alliance.

The formation of the Ulster Plantation and other plantations in Ireland during the sixteenth and seventeenth centuries led to more displacement of the Scottish. The English government wanted to make sure that the Irish were subdued by spreading English and Scottish people and ideas in their midst. They disestablished many Irish communities, particularly those that fell on the lands of nobles who had supported anti-English movements. Not only was it useful for the government to bring a more direct non-Irish presence in their homeland but it was used as an opportunity to get rid of people who were causing trouble in Scotland. Many of the more independent-minded people of the Highlands were forcibly removed to the plantations where they were to establish their own communities among the Irish and English.

The number increased during the time of the Industrial Revolution. Many of the people involved in trade or being agents of other people or organizations (such as in the tobacco trade) found that they could establish comfortable lives abroad for themselves and their families. Permanent settlement wasn't too uncommon an occurrence. Add to this the exodus of people from northern and western Scotland during the Highland Clearances, and many people jumped on opportunities to settle where they would have better chances of comfortable living. The fact remains, however, that there were people from other regions of Scotland who also wanted to seek their own place in the wide world.

Immigration from Scotland has remained steady throughout the Late Modern Era. People leave the country mainly to move to other parts of the United Kingdom, Canada, Australia, or New Zealand. People's reasons vary, but the fact remains that even at present more than 20% of those born in Scotland have immigrated (The Scotsman, 2016).

The Rise of Scottish Nationalism and the Current Political Situation in Scotland

Nationalism existed throughout the history of Scotland. Support of the identity of the nation was important to individuals throughout the ages. This started right from the creation of Alba, or perhaps earlier. National pride increased through the centuries, and symbols of the Scottish nation served to unify its people.

The crown (and royal family) was one such symbol, the Stone of Destiny another, as well as the Scottish flag. There were many others. Their unique identity set them apart from neighbors like the Irish, English, or groups that could have been their predecessors (e.g., the Picts). It united all people of the nation, from the townies in southern Scotland to the Highlanders of the north.

The Scottish nation's sense of self remained in spite of the trouble it had faced with English overlordship since before the Wars of Scottish Independence. When the crown was joined with that of England under James VI, the Scottish identity remained. The unification of Parliaments under Queen Anne didn't sway the distinctiveness of the Scottish nation. Neither did intermarrying the royal family with other regal families—such as Mary's (Queen of Scots) marriage to Francis II of France.

Failure to establish a colony in Panama (in the seventeenth century), known as the Darien scheme, could have destroyed the country's morale. However, it served to bring its citizens closer because they knew they weren't helped in their hour of need and they knew their English-centered monarch wasn't going to advance their well-being as much as they could themselves. The Darien scheme involved investments from almost every individual in Scotland who was able to donate a bit of money. When the settlement failed because of financial trouble (from English and foreign investors pulling out), illness, and a rough environment, the Scottish rallied and focused on forming a strong nation locally.

The Jacobite risings of the seventeenth and eighteenth centuries were an endeavor largely the result of Scottish nationalism. The forces of the risings were made up largely of Highlanders who were loyal to the Stuart (Stewart) family as it originally held power in Scotland. When these failed and the union was sealed, the Kirk (Church of Scotland) became the nation's uniting symbol by enforcing its separateness from the Anglican church and becoming a center of guidance for both nobles and common people. The Industrial Revolution of the eighteenth century also became a uniting force.

Scotland started advancing faster than almost any other nation in the world in science and other spheres. They were miles ahead of England in terms of new discoveries and the presence of tertiary education institutions. The nation was becoming highly urbanized and had become a world leader in the linen, sugar, and tobacco trades. Infrastructure was being implemented at a rate never seen before, with Scottish cities becoming global urban front-runners.

Home rule became a more enticing prospect during the nineteenth century. Scotland had been an active member of the United Kingdom during the advances of the Industrial Revolution and Late Modern Period, with benefits from England and its Commonwealth being clear. Despite the benefits, a locally based government would possibly be more accountable and provide better service to its people, and a local parliament would bring more relevant legislation. Further, warfare with Ireland as it was fighting for independence showed that there weren't as many benefits to staying in the United Kingdom as they had thought. The independence that Ireland won at the start of the twentieth century showed independence to have its own benefits, even for a nation that had been a long-term member of the United Kingdom.

The Scottish Nationalist Party was formed in 1934. It gained gradual support over the next two decades, with infighting being the major problem to its initial growth. The expansion of the party slowed, and it didn't hold much influence until the 1970s when oil was discovered off the Scottish coast—oil that could provide a veritable economic goldmine. The referendum of 1979 for devolution of Parliament garnered a lot of support, but not enough for anything to materialize. A referendum was executed again in 1997, this time with a successful vote.

Parliament was devolved, with its first sitting in 1999 in Edinburgh. Progress started snowballing, with the Scottish Nationalist Party gaining the majority government of Scotland in 2011, resulting in another referendum in 2014 for total independence. The referendum had 45% support from voters, showing that nearly half of the country wanted full autonomy. Despite not gaining full independence, further powers were given to the Scottish Parliament to regulate its own affairs. While it's not clear whether full autonomy will occur or not, the topic is certainly an engaging one to observe.

CONCLUSION

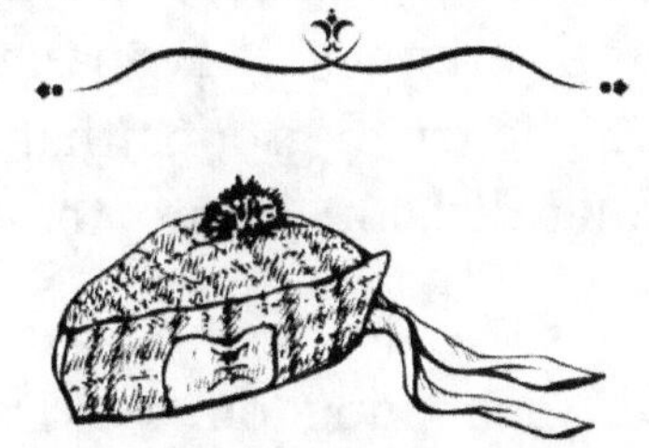

This book delved into the deepest parts of Scottish history. The prehistoric people who settled in the area of the modern nation were examined in depth. You were shown how they lived their lives and what types of tools they used to survive. The development of those people and further migrations into the area during the New Stone Age, Bronze Age, and Iron Age were surveyed. Once the prehistoric peoples had been analyzed, we looked at the prehistoric Celtic tribes that settled where Scotland is today.

The Celtic tribes were scanned one by one. Not much is known about the tribes as they used oral traditions rather than written records. That said, archeological evidence and writings from Roman records gave some idea about their identities. The attempts of the Romans to overcome the northernmost tribes of Britain showed that they might have had some military success, but they were never able to keep the tribes completely under their control. The tribal groups that managed to keep their identities strong developed into the Scotti, Picts, and Britons.

The Scotti and their kingdom of Dalriada were the predecessors of the Scottish nation today. While the Picts provided strong opponents, they seemed to have been absorbed into the Scotti kingdom, resulting in the formation of Alba. The Brittonic tribes of the Scottish regions—mainly Strathclyde—were overcome and likewise absorbed into the cultural union of the Scotti and Picts. The kingdom that emerged was first called Alba, and then the name gradually changed to Scotland.

The royal line of Alba and Scotland was documented, showing the major impacts of each monarch. The historical developments, uprisings, and periods that took place during their reigns were linked to each other. The main characters of those events, such as the Scottish Reformation, were briefly discussed to give a more complete understanding of the times. This culminated in a review of the end of the monarchy's presence in Scotland with the union of the crowns and the union of Parliaments.

The birth of Scotland as a nation without a figurehead in the country meant the Kirk became its central institution. The warfare that resulted to protect the Kirk and attempts to bring the Stewart line of monarchs back into power showed how the identity of the nation had remained prominent throughout the centuries. This led to looking at the developments of the Modern Era that impacted Scotland as a state—the Industrial Revolution, the Highland Clearances, and strengthened Scottish nationalism.

Scotland was a key player in the Industrial Revolution. There were so many discoveries made, with some of the ones included in the book being isolation of chemical elements, enhancement of production with the factory process, and improved linen and cotton production methodologies. The wealth this brought into the nation led to a focus on efficiency and building the wealth of the nation. One of the unfortunate effects of this was the Highland Clearances, in which the rights of humans were relegated to a junior level next to efficient use of land and financial profits.

As a result of the Highland Clearances and other circumstances, both nationally and internationally, immigration became a norm. This was partly due to the opportunities that were available as a result of being a member of the United Kingdom and reaping the benefits of her colonies. Despite this, the identity of Scotland as a sovereign state gradually regained support. Over the last century, nationalism has become a more relevant issue, resulting in the devolution of the Scottish Parliament in 1999 and more than one referendum regarding independent governance.

This book showed the key historical events and figures of Scotland. The information wasn't made unnecessarily complex, yet it also wasn't presented in an oversimplified manner. The aim was to present the material in a neutral fashion, but focusing mainly on Scottish history itself, rather than the history of the United Kingdom, England, or other players. Where information about other nations was included, it was to provide context of impacts directly within Scotland. With a deeper understanding of its history, it was shown that the Scottish people have a far more complex and sophisticated heritage than they are often made out to have.

With this book, it is our hope that you both enjoyed learning about the past of this nation and gained a perspective as to where the nation is advancing toward. There are many nuances to the Scottish race, whom you now have a well-rounded perspective about.

LIST OF SCOTTISH KINGS AND QUEENS

Scota (with the Egyptian name Neferubity, who was a daughter of the fictional pharaoh Chencres, who is possibly the historical pharaoh Thutmose I) and Gaythelos (a Greek prince) were said to be the original founders of what would become the Scottish nation. They sailed away from Egypt and landed in the Iberian Peninsula. The couple had, among other children, a son named Hyber. He was said to be the one whom the ancient name of Ireland—Hibernia—comes from. They established a city named Brigancia (possibly the modern city of A Coruña).

It is said that there were multiple generations that lived in Brigancia. A lot of warfare took place with the local people of Iberia, with some of Scota's descendants and their followers deciding to leave. Some settled in Ireland, and others traveled further to settle in Scotland. Scota and Gaythelos were thus thought to be the progenitors of the Scottish nation, including the monarchs.

Mythical monarchs prior to the founding of alba

Before common era

- Fergus I (330–305)

- Feritharis (305–290)

- Mainus (290–261)

- Dornadilla (261–233)

- Nothatus (233–213)

- Reutherus (213–187)

- Reutha (187-170)

- Thereus (170–161)

- Josina (161–137)

- Finnanus (137–107)

- Durstus (107–98)

- Evenus I (98–79)

- Gillus (79–77)

- Evenus II (77–60)

- Ederus (60–12)

- Evenus III (12–4)

- Metallanus (4 B.C.E.-35)

Common era

- Caratacus (35–55)

- Corbred I (55–72)

- Dardanus (72–76)

- Corbred II (76–110)

- Luctacus (110–113)

- Mogaldus (113–149)

- Conarus (149–163)

- Ethodius I (163–195)

- Satrael (195–199)

- Donald I (199–216)

- Ethodius II (216–231)

- Athirco (231–242)

- Nathalocus (242–253)

- Indochus (253–264)

- Donald II (264–265)
- Donald III (265–277)
- Crathilinthus (277–301)
- Fincormachus (301–348)
- Romachus (348–351)
- Angusianus (351–353)
- Fethelmacus (353–357)
- Eugenius I (357–404)
- Fergus II (404–420)
- Eugenius II (420–452)
- Dongardus (452–457)
- Constantine I (457–479)
- Congallus I (479–501)
- Goranus (501–535)
- Eugenius III (535–558)
- Congallus II (558–568)
- Kinnatellus (568–569)
- Aidanus (569–604)
- Kenneth I (604–605)
- Eugenius IV (605–622)
- Ferchard I (622–635)
- Donald IV (635–648)
- Ferchard II (648–668)

- Maldvinus (668–684)

- Eugenius V (684–688)

- Eugenius VI (688–698)

- Amberkelethus (698–699)

- Eugenius VII (699-716)

- Mordacus (716–731)

- Etfinus (731–761)

- Eugenius VIII (761–764)

- Fergus III (764–767)

- Solvathius (767–787)

- Achaius (787–819)

- Congallus III (819–824)

- Dongallus (824–830)

- Alpinus (830–833)

Monarchs from the founding of alba to the unification of the crowns

- Kenneth I MacAlpin (843–858)

- Donald I (858–862)

- Constantine I (862–877)

- Aed (877–878)

- Eochaid and Giric (878-889)

- Donald II (889–900)

- Constantine II (900–943)

- Malcolm I (943–954)
- Indulf (954–962)
- Dub (962–967)
- Culen (967–971)
- Kenneth II (971–995)
- Constantine III (995–997)
- Kenneth III (997–1005)
- Malcolm II (1005–1034)
- Duncan I (1034–1040)
- Macbeth (1040–1057)
- Lulach (1057–1058)
- Malcolm III Canmore (1058–1093)
- Donald Bane (1093–1094)
- Duncan II (1093–1094)
- Donald Bane (1094–1097)
- Edgar (1097–1107)
- Alexander I (1107–1124)
- David I (1124–1153)
- Malcolm IV (1153–1165)
- William I the Lion (1165–1214)
- Alexander II (1214–1249)
- Alexander III (1249–1286)
- Margaret, Maid of Norway (1286–1290)

- John Balliol (1292–1296)

- Robert I the Bruce (1306–1329)

- David II (1329–1371)

- Robert II (1371–1390)

- Robert III (1390–1406)

- James I (1406–1437)

- James II (1437–1460)

- James III (1460–1488)

- James IV (1488–1513)

- James V (1513–1542)

- Mary, Queen of Scots (1542–1567)

- James VI (1567–1625)

- (The union of the crowns occurred under James VI, resulting in a joint monarchy between England and Scotland.)

LIST OF MAJOR BATTLES AND WARS

- Mons Graupius (84)

- Battle of Degsastan (603)

- Battle of Nechtansmere (685)

- Battle of Athelstaneford (832)

- McAlpin's Treason (841) (legend—likely untrue)

- Battle of Brunanburh (937)

- Battle of Luncarty (980)

- Battle of Mortlach (1010)

- Battle of Carham (1018)

- Battle of Lumphanan (1057)

- Battle of Essie (1058)

- Battle of Alnwick (1093)

- Battle of Mondynes (1094)

- Battle of the Standard (1138)

- Battle of Largs (1263)

- Battle of Dunbar (1296) (First War of Scottish Independence)

- Capture of Kinclaven Castle (1297) (First War of Scottish Independence)

- Battle of Stirling Bridge (1297) (First War of Scottish Independence)

- Battle of Falkirk (1298) (First War of Scottish Independence)

- Siege of Caerlaverock Castle (1300) (First War of Scottish Independence)

- Battle of Roslin Glen (1303) (First War of Scottish Independence)

- Siege of Stirling Castle (1304) (First War of Scottish Independence)

- Battle of Methven (1306) (First War of Scottish Independence)

- Battle of Dalry (1306)

- Battle of Loudoun Hill (1307) (First War of Scottish Independence)

- Battle of Glentrool (1307) (First War of Scottish Independence)

- Battle of Barra (1308) (First War of Scottish Independence)

- Battle of the Pass of Brander (1308) (First War of Scottish Independence)

- Battle of Bannockburn (1314) (First War of Scottish Independence)

- Battle of Dundalk (1318) (First War of Scottish Independence)

- Battle of Old Byland (1322) (First War of Scottish Independence)

- The Weardale Campaign (1327) (First War of Scottish Independence)

- Battle of Teba (1330)

- Battle of Dupplin Moor (1332) (Second War of Scottish Independence)

- Battle of Annan (1332) (Wars of the Three Kingdoms)

- Battle of Kinghorn (1332)

- Battle of Halidon Hill (1333) (Second War of Scottish Independence)

- Battle of Culblean (1335) (Second War of Scottish Independence)

- Battle of Neville's Cross (1346) (Second War of Scottish Independence)

- Battle of Nesbit Moor (1355)

- Battle of Benrig (1380) (Second War of Scottish Independence)

- Battle of Otterburn (1388) (Anglo-Scottish Wars)

- Battle of the Clans (1396)

- Battle of Nesbit Moor (1402)

- Battle of Homildon Hill (1402) (Hundred-Year War)

- Battle of Harlaw (1411)

- Battle of Yeavering (1415)

- Battle of Lochaber (1429)

- First Battle of Inverlochy (1431)

- Battle of Piperdean (1436)

- Battle of Sark (1448) (Hundred-Year War)

- Battle of Brechin Muir (1452)

- Battle of Clachnaharry (1454)

- Battle of Arkinholm (1455)

- Siege of Roxburgh (1460)

- Battle of Tannach Moor (1464)

- Battle of Bloody Bay (1480)

- Battle of Lochmaben Fair (1484)

- Battle of Sauchieburn (1488)

- Battle of Gartalunane (1489)

- Battle of Flodden (1513)

- Battle of Hornshole (1514)

- Battle of Melrose (1526)

- Battle of Linlithgow Bridge (1526)

- Battle of Solway Moss (1542)

- Battle of the Shirts (1544)

- Battle of Ancrum Moor (1545) (War of the Rough Wooing)

- Battle of Pinkie Cleugh (1547)

- Siege of Haddington (1548) (War of the Rough Wooing)

- Battle of Corrichie (1562)

- Battle of Carberry Hill (1567)

- Battle of Langside (1568) (Marian Civil War)

- Lang Siege (1571) (Marian Civil War)

- Battle of Tillieangus (1571) (Marian Civil War)

- Redeswire Raid (1575)

- Eigg Massacre (1577)

- Blar Na Leine (1578)

- Blar Milleadh Garaidh (1578)

- Battle of Glenlivet (1594)

- Battle of Glenfruin (1603)

- Loch Earn Raid (1620)

- Battle of Megray Hill (1639) (First Bishops' War)

- Battle of Newburn Ford (1640) (Second Bishops' War)

- Battle of Tippermuir (1644) (Wars of the Three Kingdoms)

- Battle of Aberdeen (1644) (Wars of the Three Kingdoms)

- Battle of Inverlochy (1645) (Wars of the Covenant)

- Battle of Auldearn (1645) (Scottish Civil War)

- Battle of Alford (1645) (Scottish Civil War)

- Battle of Kilsyth (1645) (Scottish Civil War)

- Battle of Philiphaugh (1645) (Scottish Civil War)

- Battle of Mauchline Moor (1648) (Scottish Civil War)

- Battle of Preston (1648) (English Civil Wars)

- Battle of Carbisdale (1650) (Wars of the Three Kingdoms)

- Battle of Dunbar (1650) (English Civil Wars)

- Battle of Worcester (1651) (English Civil Wars)

- Battle of Pitreavie (1651)

- Battle of Dundee (1651) (English Civil Wars)

- Battle of Inverkeithing (1651) (Wars of the Three Kingdoms)

- Battle of Dalnaspidal (1654) (Wars of the Three Kingdoms)

- Battle of Strone Nevis (1654)

- Battle of Rullion Green (1666) (Wars of the Three Kingdoms)

- Battle of Drumclog (1679) (Scottish Covenanter Wars)

- Battle of Bothwell Bridge (1679) (Scottish Covenanter Wars)

- Battle of Airds Moss (1680)

- The Glorious Revolution (1688) (nobody died, giving it the alternate name of the Bloodless Revolution)

- Battle of Mulroy (1688)

- Battle of Killiecrankie (1689) (Jacobite risings)

- Battle of Dunkeld (1689) (Jacobite risings)

- Battle of Boyne (1690) (Jacobite risings)

- Battle of Cromdale (1690) (Jacobite risings)

- Glencoe Massacre (1692)

- Battle of Sheriffmuir (1715) (Jacobite risings)

- Battle of Preston (1715) (Jacobite risings)

- Battle of Glenshiel (1719) (Jacobite risings)

- Glasgow Malt-Tax Riots (1725)

- Porteous Riots (1736)

- Battle of Prestonpans (1745) (Jacobite risings)

- Battle of Inverurie (1745) (Jacobite risings)

- Battle of Falkirk Muir (1746) (Jacobite risings)

- Battle of Culloden (1746) (Jacobite risings)

- Battle of the Braes (1882)

WALES HISTORY

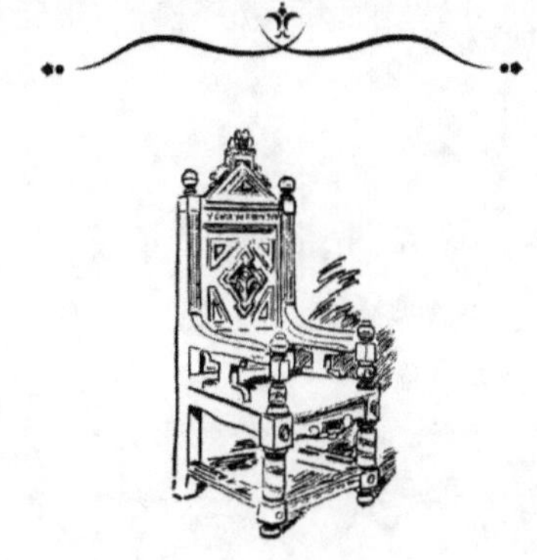

INTRODUCTION

Nestling between rugged mountains and sweeping coastlines lies a land steeped in legend and lore, where the echoes of centuries past resonate in every valley and hillside. This is Wales, a unique nation that is as rich and varied as its rugged landscape. From the ancient Celts who left such a mark on its history and culture to the bustling modern cities of today, Wales has a colourful history to discover as it has witnessed the rise and fall of kingdoms and the clash of empires. Through all these difficult times, the Welsh continued to forge their own strong and incomparable national identity.

Wales (Cymru) is one of the four countries in the United Kingdom. Wales is known for its beautiful countryside that is dotted with castles and other fortifications that are the legacy of the country's long and rich history. Wales is situated in the western part of Great Britain and is surrounded on three sides by water, with its border with England running down its eastern side. Wales is not a large country, as it has an area covering just 20,779m². Nevertheless, it is a memorable one with valleys, misty mountains and dramatic rocky coastlines.

Its people are rightly proud of their Welsh heritage and it is something they have fought hard to maintain over the centuries.

The story of Wales begins many centuries ago in prehistoric times. Archaeologists have discovered that the first footprints on Welsh soil were made by pre-Celtic tribes. During the Iron Age, the country saw the emergence of Celtic tribes that would not only leave their distinctive mark on the countryside, but also on its culture.

Britain was invaded by the Romans in the 1st century AD. They marched westwards to Wales and swept the country into the Roman Empire. The Romans left their marks on the country as during their occupation, they constructed excellent roads, forts and settlements. Notable sites like Caerwent and Caerleon were built and can still be seen today.

Following the fall of the Roman Empire, Wales witnessed the incursions of the Anglo-Saxons and other Germanic tribes. This era was marked by political fragmentation and saw the emergence of many native Welsh kingdoms - each one vying for supremacy. The story of Wales is one of resilience and resistance, as the Welsh people stood firmly against both the Roman invaders and Norman conquerors, fiercely defending their language, culture, and way of life.

It was during the Mediaeval period that Wales became a nation in its own right, with the Welsh princes ruling from powerful castles like Caernarfon and Harlech. Wales was caught in the middle between ambitious English kings and the bitter rivalries of its own princes. Despite all the conflict, this was a time that was rich in music, poetry and dance. The situation culminated in the conquest of much of the country by Edward I and this resulted in much of Wales being brought under English law.

As well as conflict and conquest, the history of Wales is also defined by the steadfast determination of its people to preserve their identity and traditions. Throughout the centuries of English domination that followed, the Welsh language has endured and is still proudly spoken by millions of people across the country. From the industrial heartlands of South Wales to the remote rural communities of the north, Wales remains a nation united by its common heritage and a strong sense of belonging.

As the 20th century drew to a close, it marked a new chapter in the history of Wales. 1999 saw the devolution of powers to the National Assembly for Wales (Senedd Cymru) and the promise of more significant social and political changes for the country. Today, Wales remains a proud and now independent nation within the United Kingdom that embraces its own unique and vibrant history and culture.

Every year more than one million visitors explore the beautiful landscapes of Wales and discover the country's colourful cultural tapestry. They find that Wales is steeped in history at every turn. From the peaks of Snowdonia to the sandy beaches of the Gower peninsula, there are traces of the country's history and visitors soon become immersed in its vivid myths and legends.

You too can make this fascinating journey. Join me now as we embark on a journey through the centuries where the country's ancient landscapes resonate with the words of the Welsh national anthem 'Hen Wlad Fy Nhadau" - "Land of my Fathers" – which reveals the passionate and enduring spirit of its people.....

CHAPTER 1
ANCIENT BEGINNINGS

The story of Wales begins millions of years ago, during the last Ice Age, when massive sheets of ice covered much of the Northern Hemisphere. Glaciers sculpted the Welsh landscape and left behind numerous iconic features that can still be seen today. Such classic glacial features as u-shaped valleys, cirques, and rugged mountainous terrain, demonstrate the force of the glaciers that shaped the hills and valleys of Wales.

The geography of Wales has changed very little since then and the features carved by the glacial ice can still be seen today. The country has a mountainous backbone with Snowdonia in the north-west which includes the five peaks of Mt Snowdon. At 1,085m (3,560 feet) Yr Wyddfa, is the highest of these peaks and the highest in Wales. The Brecon Beacons in the south of the country have been carved from red sandstone with Pen y Fan (886m/ 2,906 feet) being its highest peak.

The best place to study the features of glaciation is the Snowdonia National Park, which is home to Mount Snowdon.

The park showcases all the classic features of glaciation including pyramidal peaks, striated rock surfaces, and glacial moraines.

Earliest civilisations

The earliest civilisations in Wales pre-date the arrival of the Celts, but information about them is shrouded in mystery because of limited archaeological evidence. These early inhabitants are often referred to as 'pre-Celtic' or the indigenous people of Wales and their communities evolved over several millennia. There are scant remnants of their existence, so it is hard for historians and archaeologists to give a comprehensive narrative of their lives. Nonetheless, ongoing research and archaeological excavations continue to provide more insight into the ancient communities of Wales.

The oldest archaeological find

The oldest artefact found to date is believed to be 230,000 years old. It is a jawbone of the Neanderthal species of humans that was found in the Valley of Elwy in Northern Wales. Excavations that took place in the Pontnewydd Cave which is situated near St Asaph uncovered simple stone tools as well as some human teeth – both are now exhibited in the National Museum of Wales.

One of the prominent pre-Celtic groups who lived in ancient Wales was closely linked with the Beaker culture, which was named after their distinctive pottery vessels. This culture emerged during the late Neolithic and early Bronze Age (2,500 BC – 1,800 BC). The Beaker people are believed to have originated from continental Europe - possibly from the Iberian Peninsula. They were talented and introduced the use of bronze for making hand tools and weapons. Archaeological sites including Penywyrlod in Powys and Gaer Fawr in Pembrokeshire have both revealed artefacts that are characteristic of the Beaker culture and also revealed their burial traditions. It is believed that Wales was not continuously inhabited until about 9,000BC.

Mesolithic habitants

Another pre-Celtic group that habited Wales in ancient times is associated with the Mesolithic period (8,800BC - 4,500BC) and marked by the construction of huge stone structures. Wales has numerous megalithic sites, some of which can be explored today. with burial chambers and standing stones. A number of ancient burial chambers, standing stones, and stone circles are dotted across the Welsh landscape. Pentre Ifan, is a Neolithic burial chamber in Pembrokeshire. These sites give archaeologists a greater understanding of the community's rituals, spirituality, and possibly its social structure.

The Iron Age

The Iron Age in Wales began around 700 BC and saw the construction of numerous hill forts as cultural and defensive centres. The people of this era are often referred to as the

Celtic tribes (more about the Celtic period in Chapter 2), although their distinct identities and cultural practices varied across regions. The hill fort at Tre'r Ceiri on the Llŷn Peninsula is one of the most well-preserved and impressive examples, offering insights into the organisation of Iron Age societies in Wales.

Archaeological evidence suggests there was a degree of continuity between the pre-Celtic and Celtic periods; challenging the idea that there was an abrupt cultural shift. It is likely that the indigenous people interacted with incoming

Celts rather than experiencing a displacement. The Celtic tribes are thought to have originated from central Europe and their migration westward brought changes in language, social structures and artistic expression.

CHAPTER 2
THE ARRIVAL OF CELTS

The Celts were a number of groups of Indo-European people who shared similarities in their culture and language. They formed an extensive network right across ancient Europe. The term "Celts" is usually used to describe these various tribes and communities rather than referring to a single, homogenous group. The name Celt came from the Greek word Keltoi and the Roman Celtai, and was used to describe 'people of continental Europe' who were neither Greeks or Romans.

The Celts emerged in the late Bronze Age and Iron Age, with their influence spanning from the 8th century BC to the Roman conquests in the 1st century AD. The origin of the Celts is complex and some historians believe they originated in central Europe. Importantly, by the 8th century BC, Celtic-speaking groups had begun to expand across Europe, reaching as far west as the Iberian Peninsula, east to Anatolia, and northwards to the British Isles.

All parts of the island of Britain that lay south of the Firth of Forth, were inhabited by Celts who spoke versions of the same language – Brittonic. The Celts lived in Wales from 600BC until AD43 when the Roman Invasion of Northern Wales took place. In England, the Celts established various tribal societies. Notable among these were the Britons, who inhabited much of what is now England, and the Belgae, who settled in the south-east of England. The Celts were well-established in England by the time of Julius Caesar's expeditions in the 1st century AD.

The Celtic migration into Wales occurred during the Iron Age, with evidence suggesting a gradual and steady movement rather than a sudden influx. The exact timing and mechanisms of this migration remains unknown but archaeological findings, linguistic analysis, and historical accounts indicate that the Celts entered Wales over several centuries, starting around the 7th century BC. A number of Celtic tribes started to emerge in Wales- each with its own distinct identity and culture.

By the time the Romans began their occupation of Britain, the Celts in Wales had established a mosaic of different tribal communities, each contributing to the rich tapestry of Welsh history.

Who were the Celts?

Celtic history has significantly coloured the heritage and culture of Wales – and also Scotland and Ireland. The Celts were strong and brave warriors, who believed in spirits found in the Welsh mountains, forest, rivers and springs.

The Celts lived in four main tribes in Wales: The Ordovices were mainly in the north-west, the Deceangli in the north-east, the Silures were located in the south-east and the Demetae in the south-west.

The different tribes in Wales had the same language and traditions as other Celtic tribes in Britain. The Celts built hill forts which they surrounded with deep ditches to protect them and lived in clans – extended families. Their houses were round and made of wattle and daub with dirt floors and pitched thatched roofs. The Celts were surprisingly sophisticated and used early forms of combs, razors and hair decorations. They were also religious, worshipping many different gods.

Celtic art

The Celts were very artistic and made many beautiful stone carvings and intricate metal work. Celtic designs in precious metals can be found in museums. Celtic art gives a good insight into how they viewed their surroundings and their gods. The style of Celtic art found in Wales is called La Tène art and developed from 500 BC onwards.  Some excellent examples of this can be seen in the National Museum in Cardiff.

The earliest example of Celtic art found in Wales is the Cerrig-y-Drudion bowl which was found in a grave in the county of Conwy in 1924. Interestingly, the grave had been lined with stone. Some of the designs used in Celtic art appear very frequently. The moon-shaped plaque from Llyn Cerrig Bach is decorated with an elaborate belletrist – a three-legged design, with the legs radiating from a central point. The belletrist is thought to represent the relationship between the living, the dead and the gods.

Celtic hill forts

There are more than 1,000 Celtic hill forts to be seen today in Wales. Some of them are just outlines on hilltops, but one of the most fascinating is Castell Henllys, which has scale reconstructions of Iron Age roundhouses and runs a series of workshops with Iron Age themes. The site is located in beautiful woodland near Nevern in the Pembrokeshire National Park. (Pembrokeshire Coast National Park, 2024b) (Pembrokeshire Coast National Park, 2024c)

Among the best hill forts to see in Wales are:

- Castell Dinas Bran (near Llangollen in North Wales)
- Gaer Fawr near Welshpool in Mid Wales. Excavations
- Ffridd Faldwyn near Montgomery in Powys, mid-Wales
- For a full list of hill forts in Wales, refer to the following list.

(Wikipedia contributors, 2023)

Religion

The Celts were religious and revered many gods. They would hold religious ceremonies in woods and near sacred water. They firmly believed that a person's spiritual power was in their head so it was considered the greatest trophy to have the head of their enemy which they would proudly hang on their door.

Druids

There has been a great deal of folklore about the Druids. They were an important part of Celtic culture and their focus in Wales was the island of Anglesey. Druids were high-class priests and advisers who taught, healed and mediated. They had their own centres of learning where all knowledge was passed down from one generation to the next. Certain Druids were extremely powerful and they would be ambassadors for warring clans and were the ones to maintain the law.

Further reading: https://museum.wales/articles/1341/Who-were-the-Celts/
https://www.britainexpress.com/wales/history/iron-age.htm

The Celtic language

The native tongue of Wales is Welsh which has its roots in the Celtic language and is one of the oldest languages in the world - along with Ancient Greek and Latin. There are 29 letters in the Welsh alphabet and there are two additional vowel sounds - W and Y. In recent years, there has been a revival in the use of the Welsh language and today, it is widely spoken with one in five people living in Wales, speaking Welsh - which equates to 16% of the population. Welsh schoolchildren are taught Welsh as part of their curriculum.

Welsh shares the same linguistic roots of Brittonic as Breton spoken in Brittany and Corning, the native language of Cornwall. Brittonic was spoken in ancient times across the island of Britain. Welsh only has a few similarities with Irish

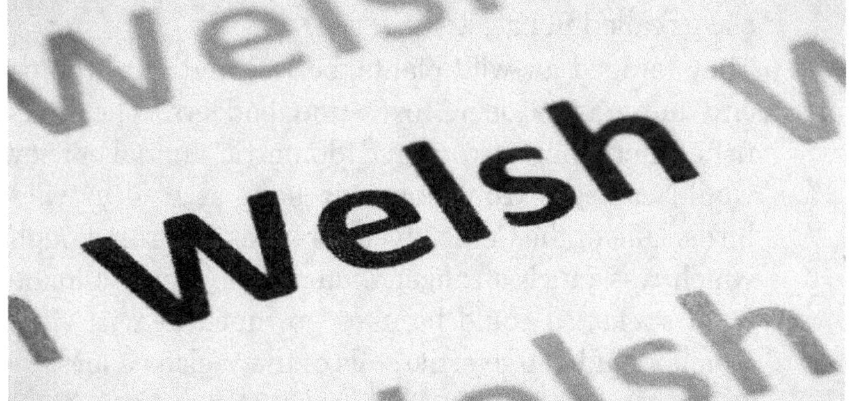

Gaelic so the written and spoken languages sound quite

different. The Welsh language really became distinctive between 400- 700 AD and the oldest known poems in Welsh, date from this period.

Wales today is very much a bilingual country. Almost all signs including road signs are written in both English and Welsh, and most schools and organisations in Wales promote the use of Welsh language'.

Ceryn Evans in https://www.twinkl.fr/blog/10-fascinating-welsh-language-facts

The modern Welsh name for Wales is Cymru and its people, Cymry. Both of these words come from the Brythonic word 'combrogi', meaning 'fellow-countrymen' and both were in use well before the 7th century.

Interesting facts about the Celts

- The Celts wore brightly-coloured clothing and some drew patterns on their skin using the blue dye from woad plants.
- The style of clothing they wore showed their status within the clan.
- The Celts are said to have been the first people in Europe to wear trousers and these were fastened by clasps called fibuales.
- They foraged for wild plants, berries and mushrooms and hunted for deer, foxes and badgers. The Celts fished and they also reared domestic animals. They would eat eggs from domestic hens as well as wild birds. One of the Celtic inventions was the iron plough which was much stronger than earlier ploughs made from sticks, so could be used on much heavier soils which included the fertile soils of the Welsh valleys.
- The Celts did not call themselves 'Celts' but they were

commonly called by the name of their tribe rather than by one collective name.

- Women were considered equal to men and could own property and choose their own husbands. They could also lead in war as Queen Boadicea did. If a woman had children, she would not raise them herself because this was the job of foster parents.

The legacy of the Celts

The Celts had a significant impact on Wales and their legacy can be found in many aspects of the country's rich history, culture and language.

The Welsh Language

The Welsh language (Cymraeg) has evolved from the language spoken by the ancient Celts in the region and has played an important role in preserving the Welsh national identity.

Celtic art and design

Celtic art and its rich use of symbols has influenced Welsh arts, crafts and jewellery to this day. As well as symbols, the Celts used intricate knotwork and made patterns by lacing threads and examples of these designs can be found in many pieces of Welsh artwork.

Celtic mythology

The Celtic pagan religion was rich in mythology and this has influenced Welsh folklore and legends over the centuries.

Welsh place Names

Many place names in Wales have Celtic origins and reflect the fact that they were once Celtic settlements.

Culture and traditions

Welsh music, dance and storytelling have all been influenced by the country's Celtic heritage. Traditional Welsh music often features Celtic instruments and melodies.

Ethnic Identity

The Welsh national identity has been strongly influenced by its Celtic roots. The Welsh are proud of their rich cultural heritage and unique language and know that they are closely connected to the Celtic legacy in Wales.

CHAPTER 3
THE ROMAN INVASION

During the first century AD, Britain was invaded by the Romans and the Celts they encountered became known as 'Britons' by them. In AD43, the Romans began a campaign to bring the whole island of Britain totally under Roman rule. The Romans believed this would be easy as they had swept through southern England, but when they reached the Welsh borders a few years later, they found the mountains challenging and the Celtic tribes ready to fight the conquering

army. The Roman conquest of Wales was to prove to be a long and brutal period in the country's history, lasting about 30 years. It is interesting to note that Wales was never totally conquered.

The Romans captured north-eastern Wales, defeating the Deceangli (known as Tegeingl in Welsh) in AD 48. The Deceangli were a Celtic tribe that lived in hill forts in the area where the city of Chester is situated today. Roman silver and lead mine workings have since been found in this area.

In AD50, the Romans defeated the Ordovices. This Celtic tribe had extensive lands in North Wales. The Celts fought the

Romans hard for 20 years- much of this time was under their leader, Caractacus, who organised the Welsh resistance. Caractacus was the son of the king of the Catuvellauni in Essex and had led the British campaign against the Romans. He had however, been forced to flee with many of his warriors when he was defeated in battle near the River Medway.

Caractacus had become the leader of the Ordovices and Silures tribes in Wales, but was defeated in battle in AD50. He was captured and sent to Rome. The Ordovices had to accept defeat when their final stronghold for both Celts and Druids in Anglesey was captured by the Romans in AD61. Wales was finally brought under the control of the Roman Empire.

'Their aim was to grow the Roman Empire by using Wales's natural resources, people, and farmland'. (HWb, n.d.)

Life under Roman rule

The Romans divided the land of Wales into lowland areas for the people and highland areas as military zones. They also established three major fortresses at York, Chester and Caerleon in Wales. The Roman establishment at Caerleon was designed with the classic Roman layout and was completed in AD78, with a sizable fortified town, which the Romans named Isca. This was to become the most important Roman site in Wales with an army of more than 5,500 men. The town had bath-houses with heated water, a hospital and an amphitheatre for regular combat with gladiators. The amphitheatre had seating for 6,000 people. Today, Caerleon is one of the best remaining military sites and is situated close to the River Usk, near Newport.

The construction of Roman forts

From Isca, the Romans developed a network of at least 30 smaller forts that stretched westwards and northwards to the island of Anglesey. The forts were linked by roads and the location of the forts ensured that they were only one day's march from each other. Military stations were also established near Caerleon and these included ones at Abergavenny, Monmouth, Neath and Loughor. The result was the establishment of an uneasy peace between the Romans and the Celts. Several of the Celtic clans in time did become Romanised.

The Romans were not particularly interested in Wales because they found its geography difficult and there was little flat and easily cultivated land. The area that they developed more than any other was south-east Wales. There were towns created and villas built in the countryside. The new forts were the focus of trade and new communities grew up around them- all with bustling markets. The largest markets sold goods from all over the Roman Empire. The Roman government was divided into administrative areas called civitates which were self-governing.

The introduction of Roman law...

There were two civitates in Wales at Carmarthen and Caerwent- which was situated just east of Caerleon. With a population of more than 3,000, Caerleon was the biggest town in Wales. The Romans did allow the Celtic ruling classes to keep their lands and customs- as long as they also supported Roman law. The Celts could also continue working on their farms. The classic round houses remained the normal type of housing, although it is estimated that 1% of the Romans lived in luxurious villas.

...And the Latin language

One of the biggest changes was that Latin became the official language of Wales, but unlike in many other European countries, Latin did not replace the native language. The majority of the Welsh continued to speak their Brythonic Celtic language. Latin became the language of the aristocracy. Brythonic did change during the Roman occupation because many Latin words were absorbed into the language. Examples of this include fort, rooms and books and these words can still be found in modern Welsh.

'The Romans brought with them different food, plants, animals, public baths, medicine, doctors, and religions. In their society, the elite learnt to read and write. The Iron Age population of Wales became "Romanised" as they took on this new culture' (HWb, n.d.-b)

Once Roman rule had been established in Wales, there is little mention of the country during the next 100 years, as the focus was on other places in the Roman Empire. In the third century, Emperor Septimius decided to divide Britain into two parts and Wales became part of Britannia Superior and was controlled from London. In AD412 Roman citizenship was given to every freeman in Wales. During the 4th century, the country was becoming prosperous but within 100 years, this was to change as the Roman Emperor began to deploy his armies elsewhere in the Empire.

In AD410, the Roman emperor Honorius decided to withdraw all Roman troops from Britain province to defend other parts of the empire. All this marked the end of Roman rule of Britain, it also left the island vulnerable to attacks from various groups - including the Anglo-Saxons and the Picts.

Interesting facts about the Romans

- The Romans spoke Latin, but many of them also spoke Greek.
- Roman armies were extremely well trained and disciplined and regularly defeated larger armies.
- Roman rulers would consume a small quantity of poison every day to help strengthen their immune systems.
- Bathing was a communal activity and everyone would get into huge baths to cleanse themselves. The Roman Baths at Caerleon (Isca) could hold 80,000 gallons (300,000 litres) gallons of water.
- The favourite sport of the Romans was gladiator fights. These took place in amphitheatres like the one at Caerleon which had wooden benches that could accommodate 6,000 spectators. As well as two gladiators fighting, often the entertainment was to watch a gladiator fight a large exotic animal.
- The Romans were clever and the first to invent many things including concrete, books, the Julian calendar, first heating system for buildings and aqueducts.

(Pwpadmin, 2023)

The Roman legacy

The Roman legacy to Wales is testament to the enduring influence of one of the greatest civilisations in history. The Romans left an indelible mark on Wales, shaping its landscape, culture and society for many centuries to come.

Travelling through Wales there is plenty of evidence of the Romans' road building skills in the well-preserved roads that criss-crossed the Welsh countryside. They established a network of roads that were built well enough to survive centuries of Welsh weather! Some of the best stretches of Roman highway to see is the 260 km (160-mile) route known collectively as 'Sarn Helen' which connects Aberconwy in the north and Carmarthen in the west.

Other Roman roads include the Fosse Way and Watling Street which both connected strategic points for ease of both trade and communication. Today, some of the Roman routes are still the major transportation routes in Wales.

Roman forts and settlements also dotted the Welsh landscape and these settlements not only contributed to the Romanisation of the local population, but also left a lasting architectural legacy that is still visible in the ruins scattered across Wales.

- Parts of Y Gaer- the largest Roman fort can still be seen standing beside the River Usk near Brecon.
- Overlooking the famous castle of Caernarfon stands the Roman fort of Segontium, which was used by the Romans for most of their occupation.
- The skill of the Roman engineers can be admired at Dolaucothi in Pumsaint, which is the only Roman gold mine in Britain and has an elaborate series of aqueducts.

(Roman Wales | Cadw, n.d.)

The influence of Latin

Latin, the language of the Romans, also left its mark on Welsh vocabulary and elements of it can still be found in the Welsh language today. Additionally, the introduction of Christianity by the Romans significantly shaped the religious landscape of Wales. The establishment of churches and the spread of Christian teachings had a profound and lasting impact on the spiritual life of the Welsh people.

The legacy of Roman law

Roman law and governance systems also played a crucial role in shaping the political structure of Wales. The Romans introduced a centralised administration, with local officials responsible for implementing Roman laws and policies. This administrative framework laid the foundation for future governance structures in Wales and influenced the development of Welsh legal and political institutions.

Post-Roman Wales

When the Roman army left Wales in the early 5th century, they left a vacuum as the country had been part of the Roman Empire for 300 years. It was a difficult time because there was no way life could return to pre-Roman times and many of the Welsh communities had become dependent on the Roman Empire. Many historians feel that both England and Wales  entered a 'Dark Ages', although this period is usually referred to as' 'Early Medieval".

The first legions had started to leave Wales in about AD

410 and within 100 years, they had all left to focus on other parts of the diminishing Roman Empire. Once the Romans had departed, Britain became divided into numerous small kingdoms. Wales became much more isolated than it had been and a decentralised society emerged. Wales was divided into the kingdoms of Brycheiniog, Dyfed, Gwent, Gwynedd, Morgannwg, Powys and Seisyllwg. The kingdoms had changing borders and lacked central authority. The strong Welsh identity did begin to take shape during this period, as the different communities developed a sense of shared culture, language, and identity.

The economy of Wales slumps

The economy of post-Roman Wales was based on subsistence farming and animal husbandry. Everyone was as self-sufficient as possible and became focused on meeting their basic needs within their community. Trade and commerce which had thrived under the Romans quickly declined. In the years that followed, the Roman infrastructure including the roads and villas fell into disrepair.

During the years 800- 900, the Welsh princes tried unsuccessfully to unite the different Welsh kingdoms, but usually ended up fighting each other. The princes were also faced with many invasions by outsiders - the Irish to the west and the Anglo-Saxons to the east. There were many conflicts over land and natural resources and these conflicts helped to define the borders of the Welsh kingdoms.

Christianity flourishes...

There was a spread of Christianity in post-Roman Wales, with the conversion of the people to Christianity steadily developing. Missionaries from Ireland and the Roman Church helped to spread the Christian faith and also established monastic communities which became great centres of learning. Britain's oldest religious school was founded in Llantwit Major and was where several Welsh saints studied. The first church was built on the site where Llandaff Cathedral stands today. As the years passed, the Welsh Church developed with its own characteristics and traditions that were quite different from the Roman Church.

An exciting current archaeological excavation....

There is currently a great deal of excitement amongst archaeologists in Wales. For the last two years they have been excavating an early mediaeval burial ground they uncovered within the grounds of Fonmon Castle near Cardiff. The graveyard dates from the 6th or 7th century and comprises about 70 graves, 18 of these have already been excavated. The site has caused interest as the excavated graves contain well-preserved skeletons, many of them placed in unconventional positions and buried with unusual artefacts including pottery, animal bones and a small carved wooden peg - probably from a game. Several imported items have also been found including fragments of glass from Bordeaux and pottery-thought to have come from North Africa.

Some skeletons are lying on their backs, but others are on their sides or even in a crouched position, with their knees drawn up to their chest. The skeletons have proved fascinating as several have front teeth that have been worn in an unusual manner - suggesting they were used like tools for a craft such as textile making or basketry.

Stability at last for post-Roman Wales

The 7th and 8th centuries saw much more stability in post-Roman Wales, as boundaries between kingdoms became well-defined and there was also a consolidation of power.

"In AD 757 - 796, the impressive linear earthwork called Offa's Dyke was built to help define the border between England and Wales – from a point near Prestatyn in the north, to Chepstow in the south. The dyke measured 82 km(132 miles) and was 20 metres(66 feet) in width." What Is the Offa's Dyke Path?, n.d.)

Peace would not last for long as the Viking raids in the 9th and 10th centuries posed new challenges. More defensive hill forts were quickly constructed as an increasing number of raids by the Vikings were made along the 600 miles of vulnerable Welsh coastline.

The impact of the Norman Conquest

During the 11th century, the Norman Conquest of England, brought new external pressures to Wales. The Norman lords were keen to expand into Welsh territories and this led to more conflict and the construction of many wooden motte-and-bailey castles for defence. The struggles between the Welsh rulers and the Normans was to continue for centuries, shaping the intricate relationships between the two societies.

CHAPTER 4
THE ARRIVAL OF THE NORMANS

In 1066, the Normans from France, successfully invaded England. During the following years 1067–1081, the Normans made several efforts at conquering Wales, but these were not undertaken with the same fervour and determination that the English invasion had been. Consequently, these first invasions failed. William the Conqueror had quickly strengthened his rule of the English kingdom and had established earldoms along the Welsh border. The Norman lords of these earldoms started to try expand their lands westwards into Wales.

In 1081, a much stronger Norman invasion of southern Wales was led by William who created a new defence point at Cardiff. During the following years, there were numerous forays by the Normans into Wales and they successfully captured and settled in the Vale of Glamorgan in the south of the country. They made Pembroke their new stronghold.

During his final years, William the Conqueror had difficulties, not only in his lands overseas, but with his son Robert and the Danes who repeatedly threatened to invade

England. William died in September 1087, during a military campaign in northern France. Before his death, William the Conqueror ensured that his sons were given power. Robert was given Normandy and England was given to his second son - who was also called William. His youngest son, Henry was given a sizable amount of money. The king also left money to the church and the poor and instructed that all prisoners should be released.

The Domesday Book

This world famous manuscript records life in much of England and parts of Wales in the 11th century. It was completed in 1086 under the orders of William the Conqueror. The king decided that the survey was necessary as many of the Norman lords were arguing about land. He also felt that it was a good way to establish where the wealth of the country lay. He was personally running short of funds and establishing how much tax-money he could get from the land would be beneficial. The script was drawn up by six scribes and then checked by a seventh.

The Domesday book lists 13,000 places and many of them still survive today. There are details of which areas were woodland, meadow and pasture. The manuscript also reveals how many buildings had been destroyed during the Norman Invasion and Interestingly, how wealthy many of the 200 Norman lords had become.

The Domesday book can be viewed online:-

https://www.nationalarchives.gov.uk/help-with-your-research/research-guides/domesday-book/#:

(The National Archives, 2023)

12th century England and Wales

William II reigned in England until August 1100, when he was accidently killed whilst out hunting in the New Forest. The crown of England passed to his younger brother Henry, who was crowned Henry I in August 1100.

Henry was keen to establish a large Norman settlement in South Wales and ordered the construction of a royal castle at Carmarthen in 1109. The Welsh princes however, were far from happy and refused to swear loyalty to the new king. Instead, they took every opportunity to take land back from the Normans, whenever they could.

Although Wales was never totally invaded by the Normans, they did firmly establish themselves in South Wales. Norman rule in England between the years 1066-1154, had a big impact on Wales – although the impact varied from one region to another - just as the allegiance of the Welsh to the Norman kings varied. In 1114, Henry I invaded Gwynedd and Gruffardap Cynan and the King of Gwynedd was defeated and forced  to pay homage to Henry. In complete contrast, the following year, Henry knighted Owain ap Cadwgan for his honourable services to the crown in Normandy. In 1116 there was another Welsh revolt led by Gruffydd who took Swansea, Carmarthen and Kidwelly castles - but failed to take Aberystwyth.

These troubles amongst the Welsh continued throughout the Norman rule of England, Wales remained divided into a number of small independent kingdoms – with some Norman lords (known as Marcher Lords) successfully expanding their territories into Wales. By building castles, the Marcher Lords were able to effectively control the English/ Welsh border.

Henry I died in December 1135 and was succeeded by his nephew, Stephen (1096 – 1154). Henry I had reared Stephen who had pledged to support Henry's daughter Matilda to become Queen. Many of the English nobles did want to be ruled by a woman and she was also resented by the Normans for marrying into the royal Angevin family. Consequently, when the king's death was declared, Stephen hurried across the Channel to claim the crown.

Stephen was a pleasant and jovial king but ineffective. He dragged England through years of civil war as he fought his rival, Matilda, for the crown. Stephen had originally had the support of the church but lost this when he arrested the powerful Bishop of Salisbury. Matilda with the support of her half-brother, Robert the Earl of Gloucester, decided to seize the opportunity to invade England. Matilda did well and brought much of the west of England under her control. Stephen gradually regained control and in 1148, Matilda, fled England.

In his final years, Stephen was happy just to do his best to protect the throne so he could pass it on to his son, Eustace. In January 1153, Henry of Anjou who was Matilda's son, invaded England to claim the throne. That summer, Eustace died and Stephen was devastated. He happily signed the Treaty of Wallingford stating that Henry would be his successor. Throughout his reign, Wales had remained an unsettled country in which he had had little interest.

Stephen I was the last Norman king and when he died, one year after signing the treaty, Henry was crowned Henry II of England.

Emergence of the Welsh princes

The Welsh princes began to rise to power during the early Middle Ages, particularly in the 9th and 10th centuries. This period saw the emergence of regional leaders who asserted authority over various territories in Wales. However, it was during the 11th and 12th centuries that Welsh princes like Gruffydd ap Llywelyn and Owain Gwynedd significantly expanded their influence and consolidated their power. They engaged in both internal conflicts with other Welsh rulers and external struggles against the invading Anglo-Normans. This period of Welsh history witnessed the formation of principalities and the assertion of Welsh autonomy before eventual integration into the kingdom of England.

During the 12th century, the Welsh princes like Owain Gwynedd and his successors spent much of their time opposing numerous attempts to seize power and land made by the Normans. Through military resistance and a number of strategic alliances, the princes managed to remain united – although there were occasions when they had conflicts amongst themselves as they vied for supremacy.

The Norman legacy

- Norman architecture has a distinctive style, the structures were large and built in stone and incorporated a variety of architectural elements. The Normans were equally artistic with metal and stone.

- Norman castles were impressive with a square keep, moats and drawbridges. The Normans built more castles across Europe than any other power.

- Chepstow Castle was one of the first Norman castles built in Wales and lies on the border between England and Wales.

- The Normans wore simple clothing but their style became more elaborate as they became wealthy.

(Historian, 2023)

Everyday life in Wales in Norman times

The influence of the Normans on the Welsh varied in the different regions. There were areas where there was interaction between the two and this to both an exchange of cultural ideas and adaption of ways. In the border areas, controlled by the Marcher Lords, a very distinctive culture emerged which was a blend of Welsh and Norman influences and traditions. Nevertheless, Wales managed to retain its individual identity and this would lead to further conflict in the future..

Throughout Norman rule the Welsh maintained their own legal and social systems. Welsh laws were known as 'Cyfraith Hywel' and were used for many aspects of everyday life. Welsh society was based on the system of tribal territories known as 'cantrefs' and 'commotes' and this practice continued.

Welsh remained the dominant language and continued to thrive and cultural heritage was enriched by a number of excellent Welsh poets and historians.

The emergence of the Welsh principalities

The Normans arrived in Wales, just one year after the Norman Conquest of England. Powerful Norman lords established themselves along the border between England and Wales and regularly made forays into Wales. The Normans established border strongholds at Chester, Shrewsbury and Hereford

William the Conqueror was keen to extend his power over Wales and captured the fertile valleys and lowlands but found much of the country had rugged terrain and was met by the fierce resistance of the Welsh. The land along the border became known as 'The Marches' and the Norman 'Marcher Lords' did their utmost to impose their rule on the Welsh lords – but were met with great resistance.

A number of Welsh principalities had evolved prior to the Norman invasion and these were strengthened. The Welsh princes fortified their strongholds and often played rival

Norman lords against each other- which was easy to do as there were many divisions amongst the Normans. The conflict was not just military but also cultural and social. A new class of Anglo- Welsh landowner appeared too. These were Welshmen who had served the Normans and were given land as a reward for their military service.

Although there were huge cultural differences, there was some cultural exchange between the Normans and Welsh- some of the Welsh princes adopted Norman customs and some Norman lords married wealthy Welsh ladies. Wales continued to be a patchwork of principalities for generations to come and the struggle for control continued well beyond the mediaeval period.

CHAPTER 5
MEDIEVAL WALES

The Plantagenet dynasty ruled mediaeval England from 1154 to 1485. There were 14 Plantagenet kings-beginning with Henry II (1154-1189) and ending with Richard III (1452-1485). The relationship between the Plantagenet kings and Wales was a complex one and shaped by military conflicts, political alliances, and attempts to integrate Wales into the English administrative and legal system. The conquest and subsequent governance of Wales had long-lasting effects on the history and identity of the country.

The House of Plantagenet is actually an 'umbrella term' coined by modern historians that covers four different royal houses from the Angevins (who were also Counts of Anjou) the main family of Plantagenet after they had loss their French lands, followed by the rival Houses of Lancaster and York – whose rivalry culminated in the War of the Roses.

The Plantagenet kings had varying degrees of involvement in Wales. Here is a brief overview of those Plantagenet kings who did have key relationships with Wales.

Wales in the 12th Century

Henry II (1154–1189)

Henry II's reign marked the beginning of the Plantagenet dynasty. He was one of the kings who was actively involved in Welsh affairs- particularly in asserting English authority over the region. Henry sought to expand his control in Wales, using both military force and diplomatic means. He initiated the construction of castles, such as those at Rhuddlan and Aberystwyth, as a way of consolidating English influence.

Richard I (1189–1199)

Better known as Richard the Lionheart and famous for his involvement in the Crusades, Richard I had limited direct engagement with Wales during his short reign. His focus was more on foreign affairs and his military campaigns in the Holy Land.

John (1199–1216)

King John faced many challenges in Wales, dealing with conflicts and power struggles among the Welsh princes. He attempted to exert control through alliances and military campaigns. The signing of the Magna Carta in 1215 (though not directly related to Wales) had broader implications for governance and law in Wales.

The Magna Carta (1215)

The Magna Carta, meaning "The Great Charter", was signed at Runnymede on June 15, 1215, by King John to deal with the grievances of the Welsh and Scottish rulers. Their main grievance was that John had more power over both countries than any English king before him. A good example of this was when in 1211 the king forced Llywelyn Farr - who was Prince of North Wales - to surrender a large area of land and give King John hostages- including Farr's own son

Gruffyd- as security. The Magna Carta was a very important document as it established the principles of limited government and the rule of law. The charter asserted the rights of the barons against the arbitrary actions of the king. Some historians describe it as setting the foundations for the development of constitutional government.

Although the Magna Carta was primarily aimed at settling the grievances of the English barons, its principles were far-reaching and it affected the governance and rights of the Welsh. Later versions of the Magna Carta included points specifically concerning Welsh law and governance.

'In chapter 56 of Magna Carta, John promised that, if had dispossessed Welshmen of their lands and liberties in England or Wales without lawful judgement of their peers— their social equals—they would be immediately restored. Any dispute was to be settled by judgement of peers.

In chapter 57, John promised to return Gruffydd immediately to Llywelyn, and also to restore all the hostages of Wales and the charters that he had extracted as security for "peace", which meant for "good"—or, as the Welsh would have thought it, "servile"—behaviour.

https://www.parliament.uk/about/living-heritage/evolutionofparliament/2015-parliament-in-the-making/2015-historic-anniversaries/magna-carta/magna-carta---wales-scotland-and-ireland/

Wales in the 13th century

Henry III (1216–1272)

Henry III's reign saw continued efforts to establish English dominance in Wales. Henry faced resistance from Welsh leaders like Llywelyn the Great. The Treaty of Montgomery in 1267 recognised Llywelyn's authority over parts of Wales, though he still owed homage to the English crown.

Edward I (1272–1307)

Edward I's rule had a significant impact on Wales. Edward's attempts to conquer Wales included the construction of the famous "Iron Ring" of castles. The castles were built in the late 13th and early 14th century to consolidate English control over Wales. The castles built include Conwy, Harlech, Caernarfon and Beaumaris. All the castles were built in carefully chosen strategic positions to suppress any Welsh uprisings. All the castles were formidable military structures which doubled as administrative centres. With their construction, Edward I was showing his determination to assert his authority over the Welsh.

Following the deaths of the powerful Welsh leaders Llewelyn and Dafydd of Gwynedd, Edward thought that to take total control of Wales would be easy, but he was wrong as there were a series of revolts. This meant that Edward had to spend much time in Wales, before finally being successful in seizing a large portion of the country.

The importance of the Statute of Rhuddlan (1284)

The Statute of Rhuddlan in 1284 was an important document as it formally annexed Wales to the English Crown-

"One of the tools Edward used to effect this change was the Statute of Rhuddlan (later, and erroneously called the Statute of Wales). According to this statute, the counties of Anglesey, Meirionnydd, and Caernarfon were created out of the remnants of Llewelyn's Gwynedd, and staffed with

sheriffs to collect taxes and administer justice.

The Statute of Rhuddlan helped define the roles of these officials and the means by which they were to enforce this essentially foreign system of law within the areas of English influence in Wales." (Britain Express, n.d.-b)

The Welsh princes during the 13th centur

The 13th century was a difficult time for the Welsh princes as it was marked by the increasing encroachment on their lands by the English – especially during the reign of Edward I. The stronger Welsh princes - such as Llywelyn the Great- resisted English domination, but in the years 1282- 1283, Edward I was finally successful and Welsh lands were brought under the English crown.

The first Prince of Wales - 1301

The title 'Prince of Wales' was created in 1301 by King Edward I and was bestowed on his son, Edward, who later became Edward II. The duties of the role have evolved through the centuries. The title is always given to the monarch's eldest son who is the heir apparent. His role as Prince of Wales helps him to prepare him for his future role as monarch as he must meet government officials and fully understand how the government works. The title is not automatic and must be bestowed by the monarch on their son.

Wales in the 14th century

Edward II (1307–1327)

Edward II faced internal strife and challenges to his rule - including discontent in Wales. His inability to effectively govern contributed to great unrest, and during his reign, there were notable uprisings in Wales, led by figures like Llywelyn Bren and later, Owain Glyndŵr. There would be further rebellions led by Owain Glyndŵr in Henry IV's reign (1399-1413) and these rebellions would have a lasting impact on the difficult relationship between England and Wales.

The Black Death (1348- 1350)

In the mid-14th century, the plague swept across Wales and was at its worst between 1348-1350. Also known as '*The Black Death*', the plague was a deadly pandemic that was spread by close contact with infected people and contaminated goods. The plague brought widespread death to Wales and this resulted in an economic upheaval that had repercussions for generations afterwards.

The symptoms of the plague were horrible with high fever, vomiting and darkened patches of skin caused by internal bleeding. Death was swift and the mortality rate was 80% in some parts of Wales. The plague affected everyone – whatever their age, social class or background and it brought with it fear and paranoia. There were food shortages, and no medicine. Trade routes were disrupted and the high death rate led to labour shortages too.

The impact on Wales was immense as entire families were wiped out, communities were shattered and a wealth of skills and talents were lost, as well as labourers and artisans and this all led to a rise in prices.

The Welsh princes during the 14th century

The Welsh were still keen to be independent and this led to regular uprisings – including those led by Owain Glyndŵr. He briefly established a Welsh parliament and gained strong support both from the Welsh nobles and a number of English rebels. The revolt did eventually fail and Wales remained under English control

Owain Glyndŵr (1359- ?1415)

Owain Glyndŵr was a nobleman who was descended from the Princes of Powys and claimed the title Prince of Wales. To many, he is a national hero. Like many, he was furious with the English, the seizure of Welsh lands and increasingly heavy taxes. In 1400, he began a revolt which proved surprisingly successful as he managed to unite various Welsh factions and win numerous battles against English soldiers. His soldiers controlled several significant parts of Wales – including the capital, Cardiff.

In 1404 he established a Welsh Parliament and was crowned Prince of Wales, which strengthened the Welsh identity. Despite these early victories, the rebellion began to falter as he received little external support and there was infighting amongst his followers. The last mention of Glyndŵr was made in historical records dated 1412. The  exact date of his death remains unknown. His rebellion left a lasting legacy for Welsh cultural identity and he remains a popular character in Welsh folklore and history and is celebrated for his defiance against English domination.

Owain Glyndŵr. (n.d.). Medieval Wales. Retrieved from https://owain-glyndwr.wales/age_of_the_princes/mediaeval_wales_detail.html

(*Wales in the Middle Ages*, n.d.)

Wales in the 15th century

Henry VI (1422–1461 and 1470–1471)

Henry VI was a weak king with poor leadership skills which led to political instability that was marked by the Wars of the Roses. These were a series of dynastic conflicts within the Plantagenet family.

The instability the conflicts caused was far reaching and indirectly affected Wales. Many of the Welsh nobility aligned themselves with either one side or the other, leading to a number of internal conflicts in Wales too. The authority of the English monarchy was greatly weakened too and Welsh leaders like Owain Glyndŵr took advantage of this to launch further uprisings against English rule in Wales. The Marcher Lords gained autonomy and power and this too increased the complexity of the country's political landscape.

Some of the Battles of the Wars of the Roses spilled over the border into Wales as a number of military actions took place on the border. This added to the instability to the area.

Richard III (1483- 1485)

Richard was a very controversial king who many believe was involved in the disappearance of his two nephews - whose father, Edward IV had been king. The young princes each had a claim to the throne. The princes were referred to as 'The

Princes in the Tower' and the elder, Edward, had already been proclaimed Edward V on the death of his father. Richard III declared that the boys' parents had not been legally married so the young Edward could not be the legitimate heir and thus claimed the throne for himself. The boys were last seen in public in June 1483 and were never seen or heard of again.

Richard's reign was brief as he was defeated and killed at the Battle of Bosworth and with him died the Plantagenet dynasty. Henry VII was the victor at Bosworth and brought the War of the Roses to an end. He was crowned King of England – and the first Tudor king.

Interesting facts about the Plantagenets

- The Plantagenet dynasty saw some of the most violent episodes in history, including the Hundred Years' War between England and France, the Peasants' Revolt and the War of the Roses. This was a civil war between the Houses of Lancaster and York and it brought an end to the dynasty.

- Drone warfare is thought of as a 21st century method, but it was first used in the 13th century between Henry III and Simon de Montfort! De Montfort planned to use cockerels with fire bombs attached to their feet to attack the capital, London. His ideas were flawed because cockerels can only fly a short distance and their feathers are inflammable! (Jones, 2022)
- The name 'Plantagenet' was first used for Geoffrey V, the Count of Anjou who always wore a sprig from a broom plant (*planta genista*) in his hat. Richard Duke of York took the name in the 15th century.
- The Plantagenets lost the 100 Years War against France. The war was a series of conflicts between 1337-1453 and was waged over the succession to the throne of France. France defeated England and this led to civil war. (*10 Fast Facts About the Plantagenets*, n.d.)

Everyday life in Medieval Wales

Life during the Plantagenet dynasty was hard for both men and women. They lived a hand -to-mouth existence and the men often died in conflict and the women in childbirth. If they survived these, then illness and infection usually killed them. Few people lived beyond their mid-40s.

Life was focused on the village and the people worked hard, wore simple clothes and ate a meagre diet. Whilst the English were farmers, the Welsh were more often herders unless they lived in the more fertile areas on the lowlands. There were fewer villages in Wales because of the challenging terrain. During 1100–1300, however, 80 towns were developed. This development was encouraged by the Welsh princes and the Marcher Lords as they would bring extra wealth. Trade in the towns also developed and the Welsh began trading animal skins and fleeces plus cheese in return for such commodities as iron, wheat and salt - but trade was often interrupted by conflict.

"There were three main social groups: the uchelwyr – the upper class, thebonheddwyr – the freemen and the taeogion – the unfree peasants. Each group had its role in society. (Sarah, 2017)

Culture in Wales

During the period 1100-1300, a group of Welsh poets known as the *Gogynfeirdd* received support from the Welsh kings and princes. One poem emerged as the best – *the Elergy of Gruffudd ab Yr Ynad Coch to Llewelyn ap Gruffudd.* Slowly as the number of princes diminished, the patronage of the poets was passed to the nobility. The poets themselves formed a society of verse called Dafydd ap Gwilym and a new style of poetry emerged rich in *cynghanedd* –which was the term given to an intricate pattern of chiming sounds.

The first Eisteddfod

Owain Gwynedd was a strong Welsh king who had built castles and defeated the English in 1136. He and his collaborator, Rhys ap Gruffudd held a magnificent music and poetry festival in Cardigan Castle in 1176 and this was regarded as the first *eisteddfod.* Traditional Welsh culture has been kept alive by these competitive music and poetry festivals which are today there are local and national events with the Royal National Eisteddfod being the largest and held each August. Today this event also includes

Welsh craftsmen. This event is held alternate years in North and South Wales.

Literature

The Mabinogion Collection is a collection of 11 stories that has been translated from Medieval Welsh manuscripts that tell tales of pre-Christian Celtic history, religion, mythology and traditions. The collection is considered to be the country's greatest contribution to European literature.

Song

Singing became a popular pastime and the natural ability of the Welsh to sing in perfect harmony soon became apparent and is a talent that has received worldwide acclaim over the centuries.

During this period, both wood carving and stone carving became highly developed – particularly in the 15th century – with the construction of castles, churches and monasteries. The parish church in Gresford is regarded as the finest example of the work of Welsh stone masons.

CHAPTER 6
WALES UNDER THE TUDORS

The Tudor kings and queens are among the most recognised of English monarchs, Richard Rex on the website - https://www.historicuk.com/HistoryUK/HistoryofEngland/The-Tudors/ suggests that they had iconic status because - "The age of print and Renaissance portraiture gave them huge advantages over the kings of earlier centuries, but they were the first English monarchs to take such pains over their public image, and it is a tribute to the success of the Tudor image-makers."

The Tudor monarchy lasted for 118 years from 1485- 1603 and comprised of five kings and queens who were of English/ Welsh descent from the Tudors of Penmynydd (Tuduriaid Penmynydd) and Catherine of Valois. They ruled the kingdom of England, Wales and the Lordship of Ireland.

Henry VII (1485-1509)

Harri's famous victory in the Wars of the Roses at the Battle of Bosworth saw the defeat of Richard and Harri becoming King Henry VII. The House of Lancaster had triumphed over the House of York. But to Welsh men and women, the victory was entirely theirs.

"Harri was the genuine article, born in Wales. He was conscious of his roots, enjoying the things the Welsh are famous for – music, poetry, literature and sport. He flew the Welsh flag, appointed Welshmen to influential government and religious posts, and returned to Wales a certain status and self-confidence that had been shattered by previous events.

(The Tudors in Wales | Cadw, n.d.)

Henry was a Welshman as his grandfather was Owen Tudor, a Welsh courtier from Anglesey and the second husband of Catherine of Valois. She had previously been married to Henry V and was mother to Henry VI. When she married Owen Tudor, they had several children including Edmund Tudor- Henry's father.

As a symbolic gesture, when he was crowned king, Henry (who was a Lancaster) married Elizabeth of York - thus uniting the two warring houses and bringing stability to England. During his reign he worked hard to strengthen royal power and to bring Wales under English control.

Henry reignited the desire to build castles which had not been seen since the reign of Edward I. Many castles were transformed from solid military strongholds into more comfortable defences modelled on the latest French designs. A good example of this is Raglan and the Octagonal tower built at Cardiff Castle. Tretower in the Brecon Beacons (Bannau Brycheiniog) is well worth seeing as it successfully combines a strong mediaeval style with a late mediaeval courthouse.

The Welsh princes in the 15th century

During the 15th century, England still dominated Wales.

There was unrest and occasional rebellions. One of the key figures during the late 15th and early 16th centuries was Rhys ap Thomas who was a powerful Welsh nobleman rather than prince who was born into the House of Dinefwr in 1449.

In 1485, Henry Tudor landed in Wales to challenge the usurper, Richard III. Rhys ap Thomas, pledged allegiance to Henry and provided him with crucial military support. At the Battle of Bosworth, Rhys ap Thomas led a strong contingent of Welsh forces and helped Henry to secure victory over Richard III and the crown of England. Local legend tells how it was Rhys ap Thomas who fatally wounded Richard. As his reward, Henry bestowed titles on him including Deputy Constable of Carmarthen Castle. Rhys ap Thomas became one of the most influential figures in Wales. He continued to support Henry and his successors. His support for the Tudor dynasty helped stabilise Wales.

Rhys ap Thomas died in 1525, leaving a lasting impact on Welsh politics.

Wales in the 16th century

Henry VIII (1509-1547)

Without a doubt, Henry VIII is the most famous of the Tudor kings - best known for his six wives and the English Reformation. Henry liked Wales, but not to the same degree as his father.

In 1536, the Act of Union was passed and this abolished the independent rule of Wales and incorporated Wales into the Kingdom of England. Henry did this because he feared a sea invasion on the Welsh coast - either by France or Spain.

When Henry died in 1547, the crown was passed to his nine year old son, Edward VI, so England was ruled by his 'Royal Advisors'. There was a concerted effort to impose Protestantism – which had been introduced by the Reformation – on the Welsh.

Mary I (1553-1558)

Mary was Henry VIII's daughter who attempted to restore Catholicism to England and Wales, and this led to great religious persecution in Wales.

Elizabeth I (1558-1603)

Elizabeth was Mary's half sister and ruled England for more than 44 years. She continued to try and fully integrate the government of Wales with England, but she was keen to maintain a stability in Wales too, so the Welsh identity and culture was allowed to thrive. However, by the time of her death in 1603 England was on the brink of civil war again and many Welsh castles would be damaged.

Interesting facts about the Tudors

- In Tudor times, people were very superstitious and also believed in magic. Some people wore an amulet such as a precious stone or piece of coloured cloth to protect them against disease. Others carried parts of an animal for good luck– with a rabbit's foot being particularly popular.
- The Tudors enjoyed playing board games and backgammon, chess, and card games all became popular.
- The wealthy enjoyed all kinds of exotic meat including badgers, otters, tortoises and dolphins.
- Tudor medicines were based on ideas from the Ancient

Greek doctor, Hippocrates. Ordinary people could not afford a doctor so would be given herbal remedies by the 'wise woman' in their community.

- One of the largest and heaviest cannons used by soldiers in Tudor times was the Mons Meg. This cannon could fire a cannon ball a distance of just under two miles (3 km) and today is displayed at Edinburgh Castle.

Everyday life in Wales under the Tudors

Life was difficult and many more people did not live more than 35 -40 years. Water was often the source of infection as it was collected from steams or pumps and was often dirty – and infected by raw sewage. Meals usually consisted of a vegetable broth and a hard grey bread made from either rye or barley. If they were lucky, some communities with animals had cheese, milk and eggs. In complete contrast, the rich Welsh princes had opulent and elegant clothes and enjoyed expensive foods including veal and venison and often French wines too. The rich enjoyed hunting, falconry and jousting.

Such games as tennis and bowls also made an appearance. In sharp contrast, poor people played football – but were only allowed to do so once a year, on Christmas Day.

The Tudor Legacy for Wales

The pivotal point for Wales in Tudor times was the Act of Union in 1536. Many historians argue that the union was not between England and the country of Wales, but between England and the March area of southern Wales. The Act was passed solely by the English Parliament, with no Welsh present. Dr John Davies is convinced though that the Act of Union was good for Wales -

It was the events of the Tudor reign that ensured that the subsequent history of Wales was a happier story than was the subsequent history of Ireland. The 'Act of Union', although it can be seen as an arbitrary act of annexation, brought about a single citizenship in Wales, a boon of immense significance. (BBC - History - Wales Under the Tudors, 2011)

CHAPTER 7
WALES IN THE 17TH CENTURY

For Wales, the Stuart period (1603- 1714) was a period of political, social, and cultural changes. These changes were closely related to the developments taking place in Britain as a whole. Wales was now incorporated into the Kingdom of England and the Welsh princes no longer had any significant power. The two Acts of Union (1536 and 1543) completed both the legal and administrative integration of Wales into the Kingdom of England. The remnants of self-government in Wales went and English law and administration was adopted throughout the country. The four Stuart kings and one queen all had difficult reigns.

James I (1603- 1625)

The reign of the Stuarts begins with the union of the crowns of Scotland and England. James VI of Scotland had been king for 36 years, when he became James I of England following the death of Queen Elizabeth I. Politically, the countries remained independent but for the first time, the King was King of the United Kingdom.

The reign of James I was a complex time for the Welsh as

he was trying to consolidate English control over Wales and he was trying to make the Welsh more English by promoting the use of English language and law and appointing English officials to all the key positions in the Welsh administration. The Welsh strongly resisted much of what James sought to achieve and worked hard to preserve their language, culture and autonomy.

Despite these tensions, there were some positive developments for Wales including modernisation of its administration and legal systems as well as advancements in education and literature.

King James was a keen theologian and during his reign ordered a new translation of the Bible. He was a tolerant man but after the Gunpowder Plot of 1605 by the Roman Catholic Guy Fawkes and his accomplices to blow up the Houses of Parliament, James introduced stiff penalties for Roman Catholics. The end of his reign was marked by financial pressures caused by the Thirty Years War in Europe and impending war with Spain.

Charles I 1625-1649

Charles I's reign was a tumultuous period in British history. His reign was marked by political strife, religious tensions, and civil war. He tried to exert control over Wales- both politically and economically- and this was met with sharp resistance by the Welsh nobles. There was great discontent amongst ordinary Welsh people too, when he imposed greater taxation and changes to land tenure.

There was religious tension between Charles and the nonconformist groups in Wales including the Calvinistic Methodists - led by preacher Vavasor Powell (1617-1670). The tensions were sparked when Charles tried to impose the Anglican liturgy on them. Powell was a key figure in the spread of dissenting religious movements in Wales. During his reign, Wales enjoyed economic growth as the country's ironworks and coal mines flourished – particularly in the south. Charles brought in new trade and taxation policies which negatively impacted Welsh merchants and landowners, causing more unrest.

Charles' reign culminated in the English Civil War (1642-1651) and this brought military campaigns and economic disruption to Wales – as well as divided loyalties to the Welsh. The Welsh found themselves fighting on both sides of the conflict. Sir Thomas Myddleton, a notable Welsh nobleman for example, supported Parliamentarians, led by Oliver Cromwell.

Civil War and Interregnum 1642- 1660

The Interregnum was the period between the execution of Charles I in 1649 and the restoration of the monarchy in 1660. This period is also referred to as the 'Commonwealth Period'.

Following the Civil War between the Royalists (Cavaliers) and the Parliamentarians (also known as Roundheads) under Oliver Cromwell – known as the Lord Protector- the monarchy was abolished and the Commonwealth established under the leadership of Oliver the Cromwell. It was a republican-style government which had power- as did the military. This was a period of great unrest with

Cromwell's forces engaged in military campaigns in Scotland and Ireland as well as several domestic revolts. Cromwell died in 1658 and his son, Richard, briefly became Lord Protector, but lacked his father's political acumen which led to the collapse of the Protectorate and the restoration of the

monarchy.

Oliver Cromwell is one of the most important men in England's history, but everything he struggled for collapsed within two decades of his death. The army, Parliament and the citizens of London grappled with each other for control of the country, and even the army no longer remained a united political force.

- Charles River Editors, taken from The Stuart Restoration, The History and Legacy of the English Monarchy's Return to Power in the Late 17th Century

Charles II (1660-1685)

Charles II was in exile when he was invited back by Parliament to be crowned. His reign brought some stability, but its most notable events were probably the Great Plague of 1665, followed by the Fire of London in 1666. The King did achieve some developments for Wales even though his primary focus was on re-establishing the monarchy and consolidating his power. He supported the development of trade and industry in Wales and the ironworks and coal mines in the south thrived once again.

Charles also granted charters to some towns in Wales to promote trade and he made efforts to improve the transport infrastructure and communication between Wales and England. He also proposed plans for a university and other educational establishments in Wales although these would not come to fruition until the 19th century.

Anne (1702- 1714)

After the troubled reign of James II (1685-1689) and the joint reign of William and Mary, Anne came to the throne as the last Stuart monarch in 1702.There had been no interaction with Wales for years as in fact none of these monarchs had visited Wales!

Queen Anne, the last monarch of the Stuart dynasty. She reigned from 1702 to 1714. Her reign was marked by significant political, military, and social developments. The War of the Spanish Succession (1701-1714) had begun the year before she was crowned and would continue throughout her reign. England played a key role and because of this, Wales was involved too.

The Acts of Union in 1707 united England and Scotland to form the Kingdom of Great Britain. Wales had already legally integrated with England by the Acts of 1535 and 1542, the Acts of Union did solidify both the political and constitutional status of Wales within the newly formed kingdom.

Anne's reign also saw the development of cultural and intellectual movements, and this had an impact on the cultural landscape of Wales.

Everyday life in Wales under the Stuarts

Many people still lived in the countryside in Stuart times, although many more had moved to the towns, where they lived in crowded conditions. In the beginning, many families had a hand-to-mouth existence but by the beginning of the 18th century, things were easier and families were living more comfortably than they had ever done. Life expectancy was still much shorter than it is today and 10- 25 women in every 100 died in childbirth. There was a clear distinction between male and female roles. Farming remained important to Wales and crops were still grown in the fertile Welsh valleys and animal husbandry continued where the soil was not so good and the terrain was more challenging. South Wales was more prosperous than the other regions in Wales because of the development of coal mining and the iron works.

For further reading about life in Stuart times https://www.historyextra.com/period/stuart/stuart-britain-what-was-life-like-for-ordinary-people/

(Evans, 2022)

The Stuart legacy for Wales

The legacy that the Stuart dynasty left in Wales was multi-faceted and changed different aspects of Welsh life. Importantly, the Acts of Union integrated Wales much more fully into the Kingdom of England and had established English law in Wales.

This was a very unsettled period with numerous military conflicts for the English and the Welsh were often drawn into them. Like in the English Civil War, the Welsh often found themselves fighting on opposing sides.

There were significant changes to land ownership in Wales and many small estates were consolidated into much larger estates – displacing many small farmers. This brought changes to both the Welsh landscape and society.

There were also significant changes in religion in Wales -

both during the English Civil War and the years of Interregnum. These changes saw a rise in Puritanism and dissenting religious movements and this had led to religious persecution and the suppression of Catholicism. The Stuarts also contributed to Welsh culture as they ardently supported the arts and literature, and this saw the emergence of many fine Welsh poets and writers.

Welsh culture in 17- 18th century

The biggest changes to the literary culture of Wales was the arrival of the Renaissance in Wales, followed by the printing press. In the 17th century the English government tried to suppress Welsh poems and books. Poets and writers were horrified as they wanted to preserve the Welsh language for future generations and many poems and books were written. There was a strong movement to ensure that Welsh was always spoken and written in church.

Poems were still written in strict metre and the anglesey poet, goronwy owen, was keen to preserve this style of poetry. The number of traditional musicians declined during this period, and it became usual for singing to be accompanied by the harp – this was the beginning of choral music. During this period there was little development in the world of welsh art or sculpture.

CHAPTER 8
18TH CENTURY WALES AND THE HOUSE OF HANOVER

The House of Hanover comprised six monarchs. Finding the correct person to be king was difficult as two descendents of James II threatened to seize the crown in 1715 and 1746 and were supported by the Jacobites – this term comes from Jacobus, the Latin name meaning 'James'. The Hanoverian years of rule did stabilise and most of the monarchs reigned for many years.

George I (1714– 27)

George I was 52nd in line to the throne of England but was the closest Protestant – as required by the Act of Settlement. George was still not the ideal choice of monarch as he did not speak English and communicated with his ministers in French. He was 54 years old - when he was crowned which also made him the oldest monarch. He spent his time stabilising England after the tumultuous Stuart period. He did not undertake any special initiatives for Wales, but he did oversee the early stages of the Industrial Revolution which brought many economic changes to Wales. In 1721, Robert Walpole became England's first Prime Minister.

George III (1760–1820)

Like his grandfather George II, whom he succeeded in 1720, the reign of George III was a period of significant change – but he did not achieve anything specific for Wales, but the changes he made did impact Wales. The 18th century had seen the beginning of the Industrial Revolution which continued through the reign of George III. The expansion of many industries including coal mining and ironworks transformed both the Welsh economy and its landscape. The steel industry would follow later. George III improved the infrastructure with new roads, railways and later trains to ensure that the coal and iron from Wales could be easily transported to other parts of Britain.

Towards the end of the 18th century, there was what many describe as a 'Welsh Renaissance' with a great revival of Welsh Culture and language. Many great literary works were published at this time and the Gwyneddigion Society was founded. This all contributed to a strengthening of the feeling of Welsh identity.

Welsh soldiers in conflict overseas

There were a number of military conflicts during George III's reign including the Napoleonic Wars and American Revolutionary War and several Welsh regiments fought with distinction in these conflicts.

Although George III did not have any specific policies for Wales, the many developments of industry, culture and transport, benefited the country tremendously.

The early 19th century in Wales and industrialisation

The reigns of the last two Hanoverian kings – George IV (1820-1830) and William IV – did not have any significant impact on Wales, but nevertheless the country saw continual development.

George IV loved buildings and architecture and instructed several impressive buildings to be constructed. There were ongoing discussions in Parliament about Welsh identity and autonomy and there was an increased interest in Welsh affairs. There was further expansion of the Welsh industries, and this saw both urbanisation and population growth in the valleys of South Wales.

William IV was keen to reform the electoral system in Britain and in 1832, the Reform Act was passed. Whilst the act focused on England and Scotland, as the redistribution of parliamentary seats was part of the act, it ensured that Wales was still represented, which was important. There were also debates and reforms about the Church of England and these had implications for Wales where the Church of England was firmly established. The Ecclesiastical Duties and Revenues Act of 1836 was tabled to reform the  allocation of church revenue and reduce inefficiencies within the church and this had direct repercussions on the Welsh.

During William's reign industrialisation in Wales continued as did an increasing awareness of Welsh identity and culture. This was fuelled by the Welsh literary revival and the activities of the various organisations that promote Welsh language and culture. This increased awareness gave many people a renewed sense of their Welsh identity.

CHAPTER 9
VICTORIAN TIMES IN WALES

During the long reign of Queen Victoria, there were significant changes and developments in Wales – just as there had been in the reigns of her predecessors. A number of key developments that took place during her reign did impact Wales.

The Industrial Revolution continues

The Industrial Revolution continued to shape Wales and new industries included steel production and slate quarrying. Wales was already well known for its coal production – especially in the valleys of South Wales. The new railways facilitated the transportation of coal and other goods – including agricultural products- and this boosted Welsh economic development.

The first mining in Wales was in Roman Times, but during the Industrial Revolution, coal mining in Wales increased dramatically and became the key industry in Wales and also for the whole of Great Britain. The coal industry was focused in the Rhondda Valley and the South Wales Valleys, but there was another coalfield in Northeast Wales. By the end of the

19th century, Barry was the largest exporting docks in the world – with Cardiff a close second. The oldest continually worked coalfield in the world was the Tower Colliery in the South Wales Valleys. Welsh coal was in high demand and commanded a good price as it was considered to be high quality coal that burned well.

There was often discontent amongst the coal workers who were unhappy with their long hours, poor working conditions and wages. There were a number of protests against employers including a large one at Merthyr in 1831. It was essential that working conditions changed – and especially child labour.

"On 4 August 1842, a law was passed that stopped women and children under ten years from working underground in mines in Britain. Before this law was passed, it was common for whole families to work together underground to earn enough money for the family to live on. "

(What Jobs Did Children Do Underground? • Coal Mining and the Victorians • MyLearning, n.d.)

Big social changes

The Victorian era also saw many social changes including improvements in health, housing and education. The Public Health Act (1848) and the Education Act (1870) were passed to address social issues and to improve the well-being of many – particularly those in poorer Welsh communities.

The Rebecca Riots (1839- 1843)

Primarily centred on the rural parts of Carmarthenshire, Cardiganshire and Pembrokeshire, the Rebecca Riots were a series of protests that had been sparked by the increasing toll charges on the roads at a time when there was great economic hardship. The riots were given the name 'Rebecca' because the rioters dressed as women to conceal their identities. Their actions reminded many of the biblical story of Rebecca by the well which is in Genesis Chapter 24. The rioters destroyed toll gates and fences so that everyone could use the roads freely. The riots were non-violent and the rioters avoided harming anyone.

The riots made a significant impact because they highlighted social and economic inequalities and the need for reform. Eventually the tolls were removed on many of the roads in Wales and discussions began about grievances in the area. The Rebecca Riots are remembered as a symbol of the Welsh resistance to injustice.

The Welsh cultural revival

The Welsh Cultural Revival continued and several organisations including Cymdeithas y Cymreigyddion (The Society of Welshmen) and the National Eisteddfod of Wales were key in promoting Welsh identity and national pride. A real boost to the Welsh was the fact that Queen Victoria took a keen interest in Wales and Welsh events and she regularly visited Wales. On one particular visit, she stayed at Penrhyn Castle, and this captured the public imagination and there was a surge in tourism to the area

and pride amongst the Welsh. The Victorian era played a crucial role in shaping Wales and its people.

Everyday life in Wales in the 19th century

At the beginning of the 19th century there was great social inequality in both England and Wales, but industrialisation brought great changes to all classes as wealth grew. The 'middle class' emerged with a huge demand for a variety of goods and services which had previously only been enjoyed by the rich. Labour was cheap, and by 1900 about one third of women aged between 15- 20 years were in service.

Changes for the poor

With their new found wealth, the middle classes bought fine clothes – purple was the exciting new colour for women's dresses. They also bought beautiful china, cutlery from Sheffield and glass from Liverpool for their homes. Importantly, these items were all made in the United Kingdom – which was good for trade.

There were still millions of poor people. They worked incredibly long hours in poor conditions in factories, mines and docks. During Queen Victoria's reign, things did change for them. Food became cheaper as imports grew. Such delights as bananas started appearing in the cities! The Factory Acts of the 1830s reduced the number of working hours and improved the working conditions for both adults and children.

A new style of housing

Cheap terraces of houses were built and these were cheaper to buy. Good examples that can be seen are the slate workers' terraced house in Bethesda in North Wales and the terrace houses overlooking the sea at Beaumaris. A Victorian terrace house in Buckley, Flintshire was voted 'Wales' Home of the Year in 2022 (https://www.dailypost. co.uk /news/north-wales-news/inside-special-victorian-terrace-named-24759756). As well as improved housing, many more people had access to clean water, drains and some homes had gas. The horrors of the early 19th century workhouses became distant memories.

Education becomes a top priority.

Education for all became more important and in 1880, it became compulsory for children to attend school until the age of ten. There were new 'board' schools and church schools established. Few children had been able to read at the beginning of the century, but by the end, almost all children were literate. Interestingly, Welsh children were not encouraged to speak Welsh and were punished if they did. Their punishment was to wear a piece of wood called a 'Welsh Not' around their neck for the rest of the day. For the first time, children and their childhood were valued. Queen Victoria and her husband, Albert had nine children and for many became 'the ideal family'.

Theatres and music halls became popular and more people enjoyed sports with the new sports of lawn tennis and croquet quickly becoming popular.

Welsh Arts in the 19th century

Until the middle of the 19th century, Welsh artists found it impossible to earn a living from the home market and many had to live away from their homeland. In 1854, an Act of Parliament was passed that would fund the creation of new art schools – which included the Cardiff School of Art, built in 1865. The Royal Cambrian Academy of Art was founded in 1881 by a group of 31 English and Welsh artists who were based in the Conwy Valley. Betws-y-Coed became a centre for art and became popular as rail travel made it easier for English artists to spend time there.

The Welsh artist, Christopher Williams (1873-1934) was born in Maesteg and was famous for his portraits and Welsh landscapes which can be seen in the Glynn Vivian Art Gallery in Swansea, Newport Museum and others. Frank Brangwyn (1867-1956) was an artist, watercolourist and printmaker. He produced more than 12,000 pieces of art during his lifetime and is best known for his brightly coloured murals with details of animals and plants. His 1890 canvas entitled 'Funeral at Sea' won a medal at the Paris Salon, the following year.

The Welsh sculptor Sir William Goscombe John (1860-1952) was born in Cardiff but split his time between the city and London. He became well known for his public memorials – especially his war memorials for the men lost in the Second Boer War and World War I.

Augustus John (1878- 1961)

Augustus John was born in Tenby in 1878 and lived much of his life in the town. He and his older sister developed a love of drawing from their mother. He studied at the Slade School of Fine Art in London where he developed his distinctive style, influenced by arts such as Van Gogh and Gauguin. His landscapes are very distinctive as he uses expansive brushstrokes and intense colours. He is well known for his portrait painting too, of politicians, writers and other artists. Augustus John had a flamboyant character and he was a central figure in the bohemian communities in the cities of London and Paris. He was a forerunner in the development of modern British art.

19th century Welsh writers and poets

The beauty of the Welsh landscape has long inspired many to reach for their pen and there were a number of prolific Welsh writers in the 19th century. Thomas Edwards (1759-1858) was born in Flintshire and wrote a book on Welsh Orthography and an English/ Welsh dictionary. Robert Williams (1830-1877) was a Welsh language poet who was born in Ty'n-yr-ardd near Llanrwst. He wrote his poems under the Bardic name of Trebor Mai.

Ann Harriet Hughes (1852-1910) was a popular Welsh language novelist who wrote under the pen name of Gwyneth Vaughan. One of her contemporaries was Rhoda Broughton (1840- 1920) who also wrote novels and short stories in the Welsh language but was side-lined by many critics as she had the reputation of being sensationalist.

Although he was a Welsh journalist, Sir Henry Morton Stanley (1841-1904) was also an explorer who became famous when he went to central Africa in search of David Livingstone. On finding him, Stanley is credited with the famous line- 'Dr. Livingstone I presume?' although this is much debated!

Important 19th century Welsh inventions

Sir William Robert Grave

This Welsh lawyer and scientist invented the fuel cell in 1839. This was to be the foundation of the development of clean energy technology which is still being developed to this day.

Richard Trevithick

Although he was born in Cornwall, which had close cultural ties with Wales, Trevithick spent much time in Wales. It was in Wales that he developed high pressure steam engines which were successfully used for early locomotives and steam powered machinery.

David Edward Hughes

Hughes was a successful Welsh- American inventor who is best known for the world's first microphone which he invented in 1878. The microphone would be used in both telecommunications industry and to advance audio recording technology.

Griffith John Griffith

Griffith was the scientist who invented flexible and transparent film – an idea patented in 1889. His invention led to the development of photographic film used in cameras and films.

The emergence of the male Welsh voice choir....

During the 19th century, the exclusively male choirs were found in many Welsh chapels. Originally, the men sang hymns but as the choir's popularity developed, their repertoire was broadened to include both traditional and modern songs as well as ballads. Often the choirs sang with no musical accompaniment, but others were accompanied by a lyre, harp or fiddle.

.... And the Welsh love of rugby

In 1823, a great new game had found its way across the Welsh borders. Rugby had been invented at Rugby School in

England. The game was an instant success with the Welsh and quickly became entwined in Welsh culture and identity.

Wales played a significant role in the development of the game. The first recorded game took place in 1875 with teams from Lampeter College and Llandovery College. Rugby became particularly popular – especially in the industrial south and it was closely associated with the working class communities.

In 1881, Wales played England in the first international rugby match at Blackheath in London. Wales won and the Welsh rugby tradition had been ignited. Over the years, Wales has produced many legendary players – especially in the 1970s, which was a golden era.

One of the most iconic moments for Welsh rugby was in 1905 when Wales defeated New Zealand – then known as the 'Original All Blacks' – in a thrilling match in Cardiff. This moment is still celebrated in Welsh history.

Today, rugby is ingrained in the Welsh culture and there is passionate support for the national team – and great rivalry whenever they play England or Scotland! The game fosters pride and camaraderie amongst the Welsh and holds a special place in their hearts. The Welsh national team continues to play at the highest level.

Somerton
NEWPORT
R. Avon
Marshf'd
R. Portishe
Caerph
Llandaff
Cleve
St.Fagans
CARDIFF
Cogan
Penarth
Yatton
Cadoxton Sta. Congresbury
Du
Weston
Mendi
Beach or Axe
Brent Knoll
Burnham
Axbrid
Bridgewater
Huntbridge

CHAPTER 10
WALES IN THE EARLY 20TH CENTURY

During the 20th century, Wales saw many changes in its political, social and cultural landscapes. There were differing relationships with the monarch as Wales was an integral part of the United Kingdom.

The early 20th century

The last year of Victoria's reign

Queen Victoria's reign was both long and settled and this brought stability to Wales. The Queen had a keen interest in politics and loved peace. She regularly visited Wales and was met with enthusiasm by the Welsh people. Her death in 1901 was seen by many as the end of an era.

Victoria's reign had been a time of increased industrialisation for Wales – particularly in coal mining and steel producing which had both developed significantly and this proved crucial for the Welsh economy. As well as coal mining, slate, gold and different metal ores were also mined in the South Wales Valleys as it had been found to be one of the richest plains in the world. The two largest slate quarries in the world were located in Wales at Penrhyn and Dinorwig and the Oakley slate mine at Blaenau Festiniog was the largest slate mine in the world. Welsh slate proved a very popular commodity for roofing, floors and tombstones.

Life for the Welsh miners was hard with long hours and many dangers – injury and even death were not unusual. The miners were often discontented but continued working hard – this is one of the popular songs from the period that they sang at the coal face and interestingly, it is in a mixture of English and Welsh- -

I am a little collier and gweithio underground

The raff will never torri when I go up and down

It's bara when I'm hungry

And cwrw when I'm dry

It's gwely when I'm tired

And nefoedd when I die

The complete English translation of the lyrics of the song are as follows:

I am a little collier and working underground

The rope will never break when I go up and down

It's bread when I'm hungry

And beer when I'm dry

It's bed when I'm tired

And heaven when I die

(Wikipedia contributors, 2024)

King Edward VII (1901-1910)

Edward was the eldest son of Queen Victoria and was born in 1941 at Buckingham Palace so at 60 years old, he was an elderly man when he was crowned king. Victoria had blamed Edward (who was nicknamed 'Bertie') for his father's death as he had been a very rebellious young prince. As the Queen's eldest son, Edward, had been bestowed the title Prince of Wales. He did make several visits to Wales for ceremonial events steeped in Welsh culture.

The nine years of Edward's reign were not easy ones for the Welsh. Although the country saw continuing industrial growth, there was both political and social unrest with a number of labour strikes and a rise in Welsh nationalism. The labour strikes were mainly in the coal mining industry to highlight the poor working conditions.

Despite the social and political unrest, Edward VII did make efforts to maintain unity with Wales. His trips to Wales were to boost morale and highlight the importance of loyalty to the crown. As well as the ceremonial occasions, he also made inspections of the most important industrial sites but did little to ease the discontent. As he spoke fluent French and German, he preferred to devote his  time to touring Europe. In doing so, he did not appreciate that there were growing aspirations for greater self-governance amongst the Welsh.

King George V (1910-1936) and the war years

Throughout his reign, George V made great efforts to maintain unity and stability in Wales. He regularly visited the country to boost morale and to emphasise the importance of national unity.

Thousands of Welsh go to war

The First World War (1914-1918) had a profound impact on Wales – both because of its contribution to the British war effort and its effects on Welsh society. Wales made a significant contribution to the war as thousands of Welsh men were enlisted into the British armed forces and filled many key roles across all three services. Welsh soldiers fought on the Western Front, in Gallipoli, Mesopotamia and all the main areas of conflict. There was a heavy toll on the Welsh soldiers and thousands were killed, wounded or missing in action. Every community in Wales was impacted and mourning the loss of loved ones and the effects of the war were both profound and long-lasting.

Industrial output is increased for the war effort

Wales also played a key role with its industrial output. Welsh coal and steel was vital and production for both was rapidly increased - with many more workers being taken on for both industries. The Welsh steelworks contributed hugely to the production of munitions.

and other war materials.

The experience of the war strengthened Welsh identity within the United Kingdom and the sacrifice of its soldiers was commemorated in poetry, literature and art.

Hedd Wyn was a popular Welsh poet who was killed in the war Hedd Wyn – whose real name was Ellis Humphrey Evans - wrote his poems in Welsh. He was posthumously awarded the Bard's Chair at the 1917 National Eisteddfod of Wales for his poem Yr Arwr – meaning' The Hero'. Hedd Wyn was killed at the Battle of Passchendaele and his death was seen as a symbol of the loss and tragedy caused by the war.

David Jones was another Welsh artist and poet, who served in World War I and his experiences on the Western Front influenced his work. His epic poem 'Parenthesis' is considered one of the finest literary works of the period. Another leading poet was Wilfred Owen who was born in England but grew up in Birkenhead. Today, Wilfred Owen is regarded as one of the leading war poets and he is also known for his powerful anti-war works.

In the years following the war, there was an increasing desire in Wales for the national identity to be redefined and for greater self-governance to be re-introduced.

David Lloyd George champions the Welsh cause

David Lloyd George became British Prime Minister in 1916 and led the nation through the latter years of the war and in the aftermath. He was born in Manchester but had strong Welsh roots. He passionately wanted Wales to be properly recognised within the United Kingdom and he played a significant role in helping to establish the country's political identity. He advocated greater self governance for Wales and greater recognition of the country's important cultural and historical heritage.

The Labour Party comes to Wales

The English Labour Party was founded in 1900 as a result of the merger of a variety of organisations and trade unions. Wales had always played a significant role in the labour movement, advocating for workers' rights and social reforms. The Labour Party's strength and influence gathered momentum in Wales and in the years between the wars, the Labour Party became one of the main political forces. The Welsh electorate liked what Labour was saying about workers' rights, healthcare and education and soon gave their backing to the new political party.

CHAPTER 11

THE MID-20TH CENTURY AND WAR ON THE HORIZON

George VI never expected to be king as his brother, Edward VIII had been crowned King in January 1936 on the death of their father, George V. However, Edward VIII's reign was a short-lived one as he abdicated the throne just 11 months later- on 11 December 1936- so that he could marry the American divorcée, Wallis Simpson. His abdication caused a constitutional crisis that affected the whole of the UK – including Wales – because it raised questions about the modern role of the monarchy and the stability of the nation. His abdication came at a time when there was significant social and political change in the years leading to the start of World War II.

George VI (1936- 1952)

The reign of George VI was a challenging one with the huge impact of World War II plus the decline of the British Empire and continuing social changes. His coronation in 1937 was a huge event that captured everyone's imagination and was important as it symbolised stability and continuity in an increasingly unsettled world.

The king made a number of visits to Wales during his reign – particularly during the war years to provide crucial moral support, to strengthen the ties between the monarchy and the Welsh people and to demonstrate the relevance of the monarchy during times of uncertainty.

Post war there were a number of social changes in Wales including the decline of the traditional industries such as coal mining and the emergence of new trades. George VI coincided his visits with these changes so that he could spend time talking to the workers who were affected.

World War II (1939-1945)

Everyone in the United Kingdom was involved in the war and made significant contributions to the war effort. When Adolf Hitler invaded Poland in September 1939, Britain and France declared war on Germany. Over the following six years, the war took more lives and destroyed more land and property than any other conflict in history.

Welsh servicemen served in all three branches of the British Armed Forces- the Royal Navy, British Army and the Royal Air Force (RAF). The Welsh regiments including the Royal Welsh Fusiliers (the oldest Welsh regiment), the Welsh Guards and the South Wales Borderers all played crucial roles in conflicts and a number of key battles:

The Battle of Dunkirk

Welsh soldiers along with other British forces were involved in the evacuation of Allied troops from the beaches of Dunkirk in 1940.

The Battle of Britain

Welsh RAF pilots took part in the 1940 operation defending British airspace from German Luftwaffe pilots.

North Africa Campaign

The Royal Welsh Fusiliers served in North Africa and fought in the battles of El Alamein and Tobruk. The South Wales Borderers also saw action in North Africa and were in the Battle of Gazala and the second Battle of El Alamein. Although the Welsh Guards was an infantry regiment used primarily for ceremonial duties, the regiment fought in several battles including the Battle of Tunis. The contribution made by Welsh soldiers fighting against the Germans and Italians, helped to secure victory for the Allied Forces.

Many Welsh soldiers distinguished themselves with great acts of bravery and heroism and were presented with the Victoria Cross and Military Cross in recognition of this.

At home in Wales

The Welsh communities also made great contributions in civil defence, air raid precautions and supporting evacuees. Welsh industries played a vital role in supplying materials for the war effort including coals for ships and steel for weapons and machinery. The Welsh workforce increased  production during the war years and many of the workers were women.

World War writers and poets

There were a number of Welsh writers and poets who contributed to the cultural heritage of Wales both during and after the war. Their work gives a clear insight into the human horrors and experiences of war and its aftermath. Dylan Thomas had been writing poetry and prose prior to the war and became a BBC scriptwriter during the war years to provide information to the public – and importantly, boost morale.

Alun Lewis served as an officer in the British Army during the war and his works reflect his experiences. As a poet he is known for his honesty and depth of emotions. Sadly, he was killed in action in Burma in 1944.

Vernon Watkins was another Welsh poet who was a friend of Dylan Thomas. He too served in the British Army and wrote poetry throughout the war years, exploring many different themes including love and nature as well as his war experiences. Gwyn Thomas was a Welsh writer and his short stories and plays were popular. During the war he worked as a teacher and served in the Home Guard so much of his writing reflects the realities of life in Wales and the impact on the community of the war.

Elizabeth II (1953- 2022)

Queen Elizabeth II's reign was one of the longest and most remarkable in the history of Great Britain. Over the years there were huge social, cultural and political changes, both in Wales and the rest of the UK

Elizabeth II was proclaimed Queen on the death of her father in February 1952. She was crowned in June 1953 when everyone was still rebuilding their lives in the aftermath of World War II. In the years that followed there were huge advancements in technology with the invention of the television and internet and digital communication – all of these completely changed everyday lives. Elizabeth embraced all the new technology, whilst working hard to maintain the traditions of the monarchy.

There were many political changes during Elizabeth's reign too, with the decolonisation of many former British colonies. Amongst the many former colonies to gain independence were India and Pakistan, which both gained independence in August 1947, Sri Lanka (formerly Ceylon) in 1948 and Uganda, Jamaica, Trinidad and Tobago all gained their independence in 1962.

During Elizabeth's reign, the European Union was created and gathered momentum. The United Kingdom joined the EU on 1 January 1973, but following a referendum, left in 2020. There was also the devolution of powers within the United Kingdom of Wales, Scotland and Northern Ireland. From 1998, all these countries were governed independently.

Elizabeth II was a significant cultural figure who represented continuity and stability in a fast-changing world. She regularly travelled abroad to visit countries in the Commonwealth and gave a number of key speeches. She was also Patron of a variety of cultural institutions. She and her husband, Philip, Duke of Edinburgh, had four children. Their marriages were great state occasions, but Elizabeth's reign was also marked by the breakdown of three of her children's marriages and the tragic death of her former daughter-in-law, Diana, Princess of Wales. Throughout her reign, the Queen remained dedicated to her duties and responsibilities as monarch.

(Face of Queen Elizabeth in Twenty Pound Sterling Banknote)

Queen Elizabeth II celebrated her Golden Jubilee, marking 50 years on the throne in 2002 and her Diamond Jubilee (60 years) in 2012 – both occasions were times for national celebration. When she died, she left a lasting legacy both in the UK and around the world.

The Welsh Language Act –1967

There had been growing concerns about the decline in the use of the Welsh language and the aim of The Welsh Language Act of 1967 was a piece of legislation that was passed to recognise, protect and promote the Welsh Language in a number of ways. It was significant to Welsh people because it recognised the cultural importance of the Welsh language and was viewed as a major step in its preservation and its promotion among the younger generations.

Equality of status:

The Act recognised the equal validity of Welsh with English for legal purposes. This meant that all legal documents could be presented in Welsh.

- Official documents and publications: All literature published by public bodies in Wales should be available in both Welsh and English.
- Education: An emphasis would be placed on the teaching of Welsh in schools and the use of Welsh in educational settings.
- Public Services: All public services such as health and local government should be conducted in Welsh whenever there was a significant demand.

The Investiture of the Prince of Wales- 1969

On 1 July 1969 there was a magnificent investiture

ceremony at Caernarfon Castle where Elizabeth II bestowed the title on her eldest son, Charles (now Charles III). Charles became the 21st Prince of Wales and the ceremony was watched on television by 500 million people worldwide. In anticipation of his new role, Charles had learnt Welsh when he was younger. There had not been a Prince of Wales since 1911. The investiture faced huge opposition from Welsh nationalists who felt that an English prince was being thrust upon them.

Consequently, when Prince William became Prince of Wales on the death of his grandmother Elizabeth II in September 2022, there was no investiture ceremony to avoid any tension. Like his father, Prince William studied Welsh as a teenager in preparation for his future role.

Duties of the Prince of Wales

- To represent the monarch at a variety of different ceremonies and events.
- To maintain and promote the Royal traditions.
- Promote British interests both at home and overseas and enhance business, cultural and diplomatic exchanges.
- To support charitable organisations and initiatives – with emphasis on education, youth development, healthcare and environmental conservation.

The roles of the Prince of Wales in modern times have become far reaching and are seen as important for preparing the Prince of Wales for his future leadership role both within the Royal Family and worldwide.

(Wikipedia contributors, 2024a)

The Welsh miners' strikes

There were several Welsh miners' strikes and the two main ones took place in 1972 and 1984- 1985. They had significant social, economic and political repercussions not only on the coal mining industry, but numerous mining communities in Wales and the wider labour movement. The strikes have left their mark on the memories of the Welsh mining communities.

The 1972 strike

This dispute started in early January following a dispute over wages. The National Union of Mineworkers (NUM) had demanded a substantial increase in wages and an improvement in working conditions. The aim of the strike was to improve both wages and working conditions for all coal miners in the UK.

The strike lasted seven weeks and resulted in a significant pay increase for miners and an improvement in working conditions and safety standards.

The 1984- 1985 strike

This strike was caused by the announcement made by Margaret Thatcher, the Prime Minister, that 20 coal mines would be closing as they were unprofitable and that the coal industry would be restructured. There was much anger amongst the Welsh miners and fear of job losses in the mining communities.

The aims of the strike were to oppose the closure of the mines and protect both the coal industry and thousands of jobs. The strike lasted nearly a year and was unsuccessful because Mrs Thatcher was determined to break the strike and the NUM lost valuable financial support from other unions.

The miners returned to work, but the coal mining industry declined even further.

New industries for Wales

Following the decline of coal mining, a number of new industries began in Wales, and these helped to diversify the economy.

Manufacturing and engineering

There has been significant growth in advanced engineering and manufacturing in Wales – particularly in the aerospace, car and electronic sectors. Companies such as Airbus, Toyota and Dynamics have all opened factories in Wales providing many skilled employment opportunities.

Information technology and digital

Wales has seen growth in both these sectors in recent years. Technology parks have been developed near cities like Cardiff, Swansea and Newport, with companies involved in software development, digital media and telecommunications. All these new industries are currently thriving.

Life sciences and healthcare

The science sector in Wales is rapidly developing with the arrival of new specialist companies in pharmaceuticals, biotechnology and medical devices. Welsh research institutions and universities are driving innovation and development in the sector.

The creative industries

Wales has a vibrant creative industry including film and television production, animation, gaming and design. Today, Cardiff is the hub for media companies with the BBC and other broadcasters all having studios located in the city.

Tourism

With its natural beauty, numerous historic sites and cultural attractions, tourism has in recent years become an important industry and a significant contributor to the Welsh economy – especially in rural areas. Wales attracts many special interest visitors who enjoy a wide range of interests including cycling, hiking and ornithology. Currently, there are a number of new initiatives promoting sustainable tourism.

Wales joins the European Union- 1973

As part of the United Kingdom, Wales joined the EU on 1 January 1973 and saw both positive and negative impacts from its membership. A significant and very positive aspect was the amount of funding that Wales received from the EU. Various EU funds have provided financial support for economic development, the improvement of infrastructure and job creation.

The EU also provided funding for urban regeneration to help revitalise communities to improve living conditions. Infrastructure of roads, railways and ports was enhanced providing Wales with better connections with other parts of the UK and Europe. The EU also helped to enhance training opportunities to develop skills in the workforce to ensure that they were both more employable and more competitive.

Agriculture and farmers also received EU funding to promote sustainable farming practices. The EU encouraged environmental protection policies and initiated changes to address climate change and preserve biodiversity. The challenges of being a member of the EU included regulatory alignment and immigration. The impact of joining the EU was certainly multi-faceted.

On 23 June 2016, a referendum was held in the UK asking voters whether the UK should remain a member of the European Union or not. In Wales, 52.5% of voters voted in favour of leaving the EU. This result was in line with the rest of the UK where 51.9% voted to leave. This decision has had significant political, economic and social ramifications for Wales – like the rest of the UK - and triggered negotiations with the EU to establish a new working relationship between the UK and EU.

CHAPTER 12
MODERN WALES AND DEVOLUTION

The devolution of powers to Wales took place steadily over several years. The National Assembly for Wales was established in 1999 and was a key moment for the country. Here are the various stages of the Welsh devolution.

The Welsh referendum

In 1997 a referendum was held in Wales and the majority of voters supported the establishment of a National Assembly with devolved powers.

1999 and the National Assembly is established

The National Assembly was officially established in 1999 but had limited legislative powers. It could make secondary legislation and oversee such areas as health, education and local government.

2014, The Wales Act

This act introduced significant changes by granting additional powers to the National Assembly. For the first time, the National Assembly could pass legislation in certain areas without seeking approval from the UK parliament. The Act also paved the way for the devolution of taxation powers so that the Welsh Government could set its own tax rates.

2020 The renaming of the National Assembly

Following the Welsh Parliament and Elections Act that was passed in 2020, the National Assembly was renamed the Senedd Cymru – meaning 'Welsh Parliament'. The act also gave the Welsh Parliament greater powers over transportation, energy and the environment.

Devolution has been warmly welcomed by the Welsh as they feel it gives them greater control over domestic affairs and policies. The Welsh Parliament can make decisions tailored to the specific needs of the Welsh population. Welsh devolution has also contributed to the preservation of Welsh culture, language and identity which in turn has strengthened the sense of Welsh unity.

Key Welsh politicians in the 20th century

Mention has already been made of David Lloyd George who has been the only Welshman to be Prime Minister, but a number of other Welsh politicians played prominent roles during the 20th century.

Aneurin Bevan (1897-1960)

Bevan was a very strong figure in the Labour Party and was the architect of the National Health Service (NHS). He was Minister of Health in the post war Labour government. The NHS was launched in 1948, providing free healthcare to all – regardless of status.

Gwynfor Evans (1912-2005)

Evans was a prominent Welsh nationalist who became the first President of Plais Cymru – the Welsh party. He played a leading role in the Welsh nationalist movement and did much to promote Welsh language and culture. He was a strong advocate for self-government and devolution for Wales.

Clement Davies (1184- 1962)

Davies was the leader of the Liberal Party between 1945-1956. He played an important part in rebuilding the party after World War II and was a keen advocate for progressive politics and civil liberties.

Neil Kinnock

Born in Tredegar in Wales, the only child of a former coal miner, Neil Kinnock was leader of the Labour Party between 1983-1992. He played a central role in modernising the party and moving it towards the political centre. He was not successful in leading the Labour Party to victory in the general elections, but paved the way to  success for Tony Blair and the continuing transformation of the Labour Party

More recently, other Welsh figures who can be added to this list include Rhodri Morgan and Carwyn Jones who have both been First Ministers of Wales since devolution.

Welsh personalities in the 20th century

Dylan Thomas (1914- 1953)

This poet's name is the one everyone mentions when asked the question to name a great Welshman! He was born in Swansea in 1914 and is considered one of the greatest poets and writers of the 20th century. His work is well known for its vivid imagery and emotional depth.

Dylan Thomas received great acclaim early on for his

collections of poetry including 18 Poems (1934) and Death and Entrances (1946). In these volumes he explored the themes of life, death and the passage of time. He also made a number of radio broadcasts and Under Milk Wood which captures the lives of people living in a fictional Welsh town.

Unfortunately, Thomas had a troubled relationship with alcohol which led to his premature death when he was aged just 39 years. His influence on modern poetry has been profound and his evocative verse has inspired both readers and writers the world over.

(Wikipedia contributors, 2024a)

Roald Dahl (1916-1990)

One of the world's most beloved children's authors is Roald Dahl. Dahl was born in Llandaff, Cardiff to Norwegian parents. During World War II, he served as a fighter pilot with the Royal Air Force. In the years that followed he became well known for his imaginative and whimsical stories. Today his work is enjoyed by readers aged nine- 90! Many of his books including Charlie and the Chocolate Factory, Matilda and The BFG have been made into successful films. His books have sold more than 325 million copies around the world.

(Wikipedia contributors, 2024d)

Richard Burton (1925 -1984)

Richard Burton was born in Pontrhydyfen and became a highly acclaimed Welsh actor – both on stage and screen. He starred in numerous films including Cleopatra, Who's Afraid of Virginia Woolf? and The Spy who Came in from the Cold. Richard Burton became almost as well-known with the public for his turbulent relationship with his second wife, Elizabeth Taylor – whom he married twice!

Laura Ashley (1925- 1985)

World famous for her quintessentially British style and fabric designs, Laura Ashley was born Laura Mountney in Dowlais, Merthyr Tydfil in 1925. She founded the iconic 'Laura Ashley' brand which is well known for its timeless floral prints and stylish traditional furniture. Over the years, the name Laura Ashley has become a global symbol of British fashion and furniture.

Sir Tom Jones OBE (Born 1940)

Well known for his powerful voice and charismatic presence, Tom Jones was born in Treforest, Pontypridd. During the 1960s he had a string of hit records including It's Not Unusual and Delilah and What's New Pussycat which was the theme song for the James Bond film Thunderball. In 1999 he was awarded the OBE and in 2006 he was knighted by Queen Elizabeth II for his services to music. Although now in his 80s, Tom Jones still regularly appears in shows.

Shirley Bassey (Born 1937-)

Known for her distinctive voice and glamorous looks,

Dame Shirley Bassey has fanned the world over. She has many memorable songs to her credit including the James Bond themes Goldfinger, Diamonds are Forever and Moonraker. She was born in Tiger Bay near Cardiff in 1937 and started performing as a teenager. She was the first Welsh person to reach the No 1 slot in the British charts with As I Love You. With the release of her most recent album, I Owe it All to You in 2020, she is the first female artist to have an album in the UK Albums Chart in seven consecutive decades. She became a Dame Commander of the British Empire in 2020. In 2022 and 2023, commemorative coins and stamps were issued in the UK in her honour.

(Wikipedia contributors, 2024c)

Charlotte Church (Born 1986)

In the late 1990s, Charlotte Church first gained widespread recognition for her angelic soprano singing voice when she was just 12 years old. Church was born in Llandaff, Cardiff. She captivated audiences with her classical repertoire and was the youngest person ever to reach Number 1 in the UK's classical music chart. Since then, she has successfully broadened her appeal as a classical crossover artist, experimenting with pop music. She still lives in rural France and runs a wellness retreat and works in broadcasting.

(Wikipedia contributors, 2024a)

Everyday life in Wales during the 20th century

Everyday life in Wales changed significantly during the 20th century due to various economic, social and political developments.

At the beginning of the century, Wales was very reliant on coal mining and other heavy industries – especially in the South Wales valleys. Communities and everyday life revolved around the coal mines. By halfway through the century, the coal mining had started to decline and younger people in the mining communities moved to the cities in search of work. All the urban communities enlarged in size and many of the mining communities became fragmented.

The Welsh mining villages underwent huge changes with the pit closures. Many villages faced financial hardship as jobs disappeared. Mining had been the primary source of employment for generations and many older people did not want to relocate to the cities but knew they faced unemployment and financial insecurity. When the mines closed there were implications for the health and well-being of the community, but luckily, free healthcare was available to all because of the inception of the NHS.

Education remained very important in Wales and the Welsh language saw a great revival in schools and efforts to promote bibilingualism. The University of Wales had been founded in 1893, but during the 20th century it grew to include a number of different colleges and constitutions. The university also underwent significant restructuring with some of the colleges becoming independent universities.

The 20th century Welsh cultural revival

Known as Y Diwygiad, this was a rhyme with interest in - and a celebration of – Welsh language, literature and music. All these elements help to bolster Welsh national identity. The movement started because it was felt that social and economic changes were threatening the survival of the Welsh language and its culture.

Revitalisation of the Welsh language

One of the main aims of the cultural revival was the revitalisation of the Welsh language (Cymraeg)There were renewed efforts to use Welsh in schools and to promote its use in literature, the media and everyday life. The Welsh Language Society – Cymdeithas yr  Iaith Gymraeg- campaigned for the use of Welsh in public life too.

S4C (Sianel Pedwar Cymru) – Channel Four Wales - is the Welsh-language television channel and during the cultural renaissance it too enjoyed an increased number of viewers and played a significant role in promoting bilingualism. It still primarily broadcasts in Welsh, but it does also have some content in English- particularly news and current affairs.

Literature and poetry

The Welsh literary scene enjoyed a huge revival with writers and poets exploring the Welsh language and a variety of themes. Dylan Thomas has been the most celebrated poet and writer in the 20th century (there is more information on him in the section Welsh Personalities in the 20th century). This was a time with many notable Welsh poets, including R.S. Thomas, Waldo Williams and T.H. Parry-Williams. R.S. Thomas was an Anglican priest whose poems often spoke of the Welsh landscape and reflected on the complexities of modern life.

Gwynn Thomas was a popular novelist and playwright who portrayed working class life with humour and compassion.

Folk music traditions

Welsh folk music and traditions enjoyed a renaissance too. Musicians and singers revived all the Welsh folk songs and hymns and rediscovered the rich musical heritage of Wales. The Eisteddfodau – the annual Welsh festivals promoted Welsh culture and also celebrated its renaissance.

Other genres of Music

Alan Hoddinott (1929- 2008)

Alan Hoddinott was a leading Welsh composer during the 20th century and his work ranged from orchestral to chamber music. He often drew on popular Welsh themes and folklore.

Karl Jenkins (Born 1944)

This highly acclaimed Welsh composer was born in Penclawdd in 1944. At first, he won acclaim as a jazz and jazz-rock musician, but later transitioned to become a classical music composer. He has a very distinctive style which includes elements of jazz, world music and ethnic influences. One of his most famous works is 'Adiemus' which is a series of vocal compositions. Over the years, Jenkins has written music scores for commercials, films and television. In 2015 he was knighted by Queen Elizabeth II.

The Arts

Welsh artists also enjoyed new interest in their work. Favourite themes in their paintings included the local countryside, Welsh history and folklore. Augustus John (1878-1961) was one of the best-known artists of the time and his work spanned the end of the 19th century and the beginning of the 20th century. His influence has lasted much longer. (also refer to the section Welsh Arts in the 19th century)

Kyffin Williams (1918-2006) was a landscape painter who captured the ruggedness of the Welsh countryside in a very distinctive style which was characterised by bold brushstrokes and the use of a sombre colour palette. Ceri Richards (1903-1971) was a popular modernist painter and printmaker who also drew inspiration from the Welsh countryside and mythology for his work.

Theatre

The Welsh National Theatre – Theatr Genedlaethol Cymru- was founded in the capital city of Cardiff. Today the company's main performance venue is located in the Wales Millennium Centre, which is a well-known landmark that overlooks Cardiff Bay.

A number of performances proved particularly popular in the late 20th century, and these included various works by Dylan Thomas and 'How Green was my Valley by Richard Llewellyn, which is based on the 1939 novel with the same name. The company also performed On the Back Hill, based on the 1982 novel by Bruce Chatwin. The novel follows the lives of twin brothers working on a farm in the Welsh borders.

Over the years, The Welsh National Theatre has regularly staged productions of Welsh language plays including adaptations of classical works and contemporary plays that all explore Welsh culture.

Dance

Wales has its own excellent dance company – the National Dance Company Wales (NDC Wales). The NDC Wales was founded in Cardiff in 1983 and is well known for its innovative and diverse productions. The company does not focus exclusively on ballet, but it does include elements of ballet in its repertoire with contemporary dance styles. The company often collaborates with Welsh dancers and choreographers as well as many from all over the world. NDC Wales also goes on international tours to showcase the talented dancers of Wales.

Great Welsh inventors in the 20th century

Thomas 'Carbide' Williams (1860- 1915)

Williams was born in Canada to Welsh parents and his work straddled the end of the19th and beginning of the 20th century. His greatest invention was the process for producing calcium carbide and this was instrumental in the development of the acetylene gas industry.

Griffith Pugh (1909-1994)

This Welsh physiologist and inventor made significant contributions to the science of human survival in extreme weather conditions. He developed specialist clothing and equipment for mountaineers and his inventions included the down suit and innovative oxygen equipment for use at high altitudes.

Sir Clive Sinclair (1940- 2021)

Sir Clive Sinclair was a prolific inventor whose name became a household name. He was born in London, and he had Welsh grandparents. His best-known invention was the ZX Spectrum home computer and a number of different consumer electronics. Sinclair also invented the pocket calculator. He made several models that would easily fit in the pocket  and was keen that they were cheaply priced and affordable to many-

Sinclair invented the pocket calculator but was best known for popularising the home computer, bringing it to British high-street stores at relatively affordable prices.

The Guardian Newspaper (Siddique, 2021)

Gordon Edge (Born 1952)

Gordon Edge is a contemporary inventor who has become well known for his pioneering work in wind energy. He has developed variable– speed wind turbines and these have significantly increased the efficiency and reliability of wind power generators.

CHAPTER 13
WALES IN THE EARLY 21ST CENTURY

The 21st century is going to be an important one for Wales and will reflect the country's ongoing development both within the United Kingdom and as part of the global community.

Devolution and Governance

The early years of the 21st century saw the consolidation of Welsh devolution with further powers being transferred to the Senedd (Welsh Parliament) by the UK government.

In 2006, the Government of Wales Act was passed providing the Senedd with greater legislative powers.

2016 – the year of Brexit

The UK's decision to leave the European Union in 2016 had significant implications for Wales, as the country had received significant EU funding for a series of development projects. The post-Brexit years certainly brought challenges for Welsh trade and agriculture as well as regional funding.

Wales is continuing to make the transition from its

reliance on heavy industries like coal mining to new sectors such as technology, renewable energy and service industries. This has become more necessary as new customers must be found post-Brexit.

Rhodi Morgan was the First Minister of Wales between 2000- 2009 and helped to shape the nation's policies and structure of governance in the early years of Welsh devolution. Leanne Wood who is the former leader of Plaid Cymru has also been an influential figure in Welsh politics – advocating further powers of devolution and for social justice.

The impact of COVID-19

The pandemic had a significant impact on Wales affecting both the economy and daily life. The economic disruption led to job losses, business closures and financial hardship for many families. Schools and universities were forced to close and learning went online. Remote learning caused challenges for teachers, parents and students. Social distancing brought loneliness to many Welsh people. Wales implemented a vaccination programme to slow the spread of COVID-19.

Looking to the future

Following Devolution, Wales began a socio-economic revitalisation that would address some of the country's long-standing problems and also seize new opportunities. The Welsh Government outlined ambitious goals that would boost the country's economy, enhance its public services, enrich its culture and promote environmental sustainability.

The key initiatives for the 21st century that were defined

Further economic diversification

Wales needed to further reduce its reliance on the

traditional heavy industries such as coal mining and to focus strongly on innovative technological, service and creative industries. The country needs to continue to try and attract new businesses to the area and stimulate economic growth across the country.

The development of education standards and new skills

The importance of education and its link with economic prosperity has been recognised and there have been a number of initiatives to improve standards in schools and provide lifelong learning opportunities. There has been great investment in several vocational training and apprenticeship programmes to help equip school leavers with the required skills for the evolving Welsh job scene.

Health and wellness

Since Devolution, the Welsh Government has been keen to address public health challenges and promote wellness. It has also worked hard to reduce regional inequalities in the health system and to improve the level of healthcare for everyone. New initiatives have recently been made to tackle current issues  including obesity, mental health and substance abuse.

Further promotion of the Welsh culture

This has been an ongoing aim for many years along with the promotion of the Welsh language, arts and traditions. There has been increasing financial support for the various Welsh festivals and cultural programmes. This is important as it not only fosters national pride in Wales, it is also key in promoting both tourism and investment in the country.

More sport for Wales

Rugby remains as popular as ever with the Welsh national team achieving great successes in the Six Nations championship and Grand Slam victories in 2005, 2008, 2012 and 2019. The Welsh national team also reached the semi-finals of the Rugby World Cup in both 2011 and 2019. Alun Wyn Jones captioned the Welsh team on many of these occasions and he is one of Wales' most iconic sportsmen.

Wales has also performed well on the football pitch with Gareth Bale gaining national pride through his achievements at club level and as a player in the Welsh national team, for Tottenham Hotspur and Real Madrid. Many of the Welsh sportsmen and women have become role models for the young and great emphasis is being placed by schools on the many health benefits gained from children taking part in sports from a young age.

Developing renewable energy

Wales has become a leading country in renewable energy and has made substantial investments in wind, solar and hydro-electric power and this is contributing to the country's positive efforts to combat climate change.

CONCLUSION

In tracing the colourful and complex tapestry of the history of Wales, one is inevitably drawn into a narrative marked by resilience, cultural richness and a relentless quest for national identity. From its ancient origins to the modern day, Wales has witnessed a myriad of events and characters that have both shaped its destiny and strengthened its national character.

The story of Wales begins in antiquity, with its earliest inhabitants carving out their cultural identity as they thrived in the country's rugged landscapes. Over the centuries, waves of migration, invasions, and conquests have washed upon its shores – each one leaving an indelible footprint on its history. The Roman occupation brought great progress, marked by infrastructure and the first urbanisation. In contrast, the arrival of the Anglo-Saxons ushered in a difficult period of political fragmentation and great strife.

During the mediaeval era Wales emerged as an individual entity for the first time. This was the result of the rise of powerful Welsh princes and the establishment of independent kingdoms. The legendary figure of Owain Glyndŵr symbolised the enduring spirit of Welsh resistance against English dominance, when he led a valiant but unsuccessful rebellion in the 15th century.

The Union of the Crowns in 1603, when James VI of Scotland was crowned James I of England, brought Wales firmly under the authority of the English monarchy. This led to centuries of political and cultural assimilation. In the 18th century, the Industrial Revolution brought profound changes to Wales, as coal mining and heavy industry completely transformed the South Wales landscape and fuelled huge economic growth. This period also brought both social upheaval and exploitation, resulting in years of struggles for the Welsh working class in the coalfields.

Throughout this turbulent history, one constant thread has remained as strong as ever - the Welsh national identity, with its unique language as its cornerstone. Despite concerted efforts to try and suppress it, the Welsh language has endured as a symbol of great cultural pride and strong resistance.

The 20th century witnessed a great renaissance of Welsh nationalism, culminating in the country's devolution in 1999 which gave Wales a greater degree of autonomy.

Today, Wales faces new challenges as it grapples with the challenges of globalisation, environmental sustainability and the preservation of its unique heritage. There are efforts to promote greater bilingualism and preserve linguistic diversity, with the ever increasing usage of the Welsh language. The debates over Welsh independence continue to simmer too and this reflects a renewed sense of confidence and assertiveness in the Welsh people.

In conclusion, delving into the history of Wales, reveals a

land brimming with tales of courage and resilience. These have all contributed to the colourful mosaic that has created the country's heritage. From its ancient legends to its modern day successes, Wales captivates the imagination and leaves an indelible mark on those who visit its rugged landscapes.

As visitors end their exploration of Wales, they take with them more than photographs of beautiful countryside. They carry with them the lesson that nurturing cultural traditions, preserving historical monuments whilst fostering a warm spirit of unity, creates a lasting legacy that will inspire many generations to come....

REFERENCES

THE HISTORY OF ENGLAND

The Age of Enlightenment. (n.d.). History Guild. https://historyguild.org/the-age-of-enlightenment/

Anglo-Saxons: A brief history. (n.d.). Historical Association. https://www.history.org.uk/primary/resource/3865/anglo-saxons-a-brief-history

Beck, E. (2022, March 3). *The impacts of the Black Death*. History Crunch. https://www.historycrunch.com/impacts-of-the-black-death.html#/

Beer, G. (2015, November 11). *The impact of On the Origin of Species*. OUPblog. https://blog.oup.com/2015/11/academic-impact-charles-darwin/

Biography.com Editors. (2020, December 2). *Margaret Thatcher*. Biography. https://www.biography.com/political-figure/margaret-thatcher

British Empire. (2022, November 2). In *Wikipedia*. https://en.wikipedia.org/w/index.php?title=British_Empire&oldid=1119562285

British Empire in World War II. (2022, November 3). In *Wikipedia*. https://en.wikipedia.org/w/index.php?title=British_Empire_in_World_War_II&oldid=1119836413

British entry into World War I. (2022, October 26). In *Wikipedia*. https://en.wikipedia.org/w/index.php?title=British_entry_into_World_War_I&oldid=1118331534

Brooke, B. (August 30, 2022). *The legend of King Arthur*. British Heritage. https://britishheritage.com/history/legend-king-arthur

Carlin, D. (2019, September 17). *Roosevelt, Churchill and the creation of the United Nations*. Forbes. https://www.forbes.com/sites/davidcarlin/2019/09/17/roosevelt-churchill-and-the-creation-of-the-united-nations/?sh=3f1378dc528e

Cartwright, M. (2019, December 18). *Henry III of England*. World History. https://www.worldhistory.org/Henry_III_of_England/

Chan Laddaran, K. (2015, November 11). Poll says Charles Darwin's 'On the Origin of Species ' is the most influential book. CNN. https://www.cnn.com/2015/11/11/world/charles-darwin-irpt/index.html

The Editors of Encyclopedia Britannica. (n.d.). Restoration. In *Encyclopedia Britannica*. https://www.britannica.com/topic/Restoration-English-history-1660

Education Act 1944. (2022, October 31). In *Wikipedia*.

https://en.wikipedia.org/w/index.php?title=Education_Act_1944&oldid=1119151657

Elisha Sawe, B. (2019, April 23). *Biggest religions in England.* WorldAtlas. https://www.worldatlas.com/articles/biggest-religions-in-england.html

The end of the British Empire after the Second World War. (n.d.). Imperial War Museums. https://www.iwm.org.uk/history/the-end-of-the-british-empire-after-the-second-world-war

The English Renaissance. (n.d.). Study Smarter. https://www.studysmarter.us/explanations/history/the-tudors/the-english-renaissance/

European Theater of World War II. (n.d.). History Crunch. https://www.historycrunch.com/european-theater-of-world-war-ii.html#/

Fairy tale origins thousands of years old, researchers say. (2016, January 20). BBC. https://www.bbc.com/news/uk-35358487

Frum, D. (2016, June 24). *Why Britain left.* The Atlantic. https://www.theatlantic.com/international/archive/2016/06/brexit-eu/488597/

Harrison, J. (n.d.). *Who were the Anglo-Saxons?* British Library. https://www.bl.uk/anglo-saxons/articles/who-were-the-anglo-saxons

History.com Editors. (2018, August 21). *Hundred Years' War.* History. https://www.history.com/topics/middle-ages/hundred-years-war

History.com Editors. (2019, June 7). *Winston S. Churchill - Biography, death and speeches.* History. https://www.history.com/topics/british-history/winston-churchill

History.com Editors. (2020a, May 21). *The English Restoration.* History. https://www.history.com/this-day-in-history/the-english-restoration

History.com Editors. (2020b, June 30). *War of the Roses.* History. https://www.history.com/topics/british-history/wars-of-the-roses

History.com Editors. (2021a, September 20). *English civil wars.* History. https://www.history.com/topics/british-history/english-civil-wars

History.com Editors. (2021b, October 21). *Magna Carta.* History. https://www.history.com/topics/british-history/magna-carta

History.com Editors. (2022, September 20). *Revolutionary War.* History. https://www.history.com/topics/american-revolution/american-revolution-history

History.com Staff. (2018, August 29). *Was King Arthur a real person?* History. https://www.history.com/news/was-king-arthur-a-real-person

History of the United Kingdom during the First World War. (2022, October 26). In *Wikipedia.* https://en.wikipedia.org/w/index.php?title=History_of_the_United

Kingdom during the First World War&oldid=1118271438

How many Catholics are there in Britain? (2010, September 15). BBC. https://www.bbc.com/news/11297461

Interwar Britain. (2022, September 13). In *Wikipedia.* https://en.wikipedia.org/w/index.php?title=Interwar_Britain&oldid=1110032981

An introduction to Victorian England. (n.d.). English Heritage. https://www.english-heritage.org.uk/learn/story-of-england/victorian/

Japan-United Kingdom relations. (2022, October 27). In *Wikipedia.* https://en.wikipedia.org/w/index.php?title=Japan%E2%80%93United_Kingdom_relations&oldid=1118523371

Johnson, B. (n.d.). *Robin Hood.* Historic UK. https://www.historic-uk.com/HistoryUK/HistoryofEngland/Robin-Hood/

Kidadl Team. (2022, October 14). *Vikings and Anglo-Saxons facts you should definitely know.* Kidadl. https://kidadl.com/facts/vikings-and-anglo-saxons-facts-you-should-definitely-know#:~:text=Vikings%20and%20Anglo%20Saxons%20were%20t

Knowles, R. (2015, April 21). *The Whigs and the Tories.* Regency History. https://www.regencyhistory.net/2015/04/the-whigs-and-tories.html

Lambert, T. (2021, June 22). *Britain in the 20th century.* Local Histories. https://localhistories.org/britain-in-the-20th-century/#:~:text=Britain%20changed%20hugely%20during%20the%2020th%20century.%20Life,class%20at%20the%20beginning%20of%20the%2020th%20century.

List of prime ministers of the United Kingdom. (2022, November 3). In *Wikipedia.* https://en.wikipedia.org/w/index.php?title=List_of_prime_ministers_of_the_United_Kingdom&oldid=1119823727

Longley, R. (2019, July 28). *Glorious Revolution: Definition, history and significance.* ThoughtCo. https://www.thoughtco.com/glorious-revolution-definition-4692528

Mahabal, P. (n.d.). *Interesting facts about the Tudor and Henry VIII Navy.* Elizabethan England Life. https://elizabethanenglandlife.com/thetudorsfacts/interesting-facts-about-the-tudor-and-henry-viii-navy.html

Mauldin, J. (2016, July 5). 3 reasons Brits voted for Brexit. Forbes. https://www.forbes.com/sites/johnmauldin/2016/07/05/3-reasons-brits-voted-for-brexit/?sh=756103661f9d

Medieval England history: Life in the Middle Ages. (n.d.). Medieval Ages. https://www.middleages.org.uk/medieval-england/

Mediterranean and Middle East theatre of World War II. (2022, October 23). In *Wikipedia.* https://en.wikipedia.org/w/index.php?title=Mediterranean_and_M

iddle_East_theatre_of_World_War_II&oldid=1117784696

National Geographic Society. (2022, May 20). Norman Conquest. In *National Geographic.* https://education.nationalgeographic.org/resource/norman-conquest

Nollason, N. (n.d.). *Who were the Dane Vikings?* Vikings Brand. https://www.vikingsbrand.co/blogs/norse-news/danes-vikings

Ohlmeyer, J.H. (2022, September 6). English civil wars. In *Encyclopedia Britannica.* https://www.britannica.com/event/English-Civil-Wars

The Peasants' Revolt. (n.d.). BBC. https://www.bbc.co.uk/bitesize/topics/z93txbk/articles/zyb77yc

Perkins, M. (2019, August 27). *Scotland's Jacobite Rebellion.* ThoughtCo. https://www.thoughtco.com/jacobite-rebellion-4766629

Pierce, D. (2009). Decolonization and the collapse of the British Empire. *Inquiries Journal, 1*(10), 1. http://www.inquiriesjournal.com/articles/5/decolonization-and-the-collapse-of-the-british-empire

Population in the Victorian era. (n.d.). The Circumlocution Office. https://www.thecircumlocutionoffice.com/times/population/

Population of England 2016. (n.d.). UK Population 2016. https://ukpopulation2016.com/england/#:~:text=POPULATION%20OF%20ENGLAND%20IN%202016%3A%20With%20more%20than,United%20Kingdom%2C%20representing%2084%25%20of%20the%20joined%20total

Pym, H. (2013, April 8). Margaret Thatcher: How the economy changed. BBC. https://www.bbc.com/news/business-22073527

Queen Elizabeth I: Colonising America. (n.d.). Royal Museums Greenwich. https://www.rmg.co.uk/stories/topics/queen-elizabeth-i-colonising-america

Soaft, L. (2022, March 2). *Tudor history: The complete overview.* The Collector. https://www.thecollector.com/tudor-history-overview/

SociologyBri. (n.d.). *The British Welfare State 1945–1979.* Time Toast. https://www.timetoast.com/timelines/the-british-welfare-state-1945-1979

Staff Writer. (2020, March 27). *What were the major turning points of WWI?* Reference. https://www.reference.com/history/were-major-turning-points-wwi-8220d1d85253a1ba

Staff Writer. (2020, April 4). *What were the causes and effects of the Glorious Revolution?* Reference. https://www.reference.com/history/were-cause-effects-glorious-revolution-2c5929b7d08654eb

Steinbach, S. (2022, August 24). Victorian era. In *Encyclopedia Britannica.* https://www.britannica.com/event/Victorian-era

United Kingdom home front during World War II. (2022, September 16). In *Wikipedia.*

https://en.wikipedia.org/w/index.php?title=United_Kingdom_home_front_during_World_War_II&oldid=1110641279

Vaijayanti, P.M. (n.d.). *British Empire during Victorian era*. Victorian Era. https://victorian-era.org/british-empire-victorian-era.html

Vaijayanti, P.M. (n.d.). *Victorian era poetry characteristics & salient features*. Victorian Era. https://victorian-era.org/victorian-era-poetry-characteristics.html

Wallenfeldt, J. (n.d.). Acts of Union: Uniting the United Kingdom. In *Encyclopedia Britannica*. https://www.britannica.com/story/acts-of-union-uniting-the-united-kingdom

Wand, H. (2020, April 7). *Jack and the Beanstalk origins*. Fairy Tale Central. https://thefairytalecentral.com/jack-and-the-beanstalk-origins/

White, M. (2018, June 21). *The Enlightenment*. The British Library. https://www.bl.uk/restoration-18th-century-literature/articles/the-enlightenment/

Whitelock, D., & Chaney, W.A. (n.d.). Anglo-Saxon England. In *Encyclopedia Britannica*. https://www.britannica.com/place/United-Kingdom/Anglo-Saxon-England

World War I (1914–1918) - Introduction. (n.d.). History of England. https://www.historyofengland.net/wwone

World War 2 Allies. (2014, August 24). World War 2. https://worldwar2.org.uk/world-war-2-allies

Young, C. (Ed.). (2017, November 21). *England during the war: How the home front did its bit*. England Explore. https://englandexplore.com/england-during-world-war-ii/

IRISH HISTORY & MYTHOLOGY

About: Fiacha mac Delbaíth. (n.d.). DBPedia. Retrieved February 11, 2023, from https://dbpedia.org/page/Fiacha_mac_Delba%C3%ADth

About: Mag Mell. (n.d.). DBPedia. Retrieved February 13, 2023, from https://dbpedia.org/page/Mag_Mell

Áine the goddess who took revenge on a king. (n.d.). Ireland Information. https://www.ireland-information.com/irish-mythology/aine-irish-legend.html

All about Eostre - The Pagan goddess of dawn. (2020, March 5). Arcane Alchemy. http://www.arcane-alchemy.com/blog/2020/3/5/all-about-eostre-the-pagan-goddess-of-dawn#:~:text=Eostre%20is%20the%20Germanic%20goddess

All about Eostre || The Pagan goddess of dawn. (2020). [Video]. YouTube. https://www.youtube.com/watch?v=h57XfAeX9F0&t=449s

Allen, R. (2019a, May 22). Dechtire. God checkers. https://www.godchecker.com/irish-mythology/DECHTIRE/#:~:text=She%20is%20the%20daughter%2oof,So%20she%20did.

Allen, R. (2019b, May 23). Fúamnach (P. J. Allen & C. Saunders, Eds.). God Checker. https://www.godchecker.com/irish-mythology/FUAMNACH/

Allen, R. (2019c, May 23). Fúamnach (P. J. Allen & C. Saunders, Eds.). God Checker. https://www.godchecker.com/irish-mythology/FUAMNACH/

Alp-Luachra. (n.d.). Emerald Isle. https://emeraldisle.ie/alp-luachra-

Ancient Irish Games. (n.d.). Twinkl. https://www.twinkl.co.za/teaching-wiki/ancient-irish-games

Angevin Empire. (2023). Encyclopedia Britannica. https://www.britannica.com/place/Angevin-empire

Aos Si. (n.d.). Mythical Creatures Guide. https://www.mythicalcreaturesguide.com/aos-si/

Aos Sí. (2021, August 24). Wikipedia. Retrieved February 2, 2023 from https://en.wikipedia.org/wiki/Aos_S%C3%AD

Art of dry stone walling, knowledge and techniques. (n.d.). UNESCO. https://ich.unesco.org/en/RL/art-of-dry-stone-walling-knowledge-and-techniques-01393

Atma Flare. (2019, August 22). Indech, treacherous fomorian general. Tumblr. https://atmaflare.tumblr.com/post/187181853478/indech-treacherous-fomorian-general-in-irish

Augustyn, A. (2023). Bronze Age. Britannica. https://www.britannica.com/event/Bronze-Age

Barone, F. (2020, March 12). Luck of the Irish: Folklore and fairies in rural Ireland. Human Relations Area Files. https://hraf.yale.edu/luck-of-the-irish-folklore-and-fairies-in-rural-ireland/#:~:text=Known%20to%20the%20islanders%20as

Bhagat, D. (2018, October 30). The origins and practices of: Samhain, Día de los Muertos, and All Saints Day. Boston Public Library. https://www.bpl.org/blogs/post/the-origins-and-practices-of-holidays-samhain-dia-de-los-muertos-and-all-saints-day/#:~:text=Samhain%20is%20observed%20from%20sunset

Bhagat, D. (2019, June 18). The origins and practices of Litha. Boston Public Library. https://www.bpl.org/blogs/post/the-origins-and-practices-of-litha/

Blackie, S. (2016, November 15). The dangerous women of Irish Mythology. Dangerous Women Project. https://dangerouswomenproject.org/2016/11/15/the-dangerous-women-of-irish-mythology/

Blakely, S. (2021, May 14). Copper age history & society | Chalcolithic age features. Study. https://study.com/academy/lesson/copper-age-history.html

Boan, Goddess of the Boyne. (n.d.). Discover Boyne Valley. https://www.discoverboynevalley.ie/boyne-valley-drive/heritage-sites/boann-goddess-boyne

Brehon Academy. (2022). Irish mythology deep dive: The mythological cycle 6+ hours. [Video]. YouTube. https://www.youtube.com/watch?v=fZhYc8l6voo&t=488s

Brú na Bóinne - Archaeological ensemble of the Bend of the Boyne. (n.d.). UNESCO World Heritage Convention. https://whc.unesco.org/en/list/659/#:~:text=The%20three%20main%20prehistoric%20sites

Buckles, N. (n.d.). The legend of Ellén Trechend. Nifty Buckles. https://niftybuckles.buzz/2018/07/26/aillen-trechenn/

Bunbury, T. (2020, March 21). What did the Romans ever do for Ireland? The Irish Times. https://www.irishtimes.com/culture/books/what-did-the-romans-ever-do-for-ireland-1.4205876#:~:text=The%20Romans%20never%20conquered%20Ireland,%E2%80%9Ctrackless%20wastes%E2%80%9Dof%20Galloway

Butler, I. (2020, January 13). Ireland's ancient burial mounds. Europe up Close. https://europeupclose.com/article/irelands-ancient-burial-mounds/

BYU Department of Anthropology. (2014). Barry Cunliffe: Who were the Celts? [Video]. YouTube. https://www.youtube.com/watch?v=G8FM9nMFbfI&t=17s

Caitlin. (2021, September 7). Cat sìth: including 5 legendary tales. Highland Titles. https://www.highlandtitles.com/blog/cat-sith/

Caitlin. (2022, February 11). Everything you need to know about Tír na nÓg. Celtic Titles. https://www.celtictitles.com/blog/tir-na-nog/

Campbell, J. F. (1890). Fachan. Popular tales of the west Highlands (Vol. IV, pp. 297–298). Encyclopedia Mythica. https://pantheon.org/articles/f/fachan.html

Cannon, J. (2015). Overview: Kingdom of the Isles. A Dictionary of British History. Oxford University Press. https://www.oxfordreference.com/display/10.1093/oi/authority.20110803100012518

Carmody, I. Ób. (2016, April 16). The story of Rúadán from Cath Maige Tuired. Story Archeology. https://storyarchaeology.com/the-story-of-ruadan-from-cath-maige-tuired-2/

Casey, L. (2022, December 4). The Irish legend of the pooka. Irish Central. https://www.irishcentral.com/roots/history/irish-legend-pooka#:~:text=The%20Pooka%2C%20or%20in%20Irish,%2C%20Channel%20Islands%2C%20and%20Brittany

Castlehunter. (2012, May 27). The fairy castle co Dublin. Ireland in Ruins. http://irelandinruins.blogspot.com/2012/05/fairy-castle-co-dublin.html

Cataliotti, J. (2022, November 11). Copper age tools. Study.com. https://study.com/academy/lesson/copper-age-weapons-tools.html#:~:text=The%20metal%20was%20far%20more

Celtic art. (n.d.). The Artist. https://www.theartist.me/art-movement/celtic-art/

Celtic Otherworld. (2022, March 25). Celtic Life. https://celticlifeintl.com/celtic-otherworld/

Cermait. (n.d.). Myths and Folklore Wiki. Retrieved February 11, 2023, from https://mythus.fandom.com/wiki/Cermait

Cermait. (2022, April 14). Wikipedia. Retrieved February 11, 2023 from https://en.wikipedia.org/wiki/Cermait

Christianity arrives in Ireland. (2020, March 2). Your Irish Culture. https://www.yourirish.com/history/christianity/arrival-of-christianity

Cist. (n.d.). Merriam-Webster. https://www.merriam-webster.com/dictionary/cist

Cliodhna. (n.d.). Bard Mythologies. https://bardmythologies.com/cliodhna/

Clíodhna of the banshees. (n.d.). Ireland Information. https://www.ireland-information.com/irish-mythology/cliodhna-irish-legend.html

Copper. (n.d.). National Museum of Ireland. https://microsites.museum.ie/bronzeagehandlingbox/object-copper.html

Corbel. (n.d.). Merriam-Webster. https://www.merriam-webster.com/dictionary/corbel

Court tomb. (n.d.). Dictonary.com. https://www.dictionary.com/browse/court-tomb

Creidhne. (n.d.). The White Goddess. http://www.thewhitegoddess.co.uk/divinity_of_the_day/irish/creidhne.asp

Crom Cruach, the dark god of the burial mound. (2016, October 1). An Sionnach Fionn. https://ansionnachfionn.com/2016/10/01/crom-cruach-the-dark-god-of-the-burial-mound/

Cú Chulainn. (2022). A. Tikkanen (Ed.), Encyclopedia Britannica. https://www.britannica.com/topic/Cu-Chulainn

Cummings, V. (2015). Dolmen. Britannica. https://www.britannica.com/topic/dolmen

Cymres, W. (n.d.). Brigid: Survival of a goddess. Druidry. https://druidry.org/resources/brigid-survival-of-a-goddess

D'Costa, K. (2013, March 31). Beyond Ishtar: The tradition of eggs at Easter. Scientific American. https://blogs.scientificamerican.com/anthropology-in-practice/beyond-ishtar-the-tradition-of-eggs-at-easter/

Delbáeth. (n.d.). People Pill. https://peoplepill.com/people/delbaeth

Devine, B. (2013, August 27). Not all Celts are Gaels. The Wild Geese. https://thewildgeese.irish/profiles/blogs/not-all-celts-are-gaels#:~:text=%22Celt%22%20is%20the%20broader%20term

DHWTY. (2017, December 28). The Fomorians: Destructive giants of Irish legend. Ancient Origins. https://www.ancient-origins.net/myths-legends-europe/fomorians-destructive-giants-irish-legend-009349

Dian Cécht. (2018, February 15). Encyclopedia Britannica. https://www.britannica.com/topic/Dian-Cecht

Dowd, M. (2015). The Archaeology of Caves in Ireland. Oxbow Books.

Duna. (2017). Encyclopedia Britannica. https://www.britannica.com/topic/Danu

E, I. (2022a, September 20). They might be giants: 10 colossal Celts of Irish myth & legend. Irish Myths. https://irishmyths.com/2022/09/20/giants/

E, I. (2022b, September 26). Who is Balor of the Evil Eye? A brief biography of Irish mythology's "big Bbd." Irish Myths. https://irishmyths.com/2022/09/26/balor/

Early Christian Ireland. (n.d.). Ask about Ireland. Retrieved January 20, 2023 from https://www.askaboutireland.ie/learning-zone/primary-students/subjects/history/history-the-full-story/early-christian-ireland/#:~:text=Early%20Christian%20Ireland%20is%20the

Early Christian Ireland facts. (2022, January 11). Twinkl. https://www.twinkl.co.za/blog/early-christian-ireland-facts

Easter Rising. (n.d.). History. https://www.history.com/topics/british-history/easter-rising

Ehistoryadmin. (2014, May 9). "Ireland's greatest family": The Fitzgeralds, earls of Kildare. Kildare. https://kildare.ie/ehistory/index.php/irelands-greatest-family-the-fitzgeralds-earls-of-kildare/#:~:text=The%20earldom%20was%20created%20on

Elatha, Bres, Indech & Tethra: Rulers of the Fomorians. (n.d.). Atlas Mythica. https://atlasmythica.com/elatha-bres-indech-tethra-rulers-fomorians/

Ellén Trechend. (2009). Monstropedia. https://www.monstropedia.org/index.php?title=Ell%C3%A9n_Trechend

Ernmas. (2022, June 8). Wikipedia. Retrieved February 11, 2023 from https://en.wikipedia.org/wiki/Ernmas

Esus. (2015). Encyclopedia Britannica. https://www.britannica.com/topic/Esus

Etain. (n.d.). Bard Mythologies. https://bardmythologies.com/etain/

Far darrig facts for kids. (2022). Kiddle Encyclopedia. https://kids.kiddle.co/Far_darrig

Fergus. (2017, February 20). Enigmatic structures: Ireland's megalithic wedge tombs. The Irish Place. https://www.theirishplace.com/heritage/enigmatic-structures-irelands-megalithic-wedge-tombs/

FilmRise Documentaries. (2014a). The Celts - BBC series, episode 1 - In the beginning - Full episode. [Video]. YouTube. https://www.youtube.com/watch?v=AU1dKfMIEUQ&t=7s

FilmRise Documentaries. (2014b). The Celts - BBC series, Episode 2 - Heroes in defeat - Full episode. [Video]. YouTube. https://www.youtube.com/watch?v=OVovskAh5QA

FilmRise Documentaries. (2014c). The Celts - BBC series, episode 3 - Sacred groves - Full episode [Video]. YouTube. https://www.youtube.com/watch?v=GsHghGwdWNg

FilmRise Documentaries. (2014d). The Celts - BBC series, episode 4 - From Camelot to Christ - Full episode [Video]. YouTube. https://www.youtube.com/watch?v=lfY4-2zKY-g

FilmRise Documentaries. (2014e). The Celts - BBC series, episode 5 - Legend and reality - Full episode [Video]. YouTube. https://www.youtube.com/watch?v=W_l5yFlEYds

FilmRise Documentaries. (2014f). The Celts - BBC series, episode 6 - A dead song? - Full episode. [Video]. YouTube. https://www.youtube.com/watch?v=wl7X4A_mNeU

Fionn mac Cumhail. (n.d.). Discovering Ireland. https://www.discoveringireland.com/fionn-mac-cumhail/

Fire of Learning. (2018a). History of Ireland - Documentary. [Video]. YouTube. https://www.youtube.com/watch?v=fbJKanTrf8c

Fire of Learning. (2018b). History of Ireland (Part 2) documentary. [Video]. YouTube. https://www.youtube.com/watch?v=vFoxstHK-Kg&t=9s

Forsyth, S. (n.d.). Irish fairies. Celtic Wedding Rings. https://www.celtic-weddingrings.com/fairy-stories/irish-fairies

Fortress of Lugh. (n.d.). The Dagda - (Celtic mythology explained). [Video]. YouTube. https://www.youtube.com/watch?v=62DBOC5CQG0&t=10s

From hunger to harvest - The history of the ancient Celtic festival Lughnasa. (2022, July 29). IrishCentral. https://www.irishcentral.com/culture/history-celtic-festival-lughnasa

Gaelic Ireland: The unfolded exciting history throughout the centuries. (2022, August 4). Connolly Cove. https://www.connollycove.com/gaelic-ireland/

Goibhniu. (1998). Encyclopedia Britannica. https://www.britannica.com/topic/Goibhniu

Good Friday Agreement: What is it? (2022, December 16). BBC News. https://www.bbc.com/news/uk-northern-ireland-61968177

Graham, H. (n.d.). Celtic Reconstructionism. Druidry. https://druidry.org/resources/celtic-reconstructionism

Greenberg, M. (2020, November 3). Who was Midir in Irish mythology? Mythology Source. https://mythologysource.com/midir-irish-mythology/

Greenberg, M. (2021, January 18). Who was the Dagda in Irish mythology. Mythology Source. https://mythologysource.com/dagda-celtic-god/

Hare, J. B. (1911). The fairy-faith in Celtic countries by W. Y. Evans-Wentz [1911] [Review of the fairy-faith in Celtic countries, by W. Y. Evans-Wentz]. https://www.sacred-texts.com/neu/celt/ffcc/index.htm

Harris, K. (2019, April 1). Legendary grannies: Hags in Celtic myths. Curious Historian. https://curioushistorian.com/legendary-grannies-hags-in-celtic-myths#:~:text=According%20to%20Celtic%20folklore%2C%20hags

Haynie, D. (2016, March 17). 10 countries with the most Irish emigrants. US News. https://www.usnews.com/news/best-countries/articles/2016-03-17/10-countries-with-the-most-irish-emigrants

Hirst, K. K. (2019, April 29). Mount Sandel - Mesolithic Settlement in Ireland. Thought Co. https://www.thoughtco.com/mount-sandel-mesolithic-settlement-in-ireland-171665

How the Irish predict the weather. (n.d.). Ireland's Own. https://www.irelandsown.ie/how-the-irish-predict-the-weather/

Howells, C. (2022, October 18). The questing beast: The legendary Arthurian creature. Myth Bank. https://mythbank.com/the-questing-beast/

Iaconangelo, D. (2016, June 15). Why ancient butter keeps turning up in Irish bogs. The Christian Science Monitor. https://www.csmonitor.com/Science/Science-Notebook/2016/0615/Why-ancient-butter-keeps-turning-up-in-Irish-bogs

Ian. (2008, September 19). Fachan. Mysterious Britain and Ireland. https://www.mysteriousbritain.co.uk/folklore/fachan/

Illes, J. (2009). Nemain. Encyclopedia of Spirits: The Ultimate Guide to the Magic of Fairies, Genies, Demons, Ghosts, Gods & Goddesses. https://occult-world.com/nemain/

Incredible history of the Tuatha de Danann: Ireland's Most Ancient Race. (2023, January 15). Connolly Cove. https://www.connollycove.com/tuatha-de-danann/

Innes, A. D. (1912). A history of the British nation. TC & EC Jack. https://www.britainexpress.com/History/Henry-VII-and-Ireland.htm

Insular hand. (n.d.). Merriam-Webster. https://www.merriam-webster.com/dictionary/Insular%20hand

Ipbestiary. (2020, August 30). Ethniu. Tumblr. https://www.tumblr.com/lpbestiary/627909588308639744/ethniu-is-a-fomorian-from-irish-mythology-the

Ireland in the 19th century. (n.d.). Ask about Ireland. https://www.askaboutireland.ie/learning-zone/primary-students/subjects/history/history-the-full-story/ireland-in-the-19th-centu/#:~:text=Ireland%20in%20the%20early%201800s

Ireland: 4 reasons why its culture is important. (n.d.). Pruvo. https://www.pruvo.com/blog/ireland-4-reasons-why-its-culture-is-important/

Ireland's bog bodies. (2015, July 2). Claddagh Design. https://www.claddaghdesign.com/blogs/irish-interest/ireland-bog-bodies#:~:text=A%20total%20of%2017%20bog,of%20ritual%20sacrifice%20described%20above.

Irish folklore: Mythical monsters and terrifying creatures. (2022, November 11). Connolly Cove. https://www.connollycove.com/mythical-monsters-in-irish-folklore/

Irish Free State declared. (2020, October 4). History. https://www.history.com/this-day-in-history/irish-free-state-declared

Irish mythological creatures. (n.d.). Twinkl. https://www.twinkl.co.za/teaching-wiki/irish-mythological-creatures

Irish myths and legends 101. (n.d.). Ireland 101. https://www.ireland101.com/page/irish-legends#:~:text=The%20Pooka%20(also%20known%20as

Irish weather lore and traditions. (n.d.). Twinkl. https://www.eskeretns.ie/uploads/1/2/7/1/127165924/roi-gy-29-irish-weather-lore-and-traditions_ver_1.pdf

Ireland. (n.d.). The magical east of Ireland – ancient places, scenic lakes and Rocky Mountains. Komoot. https://www.komoot.com/collection/1255857/the-magical-east-of-ireland-ancient-places-scenic-lakes-and-rocky-mountains

Iron. (n.d.). Royal Society of Chemistry. https://www.rsc.org/periodic-table/element/26/iron#:~:text=Iron%20is%20the%20fourth%20most

Iron Age people: Celts. (n.d.). Ask about Ireland. https://www.askaboutireland.ie/learning-zone/primary-students/subjects/history/history-the-full-story/irelands-early-inhabitant/iron-age-people-celts/

Join Tia McCaughey and Darragh Finlay for our Mabon/Autumn equinox celebration and retreat on Sunday the 8th of September, Anaverna House and Estate Ravensdale Co. Louth. (n.d.). Darragh Finlay. https://darraghfinlay.ie/mabon-autumn-equinox-celebration-and-retreat/

Jones, M. (2004). Bean Sídhe. Jones' Celtic Encyclopedia. https://www.ancienttexts.org/library/celtic/jce/beansidhe.html

Joyce, P. W. (1911). The man-wolves of Ossory. Library Ireland. https://www.libraryireland.com/Wonders/Man-Wolves.php

Kaushik, N. (2011, October 24). Difference between Norse and Viking. Difference between Similar Terms and Objects. http://www.differencebetween.net/miscellaneous/culture-miscellaneous/difference-between-norse-and-viking/

Kesp, B. (2014, August 4). Tuatha Dé Danann - a Family Tree. Literature and Culture Corner. http://kespwriting.blogspot.com/2014/08/tuatha-de-danann-family-tree.html

Klein, C. (2018, September 4). Globetrotting Vikings: The raiding of Ireland. History. https://www.history.com/news/globetrotting-vikings-the-raiding-of-ireland

Klimczak, N. (2016, November 24). Bronze treasures beyond belief: The fabulous Dowris hoard of Ireland. Ancient Origins. https://www.ancient-origins.net/artifacts-other-artifacts/bronze-treasures-beyond-belief-fabulous-dowris-hoard-ireland-007067

Knowth megalithic passage tomb. (n.d.). New Grange. https://www.newgrange.com/knowth.htm

Lancor, K., & Lancor, M. (2022, December 28). The ancient stone circles and dolmens scattered across Ireland. Irish Central. https://www.irishcentral.com/travel/ireland-ancient-stone-circles-dolmens

Leanan Sidhe. (n.d.). Encyclopedia of Occultism and Parapsychology. Encyclopedia.com. https://www.encyclopedia.com/science/encyclopedias-almanacs-transcripts-and-maps/leanan-sidhe

Leeming, D. (2006). Nemain. The Oxford Companion to World Mythology. Oxford University Press. https://www.oxfordreference.com/display/10.1093/oi/authority.201 10810105455960

Life in Celtic Ireland – Ancient to modern Celticism. (2022, March 14). Connolly Cove. https://www.connollycove.com/life-in-celtic-ireland-ancient-to-modern/

Lir. (n.d.). Bard Mythologies. https://bardmythologies.com/lir/

Little, B. (2021, September 9). 5 Iron Age tools and innovations. History. https://www.history.com/news/iron-age-tools-innovations

Longáin, S. Ó. (2022, December 9). The púca (pooka) in Irish folklore. Your Irish Culture. https://www.yourirish.com/folklore/irish-pookas

Lucharacháin. (n.d.). An Sionnach Fionn. https://ansionnachfionn.com/seanchas-mythology/lucharachain/

Luchtaine. (n.d.). Academic Kids.

http://academickids.com/encyclopedia/index.php/Luchta

mac Cecht. (2022). Wikipedia. Retrieved February 11, 2023 from https://en.wikipedia.org/wiki/mac_Cecht

mac Mathúna, L. (Ed.). (2021). Éigse: A journal of Irish studies (Vol. 41). National University of Ireland. chrome-extension://efaidnbmnnnibpcajpcglclefindmkaj/http://www.nui.ie/eigse/pdf/vol41/Eigse_Vol_XLI_2021_Mills.pdf

macalister, R. A. S. (1918). Pre-Celtic Ireland. The Irish Monthly, 46(536), 86–95. JStor. https://www.jstor.org/stable/20504982

macha. (n.d.). Bard Mythologies. https://bardmythologies.com/macha/

mackenzie, L. (2018, May 15). Who were the Normans and why did they conquer England? History Hit. https://www.historyhit.com/who-were-the-normans-and-why-did-they-conquer-england/#:~:text=The%20Normans%20were%20Vikings%20who

macKillop, J. (2004a). Banba. A Dictionary of Celtic Mythology. Oxford University Press. https://www.oxfordreference.com/display/10.1093/oi/authority.201 10803095444436

macKillop, J. (2004b). Bodb. A Dictionary of Celtic Mythology. Oxford University Press. https://www.oxfordreference.com/display/10.1093/oi/authority.201 10803095514712

macKillop, J. (2004c). Caoránach. A Dictionary of Celtic Mythology. https://www.oxfordreference.com/display/10.1093/oi/authority.201 10803095547214

macKillop, J. (2004d). Domnu. A Dictionary of Celtic Mythology. Oxford University Press. https://www.oxfordreference.com/display/10.1093/oi/authority.201 10803095726564

macKillop, J. (2004e). Elmar. A Dictionary of Celtic Mythology. Oxford University Press. https://www.oxfordreference.com/display/10.1093/oi/authority.201 10803095745503

macKillop, J. (2004f). Ernmas. A Dictionary of Celtic Mythology. Oxford University Press. https://www.oxfordreference.com/display/10.1093/oi/authority.201 10810104841717

macKillop, J. (2004g). Fódla. A Dictionary of Celtic Mythology. Oxford University Press. https://www.oxfordreference.com/display/10.1093/oi/authority.201 10803095825980

macKillop, J. (2004h). Indech. A Dictionary of Celtic Mythology. Oxford University Press. https://www.oxfordreference.com/display/10.1093/oi/authority.201 10803100000698 macKillop, J. (2004i). Luchta. A Dictionary of Celtic Mythology. Oxford University Press. https://www.oxfordreference.com/display/10.1093/oi/authority.201 10803100117787

macKillop, J. (2004j). Nemedians. A Dictionary of Celtic Mythology. Oxford University Press. https://www.oxfordreference.com/display/10.1093/oi/authority.201 10803100228273

macKillop, J. (2004k). Overview: Brí Léith. A Dictionary of Celtic Mythology. Oxford University Press. https://www.oxfordreference.com/display/10.1093/oi/authority.201 10803095527570;jsessionid=0C049D44D19452CE696BCDAA24991 D25?rskey=UMDSU5&result=11

macKillop, J. (2004k). Tethra. A Dictionary of Celtic Mythology. Oxford University Press. https://www.oxfordreference.com/display/10.1093/oi/authority.201 10803103251488

Mag Tuired. (2018). Encyclopedia Britannica. https://www.britannica.com/topic/Mag-Tuired

Magan, M. (2017, August 9). Fairy forts: Why these "sacred places" deserve our respect. The Irish Times. https://www.irishtimes.com/culture/heritage/fairy-forts-why-these-sacred-places-deserve-our-respect-1.3181259

Magan, M. (2021, March 13). From ringfort to ring road: The destruction of Ireland's fairy forts. The Irish Times. https://www.irishtimes.com/culture/heritage/from-ringfort-to-ring-road-the-destruction-of-ireland-s-fairy-forts-1.4496069

Manannán mac Lir. (2006, December 27). Encyclopedia Britannica. https://www.britannica.com/topic/Manannan-mac-Lir

Mark, J. J. (2015). Ancient Ireland. World History Encyclopedia. https://www.worldhistory.org/ireland/

Mark, J. J. (2018). Kingdom of West Francia. World History Encyclopedia. https://www.worldhistory.org/Kingdom_of_West_Francia/

Martinsson-Wallin, H. (n.d.). Monuments and people - An introduction. Studies in Global Archaeology, 20. chrome-extension://efaidnbmnnnibpcajpcglclefindmkaj/https://www.diva-portal.org/smash/get/diva2:926765/FULLTEXT01.pdf

McCormick, K. (2017, October 9). Dragons of Fame: Ollipeist/Ollepheist/Ollipheist/Uilepheist. The Circle of the Dragon. http://www.blackdrago.com/fame/ollipeist.htm

McKeown, M. (2022, July 17). Forgotten fairies of Irish folklore. Owlcation. https://owlcation.com/humanities/Forgotten-Irish-Fairies

McNamara, R. (2020, January 29). Irish history: The 1800s. ThoughtCo.

https://www.thoughtco.com/irish-history-the-1800s-1773853

McNamara-Wilson, K. (n.d.). Irish faerie folk of yore and yesterday – The gancanagh. Got Ireland. http://gotireland.com/2013/10/04/irish-faerie-folk-of-yore-and-yesterday-the-gancanagh/

Medieval Ireland and early Gaelic Ireland. (n.d.). Discovering Ireland. https://www.discoveringireland.com/early-gaelic-ireland-and-medieval-ireland/

Megalithic Ireland. (n.d.). Megalithic Ireland. http://www.megalithicireland.com/

Mesolithic Stone Age in prehistoric Ireland. (n.d.). Travel through the Ireland Story. https://www.wesleyjohnston.com/users/ireland/past/pre_norman_history/mesolithic_age.html

Midir. (n.d.). Bard Mythologies. https://bardmythologies.com/midir/

Military History. (2022, November 7). Born in blood: the Irish Free State. The Past. https://the-past.com/feature/born-in-blood-the-irish-free-state/

Moloney, C. (2011, February 16). Know thy monuments: Barrow/tumulus. Know Thy Place Blog. https://knowthyplace.wordpress.com/2011/02/16/know-thy-monuments-barrowtumulus/

Moody, S. (2022, March 31). Meanwhile, in Ireland: Ostara. The Comenian. https://comenian.org/7527/news/meanwhile-in-ireland-ostara/

Morus-Baird, G. (2022, August 2). The goddess of sovereignty. Celtic Source. https://celticsource.online/the-goddess-of-sovereignty/

Mould, D. P. (2001). The sailing-ships of Ancient Ireland. Archaeology Ireland, 15(1), 14–18. JStor. https://www.jstor.org/stable/20562472

Mount, C. (2011, August 9). The houses of the Irish copper age 1.1. Dr. Charles Mount. http://charles-mount.ie/wp/index.php/the-houses-of-the-irish-copper-age/#:~:text=In%20Ireland%20the%20use%20of

Mythology Storyteller. (2021). Celtic gods and goddesses of mythology. [Video]. YouTube. https://www.youtube.com/watch?v=BalDcKUboDQ

Mythology Unleashed. (2022). Monsters of Celtic mythology. [Video]. YouTube. https://www.youtube.com/watch?v=OeyP8tAMWsE

Native games of Ireland. (n.d.). Mayo Ireland. https://www.mayo-ireland.ie/en/about-mayo/sports/native-games-of-ireland.html

Nave, R. (n.d.). Atmospheric refraction. Hyper Physics. http://hyperphysics.phy-astr.gsu.edu/hbase/atmos/mirage.html

Neary, C. (2021, May 30). The Irish folklore of the Celtic merrow. Beach Combing. https://www.beachcombingmagazine.com/blogs/news/the-irish-folklore-of-the-celtic-merrow#:~:text=Merrow%20(from%20the%20Irish%20Muruch

Nechtan - God of the Underworld. (n.d.). The White Goddess. http://www.thewhitegoddess.co.uk/divinity_of_the_day/irish/nechtan.asp

Nemid (or Nemed) and the Nemedians in Ireland. (1884). The Irish Fireside, 2(30). Library Ireland. https://www.libraryireland.com/articles/NemidIF2-30/index.php

Norman invasion of Ireland. (n.d.). New World Encyclopedia. https://www.newworldencyclopedia.org/entry/Norman_invasion_of_Ireland

Norman Ireland. (n.d.). New World Encyclopedia. https://www.newworldencyclopedia.org/entry/Norman_Ireland

Nuada. (2017). Encyclopedia Britannica. https://www.britannica.com/topic/Nuadu

Nugent, L. (2022, September 26). Mountains, wells, and caves: A look at Ireland's sacred landscape. The Irish Spirit. https://theirishspirit.com/mountains-wells-and-caves-a-look-at-irelands-sacred-landscape/

O'Cathasaigh, L. (2030, September 9). Tír Na nÓg - The legend of the land of eternal youth. Irish Central. https://www.irishcentral.com/roots/history/tir-na-nog-legend-eternal-youth

O'Hara, K. (2023a, January 4). The abhartach: The terrifying tale of the Irish vampire. The Irish Road Trip. https://www.theirishroadtrip.com/the-abhartach/

O'Hara, K. (2023b, January 4). The legend of the Fianna: Some of the mightiest warriors from Irish mythology. The Irish Road Trip. https://www.theirishroadtrip.com/the-fianna/

O'Keeffe, C. (n.d.). Monster/faery page. Tartan Place. http://www.tartanplace.com/faery/goddess/aeb.html

O'Neill, B. (2020, March 2). Saint Finnian of Clonard. Your Irish Culture. https://www.yourirish.com/history/christianity/st-finnian-of-clonard

O'Raifeartaigh, T. (2022). St. Patrick. Encyclopedia Britannica. https://www.britannica.com/biography/Saint-Patrick

Odekirk, S. (2021, January 29). A look at Irish culture and traditions. Family Search. https://www.familysearch.org/en/blog/irish-culture-and-traditions

Ogma. (2015). Encyclopedia Britannica. https://www.britannica.com/topic/Ogma

Onchwari, G., & Keengwe, J. (n.d.). What is an ethnolinguistic group? In Handbook of Research on Engaging Immigrant Families and Promoting Academic Success for English Language Learners. University of North Dakota. https://www.igi-global.com/dictionary/ethnolinguistic-group/72624

Orthostat. (n.d.). Collins. https://www.collinsdictionary.com/dictionary/english/orthostat#:~:text=orthostat%20in%20American%20English,lower%20part%20of%20the%20cella

Ossory. (2020). Encyclopedia Britannica. https://www.britannica.com/place/Ossory

Overly Sarcastic Productions. (2019). History summarized: Ireland. [Video]. YouTube. https://www.youtube.com/watch?v=RCCUEt8S61k

Paciorek, A. L. (n.d.). Solitary fays. Strange Lands. http://www.batcow.co.uk/strangelands/solitary.htm

Parable - Religious History Documentaries. (2020). The mysterious world of the Celtic gods | Lost gods | Parable. [Video]. YouTube. https://www.youtube.com/watch?v=NZon-IW8VSg&t=11s

Parkes, V. (2018, July 28). Grange stone circle: A place of ritual gatherings, sacrifice and worship from prehistoric times to the modern day. Ancient Origins. https://www.ancient-origins.net/ancient-places-europe/grange-stone-circle-021993

Passage tomb people. (n.d.). Passage Tomb People. https://passagetombpeople.com/

Perkins, M. (2019, September 24). Irish mythology: History and legacy. Thought Co. https://www.thoughtco.com/irish-mythology-4768762

Petruzzello, M. (2022). St. Brigid of Ireland. Encyclopedia Britannica. https://www.britannica.com/biography/Saint-Brigit-of-Ireland

Prehistoric Ireland. (n.d.). National Museum of Ireland. https://www.museum.ie/en-IE/Museums/Archaeology/Exhibitions/Prehistoric-Ireland

Prehistoric monuments. (n.d.). Heritage Ireland. https://heritageireland.ie/visit/prehistoric-monuments/#:~:text=Our%20prehistoric%20monuments%20include%20Stone

Prehistoric period (until 1050 AD) / The Viking Age. (n.d.). National Museum of Denmark. https://en.natmus.dk/historical-knowledge/denmark/prehistoric-period-until-1050-ad/the-viking-age/

Quenching. (1998, July 20). Encyclopedia Britannica. https://www.britannica.com/technology/quenching-materials-processing

Quintanilla, M. (2010). Review of the book Ireland, slavery and anti-slavery: 1612–1865 Review of Review of the book Ireland, slavery and anti-slavery: 1612–1865, by N. Rodgers. New Hibernia Review, 14(4), 153–154. muse.jhu.edu/article/412036.

Radford, B. (2017, March 8). Leprechauns: Facts about the Irish trickster fairy. Live Science. https://www.livescience.com/37626-

leprechauns.html

Rafferty, J. P. (2022). Neolithic. Encyclopædia Britannica. https://www.britannica.com/event/Neolithic

Rafferty, R. (2021, May 30). The myths and legends of Ireland's hound of deep, the dobhar chu. Irish Central. https://www.irishcentral.com/roots/irelands-hound-dobhar-chu

Rainbolt, D. (2022, January 20). The wee folk of Ireland. Wilderness Ireland. https://www.wildernessireland.com/blog/irish-folklore-fairies/

Ring fort. (n.d.). Britannica Kids. https://kids.britannica.com/kids/article/ring-fort/487545

Ryan, W. G. (n.d.). A survey of monuments of archaeological and historical interest in the Barony of Bunratty Lower, Co. Clare. Clare Country Library. https://www.clarelibrary.ie/eolas/coclare/archaeology/ryan/part1_ring_barrows.htm#:~:text=In%20general%20ring%2Dbarrows%20may

Samhain. (2022, October 5). History. https://www.history.com/topics/holidays/samhain#:~:text=Ancient%20Celts%20marked%20Samhain%20as

See U in History / Mythology. (2022). Irish mythology: The arrival of the Celtic gods - Complete - The Tuatha Dé Danann - See u in history. [Video]. YouTube. https://www.youtube.com/watch?v=mwLuVo3N1fY&t=19s

Shaw, J. (2014, January 30). Etain, the shining one – Celtic sun goddess/goddess of transformation by Judith Shaw. Feminism and Religion. https://feminismandreligion.com/2014/01/30/etain-the-shining-one-celtic-sun-goddess-by-judith-shaw/

Sleeping Ulstermen. (n.d.). Bard Mythologies. https://bardmythologies.com/sleeping-ulstermen/

Sluagh. (n.d.). Emerald Isle. https://emeraldisle.ie/sluagh

Snell, M. (2021, February 17). The Early, High, and Late Middle Ages. ThoughtCo. https://www.thoughtco.com/defining-the-middle-ages-part-6-1788883

St. Enda. (n.d.). Catholic News Agency. https://www.catholicnewsagency.com/saint/st-enda-700

Standing stones. (n.d.). As about Ireland. https://www.askaboutireland.ie/reading-room/environment-geography/physical-landscape/man-and-the-landscape-in/dun-laoghaire-rathdown-ea/megalithic-monuments-4/#:~:text=Standing%20Stone%2C%20Glencullen%20(location)

Stone Age. (n.d.). National Museum of Ireland. https://www.museum.ie/en-ie/collections-research/irish-antiquities-division-collections/collections-list-(1)/stone-age

Stone, R., & Winters, R. (2019, March 22). The wooing of Etain: An Irish tale of love, loss, and jealousy. Ancient Origins. https://www.ancient-origins.net/myths-legends-europe/wooing-etain-irish-tale-love-loss-and-jealousy-003077

Study of antiquity and the Middle Ages. (2022). Irish origins | The genetic history of Ireland. [Video]. YouTube. https://www.youtube.com/watch?v=HxivGM_LESk&t=641s

Subtracting insult from injury: the medical judgements of the Brehon Law. (n.d.). History Ireland. https://www.historyireland.com/subtracting-insult-from-injury-he-medical-judgements-of-the-brehon-law/#:~:text=The%20Brehon%20Law%20was%20the,complexity%20of%20early%20Irish%20society.

Suibhne. (2017). The animated history of Ireland. [Video]. YouTube. https://www.youtube.com/watch?v=dQvaGt9B6H0&t=488s

Teutates. (2018). Encyclopedia Britannica. https://www.britannica.com/topic/Teutates

The adventures of Connla the Fair. (1936). T. P. Cross & C. H. Slover (Trans.), Ancient Irish Tales. Henry Holt & Co. https://www.maryjones.us/ctexts/connla.html

The Bodach. (n.d.). Emerald Isle. https://emeraldisle.ie/the-bodach

The Bronze Age. (n.d.). Travel through the Ireland Story. https://www.wesleyjohnston.com/users/ireland/past/pre_norman_history/summary2.htm#:~:text=The%20Bronze%20Age%20in%20Ireland

The Bronze Age in Ireland. (n.d.). National Museum of Ireland. https://microsites.museum.ie/bronzeagehandlingbox/bronze-age.html

The Celts. (n.d.). Knowth. https://www.knowth.com/celts.htm

The chase of Slieve Faud. (1920). Old Celtic romances (pp. 362–385). The Educational Company of Ireland. https://storyarchaeology.com/wp-content/uploads/The_Chase_of_Slieve_Fuad=Joyce.rtf

The Cú Sidhe. (n.d.). Emerald Isle. https://emeraldisle.ie/the-cu-sidhe

The demna aeoir. (n.d.). Emerald Isle. https://emeraldisle.ie/the-demna-aeoir

The dream of Aengus. (n.d.). Mythopedia. https://mythopedia.com/topics/aengus

The fear gorta. (n.d.). Emerald Isle. https://emeraldisle.ie/the-fear-gorta

The four jewels or treasures of the Tuatha Dé Danann. (2016, May 11). An Sionnach Fionn. https://ansionnachfionn.com/2016/05/12/the-four-jewels-or-treasures-of-the-tuatha-de-danann/

The great wyrms of Ireland. (n.d.). Emerald Isle. https://emeraldisle.ie/the-great-wyrms-of-ireland

The Histocrat. (2020). The druids. [Video]. YouTube. https://www.youtube.com/watch?v=8JBW-_zq4xM&t=4781s

The history of Ireland: 11 milestone moments. (2019, February 5).

HistoryExtra. https://www.historyextra.com/period/20th-century/the-history-of-ireland-11-milestone-moments/

The Irish Jewelry Company. (2022, August 10). Celebrating the Autumn equinox called Mabon. Irish Culture and Traditions. https://irishcultureandtraditions.org/2022/08/10/celebrating-the-autumn-equinox-called-mabon/

The last dragon in Ireland. (n.d.). Emerald Isle. https://emeraldisle.ie/the-last-dragon-in-ireland

The legend lives on. (n.d.). Old Church Visitor Centre. https://www.oldchurchvisitorcentre.com/about/tuatha-de-danann-clan

The Legend of the selkies | Ultimate mythology blog - top selkie facts. (2022, June 24). Connolly Cove. https://www.connollycove.com/the-legend-of-the-selkies/

The Neolithic, or New Stone Age. (n.d.). Travel through the Ireland Story. https://www.wesleyjohnston.com/users/ireland/past/pre_norman_history/neolithic_age.html

The ninety-seven Kerbstones at Newgrange. (n.d.). The Fr. O'Flanagan Heritage Centre. http://www.carrowkeel.com/sites/boyne/newkerbstones.html

The Protestant Ascendency. (n.d.). Discovering Ireland. https://www.discoveringireland.com/the-protestant-ascendency/

The Red Branch knights. (1906). A smaller social history of ancient Ireland. Longmans, Green, and Co. https://www.libraryireland.com/SocialHistoryAncientIreland/I-III-3.php

The River Boyne. (n.d.). Boyne Valley Tours. https://boynevalleydaytours.com/boyne-river.htm

The Roman Empire in the first century: Early Christians. (n.d.). Public Broadcasting Service. https://www.pbs.org/empires/romans/empire/christians.html#:~:text=In%20313%20AD%2C%20the%20Emperor

The Storm Hag. (n.d.). Emerald Isle. https://emeraldisle.ie/the-storm-hag

The voyage of Bran. (n.d.). Bard Mythologies. https://bardmythologies.com/voyage-of-bran/

The water horse. (n.d.). Emerald Isle. https://emeraldisle.ie/the-water-horse

Thomond. (2022, November 3). Wikipedia. Retrieved December 24, 2022 from https://en.wikipedia.org/wiki/Thomond

Thompson, T. F. (n.d.). Ireland's pre-Celtic archaeological and anthropological heritage. Knowth. https://www.knowth.com/ireland_pre-celtic.htm

Timeline - World History Documentaries. (2021). The mysteries of the

Celtic Otherworld | Myths and monsters | Timeline. [Video]. YouTube. https://www.youtube.com/watch?v=iuKVQHyWxqA&t=14s

Toner, E. (2019). The secret world of life (and death) in Ireland's peat bogs. The New York Times. https://www.nytimes.com/interactive/2019/10/19/multimedia/ireland-peat-bogs.html

Tuatha Dé Danann. (2023). Wikipedia. Retrieved February 10, 2023 from https://en.wikipedia.org/wiki/Tuatha_D%C3%A9_Danann

Tuatha Dé Danann. (2023, January 27). Encyclopedia Britannica. https://www.britannica.com/topic/Tuatha-De-Danann

Tudor conquest of Ireland. (2023). Wikipedia. Retrieved February 5, 2023 from https://en.wikipedia.org/wiki/Tudor_conquest_of_Ireland

Tudor Ireland. (n.d.). Ask about Ireland. https://www.askaboutireland.ie/learning-zone/secondary-students/history/tudor-ireland/

Uyeno, G. (2019, June 10). What are rock cairns? Live Science. https://www.livescience.com/65687-rock-cairns.html

VendettaVixen. (2022, August 23). Types of Irish fairies: Leprechauns, grogochs, and other species. Exemplore. https://exemplore.com/magic/typesofirishfairies

Viking. (2022). A. Augustyn (Ed.), Encyclopedia Britannica. https://www.britannica.com/topic/Viking-people

Walter, R., Fanning, R., Kay, S., O'Beirne Ranelagh, J., & Edwards, D. (2023). Ireland. Encyclopædia Britannica. https://www.britannica.com/place/Ireland

Webb, A. (1878). Saint Columcille. Library Ireland. https://www.libraryireland.com/biography/SaintColumcille.php

Weebush. (2020, November 17). The red cap. Ireland's Lore and Tales. https://irelandsloreandtales.com/2020/11/17/the-red-cap/

Wheel of the year. (2022). Wikipedia. Retrieved 8 February, 2023 from https://en.wikipedia.org/wiki/Wheel_of_the_Year#:~:text=The%20Wheel%20of%20the%20Year,and%20the%20midpoints%20betwe en%20them.

Who was St. Brendan. (n.d.). St. Brendan Parish. https://www.stbrendannortholmsted.org/WhoWasStBrendan.aspx#:~:text=He%20is%20known%20as%20one

Wigington, P. (2019, June 25). The magic of stone circles. Learn Religions. https://www.learnreligions.com/what-are-stone-circles-2562648

Williams, A. (2022, November 29). Morrigan. Mythopedia. https://mythopedia.com/topics/morrigan

Wright, G. (2022a). Aengus. Mythopedia. https://mythopedia.com/topics/aengus

Wright, G. (2022b, November 29). Badb. Mythopedia. https://mythopedia.com/topics/badb

Wright, G. (2022c). Lugh. Mythopedia.

https://mythopedia.com/topics/lugh

Wright, G. (2022d, November 29). Medb. Mythopedia. https://mythopedia.com/topics/medb

Wright, G. (2022e). Neit. Mythopedia. https://mythopedia.com/topics/neit

Wright, G. (2022f). Nuada. Mythopedia. https://mythopedia.com/topics/nuada

Wright, G. (2022g). Taranis. Mythopedia. https://mythopedia.com/topics/taranis

Yeats, W. B. (n.d.). Irish court cairns. The Fr. O'Flanagan Heritage Centre. http://www.carrowkeel.com/files/courtcairns.html

Young, E. (1909). The coming of Lugh: A Celtic wonder-tale. The Fr. Michael O'Flanagan History and Heritage Centre; Maunsel & Co., LTD. http://www.carrowkeel.com/sites/moytura/lugh.html

Zhelyazkov, Y. (n.d.). Far darrig – The leprechaun's evil cousin. Symbol Sage. https://symbolsage.com/far-darrig-celtic-mythology/

(n.d.). Ask about Ireland. https://www.askaboutireland.ie/narrative-notes/the-ice-age-in-ireland/index.xml#:~:text=This%20last%20major%20period%20of

SCOTLAND

Abernethy, S. (2018, July 13). *Joan of the Tower, Queen of Scots*. The Freelance History Writer. https://thefreelancehistorywriter.com/2018/07/13/joan-of-the-tower-queen-of-scots/

About: Battle of Aberdeen (1644). (n.d.). DBpedia. https://dbpedia.org/page/Battle_of_Aberdeen_(1644)

About: Battle of Alford. (n.d.). DBpedia. https://dbpedia.org/page/Battle_of_Alford

About: Battle of Annan Moor. (n.d.). DBpedia. https://dbpedia.org/page/Battle_of_Annan_Moor

About: Battle of Dalnaspidal. (n.d.). DBpedia. https://dbpedia.org/page/Battle_of_Dalnaspidal

About: Battle of Dalrigh. (n.d.). DBpedia. https://dbpedia.org/page/Battle_of_Dalrigh

About: Battle of Kinghorn. (n.d.). DBpedia. https://dbpedia.org/page/Battle_of_Kinghorn

About: Dub, King of Scotland. (n.d.). DBpedia. https://dbpedia.org/page/Dub,_King_of_Scotland

A brief history of the Jacobite risings. (n.d.). Sky HISTORY. https://www.history.co.uk/articles/a-brief-history-of-the-jacobite-risings

Act of Union 1707. (n.d.). UK Parliament.

https://www.parliament.uk/about/living-heritage/evolutionofparliament/legislativescrutiny/act-of-union-1707/#:~:text=The%20Acts%20of%20Union%2C%20passed

Act of Union 1707: Contemporary context. (2016, August). UK Parliament. https://www.parliament.uk/about/living-heritage/evolutionofparliament/legislativescrutiny/act-of-union-1707/contemporary-context/

Aed (877–878). (n.d.). ScotClans. https://www.scotclans.com/pages/aed-877-878

Aidan. (2020, June 24). *The lost kingdom of the Britons in Scotland.* Celtic Cross. https://www.celticcrossonline.com/the-lost-kingdom-of-the-britons-in-scotland/

Ashley, M. (2023). *Charles I.* Britannica. https://www.britannica.com/biography/Charles-I-king-of-Great-Britain-and-Ireland

Augustyn, A. (2023). *William II.* Britannica. https://www.britannica.com/biography/William-II-king-of-England

Battle of Auldearn. (n.d.). Wikiwand. https://www.wikiwand.com/en/Battle_of_Auldearn

Battle of Carbisdale. (n.d.). Military Wiki. https://military-history.fandom.com/wiki/Battle_of_Carbisdale

Battle of Homildon Hill. (n.d.). British Battles. https://www.britishbattles.com/one-hundred-years-war/battle-of-homildon-hill/

Battle of Inverkeithing. (n.d.). Military Wiki. https://military-history.fandom.com/wiki/Battle_of_Inverkeithing

Battle of Kilsyth. (n.d.). Historic Environment Scotland. http://portal.historicenvironment.scot/designation/BTL13

Battle of Luncarty. (n.d.). Electric Scotland. https://electricscotland.com/history/wars/04BattleOfLuncarty980.pdf

Battle of Philiphaugh. (n.d.). Battlefields Hub. https://www.battlefieldstrust.com/resource-centre/civil-war/battleview.asp?BattleFieldId=74

Battle of Sark. (n.d.). Historic Environment Scotland. http://portal.historicenvironment.scot/designation/BTL40

Battle site of Athelstaneford (832). (n.d.). Scotland's Finest. https://www.scotlandsfinest.nl/what-s-to-see/scotland-s-finest-battle-sites/battle-site-of-athelstaneford

Baury, R., Legay, M. (2009). *L'invention de la décentralisation: Noblesse et pouvoirs intermédiaires en France et en Europe xviie-xixe siècle.* Presses universitaires du Septentrion.

Bloks, M. (2017, November 23). *Gruoch – The real Lady Macbeth.* History of Royal Women. https://www.historyofroyalwomen.com/gruoch/gruoch-real-lady-macbeth/

Brain, J. (n.d.). *William of Orange*. Historic UK. https://www.historic-uk.com/HistoryUK/HistoryofEngland/William-Of-Orange/

Bronze Age. (n.d.). ScotClans. https://www.scotclans.com/pages/bronze-age

Buchanan, G. (1799). *The history of Scotland from the earliest accounts of that nation, to the reign of king James VI*. https://ia800205.us.archive.org/26/items/historyofscotlan02buch/historyofscotlan02buch.pdf

Buchanan, G. (1799). *The history of Scotland: from the earliest accounts of that nation, to the reign of King James VI*. Internet Archive. https://archive.org/details/historyofscotlan01buch/page/10/mode/2up

Buchanan, G. (n.d.). *The history of Scotland written in Latin by George Buchanan ; faithfully rendered into English*. Early English Books Online. https://quod.lib.umich.edu/e/eebo/A29962.0001.001/1:7?rgn=div1

Butler, J. (n.d.). *The Great Heathen Army*. Historic UK. https://www.historic-uk.com/HistoryUK/HistoryofEngland/Great-Heathen-Army/

Campbell, M. (n.d.). *History and heritage of Cumbria and the Lake District*. Kingfisher Visitor Guides. https://kingfishervisitorguides.com/features/history-and-heritage-of-cumbria-and-the-lake-district/

Cannon, J. A. (n.d.). *Gododdin, kingdom of the*. Encyclopedia.com. https://www.encyclopedia.com/history/encyclopedias-almanacs-transcripts-and-maps/gododdin-kingdom

Cartwright, M. (2022, January 25). *Battle of Preston in 1648*. World History Encyclopedia. https://www.worldhistory.org/article/1934/battle-of-preston-in-1648/

Castelow, E. (n.d.-a). *The Battle of Ancrum Moor*. Historic UK. https://www.historic-uk.com/HistoryMagazine/DestinationsUK/The-Battle-of-Ancrum-Moor/

Castelow, E. (n.d.-b). *The Battle of Bothwell Bridge*. Historic UK. https://www.historic-uk.com/HistoryMagazine/DestinationsUK/The-Battle-of-Bothwell-Bridge/

Castelow, E. (n.d.-c). *The Battle of Dupplin Moor*. Historic UK. https://www.historic-uk.com/HistoryMagazine/DestinationsUK/The-Battle-of-Dupplin-Moor/

Castelow, E. (n.d.-d). *The Battle of Otterburn*. Historic UK.

https://www.historic-uk.com/HistoryMagazine/DestinationsUK/The-Battle-of-Otterburn/

Castelow, E. (n.d.-e). *The Battle of Worcester*. Historic UK. https://www.historic-uk.com/HistoryMagazine/DestinationsUK/The-Battle-of-Worcester/

Cheney, B., Thompson, P. M., Ingram, S. N., Hammond, P. S., Stevick, P. T., Durban, J. W., Culloch, R. M., Elwen, S. H., Mandleberg, L., Janik, V. M., Quick, N. J., ISLAS-Villanueva, V., Robinson, K. P., Costa, M., Eisfeld, S. M., Walters, A., Phillips, C., Weir, C. R., Evans, P. G. H., & Anderwald, P. (2012). Integrating multiple data sources to assess the distribution and abundance of bottlenose dolphins Tursiops truncatus in Scottish waters. *Mammal Review*, 43(1), 71–88. https://doi.org/10.1111/j.1365-2907.2011.00208.x

Clan Bruce. (n.d.). VisitScotland. https://www.visitscotland.com/info/see-do/clan-bruce-p1475091#:~:text=Clan%20Bruce%20was%20one%20of

Consequences of union. (n.d.). NLS Digital Gallery. https://digital.nls.uk/unionofcrowns/consequences.html

Cracknie souterrain. (n.d.). Forestry and Land Scotland. https://forestryandland.gov.scot/what-we-do/biodiversity-and-conservation/historic-environment-conservation/investigation/cracknie-souterrain#:~:text=The%20word%20comes%20from%20the

Cromdale battlefield. (n.d.). The Jacobite Trail. https://www.jacobitetrail.co.uk/cromdale-battlefield

Dalriada. (n.d.). The Scottish History Society. https://scottishhistorysociety.com/dalriada/

Damnoni Celtic tribe. (n.d.). Roman Britain. https://www.roman-britain.co.uk/tribes/damnoni/

Damnonii. (n.d.). Encyclopedia.com. https://www.encyclopedia.com/history/encyclopedias-almanacs-transcripts-and-maps/damnonii

Davies, J. R. (2019, August 18). *The absolution of Robert I, 1310*. The Community of the Realm of Scotland, 1249–1424. https://cotr.ac.uk/blog/absolution-robert-i-1310/

Devorgilla, Lady of Galloway. (n.d.). Undiscovered Scotland. https://www.undiscoveredscotland.co.uk/usbiography/d/devorgilla.html

Documenting the Union of Parliaments. (n.d.). National Library of Scotland. https://www.nls.uk/collections/rare-books/collections/union-of-parliaments/

Donald I (860-863). (n.d.). ScotClans. https://www.scotclans.com/pages/donald-i-860-863

Dumbarton Castle. (n.d.). Historic Environment Scotland. https://www.historicenvironment.scot/visit-a-place/places/dumbarton-castle/history/#:~:text=Its%20recorded%20history%20goes%20back

Duncan, Brian. (2012). *Scottish nationalism: The symbols of Scottish distinctiveness and the 700 Year continuum of the Scots' desire for self determination.* JMU Scholarly Commons. https://commons.lib.jmu.edu/master201019/192

English heritage battlefield report: Newburn Ford 1640. (1995). Historic England. https://historicengland.org.uk/content/docs/listing/battlefields/newburn-ford/

Epidii Celtic tribe. (n.d.). Roman Britain. https://www.roman-britain.co.uk/tribes/the-epidii-or-epidi/

Erik II. (n.d.). Britannica. https://www.britannica.com/biography/Erik-II

Family tree Cromer/Russell/Buck/Pratt» Kenneth I McAlpin of Scotland (810--858). (n.d.). Genealogy Online. https://www.genealogieonline.nl/en/family-tree-cromer-russell-buck-pratt/P23470.php

Fergus I, king of Scotland (330–305 B.C.). (n.d.). Royal Collection Trust. https://www.rct.uk/collection/403322/fergus-i-king-of-scotland-330-305-b-c

FlikeNoir. (2018, May 22). *What happened to the Scottish monarchy?* Random Scottish History. https://randomscottishhistory.com/2018/05/22/what-happened-to-the-scottish-monarchy/

Fraser, A. (2023). *Mary.* Britannica. https://www.britannica.com/biography/Mary-queen-of-Scotland

Gaels and Scots. (n.d.). The Book of Deer Project. http://bookofdeer.co.uk/historical-background/gaels-and-scots/

Garlinghouse, T. (2022, August 17). *Who were the Picts, the early inhabitants of Scotland?* Live Science. https://www.livescience.com/who-were-picts-scotland

Hayes, A. (2022, June 8). Adam Smith and "the wealth of nations." Investopedia. https://www.investopedia.com/updates/adam-smith-wealth-of-nations/

Hepburn, D. (2023, March 17). *Biggest towns in Scotland: Here are the 21 largest Scottish towns by population – from Paisley to Newton Mearns.* The Scotsman. https://www.scotsman.com/lifestyle/family-and-parenting/biggest-towns-in-scotland-here-are-the-21-largest-scottish-towns-by-population-from-paisley-to-newton-mearns-4069525

History. (n.d.). Scotland. https://www.scotland.org/about-scotland/history-timeline

History of the Stewarts | Battles and historic events. (n.d.). The Stewart Society. https://www.stewartsociety.org/history-of-the-stewarts.cfm?section=battles-and-historical-events&subcatid=1&histid=443

Hosch, W. L. (2023). *Bishops' Wars.* Britannica. https://www.britannica.com/event/Bishops-Wars

Iron Age – Celts, Picts and Romans. (n.d.). ScotClans. https://www.scotclans.com/pages/iron-age-celts-picts-and-romans

Israrkhan. (2021, June 16). *Scots trace their lineage to Egyptian Queen Scotia—yths and reality.* Medium. https://medium.com/lessons-from-history/scots-trace-their-lineage-to-egyptian-queen-scotia-myths-and-reality-5e8bbbd33310

James Stewart, 1st earl of Moray. (n.d.). Undiscovered Scotland. https://www.undiscoveredscotland.co.uk/usbiography/s/jamesstewartmoray.html

James VI and I: Life story – Chapter 3: Regents. (n.d.). Tudor Times. https://www.tudortimes.co.uk/people/james-vi-i-life-story/regents

James VI and I: Life Story – Chapter 4: Coming of age. (n.d.). Tudor Times. https://www.tudortimes.co.uk/people/james-vi-i-life-story/coming-of-age

James VII (1633–1701). (n.d.). National Library of Scotland. https://www.nls.uk/exhibitions/jacobites/james-vii/

Jill, Duchess of Hamilton. (2010, August 13). *Benedict XVI should address the papacy's treatment of Robert the Bruce.* Catholic Herald. https://catholicherald.co.uk/benedict-xvi-should-address-the-papacys-treatment-of-robert-the-bruce/

Johnson, B. (n.d.-a). *Queen Anne.* Historic UK. https://www.historic-uk.com/HistoryUK/HistoryofBritain/Queen-Anne/

Johnson, B. (n.d.-b). *The Anglo-Scottish Wars (or Wars of Scottish Independence.* Historic UK. https://www.historic-uk.com/HistoryUK/HistoryofScotland/The-AngloScottish-Wars-or-Wars-of-Scottish-Independence/

Johnson, B. (n.d.-c). *The Darien scheme.* Historic UK. https://www.historic-uk.com/HistoryUK/HistoryofScotland/The-Darien-Scheme/

Johnson, B. (n.d.-d). *The Jacobite revolts: Chronology.* Historic UK. https://www.historic-uk.com/HistoryUK/HistoryofScotland/The-Jacobite-Revolts-Chronology/

Kennedy, L. (2019, October 21). *The prehistoric ages: How humans lived before written records.* History. https://www.history.com/news/prehistoric-ages-timeline#:~:text=In%20the%20Paleolithic%20period%20(roughly

Kenneth II (971–995). (n.d.). ScotClans. https://www.scotclans.com/pages/kenneth-ii-971-995

Kessler, P. L. (n.d.). *Rheged (Recet).* The History Files.

https://www.historyfiles.co.uk/KingListsBritain/BritainRheged.htm

Kinclaven Castle, Perthshire. (n.d.). Castle Finders. https://castle-finders.co.uk/Scotland/kinclaven-castle.html

King Charles II | The public and personal life of a British monarch. (n.d.). Royal Museums Greenwich. https://www.rmg.co.uk/stories/topics/king-charles-ii-public-personal-life-british-monarch#:~:text=Venue%20ohire-

King Culen. (n.d.). Undiscovered Scotland. https://www.undiscoveredscotland.co.uk/usbiography/monarchs/culen.html

King Eochaid and King Giric. (n.d.). Undiscovered Scotland. https://www.undiscoveredscotland.co.uk/usbiography/monarchs/eochaidgiric.html

King Indulf. (n.d.). Undiscovered Scotland. https://www.undiscoveredscotland.co.uk/usbiography/monarchs/indulf.html

Kinnatellus, king of Scotland (574–5). (n.d.). Royal Collection Trust. https://www.rct.uk/collection/403274/kinnatellus-king-of-scotland-574-5

Late Modern Period | History, timeline, and significant events. (2023, March 12). https://study.com/academy/lesson/late-modern-period-history-timeline-significant-events.html.

List of child brides. (2023). Wikipedia. https://en.wikipedia.org/wiki/List_of_child_brides

Local authority areas in Scotland. (n.d.). The Scottish Government. https://www.gov.scot/binaries/content/gallery/publications/statistics-publication/2015/02/scottish-local-government-financial-statistics-2013-14/00471983.gif

Lulach (The Fool) (1057–1058). (n.d.). ScotClans. https://www.scotclans.com/pages/lulach-the-fool-1057-1058

Mac, E. (2011, April 15). *Luguwalos: Carlisle's ancient roots.* Esmeralda's Cumbrian History & Folklore. https://esmeraldamac.wordpress.com/2011/04/15/carlisles-ancient-british-heritage-luguwalos/

MacInnes, A. (1990, May). *Covenanting Revolution and municipal enterprise.* History Today. https://www.historytoday.com/archive/covenanting-revolution-and-municipal-enterprise

MacInnes, I. A. (n.d.). *Scotland's second war of independence, 1332–1357* . Boydell and Brewer. https://boydellandbrewer.com/9781783271443/scotlands-second-war-of-independence-1332-1357/#:~:text=The%20Second%20Scottish%20War%20of,Scottish%20crown%20recommenced%20once%20more

Maeatae. (2017, January 8). Eagles and Dragons Publishing. https://eaglesanddragonspublishing.com/tag/maeatae/

Maldonado, A. (2020, July 21). *Looting Scotland in the Viking age.* National Museums Scotland. https://blog.nms.ac.uk/2020/07/21/looting-scotland-in-the-viking-age/#:~:text=In%20795%20AD%20one%20of

Manning, R. B. (2006, May). *An Apprenticeship in Arms: The Origins of the British Army 1585–1702.* Oxford Academic

Manning, S. (2023). *Battle of Bannockburn.* Britannica. https://www.britannica.com/event/Battle-of-Bannockburn

McGraw, J. (n.d.). *The easiest guide to Scotland's archaeological time periods and ages.* Dig It! https://www.digitscotland.com/an-easy-guide-to-scotlands-archaeological-time-periods-and-ages/#:~:text=When%20was%20the%20Iron%20Age

McNeil, G. P. (2022, April 28). *Scota, queen of the Gadelians {fictitious}.* Geni. https://www.geni.com/people/Scota-Queen-of-the-Gadelians-fictitious/6000000000077265812

Morrill, J. S. (2023a). *Margaret Tudor.* Britannica. https://www.britannica.com/biography/Margaret-Tudor

Morrill, J. S. (2023b). *James V.* Britannica. https://www.britannica.com/biography/James-V

Neolithic farmers and monument builders. (n.d.). ScotClans. https://www.scotclans.com/pages/neolithic-farmers-and-monument-builders

Novantae Celtic tribe. (n.d.). Roman Britain. https://www.roman-britain.co.uk/tribes/novantae/

Ohlmeyer, J. H. (2023). *English civil wars.* Britannica. https://www.britannica.com/event/English-Civil-Wars

Parker, N. G. (2022). *Battle of Dunbar.* Britannica. https://www.britannica.com/event/Battle-of-Dunbar

Parrott-Sheffer, C. (2023). *James Stewart, 1st earl of Moray.* Britannica. https://www.britannica.com/biography/James-Stewart-1st-Earl-of-Moray

Parrott-Sheffer, C. (2023, February 21). *Pict.* Britannica. https://www.britannica.com/topic/Pict

Paxton, J. (2020, May 7). *Roman conquest of Britain: Caesar's expedition to Hadrian's Wall.* Wondrium Daily. https://www.wondriumdaily.com/roman-conquest-of-britain-caesars-expedition-to-hadrians-wall/#:~:text=So%2C%20Romans%20first%20encountered%20Britain

Pettit, H., Weston, P. (2018, June 4). *Exclusive: What Britain looked like during the last ice age: Interactive map reveals where ice corridors and glacial lakes formed 22,000 years ago.* MailOnline. https://www.dailymail.co.uk/sciencetech/article-

5803855/Interactive-map-reveals-Britain-looked-like-ice-age.html

Prehistoric Scotland. (n.d.). ScotClans. https://www.scotclans.com/pages/prehistoric-scotland

Readman, K. (2021, April 25). *The first Scottish war of independence: Robert the Bruce vs Edward I.* The Collector. https://www.thecollector.com/the-first-scottish-war-of-independence-robert-the-bruce-vs-edward-i/

Reid, B. (n.d.). *The Siege of Stirling Castle.* Hidden Scotland. https://hiddenscotland.co/the-siege-of-stirling-castle/

Reid, B. (n.d.). *The Siege of Caerlaverock Castle.* Hidden Scotland. https://hiddenscotland.co/the-siege-of-caerlaverock-castle/

Renaissance and Reformation – Introduction. (n.d.). BBC. https://www.bbc.co.uk/history/scottishhistory/renaissance/intro_renaissance.shtml

Renaissance. (n.d.). National Galleries Scotland. https://www.nationalgalleries.org/art-and-artists/glossary-terms/renaissance

Restoration. (n.d.). UK Parliament. https://www.parliament.uk/about/living-heritage/evolutionofparliament/legislativescrutiny/act-of-union-1707/overview/restoration/

Revolution and civil war. (n.d.). UK Parliament. https://www.parliament.uk/about/living-heritage/evolutionofparliament/legislativescrutiny/act-of-union-1707/overview/revolution-and-civil-war/

Ring hill, fort. (n.d.). Ancient Monuments. https://ancientmonuments.uk/126000-ring-hill-fort-mid-galloway-and-wigtown-west-ward#.ZBhL5exBxQI

Roller, S. (2020, October 14). *6 key battles in the Wars of Scottish Independence.* History Hit. https://www.historyhit.com/key-battles-in-the-wars-of-scottish-independence/

Romans in Scotland. (n.d.). Travel Scotland. https://www.scotland.org.uk/history/romans-in-scotland

Roseveare, H. G. (2023). *Charles II.* Britannica. https://www.britannica.com/biography/Charles-II-king-of-Great-Britain-and-Ireland

Savage, L. R. (n.d.). *John Knox and the Scottish Reformation.* Historic UK. https://www.historic-uk.com/HistoryUK/HistoryofScotland/John-Knox-Scottish-Reformation/

Scottish battles and conflicts timeline. (n.d.). orgfree.com. http://skyelander.orgfree.com/sbattles.html

Scottish battles – the Second War of Scottish Independence. (n.d.). Scots Connection. https://www.scotsconnection.com/t-battles4.aspx

Selgovae Celtic tribe. (n.d.). Roman Britain. https://www.roman-britain.co.uk/tribes/selgovae/

Siege of Dundee (1651). (n.d.). Military Wiki. https://military-history.fandom.com/wiki/Siege_of_Dundee_(1651)

Siege of Haddington. (2021, April 26). Military Wiki. https://military-history.fandom.com/wiki/Siege_of_Haddington

Significant battles in Scottish history – Preston to Culloden. (n.d.). Scots Connection. https://www.scotsconnection.com/t-battles9.aspx

1603 – The Union Of The Crowns. (n.d.). ScotClans. https://www.scotclans.com/pages/1603-the-union-of-the-crowns

Snow, D. R. (2001). *Scotland's Irish origins.* Archeology Archive. https://archive.archaeology.org/0107/abstracts/scotland.html

Solly, M. (2020, January 30). *A not-so-brief history of Scottish independence.* Smithsonian Magazine. https://www.smithsonianmag.com/history/brief-history-scottish-independence-180973928/

Stirling Castle. (2023). Historic Environment Scotland. https://www.historicenvironment.scot/visit-a-place/places/stirling-castle/history/#:~:text=Stirling%20Castle%20has%20been%20likened

Succession problem: Edward I and the decision at Norham. (n.d.). BBC Bitesize. https://www.bbc.co.uk/bitesize/guides/zrxcwmn/revision/4#:~:text=The%20Guardians%20invited%20Edward%20to

Succession problem: The Great Cause and Edward's choice. (n.d.). BBC Bitesize. https://www.bbc.co.uk/bitesize/guides/zrxcwmn/revision/6#:~:text=Edward%20I%20chose%20John%20Balliol

Sundberg, A. (2022). Natural Disaster at the Closing of the Dutch Golden Age . Cambridge University Press.

The Auld Alliance. (n.d.). Historic UK. https://www.historic-uk.com/HistoryUK/HistoryofScotland/The-Auld-Alliance-France-Scotland/

The Battle of Dunbar, 1296. (n.d.). BBC Bitesize. https://www.bbc.co.uk/bitesize/topics/z8g86sg/articles/zh3fmfr

The Battle of Inverlochy: February 2, 1645. (n.d.). Clan Cameron Online. http://www.clan-cameron.org/battles/1645.html

The Britons of Strathclyde. (n.d.). English Monarchs. https://www.englishmonarchs.co.uk/britons.html

The Bruces and the Balliols. (n.d.). Undiscovered Scotland. https://www.undiscoveredscotland.co.uk/usbiography/monarchs/balliolsbruces.html

The Caledonii tribe. (n.d.). The Romans in Britain. https://www.romanobritain.org/4-celt/clb_tribe_caledonii.php

The Declaration of Arbroath. (n.d.). National Records of Scotland. https://www.nrscotland.gov.uk/Declaration#:~:text=The%20Declar

ation%20is%20a%20letter

The Editors of Encyclopaedia Britannica. (n.d.). *Alba*. Britannica. https://www.britannica.com/place/Alba-historical-kingdom-Scotland

The Editors of Encyclopaedia Britannica. (n.d.). *Kenneth I*. Britannica. https://www.britannica.com/biography/Kenneth-I

The Editors of Encyclopaedia Britannica. (2018). *Constantine I*. Britannica. https://www.britannica.com/biography/Constantine-I-king-of-Scotland

The Editors of Encyclopaedia Britannica. (2018). *Donald Bane*. Britannica. https://www.britannica.com/place/Dalriada

The Editors of Encyclopaedia Britannica. (2018). *Dalriada*. Britannica. https://www.britannica.com/biography/Donald-Bane

The Editors of Encyclopaedia Britannica. (2018). *Kings and queens of Scotland*. Britannica. https://www.britannica.com/topic/Kings-and-Queens-of-Scotland-1856934

The Editors of Encyclopaedia Britannica. (2018). *Scot*. Britannica. https://www.britannica.com/topic/Scot

The Editors of Encyclopaedia Britannica. (2018, December 21). *Strathclyde*. Britannica. https://www.britannica.com/place/Strathclyde

The Editors of Encyclopaedia Britannica. (2019, July 15). *Lothian*. Britannica. https://www.britannica.com/place/Lothian

The Editors of Encyclopaedia Britannica. (2020). *Wessex*. Britannica. https://www.britannica.com/place/Wessex-historical-kingdom

The Editors of Encyclopaedia Britannica. (2022). *Alexander III*. Britannica. https://www.britannica.com/biography/Alexander-III-king-of-Scotland

The Editors of Encyclopaedia Britannica. (2022). *Balliol family*. Britannica. https://www.britannica.com/topic/Balliol-family

The Editors of Encyclopaedia Britannica. (2022). *David I*. Britannica. https://www.britannica.com/biography/David-I

The Editors of Encyclopaedia Britannica. (2022). *Duncan I*. Britannica. https://www.britannica.com/biography/Duncan-I

The Editors of Encyclopaedia Britannica. (2022). *George I*. Britannica. https://www.britannica.com/biography/George-I-king-of-Great-Britain

The Editors of Encyclopaedia Britannica. (2022). *Heptarchy*. Britannica. https://www.britannica.com/topic/Heptarchy

The Editors of Encyclopaedia Britannica. (2022). *James II*. Britannica. https://www.britannica.com/biography/James-II-king-of-Scotland

The Editors of Encyclopaedia Britannica. (2022). *James III*. Britannica. https://www.britannica.com/biography/James-III-king-of-Scotland

The Editors of Encyclopaedia Britannica. (2022). *John*. Britannica.

https://www.britannica.com/biography/John-king-of-Scotland-1250-1313

The Editors of Encyclopaedia Britannica. (2022). *John Stewart, 2nd duke of Albany*. Britannica. https://www.britannica.com/biography/John-Stewart-2nd-duke-of-Albany

The Editors of Encyclopaedia Britannica. (2022). *Malcolm II*. Britannica. https://www.britannica.com/biography/Malcolm-II

The Editors of Encyclopaedia Britannica. (2022). *Malcolm IV*. Britannica. https://www.britannica.com/biography/Malcolm-IV

The Editors of Encyclopaedia Britannica. (2022). *Mary of Lorraine*. Britannica. https://www.britannica.com/biography/Mary-of-Lorraine

The Editors of Encyclopaedia Britannica. (2022). *Michael III Canmore*. Britannica. https://www.britannica.com/biography/Malcolm-III-Canmore

The Editors of Encyclopaedia Britannica. (2022, August 28). *Margaret*. Britannica. https://www.britannica.com/biography/Margaret-queen-of-Scotland

The Editors of Encyclopaedia Britannica. (2023). *Archibald Douglas, 6th earl of Angus*. Britannica. https://www.britannica.com/biography/Alexander-I-king-of-Scotland

The Editors of Encyclopaedia Britannica. (2023). *Charles Edward, the young pretender*. Britannica. https://www.britannica.com/biography/Charles-Edward-the-Young-Pretender

The Editors of Encyclopaedia Britannica. (2023). *Constantine III*. Britannica. https://www.britannica.com/biography/Constantine-III-king-of-Scotland

The Editors of Encyclopaedia Britannica. (2023). *David II*. Britannica. https://www.britannica.com/biography/David-II

The Editors of Encyclopaedia Britannica. (2023). *Donald II*. Britannica. https://www.britannica.com/biography/Donald-II

The Editors of Encyclopaedia Britannica. (2023). *Edward: King of Scotland*. Britannica. https://www.britannica.com/biography/Edward-king-of-Scotland

The Editors of Encyclopaedia Britannica. (2023). *James I*. Britannica. https://www.britannica.com/biography/James-I-king-of-Scotland

The Editors of Encyclopaedia Britannica. (2023). *James IV*. Britannica. https://www.britannica.com/biography/James-IV-king-of-Scotland

The Editors of Encyclopaedia Britannica. (2023). *Kenneth III*. Britannica. https://www.britannica.com/biography/Kenneth-III

The Editors of Encyclopaedia Britannica. (2023). *Macbeth*. Britannica. https://www.britannica.com/biography/Macbeth-king-of-Scots

The Editors of Encyclopaedia Britannica. (2023). *Malcolm I*. Britannica.

britannica.com/biography/Malcolm-I

The Editors of Encyclopaedia Britannica. (2023). *Robert II*. Britannica. https://www.britannica.com/biography/Robert-II-king-of-Scotland

The Editors of Encyclopaedia Britannica. (2023). *Robert III*. Britannica. https://www.britannica.com/biography/Robert-III

The Editors of Encyclopaedia Britannica. (2023). *William I*. Britannica. https://www.britannica.com/biography/William-I-king-of-Scotland

The Editors of Encyclopaedia Britannica. (2023, January 1). *Constantine II*. Britannica. https://www.britannica.com/biography/Constantine-II-king-of-Scotland

The Editors of Encyclopaedia Britannica. (2023, February 27). *Caledonia*. Britannica. https://www.britannica.com/place/Caledonia-ancient-region-Britain

The Editors of Encyclopaedia Britannica. (2023, March 28). *Alexander I*. Britannica. https://www.britannica.com/biography/Alexander-I-king-of-Scotland

The Enlightenment and Industrial Revolution – the Industrial Revolution. (n.d.). BBC. https://www.bbc.co.uk/history/scottishhistory/enlightenment/features_enlightenment_industry.shtml

The first hunter gatherers. (n.d.). ScotClans. https://www.scotclans.com/pages/the-first-hunter-gatherers

The Highland Clearances. (n.d.). Scottish History Society. https://scottishhistorysociety.com/the-highland-clearances/

The kingdom of the Angles. (n.d.). BBC. https://www.bbc.co.uk/scotland/history/articles/kingdom_of_the_angles/#:~:text=The%20Angles%20were%20Germanic%20invaders

The kingdom of the Britons. (n.d.). BBC. https://www.bbc.co.uk/scotland/history/articles/kingdom_of_the_britons/

The Newsroom. (2017, March 1). *Roslin 1303: Scotland's forgotten battle.* The Scotsman. https://www.scotsman.com/whats-on/arts-and-entertainment/roslin-1303-scotlands-forgotten-battle-604343

The Romans in Scotland. (n.d.). National Museums Scotland. https://www.nms.ac.uk/explore-our-collections/stories/scottish-history-and-archaeology/the-romans-in-scotland/

The Scotti. (n.d.). British Isles: Past and Present. https://www.islandguide.co.uk/history/scotti.htm

The Scottish diaspora: How Scots spread across the globe. (2016, January 25). The Scotsman. https://www.scotsman.com/whats-on/arts-and-entertainment/scottish-diaspora-how-scots-spread-across-globe-1484633

The Scottish Reformation. (n.d.). BBC. https://www.bbc.co.uk/scotland/history/articles/scottish_reformati

on/#:~:text=The%20Reformation%20split%20the%20Church

The Scottish Reformation, c.1525–1560. (n.d.). The Scottish History Society. https://scottishhistorysociety.com/the-scottish-reformation-c-1525-1560/

The Selgovae tribe. (n.d.). The Romans in Britain. https://www.romanobritain.org/4-celt/clb_tribe_selgovae.php

The Stewarts. (n.d.). The Royal Family. https://www.royal.uk/stewarts-0#:~:text=The%20Stewart%20dynasty%20descended%20from,flourished%20for%20over%20three%20centuries

The Taexali tribe. (n.d.). The Romans in Britain. https://www.romanobritain.org/4-celt/clb_tribe_taexali.php

The Treaty of Edinburgh-Northampton, 1328. (n.d.). Scottish Archives for Schools. https://www.scottisharchivesforschools.org/WarsOfIndependence/Edinburgh-Northampton.asp

The Union of 1603. (n.d.). The Scottish History Society. https://scottishhistorysociety.com/the-union-of-1603/

The Vacomagi tribe. (n.d.). The Romans in Britain. https://www.romanobritain.org/4-celt/clb_tribe_vacomagi.php

The Venicones tribe. (n.d.). The Romans in Britain. https://www.romanobritain.org/4-celt/clb_tribe_venicones.php

The Wars of Independence. (n.d.). The Scottish History Society. https://scottishhistorysociety.com/the-wars-of-independence/

Tikkanen, A. (2022). *Robert Stewart, 1st duke of Albany.* Britannica. https://www.britannica.com/biography/Robert-Stewart-1st-duke-of-Albany

Toolis, R. (2022, February 27). *Beyond the wall: exploring the prehistoric origins of Scotland.* The Past. https://the-past.com/feature/beyond-the-wall-exploring-the-prehistoric-origins-of-scotland/

Union between Scotland and England? (n.d.). UK Parliament. https://www.parliament.uk/about/living-heritage/evolutionofparliament/legislativescrutiny/act-of-union-1707/overview/union-between-scotland-and-england/

Union of the crowns. (n.d.). UK Parliament. https://www.parliament.uk/about/living-heritage/evolutionofparliament/legislativescrutiny/act-of-union-1707/overview/union-of-the-crowns/#:~:text=Because%20the%20Queen%20had%20died,a%20union%20of%20the%20crowns.

Votadini Celtic tribe. (n.d.). Roman Britain. https://www.roman-britain.co.uk/tribes/votadini/

Webster, B. (2022). *Robert the Bruce.* Britannica. https://www.britannica.com/biography/Robert-the-Bruce

What is a crannog? (n.d.). The Scottish Crannog Centre. https://crannog.co.uk/what-is-a-crannog/#:~:text=Crannogs%20are%20found%20across%20Scotlan d

Who were the nine tribes of ancient Scotland? (2016, October 25). The Scotsman. https://www.scotsman.com/whats-on/arts-and-entertainment/who-were-nine-tribes-ancient-scotland-865992

Wiener, J. (2018). *Scota: Mother of the Scottish people.* World History Et Cetera. https://etc.worldhistory.org/uncategorized/scota-mother-of-the-scottish-people/

Wolff, A. (2023). *Edgar.* Britannica. https://www.britannica.com/biography/Edgar-king-of-Scotland

Yodamo. (2021, February 13). *B.C. 1526–1513: Thutmose, Gaythelos and Scota.* The Chisper Effect. https://chisper256891285.wordpress.com/2021/02/13/b-c-1526-1513-thutmose-gaythelos-scota/

WALES HISTORY

Pembrokeshire Coast National Park. (2024c, February 16). Castell Henllys Iron Age Village - Pembrokeshire Coast National Park. https://www.pembrokeshirecoast.wales/castell-henllys/

- Wikipedia contributors. (2023, February 20). List of hillforts in Wales. Wikipedia.
  https://en.wikipedia.org/wiki/List_of_hillforts_in_Wales

- Who were the Celts? Understanding the history and culture of Celtic tribes. (n.d.). Museum Wales. https://museum.wales/articles/1341/Who-were-the-Celts/

- Britain Express. (n.d.). Celtic Wales - history of Wales in the Iron Age. https://www.britainexpress.com/wales/history/iron-age.htm

- HWb. (n.d.). https://hwb.gov.wales/

- HWb. (n.d.-b). https://hwb.gov.wales/

- Pwpadmin. (2023, March 6). 10 inventions to thank the Roman Empire for. Gray Line - I Love Rome. https://graylinerome.com/10-inventions-thank-roman-empire/

- Roman Wales | Cadw. (n.d.). Cadw. https://cadw.gov.wales/learn/sites-through-centuries/roman-wales

- What is the Offa's Dyke Path? (n.d.). VisitWales. https://www.visitwales.com/things-do/adventure-and-activities/walking/offas-dyke-walks

- The National Archives. (2023, June 12). Domesday Book - The National Archives. https://www.nationalarchives.gov.uk/help-with-your-research/research-guides/domesday-book/#:

- Historian. (2023, September 9). 10 Facts about the Normans - Have fun with history. Have Fun With History. https://www.havefunwithhistory.com/facts-about-the-normans/
- Britain Express. (n.d.-b). The Statute of Rhuddlan | History of Wales. https://www.britainexpress.com/wales/history/rhuddlan.htm
- Wales in the Middle Ages. (n.d.). https://owain-glyndwr.wales/age_of_the_princes/mediaeval_wales_detail.html
- Jones, D. (2022, August 30). 5 things you (probably) didn't know about the Plantagenets. https://www.historyextra.com/period/plantagenet/5-things-you-probably-didnt-know-about-the-plantagenets/
- 10 Fast facts about the Plantagenets. (n.d.). Sky HISTORY TV Channel. https://www.history.co.uk/shows/britains-bloodiest-dynasty/articles/10-fast-facts-about-the-plantagenets
- Sarah. (2017, August 3). Daily Living in the Middle Ages - Sarah Woodbury. Sarah Woodbury. https://www.sarahwoodbury.com/living-in-the-past/
- The Tudors in Wales | Cadw. (n.d.). Cadw. https://cadw.gov.wales/learn/sites-through-centuries/tudors-wales
- BBC - History - Wales under the Tudors. (2011, February 17). https://www.bbc.co.uk/history/british/tudors/wales_tudors_01.shtml
- Evans, E. (2022, August 30). Stuart Britain: what was life like for ordinary people? https://www.historyextra.com/period/stuart/stuart-britain-what-was-life-like-for-ordinary-people/
- What Jobs did Children do Underground? • Coal Mining and the Victorians • MyLearning. (n.d.). https://www.mylearning.org/stories/coal-mining-and-the-victorians/236?
- Wikipedia contributors. (2024, February 15). Mining in Wales. Wikipedia. https://en.wikipedia.org/wiki/Mining_in_Wales
- Hedd Wyn (1887-1917) - Literature Wales. (2017, June 12). Literature Wales. https://www.literaturewales.org/our-projects/poetry-of-loss/hedd-wyn-1887-1917/
- Wikipedia contributors. (2024a, February 12). Investiture of Charles, Prince of Wales. Wikipedia. https://en.wikipedia.org/wiki/Investiture_of_Charles,_Prince_of_Wales
- Wikipedia contributors. (2024a, February 9). Dylan Thomas.

Wikipedia. https://en.wikipedia.org/wiki/Dylan_Thomas
- Wikipedia contributors. (2024d, February 20). Roald Dahl. Wikipedia. https://en.wikipedia.org/wiki/Roald_Dahl
- Wikipedia contributors. (2024c, February 14). Shirley Bassey. Wikipedia. https://en.wikipedia.org/wiki/Shirley_Bassey
- Wikipedia contributors. (2024a, February 6). Charlotte Church. Wikipedia. https://en.wikipedia.org/wiki/Charlotte_Church
- Siddique, H. (2021, September 17). Home computing pioneer Sir Clive Sinclair dies aged 81. The Guardian. https://www.theguardian.com/technology/2021/sep/16/home-computing-pioneer-sir-clive-sinclair-dies-aged-81

FREE BONUS FROM HBA: EBOOK BUNDLE

Greetings!

First of all, thank you for reading our books. As fellow passionate readers of History and Mythology, we aim to create the very best books for our readers.

Now, we invite you to join our VIP list. As a welcome gift, we offer the History & Mythology Ebook Bundle below for free. Plus you can be the first to receive new books and exclusives! Remember it's 100% free to join.

Simply scan the QR code down below to join.

OTHER BOOKS BY HISTORY BROUGHT ALIVE

Available now in Ebook, Paperback, Hardcover, and Audiobook in all regions.

Other books:

For Kids:

THE HISTORY OF ENGLAND FOR KIDS
HISTORY BROUGHT ALIVE

GREEK MYTHOLOGY FOR KIDS
HISTORY BROUGHT ALIVE

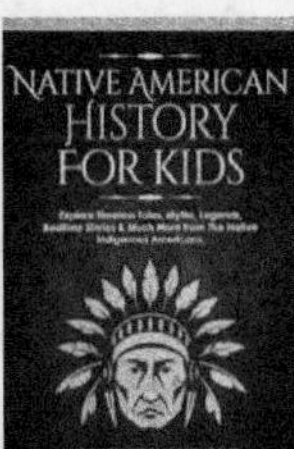

NATIVE AMERICAN HISTORY FOR KIDS
HISTORY BROUGHT ALIVE

WORLD WAR 1 & 2 HISTORY FOR KIDS
HISTORY BROUGHT ALIVE

GREEK LEGENDS FOR KIDS
HISTORY BROUGHT ALIVE

ROMAN HISTORY FOR KIDS
HISTORY BROUGHT ALIVE

WORLD WAR 1 HISTORY FOR KIDS
HISTORY BROUGHT ALIVE

WORLD WAR 2 HISTORY FOR KIDS
HISTORY BROUGHT ALIVE

MYTHOLOGY FOR KIDS
HISTORY BROUGHT ALIVE

HISTORY & MYTHOLOGY FOR KIDS
HISTORY BROUGHT ALIVE

HISTORY & MYTHOLOGY FOR KIDS
HISTORY BROUGHT ALIVE

EGYPTIAN MYTHOLOGY FOR KIDS
HISTORY BROUGHT ALIVE

CELTIC HISTORY & MYTHOLOGY FOR KIDS
HISTORY BROUGHT ALIVE

NORSE MYTHOLOGY FOR KIDS
HISTORY BROUGHT ALIVE

THE COMPLETE BRITISH ISLES COLLECTION

We sincerely hope you enjoyed our new book *"The Complete British Isles Collection"*. We would greatly appreciate your feedback with an honest review at the place of purchase.

First and foremost, we are always looking to grow and improve as a team. It is reassuring to hear what works, as well as receive constructive feedback on what should improve. Second, starting out as an unknown author is exceedingly difficult, and Amazon reviews go a long way toward making the journey out of anonymity possible. Please take a few minutes to write an honest review.

Best regards,

History Brought Alive

http://historybroughtalive.com/